PALM BEACH
POWER & GLORY
WIT & WISDOM

The Insider's Guide to the
Passions, Possessions and Pleasures
of the World's Richest Society

by

James Jennings Sheeran

Sixth Edition

Published by
Palm Beach Publishing Group©

Library of Congress Cataloging-in-Publication Data
1. Palm Beach   2. Personalities   3. Philanthropy   4. Business
I. Sheeran, James J.   II. Title
2000-090814
ISBN 1-893449-00-9
ISSN 1042-637X

Printed in the United States of America

First Edition (March 1988)
Second Edition (December 1989)
Third Edition (November 1991)
Fourth Edition (January 1995)
Fifth Edition (June 1997)
Sixth Edition (September 2000)

1 2 3 4 5 6 7 8 9 10

This book is dedicated
to the many
PALM BEACHERS
who help make
the world a better place
by their extraordinary
contributions to charity.

To those
who celebrate life's joy
share their treasures
gladden the hearts of children
laugh, build, love, grow. . .
and understand the purity
of
GIVING.

ALSO BY THE AUTHOR

Six-Figure Lifestyle

Skyrocketing Your Income

The Opportunist

The Gift of Death

The Palm Beach Book of Facts & Firsts (3 Editions)

Palm Beach Wit & Wisdom

Washington Facts & Fancies, Caprices & Curiosities

Chicago Facts & Fancies, Caprices & Curiosities

Palm Beach Facts & Fancies, Wit & Wisdom (2 Editions)

Palm Beach Power & Glory, Wit & Wisdom

—CONTENTS—

Acknowledgments x
Introduction xi

—ACKNOWLEDGEMENTS—

A book like this cannot be written in a vacuum; it is the result of hundreds of interviews seeking the insights and opinions of many of Palm Beach's most prominent residents and professionals. It is also the subjective expression of the Editor in that much of the material presented is purely a matter of personal perception. As in many literary works that entertain yet are considered reference books, there is a fine line between fact and fiction; we beg your indulgence for whatever fine shadings have been placed on certain **Facts & Fancies**. While every effort has been made to assure accuracy, no responsibility can be assumed by the author or the publisher for errors or misinterpretations.

In view of the foregoing, we gratefully acknowledge dozens of Islanders who gave so generously of their understanding and knowledge of Palm Beach; they are listed in the Contributors section.

—INTRODUCTION—

*I*t is customary to think of **Palm Beach** as a social microcosm—one culture, one level of wealth, one aging citizenry, one basic interest in life, all in one urbane resort area. The homogenizing forces of conspicuous consumption, dedication to philanthropy, and abundance of social top spin have created that perception of Palm Beach to the world.

Yet, this book asserts a different viewpoint; that of Palm Beach as a unique bastion of money and power intermixed with benevolence, a genteel people and a progressive history quite unparalleled anywhere on the Planet Earth. The infinite variety of backgrounds, the impressive range of achievement, freshness of spirit of its residents, and the labyrinthine social machinery by which most people fulfill themselves, make the Island the world capital of affluence; and the mecca for the orderly disposition of wealth via the many processes endemic to making the world a better place.

Dozens of books (and hundreds of articles) have been written about Palm Beach and its special orientation; each adding a new dimension to this small Island of gigantic legend. Some suggest a troubled tropic. A land of status-seekers and pyramid-climbers. Paradise Lost. A decadent environment. Or, a gracious Lady past her prime. Most such journalism has its thrust in adversity as a means of sensationalism; and most is superficial for that reason.

Palm Beach Power & Glory, Wit & Wisdom, now in its Sixth Edition, is an affirmation of Palm Beach; it is a love story about the Island. As a reference work, it highlights the many special characteristics, personalities, parameters, passions and unique features of the "Garden of Eden." It is comprehensive, fact-filled, provocative and authoritative—the result of a prodigious amount of research by dedicated Palm Beachers who, too, have a romance going with our Island. No such book about Palm Beach has ever been written.

POWER & GLORY is published regularly, with constant updatings, additions, new insights, revelations and information; in effect, it is an ongoing sociological chronicle of Palm Beach. With books of this nature, reader observations often become data for future use, and thus, the book is rewritten, in part, by audience applause/criticism and general commentary. In that context, we seek your participation in future portrayals of Palm Beach **as it is**.

Come, let us begin our romance . . .

CHAPTER I

THE LUCKIEST PEOPLE IN THE WORLD
(Palm Beach Players, Partisans & Pilgrims)

Photo:Mort Kaye Studios

LESLY SMITH AND JOHN WALSH
informed, idealistic and inspired

—PALM BEACHER PORTRAIT—

*D*espite Ladies and Lads Bountiful, the quintessential patina of Old Guard money and upper class, Croeses-rich mates and dates, unassailable WASP credentials coupled with the ultimate in glamour and chic, dazzling patrician beauties and devilishly attractive rogues—all guided by the law of social primacy, **Palm Beachers** are quite normal!

They live on a gloriously Edenesque tropical island with a land area of 3.75 square miles; and most of the 9,800 residents sniff flowers year around. The median age of Palm Beachers is 60.1 years; 36.6% of the population is 65 or over, slightly more females than males. The average household size is 2.1; 69% are married with 27% widowed, divorced or separated and 4% single. The median family income is $286,450 with a median home value of $825,000. Many retired captains of industry, statesmen, professionals and financiers enjoy their treasures and pleasures on the Island; 87% have net worths of $2.8 million or more and some 45% own three or more cars. Real estate is the major contributor to wealth but dozens of Island families made their fortunes the hard way—through **inheritance**, "generational" monies passed down for one hundred years or more. The population is largely passive, genteel, dedicated to a good lifestyle, and a perfect balance of Christians and Jews.

Palm Beach has enormous visibility and power on the world scene. Since its inception, it has been canonized as the world's richest society, appealing to an international cast of affluent players and pretenders. In fact, the Town is a micromarket, painstakingly scrutinized by the press and overlords from other societies, but it is true to its charter, which simply charges all those who cross the bridge to regard Palm Beach as a **gem**—dazzling, breathtaking, pristine and matchless, and to treat it accordingly, as the ultimate monied resort capital of the world!

—PALM BEACHER PROFILE—

*H***E:** Charming/disarming, good neurocepters, superb looks—like an old Roman coin • *can be huffy/puffy/stuffy but generally easygoing sophisticated* • great at exclamations and proclamations • *understands the waltz of people, very comfortable with the privileged set and their superior cosmos where territorial rights are taken for granted* • has first dibs on most everything via winking or waving a Ben Franklin • *occasionally has the look of someone who would like to slip off and gnaw on a bone* • can be raffish and casual beneath the inner circle complex • *capable of triggering a domino effect, action-*

14

oriented and understands that if you wait all that happens is that you get older • knows he can't be chic of the week forever • *honest and willing, proud and lonely (they go together), aware that sometimes in life we say yes just because we're tired of saying no* • senses that under the parade of human work and noise, today is much like yesterday and tomorrow will be like today. Existence is a wheel of recurring patterns, and all we can do is live for a while, do our best, then die for good, without finding out much.

She: Lovely Lady with a twinkly presence and a sweet soul, not likely to shuffle off to Buffalo • *has a superb truth-radar allowing her to skip the palaver and cut to the motive quickly while accepting the merry-go-round as part of the package* • can mesmerize with her eyes, is too smart to buy a dream or engage in much cognac and cogitation • *demonstrates a high level of aloofness, not good at making a Greek tragedy of everything* • is fully aware that the shark is the only animal that never sleeps • *gets a lot of appraising and deeply approving glances, completely aware that most people live more in their fiction than in their fact* • fully capable of—you're my lamb, I'm your shepherd behavior • likes the Sean O'Casey line—"the theater is no place for a person who bleeds easily" • *has an abundance of general love and a great way with conversation—she never makes it, but is genuinely interested in comments and when one is finished talking to her, he usually knows more about the subject than when he started* • is reputed to be great at yawning, stretching, purring, as well as being on an adrenaline high • *is freshly-scrubbed, spunky, brave, decent with a smile so radiant her legions would throw themselves on swords for her (so the Irish say)* • People who know her feel gratitude that she is a friend, pride in being supportive of her—mostly they rejoice in being part of her world in which there's a legal limit to the snow!

—ANCIEN REGIME—

A more appropriate name for world-class sophisticates who have enjoyed the galaxy of human experiences at the highest levels, would be hard to find; **Old Guard** as a name, despite its historical relevance to the **Cave Dwellers** (in Washington, D.C.) connotes all the right things about those who dwell in the world's richest enclave.

Old Guard, historically, is a term for the conservative wing of a political party, or anyone who opposes change; it dates back to Napoleon's Imperial Guard, troops chosen in 1804 to be the elite of the French military. Devoted to Napoleon, they were given preferential treatment and thus opposed any change in the *status quo*; the French called them the

"Vieille Garde" or "Old Guard." In their bearskin hats and colorful uniforms they made the last charge at Waterloo.

How the term was translated to a social classification is unknown, but it's obvious that "vintage" is presumed; probably the term was reinvented when some literary observer decided to lay an accolade on those pioneers who created and massaged Palm Beach society to its current *ne plus ultra* status. In a strict sense, a member of the Old Guard is someone born to a patrician family and bred in the area; someone born to the manner with an abnormal love of the tropics and the perseverance to tolerate revolving economics and social aspirants. In other cities, the **Old Guard** is equivalent to a **Cave Dweller** or a **Brahmin** or a **Blueblood**, but despite nomenclature, members of that sacrosanct classification do, usually, have great breeding, genes and a special *joie de vivre* (even if it is conservatively concealed). They often have streets, parks and museums named after their ancestors but their names rarely appear in newspapers; they shrink from publicity, party at home and live on inherited money.

Credentials include the right **birthplace** (an adroit midwife or the original St. Mary's or Good Sam), **schools** (PB Day School and Rosarian Academy), **charities** (Preservation Foundation, Four Arts), **hangouts** (B&T, Everglades), **churches** (St. Edward's or Bethesda); and as the Game gets played out, even the proper **undertaker** (Quattlebaum) and **cemeteries** (the Columbarium at Bethesda).

—CLASS DISTINCTIONS—

These preferences define the classes:

	OLD GUARD	NOUVEAU RICHE
Art	Hunt prints, landscapes, family portraits in oil, Monet, Renoir, old masters	Picasso, Chagal, Miro, Botero, conceptual art, sculpture in cast bronze, mixed media installations, faux masters
Autos	American made station wagons, sedans, Jeeps, old Rolls and Bentleys, vintage classics	Rolls Corniche, Bentley Turbo, Mercedes, Volvo station wagons, Range Rovers, Ferraris, BMWs, Jaguars
Charities	Four Arts, Preservation Foundation, Red Cross, Community Chest, Cancer, Hospice, Juvenile Diabetes, Hospitals	Heart, P.B. Opera, Ballet Florida, P.B. Symphony, Lord's Place, Cystic Fibrosis, Arthritis, Mental Health, Hope House
Churches	Bethesda, Royal Poinciana Chapel, St. Edward's	Bethesda, Royal Poinciana Chapel, St. Edward's, Temple Emanu-El

16

Clubs	B&T, Everglades, Society of the Four Arts, Garden Club	Beach Club, Sailfish Club, Palm Beach Country Club, The Mar-a-Lago Club
Dress Women	Classic ensembles in cotton, linen and cashmere, Lilly Pulitzer, Adolfo, Blass, Galanos, Givenchy, Herrera, St. Laurent, de la Renta, Trigere, Vintage Couture from Schiaparelli, Norell, Chanel, Dior, mink stoles, sensible shoes	Trendy fashion, plunging decolletage, Karan, Calvin, McFadden, Scassi, Escada, Armani, Galliano, Versace, St. Laurent, de la Renta, head to toe Chanel, Prada, Gucci, Vuitton, Hermes, Ferragamo, Manolo Blahnik, Pashmina Stoles, beaucoup shoes-towering heels
Dress Men	Navy blazer a la Brooks Bros., cuffed pants in white, khaki or gray, button down shirts, shawl-collared tuxedos, club ties, polo shirts, tennis whites, cashmere sweaters, Belgian loafers	Navy blazer a la Brioni, bespoke tailoring from Huntsman, Lanvink and Cifonelli, monogrammed Turnbull Asser, and Charvet shirts, Armani, Hermes ties, Lobb, Gucci, Ferragamo cashmere everything, silk or sea island cotton dressing gowns, velvet slippers with gold embroidery
Jewelry	Treasured family heirlooms, pearls, discrete and tasteful stones, solitaire engagement rings, gold wedding bands, Fred Leighton, Greenleaf & Crosby, Tiffany, vintage Cartier and Van Cleef & Arpels	Important stones set in high mountings, multiple gold bracelets, sapphire engagement rings, David Webb, Bulgari, latest Cartier and Van Cleef & Arpels mixed with fashion-faux, suite with impressive provenance from Sotheby's and Christies
Libations	Scotch, gin martinis, bourbon, champagne, sherry, claret, bordeaux, port, brandy	Flavored vodka martinis, champagne, micro-brewed beers, single malt scotch, grand cru chateaux and Domaine wines, V.S.O.P. Cognac (with Cuban cigars)
Hobbies	Bridge, gin rummy, tennis, golf, backgammon, polo, riding, skeet shooting, fishing, sailing,	Backgammon, polo, golf, tennis, skiing, running, fishing in exotic locales, gourmet cooking, fine dining, shopping, redecorating,

17

	dressage, thoroughbred racing, hunts, gardening, flower arranging, genealogy	"Net" surfing
Habitat	Chevy Chase, New York, Newport, Saratoga, Middleburg, Palm Beach	New York, Hamptons, Aspen, Sun Valley, Westchester, Palm Beach
Orchestras/Music	Neal Smith, Lester Lavin, Peter Duchin, Marshall Grant (the late)	Joe Ricardel, Alex Donner, Mike Carney, Michael Rose, Billy Duke, Doug Verga
Pets	Labradors, Golden Retrievers, German Shepherds, Dachshunds, Poodles, Corgies, feral Cats, canaries	Jack Russell Terriers, Lhasa Apsos, Maltese, Pugs, Shih Tzus, King Charles Spaniels, exotic birds and fish
Characteristics	Unpretentious, entertains simply, shuns publicity, quiet and modest, reclusive, stiff upper lip, makes do	Cultural enthusiast, supports the arts, social climber, entertains on grand scale, courts press, retains P.R agent, does the Hustle, makes over
Society Families	Phipps, Matthews, Whitney, Maddock, Cluett, Gardiner, Smith, Fanjul, Kennedy, du Pont, Ford, Guest, Hutton, Drexel	Taubman, Goodman, Gosman, Perelman, Kohl, Trump, Mashek, Lauder, Fisher, Marden, Adler

The **Old Guard** in Palm Beach is somewhat endangered, locked in trust funds with low interest rates set up years ago, poor personal executors, inflation—whatever the cause, the prognosis for the survival of this species is questionable. Financially, those who had everything (background, breeding, proper education, glamorous lives) are now often in a position of meager existence (only by Palm Beach standards). The Old Guard presents a facade of strength, confidence, authority and status based on heritage and ancestry; unfortunately, status can't buy exorbitantly priced material goods that are so much a part of today's *nouvelle* society (but, on the other hand, ancestry is priceless and can't be bought). The question has recently become—who carries more status in Palm

Beach? Those born into the "right" family, living without extravagance yet belonging to the "elite" clubs or those who through individual personal achievement have created life in the "grand style" (the former style of the Old Guard)?

—SURNAME SCORE—

*M*any seem to think that the most popular name in Palm Beach is "**Darling**," but based on the approximately 9,200 registered voters in the town, **Smith** is the surname most frequently represented. Not far behind are **Miller, Cohen** and **Schwartz**. The Palm Beach of the 30s and 40s saw Smith again the most active name, followed by Miller, Williams and Brown.

As for first names, way back when, the most popular names were Jonathan, Christopher, Anthony, David and John; Emily, Elizabeth and Jessica. Lately, first names like Tiffany, Samantha, Alexandra, Katherine and Jennifer; Daniel, Ashley, Jason, James, Michael and Alexander are the winners.

—SOLID GOLD—

*F*orbes Magazine ("America's Four Hundred Richest People") singles out our area as having an abundance of super-rich residents. The following are the most visible:

BILLIONAIRES	NET WORTH
John Kluge, 80s, Palm Beach, Metromedia, broadcast	$11.9 billion
Edgar Bronfman, 70s, Palm Beach, Seagram, investments	$ 4.2 billion
Carl Icahn, 60s, Palm Beach, financier	$4.2 billion
Leonard Lauder, 60s, Palm Beach, cosmetics	$4.1 billion
Ronald Lauder, 50s, Palm Beach, cosmetics	$4.0 billion
Ronald Perelman, 50s, Palm Beach, financier	$3.8 billion
David Koch, 60s, Palm Beach, oil, investments	$3.4 billion
Jack Taylor, 70s, Palm Beach, rental cars	$2.8 billion
James Clark, 50s, Palm Beach, Netscape, internet	$1.8 billion
Richard deVos, 70s, Manalapan, Amway Corp.	$1.8 billion
Sydell Miller, 60s, Palm Beach, hair products	$1.7 billion
Donald Trump, 50s, Palm Beach, real estate	$1.6 billion
George Lindemann, 60s, Palm Beach, Wellington, cable TV	$1.5 billion
Robert Rich, 80s, Palm Beach, dairy products	$1.4 billion
Arthur Williams, 50s, Palm Beach, insurance	$1.4 billion
Ken Langone, 60s, Palm Beach, The Home Depot, investments	$1.2 billion
Sidney Kimmel, 60s, Palm Beach, apparel	$1.0 billion

MEGA-MILLIONAIRES

Max Fisher, 90s, Palm Beach, oil, gas	$975 million
Nelson Peltz, 50s, Palm Beach, LBOs	$890 million
Thomas Lee, 50s, Palm Beach, LBOs	$875 million
Alfred Taubmann, 60s, Palm Beach	$860 million
Diana Strawbridge Wister, 60s, Palm Beach, inheritance	$700 million
William Koch, 60s, Palm Beach, oil	$650 million
Stuart Subotnick, 50s, Palm Beach, Metromedia, broadcast	$625 million
Melvin Simon, 70s, Manalapan, shopping centers	$600 million

Palm Beacher **Mitzi Newhouse** had an estimated net worth of $8 million at the time of her death a few years ago (the IRS was heavily involved in sorting out taxable portions of the estate); she and her sons—Donald and Samuel—own Advance Publications, a communication complex of newspapers (*Newark Star-ledger*), magazines (*Parade, Glamour, Vogue, Self, Mademoiselle, Bon Appetit, Vanity Fair, Gourmet*), books and cable TV systems with annual revenues of about $4 billion. Her $8 million made her the richest woman in America at the time but in the inexorable escalation of almost everything, her monies are modest compared to the current fortunes of several women: **Alice** and **Helen Walton** each have a net worth of $16 billion, as heirs to Wal-Mart Stores; and **Barbara Cox Anthony** and **Anne Cox Chambers** are worth $10.6 billion each, inheritance from Cox Enterprises.

For the record, the richest man in America is **William Henry Gates** (Seattle; 40s) of Microsoft Corp. with an estimated net worth of $60-$90 billion; second is **Warren Buffett** (Omaha, 70s), Berkshire Hathaway at $36 billion. **Paul Allen**, also of Microsoft is third with $30 billion, followed by Microsoft CEO, **Steven Ballmer** at $20 billion.

Gates is also the richest man in the world. His formidable net worth is worth more the value of some of the world's largest corporations—at $90 billion he outperforms Chase Manhattan at $62 billion; Ford Motor Company at $60 billion; McDonalds at $57 billion; and Philip Morris at $56 billion. Yet he isn't considered the richest man of all time—John D. Rockefeller, Cornelius Vanderbilt and John Jacob Astor all had greater fortunes based on their wealth as a percentage of the country's gross national product. On a projected basis, however, Gates is likely to be the world's first trillionaire by 2005, and assuming our economy grows an average of three percent a year, his fortune will surpass the U.S. gross domestic product by 2010! (Fortunes vary widely year-to-year.)

The greatest concentration of **wealth** in the world is in the United States. Family dynasties control staggering fortunes. Among leaders are (in billions): Walton ($40); Mars ($25), du Pont ($25), Cox ($23). It is estimated that in the next 20 years, some $10 trillion in assets will be passed on from families like these to their children and grandchildren—the largest single money transfer in history.

It's up, up and away for **executive** salaries, too. In 1978, Palm Beacher David Mahoney (the late), then Chairman of Norton Simon, was the highest-paid CEO in America at $2 million (the average worker was paid $10.592). Twenty years later, Michael Eisner, CEO of Walt Disney took home $575 million in cash and stock (and the average worker's pay was $22,976). In the new century, between salary, bonus and long- term compensation, it will be routine for top executives to earn beaucoup millions annually.

Right up there in the mega-buck category are many **entertainment** and fashion industry figures: producer George Lucas made $400 million last year; Oprah Winfrey, $150 million; Giorgio Armani, $135 million; Tom Hanks, $71 million; author Tom Clancy, $66 million; Stephen King, $65 million; The Backstreet Boys, $60 million; Steven Spielberg, $60 million and Bruce Willis, $55 million. Success is a matter of performance backed by headlines, cover stories, internet exposure and access to the power elite.

In the classification of **dictators**, financial info is nebulous because of inaccurate reporting, but it is believed that Sultan Hassanai Bolkiah of Brunei is tops with a net worth of $30 billion; he is followed by King Fahd Bin Abdulaziz Alsaud of Saudia Arabia at $428 billion; Sheikh Zayed Bin Sultan Al Nahyan of UAE at $20 billion; Amir Jaber Al-Ahmed Al-Jaber Al-Sabah of Kuwait at $17 billion.

As a monarch, **Queen Elizabeth II** of the U.K. is worth $16 billion; she gets an annual allowance of $15 million for official duties, staff salaries and upkeep of Buckingham Palace. Nine other family members get allowances totaling $5 million. Charles, the Prince of Wales, and Duke of Cornwall, is worth an estimated $464 million based on his land holdings in Cornwall, which throw off more than $11 million annually. His lifestyle is quite lavish—$320,000 for an Aston Martin V8 Volante, $640,000 per year for travel, about $250,000 to keep his mistress—Camilla Parker Bowles, in proper bangles and beads, and about $80,000 for his own clothing.

Other **monarchs** don't fare as well: Queen Margarethe of Denmark gets an annual stipend of $4 million; Belgium's King Badouin makes about $3 miilion yearly; King Juan Carlos and Queen Sophie of Spain receive $3.5 million; and socialist Sweden pays $2 million yearly to King Gustav and Queen Silvia.

Among the Palm Beach-related fortunes that have not been divided so often as to have little residual value left are: **Phipps** at $6.5 billion; **Scripps**, $4.5 billion; **Wrigley**, $2.7 billion; **Ford**, $2 billion; **Donnelley**, $1.8 billion; **Pulitzer**, $1 billion and **Flagler/Kenan**, $1 billion.

Large, but lesser numbers accrue to these Palm Beach ladies who are considered the richest single women in Town: **Kathy Ford, Celia Lipton Farris, Anya Bagley, Estelle Gelman, Barton Gubelmann, Rose Sachs, Mary Alice Fortin, Carola Mandel, Aimee Heeren, Gio King, Fran Todman, Enid Haupt, Jan Hooker, Sydell Miller** and **Terry Allen Kramer.**

—DIVINE & SUBLIME—

*B*y any measurement, many Palm Beachers fit the specifications as among the world's most beautiful, vibrant and exciting women. In that league are: **Inger Anderson, Mary Baker, Tori Baker, Nancy Brinker, Virginia Burke, Kim Campbell, Caroline Cassidy, Dee Cushing, Lore Dodge, Jane Dudley, Nicole Fanjul, Celia Lipton Farris, Lisa Ferguson, Gay Gaines, Jill Gilmour, Christina Goldsmith, Judy Grubman, C.Z. Guest, Audrey Gruss, Anita Hamilton, Nicki Harris, Mai Harrison, Dina Merrill Hartley, Betty Scripps Harvey, Trish Hilton, Betsy Kaiser, Susan Keenan, Anne Keresey, Angela Koch, Renee Lickle, Hillie Mahoney, Jean Matthews, Jayne McConnell, Terry Monell, Fern de Narvaez, Nadia Oxenberg, Kit Pannill, Sue Partington, Chessy Patcevitch, Pauline Boardman Pitt, Lois Pope, Maggie Scherer, Diane Millner, Mary Schott, Lesly Smith, Jean Tailer, Mary Webster** and **Betsy Ylvisaker.**

Fellows of comparable ilk include: **H. Loy Anderson Jr., Kane Baker, Peter Broberg, Guilford Dudley, Stanley Gaines, Warry Gillet, William Gubelmann II, Alexander Guest, Paul Ilyinsky, Bob Lappin, Bob Leidy, Gary Lickle, John Mashek, Bruce McAllister, Laddie Merck, Dan Ponton, Stanley Rumbough, Warren Scherer, Frank Shields, Donald Trump** and **Ron Viejo.**

—GRANDES DAMES & DAMSELS—

By definition, a **Grande Dame** is usually an elderly woman of high social position or majestic manner. She rules her domain through an elegant routine and is generally admired, emulated and revered by her peers and followers. Yet, she is evolutionary—she grows into her role over time, fulfills her obligations during her moments of glory, evolves into a statesperson and ultimately into a sage and symbol of a "great era."

In a Town with wall-to-wall hostesses, all sophisticated, cosmopolitan and competitive, these are the stand outs (although each would deny same, preferring to pass the praise and low-key themselves):

Jean Tailer: always there, always a vision, always ready to serve, mostly for The Preservation Foundation of Palm Beach.

Celia Lipton Farris: name it, she does it! Has that humanitarian instinct from way back and has used it to serve almost every cause in Town, with class and panache.

Cathleen McFarlane: lots of top spin and pertinacity in taking the unknown into the limelight; goes for the blue moon, each and every time.

Betty Scripps Harvey: although her thrust in life takes her to many places in many roles, she is the quintessential Lady/Doer/Overseer/Incentivizer; always performs with class.

Other Grand Ladies like **Eunice Gardiner, C.Z. Guest, Audrey Gruss, Virginia Burke, Lois Pope, Ann Boutell, Betsy Matthews** and **Pauline Pitt** add lustre to our Town, too.

The Grande Dame of yesteryear really doesn't exist today. Although the Lady under the microscope may have the right *bona fides* and offer all the proper grandeur, in most cases she rejects the Grande Dame designation, because it suggests antiquity and, maybe, a certain superficial way of life. Today's woman is pragmatic, socially conscious, and aware of her role as an active contributor to society.

—STYLE SETTERS—

*T*he Winner's Circle is owned by those who follow cogent little dictates and fashions—the keystones to access, success, address and a full life. In Palm Beach, being a fastidious and elegant dresser opens eyes, doors and invitation lists. On a comparative basis, our Townies are sartorially superior and certainly rank with the world's elite in terms of being fashionable. Based on a survey of major fashion outlets in Palm Beach, here are the chosen ones (most are well-known in the community, support our Town via charitable activities, buy "locally" whenever feasible, and are workers/doers; they are admired and represent a dynamic force in our Town):

WOMEN

Catherine Adler (Mrs. Frederick): loves clothes with an attitude, elegance over easy. Very fashion savvy. Glamorous looks, tightly edited, likes colorful, dramatic and imaginative designer combinations.

Lisa Anderson (Mrs. John): the embodiment of elegance and ease; her spindle-thin waist carries the weight of voluminous lined skirts with airy grace; always a knockout.

Kathy Bleznak (Mrs. Alan): prefers eye-catching, glimmering gowns to match her effusive personality; fits the slim & trim look ideally.

Nancy Brinker: classic, tailored and elegant; powerful yet understated. Loves red.

Nicole Fanjul (Mrs. Alex): advocate of the fundamental look, with perfection in every detail; no fluffs or puffs, just basic figure-enhancing lines.

Marjorie Fisher (Mrs. Max): international good taste reflected by an extensive designer wardrobe; impeccably groomed and coiffed.

Joan Goodman (Mrs. Murray): enjoys sporting up-to-date clothes; true to traditional designers, but loves to experiment with the latest creations.

Audrey Gruss (Mrs. Martin): likes long and unforced lines with emphasis on the torso; has aerobicized her closet with chic, sleek and urbane classics, and a generous dash of jewelry.

Betsy Kaiser (Mrs. Michael): long-stemmed beauty who transforms every style into modern opulence; has an entrance-making star quality in whatever she wears. Former Galanos model (still true to his creations).

Susan Keenan (Mrs. James): superbly presented via stunning good looks and champagne personality; tends to shy away from the cold fashion icon look in favor of light and luxe tailored silhouettes.

Dorothy Kohl (Mrs. Sidney): a beauty in whatever she wears with a "perky" but elegant look, embellishing her well-proportioned athletic figure. Has an enviable cache of jewels.

Chris Marden (Mrs. Bernard): the epitome of good taste; a big Armani fan, the perfect backlight for her well-selected jewels.

Alyne Massey: internationally acclaimed for her good looks and extraordinary flair for the latest fashions. A big Blass advocate.

Betty Swope (Mrs. Herbert): always elegantly and appropriately dressed; the epitome of sophistication and charm.

Jean Tailer: transforms the tried and true into an aristocratic presentation; always in control—can affect high glamour or a natural look.

Pauline Boardman Pitt (Mrs. William): displays an easy luxurious appeal via an unerring sense of quality and taste. *"C'est grande taille ca"* has great shoulders and a demure sensuality that bewitches.

Lois Pope: understands what works perfectly, from rebellion to restraint; has a neatly seasoned look.

Celia Lipton Farris: wears designer fashions with aplomb; loves Escada by day, Mackie by night; gracious hostess, philanthropist, gently sophisticated.

Others: Known as fabulously groomed, fastidious and immaculately presented are: **Susan Bishop, Christine Curtis, Sandy Heine, Susan Partington, Nancy Tsai, Ruth Perelman** (wears Armani or Chanel with Van Cleef gloriously) and **Susan Lehrman Blank.** Equally charming in sportswear stretch or *froufrou* is **Jasmine Horowitz**, Lady of many bewitching hats and jewels. Lady with the most feminine looks (and clothes to match) is **Anita Hamilton.** Very Lady of Lady looks—**Betty Fisher** and **Tina Bilotti.** Most avant garde dresser—**Iris Apfel**, a study in imagination. Owner of the most Scaasi are **Eles Gillet** and **Barton Gubelman**; most "Oscars"—**Judy Taubman**; most Ungaros—**Estelle Gelman.** Most aware of the fine line between classy and sexy—**Linda Rossbach, Judy Grubman, Jill Rau** and **Ann Hamilton**. Finest refined power look— **Tina Flaherty**. Always well put together and on fashion alert—**Lesly Smith, Betty Scripps Harvey, Mary Schott, Kit Pannill, Kelly Brogan** and **Diane Millner**. Very trendy and tuned in—**Julia Koch, Paula Cook, Dorothy Schulman, Pam Hoffpauer, Maria Ponton, Jacquie Liggett, Wendy Meister, Nan Ourisman, Peggy Rao** and **Carol Digges**. Knowing well that fashion is fleeting but style is eternal are: **Lynn Manulis, Marla Paxson, Gay Gaines, Mary Montgomery, Nicki Harris, Christine Curtis, Leigh Larmoyeux, June Rooney** and **Patricia Kennedy**. Shortest hair in Town—**Suzette Wexner**; longest— **Etonella Christlieb**. Maddest hatter—**Dorothy Sullivan**.

MEN

Lewis Schott: urbane, stately, looks great formally or informally. Very together and tailored.

Jose "Pepe" Fanjul: international look, great flair and individual style.

F. Warrington Gillet, Jr.: debonair, tanned, an advocate of the professional look, always on the mark.

Ridgely Harrison: the look of today's Palm Beach, with traditional overtones; classy casual.

Stanley Rumbough: typifies Palm Beach in its halcyon days, sporty, elegant, tasteful, loves Island colors (pink, chartreuse, magenta).

Gary Lickle: tall, refined, sports the young "traditional" look.

Jeremy Harvey: wears blazers and formal wear exceptionally well; tall, lean, suave, neatly assembled.

Bob Leidy: understated, manly image, stylish and classy.

Robert Montgomery: conservative, strictly business look, clean cut, tight, can be sporty.

John Mashek: likes well proportioned, symmetrical clothes, tends to be formal yet dashing. Trim, tall and always well turned out.

Other gents with fashion panache are: **Charles Ranson, Harold Corrigan, Dixon Boardman, Ned Monell, Peter Summers, Pedro Morrison, Scott Snyder, Ashton de Peyster, Ron Viejo, Richard Cowell, Bill Pitt, Michael Blank, Gerald Goldsmith, Dan Ponton, George Sharoubim, Kirby Kooluris, Ray Perelman, Carlo Bilotti, Michael Brown, Harry Platt, Stanley Gaines, Harcourt Sylvester, Carl Apfel, Michael Carney, Doug Regan** and **Dean Vegosen**.

COUPLES

Terrence and Carrie Cassidy: tall, genteel; stylish clothing enhances their stature.

25

Robert and Eunice Gardiner: he's conservative, wears neatly tailored clothing, she prefers contemporary chic styles; both right on the money.

Patrick and June Rooney: he's dapper, perfectly put together, she has a tailored, classy look.

William and Renee Lickle: classic American-looking couple, sensitive, careful about their traditional yet adventurous look.

John and Lisa Anderson: always appropriately dressed for the occasion, adaptable, fitting, stylish.

Guilford and Jane Dudley: internationally stylish, a classy "Old Guard" look.

Tommy and Dee Cushing: exquisite taste, understand the power of low-key elegance.

Bill and Virginia Buckley: distinguished look, tastefully conservative.

Hunter and Helga Marston: have a "young at heart" look reflective of their zeal in living life to the fullest, both open to new styles.

Other couples with sartorial finesse are: **Jeanie and Will Matthews, Lourdes and Bob Harvey, Betsy and Bill Ylvisaker, Jackie and Dick Cowell, John and Noreen Drexel, Chris and Bernard Marden, Ruth and Ray Perelman, Sam and Marjorie Meek, Sheila and Jim Kerwin, Betsy and Wallace Turner, Jan and Harding Willinger, Laura and Lee Munder, Nancy and Jeff Smith, George and Betsy Matthews, Richard and Pat Johnson, Alma and Tony Tambone, Edie and Marvin Schur, Tina and Bill Flaherty, Lori and Harold Corrigan, Ned and Pat Cook, Sam and Joyce McLendon, Kim and Rolla Campbell, Patricia and Julian Hipwood, Laddie and Dede Merck, Brian and Eileen Burns, Norma and Simon Fireman, Chris and Leigh Larmoyeux, Angie and Paul Ilyinsky, Jim and Patsy Wearn, Jack and Nell Hight, Martin and Audrey Gruss, Sondra and David Mack, Jeanne and Frank Habicht, Katie and Leo Vecellio** and **John and Lore Dodge**.

These Palm Beachers join the illustrious ranks of their counterparts on a global basis. The International Best Dressed List, coordinated by Eleanor Lambert, and now in its fifth decade, annually selects those who dress exceptionally well. Among the Ladies are: **Brooke Astor, China Machado, Jane Dudley, Nina Griscom Baker, Aimee de Heeren, Amanda Burden, Aerin Lauder, Gwyneth Paltrow, Eliza Reed, Viscountess Linley, Jade Jagger, Marian McEvoy, Lee Radziwill Ross, Carolina Herrera, Kelly Klein, Adrienne Vittadini** and others. For the men, best dressed winners are: **King Juan Carlos** of Spain,

Tom Wolfe, Viscount Linley, Paul Newman, Mark Hampton, Count Frederic Chandon, Paul Wilmot, Henry Kravis, Pat Riley, Massimo Ferragamo, Kenneth Chenault, Lord Hindlip, Thomas Kempner, Phillip Hathaway and Prince Michael of Kent.

—SOCIAL LIONS—

Once you're inside The Circle, the same faces appear all too often; yet since a pyramid is cone-shaped, density at the top must, perforce, diminish, thus a select few: **Janna and Stanley Rumbough** (heritage, horses, dedicated to cause); **Pauline and William Pitt** (affuence, track record, willingness to do the deed); **Betsy and George Matthews** (long line, lots of franchise rights, a living landmark); **Polly and Michael Fawcett** (owners of Palm Beach's oldest house— *"Duck's Nest,"* built by Henry Maddock in 1891); **Renee and William C. Lickle** (generational family in finance and finesse); **Dee and Tommy Cushing** (class plus a trophy hunter plus "Deanna" creations); **Inger and H. Loy Anderson, Jr.** (Captain of Finance, irrepressible Townie and beautiful people); **Barton Gubelmann** (lovely lady, hostess in Newport and PB); **Fitz Eugene Dixon, Jr.** (affluent, back-of-the-scenes philanthropist); **Jesse and Rand Araskog** (big-time power players, adaptable, energetic); **Gay and Stanley Gaines** (panache, intelligence and zeal); **Cathleen McFarlane** (all things to all people with ease, affability and charm); and **Angelica and Paul Ilyinsky** (wide-ranging conversationalists and historians).

—NAME FAME—

Pillsbury, du Pont, Firestone, Whitney and **Lauder** are just a few of the august names that represent both a Palm Beach person and a product or service. Dozens of dynastic families enjoy their heritage and the food, beverage, cosmetic or whatever bears their name or their lineage. Some are:

Gregg Dodge (widow of auto heir Horace Dodge, Jr.); **Vincent De Paul Draddy** (the late: Izod and Lacoste knit shirts); **Jim Kimberly** (the late: Kimberly-Clark paper fortune); **D. Mead Johnson** (the late: Johnson & Johnson Pharmaceuticals); **Joan Bove** (Clairol co-founder); **Helen Boehm** (Boehm Porcelains); **Celia Lipton Farris** (late husband, inventor Victor Farris, gave birth to the milk carton and 275 other products); **Helen Cluett** (Cluett, Peabody & Co.); **Margaret Sanders** (Col. Sanders/Kentucky Fried Chicken); **Caroline Penney** (J.C. Penney stores); **Marshall "Doc" Rinker** (the late: Rinker Materials); **George Sturgis Pillsbury** (Pillsbury Co. heir); **Mary Sanford** (the late: widow of Bigelow-Sanford Carpet Co.); **Sue Whitmore** (the late: great-grandfather developed Listerine); **Mary Alice Firestone Asher** (former wife of Firstone Tire heir Russell Firestone); **Norman Brinker** (former CEO of Bennigan's and Chili's restaurants; once headed up Burger King); **Charles Bronfman** (co-chairman of Seagram Co. Ltd.); **Kathleen Ford** (former wife of Henry Ford II); **"Bunny" du Pont** (heir to the du Pont chemical fortune); **Estee Lauder** (cosmetic queen); **Marylou Whitney Hendrickson** (former wife of the late **Cornelius Vanderbilt Whitney**, lumber, railroad); **Fran Todman** (wife of one of the founders of Goodson-Todman, producers of TV shows like *Password, Concentration* and *I've Got A Secret*); **Willie Hutton** (grandnephew of E.F. Hutton, stock magnate) and Marjorie Merriweather Post, the late: Post cereals). Recently **Quick & Reilly Group, Inc.**, investment firm, located in Palm Beach; parents Leslie and Regina Quick with their son Tom and daughter Trish are visible socialites.

Others who qualify for people-gazing and occasion autograph requests are: **Donald Trump**, master of his universe and gate-keeper at Mar-a-Lago; **Arnold Scaasi** (designer of gowns for the world's elite); **George Hamilton** (son of glamorous Townie Ann Hamilton, TanMan actor and restaurateur); broadcaster **Rush Limbaugh, Jimmy Buffett** of Margaritaville fame; rocker **Rod Stewart; Burt Reynolds** (local boy who once was king of the mountain), crooners **Vic Damone** and **Perry Como**; queen of stock trading **Muriel Siebert**, **"Laddie" Merck** (pharmaceuticals), **Lowell "Bud" Paxson** (after whom a television network is named, now affiliated with NBC), and **Maya Swarovsky** (crystal jewelry and accessories). Billionaires like **Ronald Perelman, John Kluge, Carl Icahn, Leonard and Ronald Lauder, Donald and Samuel Newhouse**, and **James Clark** are just private enough not to be widely recognized, and usually confine their autographs to signing checks!

—MAX-MARRIAGES—

*E*ndurance in the **matrimonial state** is a rare thing; estimates suggest that 46 percent of marriages fail within the first five years. All the more reason to applaud these long-term happily married Townies (with marital unions in the 40- to 60-year range):

Nancy and Wycoff Myers (she of charitable prowess, he of banking leadership); **Virginia and Bill Buckley** (all-around do-gooders); **Alma and Tony Tambone** (always there, always a #10 in performance); **Arlette and Bob Gordon** (world-travelers, world-class hosts), **Chris and Bernie Marden** (major philanthropists and friends of the needy); **Helene and Jesse Newman** (among our Town's most visible and ad-

28

mired couples); **Carol and Claude Dimick Reese** (part of the heritage of our Island); **Gay and Stanley Gaines** (great friends of the less fortunate and enthusiastic participants in life); **Emily and Dom DiMaggio** (advocates of forward motion and superior gamemanship); **Edith and Eugene Dixon** (educated and effective role models); **Jeanne and Frank Habicht** (relentlessly pursuing excellence, in whatever); **Ruth and Ray Perelman** (originals, activists, delightful in social situations); **Angelica and Paul Ilyinsky** (tops in Town politics and praiseworthy work); **Elaine and Joe Jack Merriman** (munificent and outgoing, friends to all); **Betsy and George Matthews** (holders of a legacy, top achievers); **Evalyn and Howard Swartz** (great in devotion to family, friends and causes); **Jerre and Curt Gowdy** (long-time supporters of charities and activists on many fronts); **Jane and Guilford Dudley** (noble sense of responsibility, in or out of government); **Ruth and Ed Hennessy** (very proper and poised in everything they do, which is plenty); **Kay and Jim Morrissey** (entertaining and indefatigable Townies of rich vintage); **Betty and Alfred Fisher** (civilized and enlightened couple with good instincts for the right causes); **Renee and Bill Lickle** (distinguished and dedicated humanitarians); **Patricia and Al Haig** (fixtures in Town affairs, perfectly attuned to results); **Maria and John Cassidy** (industrious and lively social and business leaders); **Dorothy and John Sullivan** (lovely fundraisers and people-people); **Mary and Robert Montgomery** (as sure as sunrise for all the right causes in all the right ways).

Other blissful couples in the long-term classification are: **June and Tim Rooney, Nancy and Joe Dryer, Sally and Dick Robinson, Joyce and Sam McLendon, Joan and Brad Greer, Sarah and Dr. Younger Staton, Eleanor and George Hoyt, Diann and Victor Scaravilli, Anita and Herman Dubnoff, Dorothy and Milton Schulman, Babe and Bob Davidoff** and **Carol and Ted Hepburn.**

—SUPER SWORDS—

ur Town has an attractive complement of people in the category of SWORDS—single, widowed or recently divorced. They float about the galas and special events with aplomb and uninhibited enthusiasm, generally open to a possible alliance and the opportunity to tie a million dollar knot, or just to enjoy the drawing room comedy that is often presented.

Among the super-single gentlemen are: **John Brogan**, All-American humanitarian; **Michael Burrows**, real estate developer, fundraiser; **Michel de Yougoslavie**, royal realtor; **Bob Leidy**, investor and sportsman; **Garrison Lickle**, banker, social heavy-hitter; **Dan Ponton**, Club

Colette CEO; **Elliot Schnall**, financier extraordinaire; **Ron Viejo**, Van Cleef's local hero; **Mason Phelps**, United States Equestrian Team champion; kinetic energy mogul **Donald Trump; Patrick Park**, man-about-the cosmos; New Wave leader **Alfonso Landa; Judge Rex Ford**; carrier of many anecdotes **Tony Boalt**; Tiffany toast **Harry Platt**; international designer **Geoffrey Bradfield; Averell Harriman Fisk**, financialman; **Kentucky Colonel James Lesher; Allen Manning**, spokesman for many causes; preserver of tradition **John Mashek; Philip Whitacre**, Community Chest Exec Director; Dr. Graham Whitfield, physician on land and in the air; top banker **Charles Ranson; Col. Bobby Spencer**, true gent and actionary; money sage **Howard Risick**; publisher **Ron Woods**; real estate and croquet master **John Ryan**, mega-entrepreneur **Bob Cuillo** and a host of other leaders, whatever their side of the street: **Sam Whittaker, Bruce Bent, Alton O'Neil, Tom Abrams, Frank Butler, Louis Anthony, John Raimondi, Tony Rolfe, Tom Baldwin, Neil Hirsch, Billy David, Keith and Todd Meister, James Borynack, Eddy Louis, Stanton Freeman, George Sharoubim, Alexis Mersentes, Josh Gruss, Franklyn de Marco, Elliot Shaw** and **Wes Cawley.**

For the record, some of the *world's* most eligible bachelors are: **Nick Firestone**, 20s, heir to the tire fortune; **Prince Pierre D'Arenberg**, 30s, Standard Oil heir; the **Duke of Northumberland**, 30s, worth about $100 million; the **Duke of Hamilton**, 50s, Scotland's premier duke; the **Duke of Atholl**, 60s, worth about $300 million, has own private army; **Tara Getty**, 20s, only son of Paul Getty, Jr.; and **Carter Burden III**, 30s, grandson of CBS founder William Paley.

Re the **Ladies**. There are many beauties who are single but not necessarily available because of family commitment, desire, economic restraints or other conditions of humankind. **Carroll Petrie, Celia Lipton Farris, Alyne Massey, Lois Pope, Jean Tailer** and **Kathy Ford** are single, for example, but hardly available for occasional dates; most super-sophisticated women (and men) have their own social milieu and strata and don't venture far from their heritage. Yet, some delightfully single and willing-to-talk Ladies in Town are: **Antoinette Boalt, Sheila Haisfield, Anita Hamilton, Trish Hilton, Liza Leidy, Chan Mashek, Patricia McConnell, Brownie McLean, Faith Morford, Lucy Musso, Trish Quick, Susan Reymond, Carol Ruhlman, Judy Schrafft, Sandy Smith, Anita Tremain, Mary Frances Turner, Ashton Battle, Clare O'Keeffe, Beverly Wilkes, Cynthia Van Buren, Gale Brophy, Kathy Miller, Cheryl Gowdy, Maggie McCloskey, Claudia Holguin, Monique Fortinberry, Jacqueline Parker, Diane Millner, Vicki Bagley, Ashley Crystal, Maureen O'Sullivan, Jane Robinson, Judy Grubman, Christiana Shields, Sugar Rautbord, Nancy Walsh, Dale**

Coudert, Ann Appleman, Catherine Ford Brister, Skira Watson, Dee Banker, Kimberly Strauss, Patricia Sans, Caroline Marston, Becky Bruder, Susanna Cutts, Maria Ornelas, Barbara Katz, Leslie Aldrich Westoff, Bunnie Stevens, Jill Curceo, Diana Paxton and **Carol Digges.**

—THE MAIDENS—

Maiden names of Leading Ladies:

Current	Maiden
Mrs. Samuel W. Meek	Marjorie Meacham
Mrs. O. Roy Chalk	Claire Cole
Mrs. Norris Brown McFarlane	Cathleen Cox
Mrs. Joseph Lauder	Josephine Mentzer
Mrs. Sam Cook Digges	Carol Ellis
Mrs. Alex Dreyfoos	Carolyn Elmhirst Buckley
Mrs. Curtis E. Gowdy	Jerre O. Dawkins
Mrs. Jesse D. Newman	Helene DeMarco
Mrs. Robert Hurbaugh	Pat Roper
Mrs. Arthur Ruddy	Belle Ryder
Mrs. Melvin H. Shalek	Berdonna Levy
Mrs. Robert G. Gordon	Arlette Lederman
Mrs. Arthur Burck	Rutilia Poli-Sandri
Mrs. William Flaherty	Tina Santi
Mrs. Richard C. Cowell	Jackie McKissick
Mrs. Edward W. Cook	Patricia Long
Mrs. William E . Buckley	Virginia Smith
Mrs. Norberto Azqueta	Lillian Fanjul
Mrs. Earl E.T. Smith	Lesly Stockard
Mrs. Edward Marshall Boehm	Helen Francesca Franzolin
Mrs. Charles Clayton Holt	Diana B.M. Blabon
Mrs. Frederick Adler	Catherine George
Mrs. Robert Barrett	Catherine B. Moore
Mrs. Rolla Dacres Campbell	Patience Mullendore McNulty
Mrs. Nathan Appleman	Ann Maynard
Mrs. Peter Nelson Basil	Danielle Freimann
Mrs. William Pitt	Pauline Baker
Mrs. Brown Bolte	Baronessa Erminia Amaru-Landau Mrs.
Mrs. Norman Eugene Brinker	Nancy Goodman
Mrs. Phillip Tennyson Crenshaw	Jacqueline Jean Saathoff
Mrs. R. Leigh Duemler	Catherine Merrill
Mrs. Max Martin Fisher	Marjorie Switow
Mrs. Paul B. Henry	Courtaline M. Hay
Mrs. Edward Kassatly	Camille Nicholas

31

Mrs. Stanley Gaines	Gay Hart
Mrs. David Joseph Mahoney	Hildegarde Mercedes Ercklentz
Mrs. Nigel Trevor Marix	Yvelyne Gabrielle De Marcellus
Mrs. I.S.V. Patcevitch	Chesbrough Lewis
Mrs. Paul Desmarais	Jacqueline Maranger
Mrs. Guilford Dudley	Jane Anderson
Mrs. Alfonso Fanjul	Lillian Gomez Mena
Mrs. Jose Pepe Fanjul	Emilia May
Mrs. Victor W. Farris	Celia Lipton
Mrs. Alfred J. Fisher	Betty Jane Jacobs
Mrs. Warner Bishop	Susan Bragg Howard
Mrs. George E. Ford	Beatriz Algarra Cuellar
Mrs. Henry Ford	Kathleen King
Mrs. Alfred A. Taubman	Judy Mazor
Mrs. Robert D.L. Gardiner	Eunice Bailey Oakes
Mrs. Warrington F. Gillet	Elesabeth Ingalls
Mrs. Walter S. Gubelmann	Barton Green
Mrs. Winston Guest	Helen Shields
Mrs. Louis Lehr	Sherry Mann
Mrs. Page Hufty	Frances Archbold
Mrs. James Morrissey	Kay Partney
Mrs. Paul Romanoff Ilyinsky	Angelica Kauffmann
Mrs. Lester Lindow	Baroness Andree de Verdor
Mrs. Wilson C. Lucom	Toni Arias
Mrs. Leon Mandel	Carola Panerai
Mrs. John R. McLean	Mildred Brown
Mrs. George Gregory Matthews	Betsy Kelly
Mrs. Michael Allan McIntosh	Winsome Dunn
Mrs. James Henry Partington	Susan Trowbridge
Mrs. William Pannill	Alice Zimmer
Mrs. Robert Curtis Salisbury	Frances Montgomery
Mrs. Horace W. Schmidlapp	Patricia Kennedy
Mrs. John Hamilton Schuler	Elizabeth Locke
Mrs. John Stetson	Josephine DeFina
Mrs. Frederick M. Supper	Patricia McKeon
Mrs. Howard R. Swartz	Evalyn Snyder
Mrs. Clother H. Vaughn	Joyce Sanders
Mrs. John L. Volk	Lillian Jane Kinney
Mrs. Thomas Barclay Walker	Julie Wood Fitzgerald
Mrs. John Liggett	Jacqueline Torkington
Mrs. Florenz Ourisman	Nan Lawn Thompson
Mrs. Warren Edward Avis	Deborah Kah
Mrs. Henry Bagley	Anya Smolianinoff Frelinghuysen-Carey
Mrs. Anthony Kane Baker	Victoria Oelsner

Mrs. Lowry Bell	Diana Marc Anthony
Mrs. David Berger	Barbara Simmons Wainscott
Mrs. Carlo Bilotti	Margaret Schultz
Mrs. Michael Blank	Susan Miller Lehrman
Mrs. Harold Cayzer	Beatrice de Holquin Fairbanks
Mrs. Dorothy Rautbord	Dorothy Haas
Mrs. William Claggett	Barbara Clark
Mrs. William G. Cluett	Helen Mitchell Stedman
Mrs. Donald G. Conrad	Stephania Shimkus
Mrs. Enriquillo Del Rosario	Audrey Barron
Mrs. Fitz Eugene Dixon	Edith Bruen Robb
Mrs. John Dodge	Lore Hayward Moran
Mrs, Alan Drey	Roberta Beverly Leonardo
Mrs. Andres B. Fanjul	Catherine Anne Scheerer
Mrs. Michael Fawcett	Polly Vanderford
Mrs. Bernard Gewirz	Sarah Myers
Mrs. Michael Joseph Gibbons	Cynthia Hungerford
Mrs. Alexander M. Haig	Patricia Fox
Mrs. J. Ira Harris	Nikki S. Shadur
Mrs. Edward Lawrence Hennessy	Ruth Francis Shilling
Mrs. Jack Hight	Nell Walker
Mrs. Barry Hoyt	Cynthia Dellard
Mrs. William E. Hutton III	Lynn Smith
Mrs. Daniel James	Sylvia Maxine Simonson
Mrs. Eric M. Javits	Margaretha Espersson
Mrs. William Kemp	Beverly Jo Smith
Mrs. Nicholas Kirkbride	Margaret Sherston-Baker
Mrs. Christopher Larmoyeux	Leigh Thorpe
Mrs. Bernard Marden	Chris Lemlich
Mrs. Jack Massey	Alyne Queener
Mrs. Bruce McAllister	Susan Ann Davidson
Mrs. Samual McLendon	Joyce Wiley
Mrs. David Miro	Herme de Wyman
Mrs. John Nicolo	Constance J. Roeder
Mrs. Martin Purcell	Constance Neher
Mrs. Todd Weintz	Sharon Queeney
Mrs. John Rau	Jill Laurie Porvancher
Mrs. David Robb	Patricia Ann Chrupcala
Mrs. William Roosevelt	Ava Elizabeth Fichtner
Mrs. Stanley M. Rumbough	Janna Herlow
Mrs. Robert Simmons	Nancy Jean Sharigan
Mrs. T. Suffern Tailer	Jean Sinclair
Mrs. William I. Tracy	Patricia Kate Kaplan
Mrs. William Wagner	Jo-Anne Condon
Mrs. Orator Woodward	Maureen Barry

—PALM BEACH CLASS—

*A*ny man who wears a plaid suit with a striped shirt, checked tie and polka-dotted handkerchief—and looks great—has CLASS (especially when most guys spend 20 minutes picking the wrong tie). It's indefinable, but it's there.

In a Town where Class abounds, it's easier to see it than define it; easier to sense Class than understand it; and it's quite impossible to clone it, imitate it or get it by osmosis. CLASS is in a Class by itself.

Here's what true Palm Beach CLASS is:

CLASS never makes excuses. It takes its hits, learns from experience and is always ready for the next confrontation.

CLASS is very considerate of others. It knows that good manners are nothing more than a series of petty sacrifices, small "gives" in anticipation of modest receipts.

CLASS can walk with kings and keep its virtue, and talk with the masses via a common touch that reaches everyone.

CLASS bespeaks an aristocracy that has nothing to do with lineage or wealth. The most affluent blue blood can be devoid of Class while the descendant of an Irish fisherman may ooze Class from every pore.

CLASS knows whether to congratulate or to commiserate in every situation; there is never a loss for words nor is there any automatic rejoinder. Class is basically quiet, soft, sure.

CLASS never runs scared. It is sure-footed and confident in the knowledge that you can meet life head on and handle whatever comes along.

CLASS regards the "New Tycoonery" with disdain, and knows that little monkeys follow big apes without much analysis; thereby condoning greed and assuring ostracism for all.

CLASS never tries to build itself up by totaling others; Class is already up and does not strive to look better by making others look worse.

CLASS understands that people who have had the same surgery like to compare scars; and keeps its distance from private dalliances.

CLASS realizes that there is no such thing as a do-it-yourself Rex Harrison Kit; and works at self-perfection rather than perfecting the style of others.

CLASS refutes the concept that life is a tragedy wherein we sit as spectators awhile, before acting out our own part. Class believes a person is what he/she does.

CLASS realizes that there are no draws in games of power.

CLASS is aware of (but protests) the normal sequence in most projects; Exultation; Disenchantment; Confusion; Search for the guilty; Punishment of the innocent; Distinction for the uninvolved.

CLASS realizes that the higher you climb the pyramid the more southern exposure you have.

CLASS knows there is no better way to flaunt power than to appear equal when dealing with inferiors.

CLASS recognizes that it isn't proper to serve five o'clock tea at all hours.

CLASS understands that the more you complain, the longer God lets you live.

CLASS assumes that it is wasted energy to have a battle of wits with an unarmed person.

CLASS recognizes a certain truism in the credo of Napoleon: "My power is dependent on my glory, and my glory on my victories. My power would fall if I did not base it on still more glory and still more victories. Conquest made me what I am; conquest alone can keep me there." Class, however, predicates life on victory for humankind, not victories over it.

CLASS knows that money doesn't talk, it swears!

Finally, CLASS appreciates the fact that this life kneels before the next.

La Revue Balmain
by °Rene Gruau

35

WILLIAM AND KIT PANNILL AND SONDRA AND DAVID MACK
purposeful, provocative, premier

Photo: Lucien Capehart

JOHN AND NOREEN DREXEL III
masterly and matchless

CANDY VAN ALEN AND COL. ROBERT SPENCER
formidable and fashionable

Photo: Lucien Capehart

BETTY AND ALFRED FISHER
captivating and cogent

SAMUEL AND MARJORIE MEEK
masters of the great game

Photo: Mort Kaye Studios

BETTY AND HERBERT SWOPE
veddy civilized, classics

EDIE AND FITZ DIXON
artful, active and appealing

Photo: Lucien Capehart

MURRAY AND JOAN GOODMAN
testimonial to high style and standards

Photo: Lucien Capehart

CHRISTINE AND ALAN CURTIS
good news and goodness all-around

Photo: Lucien Capehart

BOB AND MARY MONTGOMERY
all harmony and heart

45

Photo: Lucien Capehart

EDWIN AND VIRGINIA BURKE
universally admired and emulated

CHAPTER II

SOCIOLOGY, STATUS & SAVOIR-FAIRE
(Spirit, Style & Success)

Photo: Mort Kaye Studios

PAUL AND ANGIE ILYINSKY
regal, resplendent and radiant

—ELITISTS—

*S*ome of the Old Dukes, Grandes Dames, Boulevardiers and Eternal Winners always seem to be in style and in control and flash their elite demeanors in all the right places: **Edie and Fitz Eugene Dixon, Jr., Mrs. John L. Volk, Mr. and Mrs. William G. Pannill, Hollis Baker, Mrs. Henry Bagley,** the Honorable **John and Noreen Drexel, Renee and William C. Lickle, Elizabeth and Herbert Bayard Swope, Jr., Elizabeth and John H. Schuler, Susan and Henry P. McIntosh IV, Mr. and Mrs. James A. dePeyster, Mrs. Robert I. Ballinger, Mrs. Jack C. Massey, Barbara and Doyle Rogers, Ogden Phipps, Joan and John Reynolds III, Mrs. Earl E. T. Smith, Mr. and Mrs. Michael Kaiser,** Ambassador and **Mrs. Guilford Dudley, Jr., Mr. and Mrs. William E. Benjamin, Mr. and Mrs. Wiley Reynolds, Mr. and Mrs. F. Warrington Gillet, Jr., Mr. and Mrs. George G. Matthews** and **Mr. and Mrs. Jeremy Harvey, Mr. and Mrs. William Pitt** and **Mrs. Earl Smith.**

—FIRST FAMILY—

George and Betsy Matthews are the reigning first family; George's mother **Jean Flagler Matthews** was the granddaughter of Henry Morrison Flagler (the man responsible for the "birth of Palm Beach"). George has continued his mother's mission restoring the Flagler Museum to its original grandeur. The Matthews have three children, so at least for another generation the Flagler lineage will continue in Palm Beach. The children are: Kelly Flagler Matthews, Mr. and Mrs. George G. Matthews, Jr. and Mrs. James Dryden Pence III (Elizabeth Matthews).

Betsy Matthews (Betsy Ellen Kelly), especially, is actively involved in Palm Beach charities, recently being chairman of the Centennial Ball to benefit Good Samaritan Medical Center and to celebrate the founding of West Palm Beach in 1894 (by Henry Morrison Flagler, great grandfather of George Matthews).

The largest family in Palm Beach belongs to **John and Betty Groth**, Island residents for almost 37 years, with a total of 11 children; nine females and two males, ranging in age from 30 to 50. Many are married and have produced multiple grandchildren; all members of the family live in the area (or the state of Florida). The family recently had a "reunion"—the entire clan (some 40 people strong) spent the holidays together at the Groth home on Queens Lane.

Married for 48 years, "Johnny" pitched for six American League baseball teams during his 13-year major league career and has been a scout for the Atlanta Braves. In addition to raising her family, Betty has been very active in St. Edward's Guild and was president of St. Mary's Hospital Auxiliary.

—POP PERSONALITIES—

*O*nce the game is over, the king and the pawn go back into the same box; but while the game is being played, some people give it such life force that they automatically rise to the top. Among our most popular Townies are:

High-visibility socialite **Celia Lipton Farris**, high-energy and scintillating **Helen Boehm**, high-and-mighty **Marjorie and Sam Meek**, all-around good guys **Jeanne and Frank Habicht**, decorator **Scott Snyder**, always trustworthy and turned out well **Nancy and Wycoff Myers**, multi-media power **Alex Dreyfoos**, former Mayor and world explorer **Deedy Marix**, work-then-fun-lover **Cathleen McFarlane**, comrades and contributors **Meredith and Tony Newton**, stylishly charitable **Betsy and Michael Kaiser,** man of broad-based benevolence **Abe Gosman** and wife **Lin**, civic leaders **Helene and Jesse Newman**, benefactor and malleteer **Pat Supper**, public spirited Islander **Brownie McLean**, internationalists and toastmasters **Susan and Michael Blank**, wonder girl **Nancy Brinker**, man with many legs and lives **John Brogan** and lovely ally **Mosse Hvide,** preservationist **Polly Earl**, young cabaretman **Dan Ponton**, underwater model and activist **Judy Schrafft**, world-class opera hosts **Ava and Barclay Coleman**, masterful **Donald Trump**, girl of many charms **Mary Schott**, dignified, ladylike **Lesly Smith**, good humorist **Bob Leidy**, historian **Jim Ponce**, holier-than-most **Rev. Frank Lechiara**, banking and citrus stars **Inger and H. Loy Anderson**, big-time gift givers **Janna and Stan Rumbough,** ballet backers and comrades **Leslie Claydon-White** and **David Veselsky**, good sports **Dr. and Mrs. Rolla Campbell**, The Honored Ones **Angelica and Paul Ilyinsky** and Woman-of-all Seasons **Kit Pannill**.

—MEGA-ACHIEVERS—

They just keep going on and on! **Doing their thing with aplomb! For the Gents: John Brogan**, retired businessman and man-about-philanthropy; **Guilford Dudley**, former Ambassador and man-of-many-honors; **Frank Wright**, charitable leader and former czar of the Round Table; **William Buckley**, superb Realtor and cause supporter; **Bill Pitt**, leader of the old boys network; **Alex Dreyfoos**, inventor, sailer, major donor and man whose name adorns many buildings; **Ray Perelman**, tireless entrepreneur and philanthropist; **Bill Lickle**, former banker now dotcom book publisher; educator and art aficionado **Artine Artinian**; **Dr. Rolla Campbell**, man of medicine, lover of animals and life; **Phil Whitacre**, energetic raconteur and social gent.

For the Ladies, notable achievers are: **Helen Cluett, Betty Swope, Fran Todman, Claire Chalk, Estee Lauder, Rose Sachs, Dorothy Rautbord, Dorothy Schulman, Kay Rybovich, Etonella Christlieb, Dorothy Sullivan, Marjorie Meek, Gio King, C.Z. Guest, Muriel Siebert** and **Gertrude Maxwell.**

—CLASS LASSES—

*I*n a Town with personalities like **Marylou Whitney Hendrickson** and **Estee Lauder**, this category takes on special meaning. They are world-class women who set standards with which it is difficult to compete. In a league of their own, are these Ladies:

Celia Lipton Farris (born to perform and produce and be a patron saint); **Eles Gillet** (perfectly in tune with the times and its needs/wants); **Hillie Mahoney** (soft-spoken charmer who does things her way and always wins); **Lesly Smith** (well versed in politics and philanthropy); **Cathleen McFarlane** (highly motivated, animated and persuasive); **Kit Pannill** (great aura, a vision of gracefulness); **Pat Schmidlapp** (gentle and generous); **Alyne Massey** (anthropologically significant in every way); **Jane Dudley** (just the right look, touch and air); **Carolyn Buckley** (bright, verve-laden); **Carol Digges** (sparkling personality backed by business acumen); **Audrey Gruss** (just the right attitude to achieve the maximum whatever); **Lisa Anderson** (witty and wise to the ways of the world); **Nancy Brinker** (the ideal balance of cause and charm); **Aimee deHeeren** (bright, beautiful, perpetual motion); **C.Z. Guest** (something of a legend, green thumb and all); **Chessie Patcevitch** (delightful, delovely and decisive); **Virginia Smith Burke** (classic beauty with great Palm Beach look); **Pauline Boardman Pitt** (chic interior designer, great smile); **Maura Benjamin** (community leader, superb sense of humor); **Jackie Cowell** (good credentials and spirit to match); **Didi Ballinger** (lady of many Town interests, an icon).

—DREAM QUEENS—

With the demise of **Mary Sanford** and **Sue Whitmore**, the job of "Queen" remains open. But the newly designated One will have to perform as well as **Eva Stotesbury**, be as charming as **Marjorie Merriweather Post** and have just enough breeding to make the grade while maintaining forward vision. In a Town characterized by change, the new queen will have to bridge the gap between preservationist and futurist.

Among those mentioned for Her Queenship are: **Lesly Smith**, everybody's favorite; **Jean Tailer**, who brings a subtle hum to her projects; **Kit Pannill**, pleasant and productive Insider; **Audrey Gruss**, who moves in/out with great dexterity; **Marylou Whit-ney Hendrickson**, divinely qualified, but probably too much of a cos-mopolite; **Eunice Gardiner**, makes the right moves, very courtly and considerate; **Pauline Boardman Pitt**, good backing, good fan club, good spokeswoman; **Betsy Matthews**, unique training, great pedigree, fits the specs; **Betty Scripps Harvey**, grand presentation, philosophy and econo-mic sophistication.

Choosing the Queen is one of those subtle matters that defies format. Somehow it gets done in the soft light of the morning and the deep shadows of night by a cast of arbiters who don't want recognition and refuse to declare their positions, and by whatever vicissitude, keep things moving with great finesse.

—"MERRY WIDOWS"—

*M*any of the high profile widows of former mega-buck husbands travel the high road and take their share of joy from life; others go into a kind of luxurious seclusion, based on the premise that the best thing money can buy is privacy. Here's a blend of both, who have traded in their Widow's Weeds for either a gown or a jumpsuit: (I = $100 million or more; II = $50 to $100 million; III = under $50 million)

Marylou Whitney Hendrickson (I), **Celia Lipton Farris** (I), **Jayne Wrightsman** (I), **Estee Lauder** (I), **"Bunny" du Pont** (I), **Lois Pope** (I), **Sydelle Miller** (I), **Kathleen Ford** (II), **Anya Bagley** (II), **Diane Norris** (II), **Barton Gubelmann** (II), **Carola Mandel** (III), **Estelle Gelman** (III), and **Aimee deHeeren** (III).

These affluent/influential women join ranks with some of America's richest Merry Widows. Among them:

Jane Engelhard (NJ, I), **Brooke Astor** (NY, I), **Kay Graham** (DC, I), **Basia Johnson** (NJ, I), **Betsy Bloomingdale** (LA, II), **Grace Dudley** (NY, II), **Courtney Sale Ross** (NY, II) and **Drue Heinz** (NY, II).

(Note: figures are estimates from public sources.)

51

—Role Models—

*P*alm Beach has an abundance of faces that graced magazine covers over the years; a notable collection of fashion models that still have their composites (and clippings) just in case. Among them are:

Inger Anderson, Pat Booth, Mary Schott, Adele Siegel, Susan Keenan, Judy Grubman, Jayne McConnell, Dee Cushing, Claudia Peltz, Cathleen McFarlane, Mary Boykin, Maria Draddy, Nancy Brinker, Dina Merrill-Hartley, Hillie Mahoney, Diane Millner, Susanna Cutts, Norma Fireman, Betsy Kaiser, Mimi Welfield and **Kathleen Ford**.

For the record, Mary Schott was a cover girl for *Vogue, Cosmopolitan, Harper's Bazaar, Elle* and the *New York Times* Magazine; Mary Boykin was featured in *Mademoiselle, Glamour* and *Life*; Inger Anderson was a favorite in Paris, London and Rome on covers for *Collection* and *Vogue*; Jayne McConnell was a top cosmetic executive who modeled her company's products; Cathleen McFarlane was an actress, television personality and cover feature for *Glamour* and *Harper's Bazaar*; and Kathleen Ford graced covers for *Vogue, McCall's* and *Family Weekly*.

—Big Talkers—

FDR in one of his classic quips noted—"Why should two bald men fight over a comb?"—that type of acute observation made him one of the great mass communicators of our time. **JFK** hit the heartbeat of Americans, too, and in his time delivered some immortal lines. **Ronald Reagan** was the perfect 10 in the 80s, scoring with every argument; his Hollywood background gave him the showmanship and aplomb to face, and face down, any and all audiences. **Clinton**, too, is masterful with the mike.

On the chicken dinner circuit today, locally, are a number of convincing orators: **Jesse Newman** offers believable and compelling copy with humor; **Allen Manning** scores with sincerity and credibility; **Gay Gaines** rates attention with a youthful exuberance; **Gary Lickle** carries a verbal tune well with logical and pragmatic offerings; **Bob Eigelberger** projects an image of substance and charisma; **Leslie Shaw** masters words and nuances and moves forward with assurance; **Paul Ilyinsky** has a certain rhythm that gets affirmative nods; **Helen Boehm** has that fresh can't-tell-a-lie directness that hits home every time; **Wiley Reynolds III** moves words with ease; **Gale Brophy** beguiles and charms audiences to the point of surrendering; **Jeanne Ford** is so firm in her convictions that people have no chance to be dissuaded; **Celia Lipton Farris** garners empathy from listeners based on her theatrical background; **Bob Mont-**

gomery has a knowledgeable approach that makes allies of his audience; **Susan Keenan** smiles and schmoozes with great authority; **Pat Cook** allows her musical background to motivate the troops, while **Curt Gowdy** tells a story with mastery; **Doyle Rogers** powers forward with glibness and compelling arguments; and **David Scaff** commands the language with skill, as does **Herbert Swope, Jr.; Amb. Henry Kimelman** is smooth and pleasantly anecdotal; **Tina Flaherty** carries on with aplomb and a wry smile as she instructs; **Adm. Phil Whitacre** has a kind of "let's storm the hill" approach which is very effective; **Mary Weiss** is soft-spoken but hard-driven in her pronouncements. Others in the communication major league are **Simon Fireman, John Brogan, Bill Brooks, Anita Dubnoff, Bob Nichols, Alex Dreyfoos, Col. Frank Randolph** and **Ira Harris.**

Although each of these Palm Beachers is notable & quotable and has dropped some memorable lines over the years, they probably can't deliver anything comparable to the 10 most famous quotes of the century:

1. *"Have you no sense of decency, sir, at long last?"* lawyer Joseph Welsh, representing the Army, against Sen. Joe McCarthy, 1954.

2. *"I have a dream...."* Rev. Martin Luther King at the March on Washington, 1963.

3. *"The only thing we have to fear is fear itself."* FDR, first inaugural address, 1933.

4. *"Ask not what your country can do for you, ask what you can do for your country."* John F. Kennedy, inaugural address, 1961.

5. *"Ich bin ein Berliner."* JFK's address to the German people, outside of city hall in West Berlin, 1963.

6. *"Are you better off than you were four years ago?"* Ronald Reagan, 1980, in a debate with Jimmy Carter.

7. *"Speak softly and carry a big stick."* Theordore Roosevelt, in an address to Congress in 1901.

8. *"The world must be made safe for democracy."* Woodrow Wilson, 1917, as he sent American troops into battle in World War I.

9. *"I will go to Korea."* Dwight Eisenhower promising to go to Korea to seek peace in 1952.

10. *"Mr. Gorbachev, tear down this wall."* Ronald Reagan deploring the Berlin Wall, 1987.

—STATESMEN—

*T*hese distinguished Ambassadors live in Palm Beach: The Honorable: **Guilford Dudley** (Denmark), **Vernon Walters** (United Nations), **Enriquillo del Rosario** (Dominican Republic), **Eric Javits** (Venezuela), **Henry Kimelman** (Haiti),

Bruce Gelb (Belgium), Jean Kennedy Smith (Ireland), the late Earl E. T. Smith (Cuba), and Dr. Norman Athill (Chile).

The origin of Ambassadors and Embassies began with the rules of diplomatic precedence, first manifest at the 1815 Congress in Vienna; the rules still stand in Catholic countries. Papal Nuncios generally represent various diplomatic delegations when a single authority is needed. In other countries the dean of the corps is the Ambassador of most seniority (in Washington, a DP-1 license plate signifies Number One ranking).

The pecking order for diplomats is: Ambassador Extraordinary and Plenipotentiary, Legate or Nuncio, Envoy or Minister, Charge d'Affaires.

Assuming a large state party, with representatives from many branches of government, here's the **official ranking** based on established protocol: The President of the U.S., The Vice-President of the U.S., The Speaker of the House of Representatives, The Chief Justice of the U.S., Former Presidents of the U.S., The Secretary of State, The Secretary General of the U.N., Ambassadors of Foreign Powers, Widows of Former Presidents of the U.S., Associate Justices of the Supreme Court of the U.S., Cabinet Members; Director—Office of Management and Budget, Chairman, Council of Economic Advisers, Special Representative for Trade Negotiations, The Senate, Governors of States, Former Vice-Presidents of the U.S., The House of Representatives, Assistants to the President, Charges d'Affaires of Foreign Powers, The Under Secretaries of the Executive Departments and the Deputy Secretaries, Administrator—Agency for International Development, Director—U.S. Arms Control and Disarmament Agency, Secretaries of the Army, the Navy, and the Air Force.

—LIVING LEGENDS—

*T*he late former Mayor of Palm Beach and former **Ambassador Earl E.T. Smith** who was honored by his friends for his decades of service to Palm Beach, who commissioned architect Edward D. Stone to design the Earl E.T. Smith Park, a peaceful corner plot centered by a fountain, cast stone benches, flower-filled urns and shade trees bordered by plant-covered columns. The park is located on South County Road opposite Town Hall and next to the offices of the Preservation Foundation of Palm Beach.

The park is one of a number of public buildings or centers in the area that are named after notable people who have moved the cause of Palm Beach forward by their inspiration and largesse. Others who have garnered public recognition are:

Harold and Sylvia Kaplan Park: dedicated in 1986; located at the corner of South Ocean Boulevard and Hammon Avenue, is named after businessman and philanthropist Harold Kaplan.

Helen L. Messic North Meadow Park: at the Charles W. Gerstenberg Hospice Center.

Thoresen Theatre: at Randolph Macon Woman's College, Lynchburg, VA, named in memory of Richard Thoresen, son of William and Kay Thoresen.

Thoresen Gallery: in Macon's Maier Museum of Art.

Raymond F. Kravis Center for the Performing Arts: named in honor of Raymond and Bessie Kravis.

McMahon Stadium: in Calgary, honoring the late Frank McMahon.

Victor Farris Pavilion: at Good Samaritan Hospital, in honor of inventor Victor Farris.

Maddock Alumni Center: at Brown University, in honor of Paul Maddock.

Eric Friedheim Library: at the National Press Club in Washington, D.C.; the Eric Friedheim Quadrangle at American University in Washington, D.C.—both named in honor of publisher Eric Friedham—and the Arthur Friedham Library at the Peabody Conservatory (Johns Hopkins University, Baltimore, MD)— in honor of the famed pianist, Maestro Friedham.

Mitzi Newhouse Theater: in Lincoln Center (New York City), honoring the many contributions of Mrs. Newhouse to theater.

Nemec Hall—at Stetson University, honoring James and Ruth Nemec.

Marden Medical Education Center: at St. Mary's Hospital, in honor of Bernard and Chris Marden.

Kimmel Outpatient Surgical Center: at St. Mary's Hospital, in honor of Edward and Lucille Kimmel.

Claudia and Nelson Peltz Building: Middle School Facility of the Benjamin School, North Palm Beach, in their honor.

Goodman Stadium: on the Lehigh University campus, donated (in part) by alumnus Murray H. Goodman, builder of the Esplanade, Phillips Point and Neiman-Marcus/Worth Avenue.

The Michael and Andrew Gosman Amphitheater: at Kravis Center, honoring the Abraham Gosman Family.

Widener Library: at Harvard University, donated by the former wife of George Widener in memory of her deceased son, a bibliophile.

Mortimer and Rose Sachs Administration Building: at Palm Beach Atlantic College, donated by Rose Sachs in honor of her husband.

Hood Free Enterprise Building: at Palm Beach Atlantic College, donated by Mary Tolerton in honor of her father and husband.

Frank and Helen Weyenberg Nurses Residence: at Good Samaritan Hospital, honoring Frank and Helen Weyenberg.

Mae Rovensky Nurses Residence: at Good Samaritan Hospital, in memory of Mae Rovensky by her husband John.

Rinker School of Business: at Palm Beach Atlantic College, in honor of Marshall Edison "Doc" Rinker who has been a continuing supporter of the college since its inception; the Rinker Playhouse at Kravis Center.

Esther Burger O'Keeffe Pavilion: at St. Mary's Hospital, honoring Mrs. O'Keeffe.

M.E. Rinker, Sr. Institute for Tax and Accounting: at Stetson University, by the M.E. Rinker Foundation.

Bernice and Cecil N. Rudnick Laboratories for Research on Alzheimer's Disease and the Cecil and Bernice Rudnick Meditation Chapel: at Yeshiva University's Albert Einstein College of Medicine by Bernice and Cecil N. Rudnick.

Jack and Pearl Resnick Center for Research on Aging of the Brain and the **Jack and Pearl Resnick Gerontology Center**: at Albert Einstein College of Medicine, by Jack and Pearl Resnick.

Harold and Sylvia Kaplan Pavillion at the Joseph L. Morse Geriatric Center: by Harold and Sylvia Kaplan.

Harold and Rita Dee Hassenfeld University Conference Center: at Brandeis University, by Harold and Rita Dee Hassenfeld.

Montgomery Hall: at the Armory Art Center, in honor of Mary and Robert Montgomery.

The Walter R. Newbern Memorial Pavilion: at Good Samaritan Hospital, honoring the late Walter R. Newbern.

Frederick and Patricia Supper Center for Excellence in Business: Palm Beach Atlantic College, in honor of the Suppers; the Supper Central Garden of The Norton Museum of Art.

Hortense and Louis Rubin Dialysis Center in Troy, N.Y.: in honor of the Rubins.

The Marjorie Meek Planned Parenthood Clinic: in West Palm Beach, donated by Gio King in memory of her late husband, Joseph.

The Harvard Mahoney Neuroscience Institute and The David Mahoney Institute of Neurological Sciences at the University of Pennsylvania: donated by David Mahoney. **The David Mahoney Center Neuro-oncology** at Dana-Farber, Boston. **The Hillie Mahoney Memory Disorders** at St. Mary's Hospital.

Wexner Center for the Visual Arts at Ohio State University: donated by Leslie Wexner in memory of his father.

Mary Rubloff (Schott) **Harmony House**: YMCA, West Palm Beach, in honor of Mary Rubloff (Schott).

Helen Boehm Building: Adam Walsh Children's Foundation, in honor of Helen Boehm.

Ray and Ruth Perelman: The Perelman Jewish Day School, in Wynnewood, PA in their honor.

The Kenan-Flagler School of Business: University of North Carolina, in honor of Mary Lily Kenan; also the Kenan Student Center, Kenan Stadium and Kenan's Institute of Private Enterprise, all at UNC.

Mary Alice Fortin Child Care Foundation (for children infected with AIDS) and the **Mary Alice Fortin Kids' Korner at St. Mary's Hospital**: donated by Mary Alice Fortin.

The Nathan Cummings 20th Century Art Building: at the Israel Museum in Jerusalem.

The Ferris P. Ellis • J. David Veselsky, Jr. • Leslie Claydon-White Building: the Ballet Florida building in West Palm Beach.

The Wish Theater Building, Bowdoin College honoring Barry and Oblio Wish.

The Norm and Sonia Gregersen Playground: at The Children's Place/Connor Nursery.

Joseph and Gioconda King Library: at The Society of the Four Arts, honoring Gioconda King.

The Simon C. Fireman Foundation Home Safe Center for Children: Lake Worth, recognizing the benevolence of Simon and Norma Fireman.

The Sylvester Family Children's Cancer Research Center: at the University of Miami, honoring the Sylvester Family.

The Leonard and Sophie Davis Gallery: at the Norton Museum of Art, in honor of the Davis Family.

The Arthur I. Meyer Jewish Academy: the Meyer Ampitheater, the Sydelle and Arthur I. Meyer Gallery (Norton); Meyer Hall (Dreyfoos School of the Arts), honoring the Arthur I. Meyer Family.

The Alexander W. Dreyfoos, Jr. Concert Hall: at The Kravis Center, honoring Alexander W. Dreyfoos, Jr. a prime mover in developing the Center; the Alexander W. Dreyfoos, Jr. School of the Arts.

Buying "immortality" is big business and can help fund a building or project in a substantial way. For example, at the Raymond F. Kravis Center for the Performing Arts, at one time, a donor could put up $15,000 to get his/her name on a water fountain; $25,000 got the honor of naming the men's lounge; $10,000 rated one's name permanently engraved on one of the 2,200 seats in the auditorium; $100,000 got one's name on a star's dressing room; and $1 million got the big prize—one's name on the stage.

Donors can also buy "category recognition." The Palm Beach Community Chest/United Way, for example, has a division called Alexis De Tocqueville Society, which recently recognized annual contributors at various levels: La Table Ronde des Millions de Dollars ($1 million or more: Mr. and Mrs. Richard D. Greenfield); Ordre de Connaissance ($500,000 - $749,999: Mr. and Mrs. J. Ira Harris); La Societe National

($100,000 - $249,999: Mrs. Francis R. Guyott, John F. Scarpa, Mr. and Mrs. Jack Taylor); Ordre de Fraternite ($75,000 - $99,000: Ann Appleman); Ordre d'Egalite ($50,000 - $74,999: Mr. and Mrs. Jeffry M. Picower; Mr. and Mrs. Carl J. Shapiro, Harcourt M. Sylvester); Ordre de Liberte ($25,000 - $49,999: Mr. and Mrs. Merrill L. Bank, Mr. and Mrs. Edward W. Cook, Mr. and Mrs. Alan Curtis, Mr. and Mrs. Thomas B. D'Agostino, Mr. and Mrs. Abraham Gosman, Mr. and Mrs. Sidney A. Kohl, Eugene J. Ribakoff, Mr. and Mrs. Morton Wiener). Last year, the Community Chest/United Way raised over $3.3 million which is distributed to 40 local health and human service agencies. Over 100 donors received special "category recognition."

—ARCHANGELS—

*P*alm Beach is famed for its eleemosynary instinct; major givers are:

Iris and Carl Apfel—$1.2 million to the Bascom Palmer Eye Institute.

John Brogan—Named Philanthropist of the Year by the National Association of Fundraising Executives; over the years he has been responsible for helping charities raise over $100 million.

Julian and Eunice Cohen—Donated $1 million to Kravis Center for the Performing Arts.

Alex Dreyfoos—Donated $5 million to the Kravis Center for the Performing Arts; $1 million to the School of Arts Foundation; $1 million to the Intracoastal Health Foundation; $250,000 to the Norton Museum; $15 million to MIT.

Celia Lipton Farris—Donated $2 million for the Victor Farris Pavilion at Good Samaritan Hospital; also contributed $1 million to the new Kravis Center, $1.6 million to benefit AIDS and a similar sum to the Capital Campaign of the Salvation Army.

Wally Findlay *(the late)*—$2 million (artwork) to Northwood University.

Norma and Simon Fireman—Many millions to various local arts, culture and medical charities.

Max Fisher—Donates up to $10 million each year to various causes.

Mary Alice Fortin—Donated her Melbourne House condominium to Paracare Association of Palm Beach; donated funds for the Mary Alice Fortin Kids' Korner at St. Mary's Hospital and $500,000 toward the Mary Alice Fortin Child Care Foundation for children infected with AIDS.

Henry and Lois Foster—Provided $1 million to the Museum of Fine Arts, Boston.

Eric Friedheim—Donated $1 million to the National Press Club; $1 million to American University; and $1 million to John Hopkins University—all for libraries.

Lorraine and Jack Friedman—Donated $1 million to the Jewish Federation of Palm Beach County for the Jewish Education Center.

Ray E. Friedman—Several million to various causes, including the Simon Wiesenthal Center and Orbis Intl.

Murray H. Goodman—Gave $3.5 million to build a new stadium at Lehigh University, his alma mater.

Abe Gosman—$1 million to Kravis Center for the Performing Arts; $8 million to the Dana-Farber Cancer Institute; plus several million to other causes, in-cluding Orbis International.

Rita Dee and Harold Hassenfeld—Provided $1 million to Brandeis University.

Enid Haupt—Gave $5 million to New York's Botanical Garden; $5 million to the New York Zoological Society; and $1.5 million to Metropolitan Museum of Art.

Marjorie Stoll Holtz—$1 million to Technion, the Israeli Institute of Technology.

Mary Hulitar—Donated $1 million toward the Charles W. Hulitar Gerstenberg Hospice Center.

Harold *(the late)* **and Sylvia Kaplan**—Over the past 10 years they donated $20 million to the Jewish Community Campus, the Joseph L. Morse Geriatric Center (The Harold & Sylvia Kaplan Pavilion), St. Mary's Hospital (Harold & Sylvia Kaplan Cancer Center), The Harold & Sylvia Kaplan Park, the Kravis Center and WPB Library.

Kenan Family—Over $40 million to the University of North Carolina for various buildings and programs.

Edward and Lucille Kimmel—$1 million to St. Mary's Hospital.

Gio King—Gave the "Marjorie Meek Planned Parenthood Clinic" in memory of her late husband Joseph; $2 million to Norton Museum of Art.

Margaret Strauss Kramer *(the late)*—$1 million to the Palm Beach Community Chest/United Way Campaign; similar gift to Technion.

Henry Kravis—Donated $10 million to the Metropolitan Museum of Art and $10 million to Mount Sinai Medical Center.

Raymond *(the late)* **and Bessie Kravis** *(the late)*—Gave $1 million toward the Kravis Center for the Performing Arts.

Blanche and A.L. *(the late)* **Levine**—$1 million to Kravis Center for the Performing Arts; also $5 million to the Metropolitan Museum of Art (NYC).

David Mahoney *(the late)*—Donated $1.7 million for The Harvard Mahoney Neuroscience Institute; supports an endowment fund for the The David Mahoney Institute of Neurological Sciences at the University of Pennsylvania.

Bernard and Chris Marden—$2 million to St. Mary's Hospital; also $1 million to Kravis Center for the Performing Arts.

Arthur and Sydelle Meyer—$1.5 million to The Jewish Federation of Palm Beach County; $1 million to Norton Museum of Art.

Melvin and Barbara *(the late)* **Nessel**—$10 million to Massachusetts General Hospital for Cancer Services Center; plus several million to the Wang Building, the Phillips House Pavilion and the Gene Therapy Center of the hospital.

Esther Burger O'Keeffe *(the late)*—$1 million to St. Mary's Hospital for expansion of their pediatric wing.

Nelson Peltz—Gave $10 million to the Jewish Community Campus for a new sports complex; also $1 million to the Middle School.

Ronald O. Perelman —Pledged $10 million to build a student center at the University of Pennsylvania (to be called the Revlon Campus Center); also $10 million to NYC's Guggenheim Museum; $2 million to the Solomon Schecter Day School (Wynnewood, PA); $2 million to U.S. Holocaust Memorial Museum in Washington, D.C.; and $2 million to the Philadelphia Museum of Art.

Lois Pope—Over $15 million to various causes, including $10 million for the Miami Project to Cure Paralysis, a program of the University of Miami School of Medicine, and $250,000 to the Jewish Guild for the Blind.

Marshall "Doc" Rinker *(the late)*—$8 million to Palm Beach Atlantic College for expansion of the Rinker School of Business and $2 million to Stetson University for the new tax and accounting institute.

Rose Sachs—$1 million to Palm Beach Atlantic College in memory of her late husband Mortimer for the Mortimer and Rose Sachs Administration Building.

Lewis M. Schott—$1 million to various causes, including $250,000 to Palm Beach Atlantic College for the Schott/Warren Wellness Center.

Fred *(the late)* **and Pat Supper**—$1 million to a museum in Greenwich, CT; $100,000 to Ballet Florida.

Alfred Taubman—Gave $15 million to create Taubman Center for State and Local Government at JFK School of Government, Harvard.

Harcourt Sylvester—$1 million to the United Way of Palm Beach; $2 million to the Florida Philharmonic Orchestra; $5 million to University of Miami medical progams; $1 million to Hope House.

Ruth C. Heede estate—$3.75 million to the Cancer Institute at Good Samaritan.

Miles Zisson—$1 million to the Comprehensive Breast Center at Good Samaritan; $1 million to Bascom Palmer Eye Institute.

Tina and Bill Flaherty—$1.5 million to the Palm Beach Zoo at Dreher Park; also $1.5 million to the Intracoastal Health Foundation.

William and Sally Soter—$1 million to the Norton Museum of Art.

Helen and Harry Gray—$3 million to the Cancer Institute at Good Sam.

Carl and Ruth Shapiro—$20 million to Brandeis University; $6 million to the Harvard Medical School-Beth Israel Deaconess Mount Auburn Institute; $5.5 million to the Museum of Fine Arts, Boston; $1 million to Wellesley College; $1 million to Boston's Brigham & Women's Hospital; $1 million to the Kravis Center.

John and Marjorie McGraw and the McGraw Foundation—$3.25 million to the Norton Museum of Art.

Anne and Harold Smith—$2 million to the Norton Museum of Art.

Raymond and Ruth Perelman—$15 million to the Philadelphia Museum of Art; $3 million to the Perelman Jewish Day School.

Peggy and Richard Greenfield—$1 million to Palm Beach Community Chest.

George Cornell—$10 million to Cornell University.

Helen and James Rosburg—$1 million to the Palm Beach Zoo at Dreher Park.

Carl DeSantis—$1 million to WXEL-Channel 42.

Michael and Howard Kessler—$1 million to Boston's Brigham & Women's Hospital.

Pat and Richard Johnson—$2 million to St. Mary's.

Laurence and Florence De George—$1 million to Juvenile Diabetes Research.

Charles Bronfman—$33 million to various Jewish charities.

The Esther B. O'Keeffe Charitable Foundation—$3.5 million to the Society of the Four Arts.

Leonard and Sophie Davis—$2 million to the Norton Museum of Art.

Ken Langone—$6.5 million to New York University.

The Kimelman Foundation—$500,000 to the Palm Beach Zoo at Dreher Park.

James Clark—$150 million to Stanford University.

Eunice and Julian Cohen—$5 million to the Boston Symphony Orchestra.

M. Mac Schwebel—$10 million to the Solomon Schecter School of Westchester.

Robert and Mary Montgomery—$1.2 million to the Armory Art Center.

Helen K. Persson—$1 million to PB Atlantic College.

Eugene and Ronnie Isenberg—$6 million to the University of Massachusetts.

Barry and Oblio Wish—$5.2 million to Bowdoin College.

Miles and Shirley Fiterman—$500,000 to the Norton Museum of Art.
Kim and Dr. Rolla Campbell—$1 million to the Palm Beach Zoo at Dreher Park.
John and Tiffany Boswell—$1.5 million to the Palm Beach Zoo at Dreher Park.
Alvin and Peggy Brown—$1.2 million to the Palm Beach Zoo at Dreher Park.
Kenan Charitable Trust—$900,000 to Flagler Museum.
Lawrence Barreca—$1 million to Bascom Palmer Eye Institute.
Ephraim Bloch—$1.2 million to Good Samaritan.
Rinker Foundation—$3 million to Palm Beach Atlantic College.
Martin and Audrey Gruss—$1 million to Lifelines, Intracoastal Health Systems, Inc.; $1 million to University of Pennsylvania's Wharton School of Business.
David Mack and family—$700,000 to Lifelines, Intracoastal Health Systems, Inc.
Sydelle Miller—$10 million to Case Weston Reserve University.
Jan Claire Kempner—$1.5 million to St. Ann School.
Mary Alice Fortin—$750,000 to St. Ann School.
Arthur Williams—$70 million to Liberty University.
The Quantum Foundation—$2 million to St. Mary's Hospital.
Spencer Partrich—$2.5 million to Wayne State University.

For the record, a number of Palm Beachers have donor-fever, tossing off millions of dollars each year to favorite causes. Examples (lifetime totals to-date):

John Kluge, Metromedia mogul: $180 million to arts and equal opportunity causes.
Ronald Perelman, takeover king: $165 million to cancer research, education and arts.
Iris Cantor, sculpture collector: $100 million to arts and medical research.
Richard and Helen DeVos, Amway Home Products: $97 million to arts, medicine and Christian outreach.
Arthur and Angela Williams, term life insurance tycoon: $70 million to Christian education.
Zachery *(the late)* **and Elizabeth Fisher**, real estate: $60 million to health care and military family services.
Alfred Taubmann, mall developer: $60 milion to education, arts and medical.
Max and Marjorie Fisher, real estate and industry: $50 million to educational and Jewish charities.
Enid Annenberg Haupt, heiress: $45 million to cancer research, botanical gardens.

Ted Forstmann, investor: $53 million to school programs.

Ron and Jo Carole Lauder, cosmetics: $36 million to arts and Jewish education.

There has been a pronounced change in the character of donors in recent years. Whereas the mega-rich or the aristocracy were the prime movers in financing charities, now corporations have assumed a benevolent role and are actively underwriting galas and special events. It's only logical that Corporate America seek alliances with charities; it allows them to interface with new business prospects, while showing their community spirit. Corporations gave a record $9.2 billion last year and spent almost $1 million promoting their largesse. Locally, Chase, Merrill Lynch, Northern Trust, Tiffany & Co., J.P. Morgan, Cartier, Seagram, Sara Lee Corporation, Chanel, Van Cleef and Arpels, and Daimler Chrysler were big spenders.

The site for fundraisers is also in transition. Many private homes are now the locus of special events. Pre-event parties are especially well-suited to homes since the crowd expectancy is in the 150 people category. Only mansions with huge lawns can accomdate the ball crowd, which easily numbers up to 500 people. Parking is the main problem— few homes have access to open areas for the influx of cars. Yet, the intrigue of attending a ball held in a pedigreed mansion can create additional ticket sales and save the charity the major expense of paying for hotel facilities.

—HONOREES—

*T*he following Palm Beachers received special recognition in the last few years for their achievements:

Winifred Clarke Anthony *(the late)*: Memorial Garden from Opportunity, Inc., a 51-year-old preschool and after-school program which she founded in 1934.

Nate Appleman *(the late)*: Alexis de Tocqueville Award.

Diane Belfer: Honorary Doctoral Degree from Yeshiva University.

William Benjamin, II: Gates of Jerusalem Medal from the Palm Beach County Israel Bonds Banking Division.

Helen Boehm: Commitment Award by Adam Walsh Children's Fund.

Mary Bolton: Ballinger Award, Preservation Foundation.

Florence Bonsuk: ARC Service Award, the Children's Place/Connor's Nursery Appreciation Award, Up and Comers Award, Price Waterhouse/South Florida, Cartier Community Leadership Award and "Florida's Finest" Award.

Nancy Brinker: Women of Distinction, Palm Beach Atlantic College; Helen Messic Humanitarian Award, Hospice of Palm Beach County.

John Brogan: Alexis de Tocqueville Award; American Free Enterprise Medal, Palm Beach Atlantic College.

Bill Brooks: Distinguished Public Service Award, Anti-Defamation League; Humanitarian Award, American Ireland Fund.

Virginia Buckley: National Medallion Award from the Boys and Girls Clubs of Palm Beach County.

Carolyn Buckley: Women of Distinction, Palm Beach Atlantic College.

Carol and Paul Chanin: Distinguished Service Award from the American Technion Society, Palm Beach Chapter.

Maurizio Ciminella: "Young Entrepreneur of the Year" Award by Northwood University.

Helen Cluett: Outstanding Community Citizen Award, Community Chest/United Way.

William S. Cohen: Distinguished Service Award from the American Technion Society, Palm Beach Chapter.

Ned Cook: The Alexis de Tocqueville Society's Outstanding Community Citizen Award (the highest honor of the Palm Beach Community Chest/United Way; previous honorees of the Award have been Doyle Rogers, Frances Hufty, Nathan Appleman *(the late)*, John Brogan, Ann Appleman and Alex Dreyfoos); **(Mrs. Pat):** Women of Distinction Award, Palm Beach Atlantic College.

Richard Cowell: Inducted into the International Water Skiing Hall of Fame.

Christine Curtis: Alexis de Tocqueville Award.

Robert Deziel: Ballinger Award, Preservation Foundation.

Shannon Donnelley: The Good Samaritan Award by the Palm Beach County Sheriff's Office.

Alex Dreyfoos, Jr.: The Florida Arts Recognition Award by the Florida Division of Cultural Affairs; the Entrepreneur Hall of Fame Award from Nova University; the Outstanding Volunteers Fundraiser Award, National Society of Fundraising Executives; Alexis de Tocqueville Award; Providencia Award, Palm Beach County Visitor's Bureau; American Business Leader by Northwood Institute.

Anita Dubnoff: Women of Distinction, Palm Beach Atlantic College, and Harmony House Achiever Award.

Eileen Burns: The Third Annual Ballinger Award, Preservation Foundation, for the Vicarage, the original Lake Trail home of Bethesda-by-the-Sea's Vicar (presently owned and restored by Mrs. Burns).

J. Pepe Fanjul: Distinguished Honoree Award from Casita Maria (the oldest settlement house in NYC serving the Hispanic Community).

Celia Lipton Farris: The Gloria Swanson Humanitarian Award from the American Cinema Awards Foundation, Beverly Hills; the

"Local Charity Drive Award," Palm Beach Chamber of Commerce. **Bidi and Albert Finkelstein:** Distinguished Public Service Award from the Anti-Defamation League.

Gwen and Lester Fisher: Albert Einstein College of Medicine Humanitarian Award from Albert Einstein College.

Max Fisher: National Alexis de Tocqueville Award.

Tina Flaherty: Gold Medallion, Animal Rescue League.

Mary Alice Fortin: Outstanding Community Citizen Award, Palm Beach Community Chest/United Way.

Isabel and Richard Furland: Ballinger Award, Preservation Foundation.

Lynette and Howard Gittis: Ballinger Award, Preservation Foundation.

J. Peter Grace: Ellis Island Medal of Honor in New York.

Walter S. Gubelmann *(the late)*: Honored by the Society of the Four Arts with a sculpture by D.H.S. Wehle called "Silver King" (a bronze Tarpon).

Jeanne P. Habicht: Clara Barton Honor Award, American Red Cross.

Anita Hamilton: Women of Distinction, Palm Beach Atlantic College. Also "Outstanding Volunteer Fund Raiser" Award by the National Society of Fund Raising Executives.

Nicki Harris: Women of Distinction, Palm Beach Atlantic College.

Sylvia Hassenfeld: Statue of Liberty Award, American Jewish Historical Society.

Edward and Ruth Hennessy: Fleur de Lis Award, United Way of America.

Frances & Page Hufty: The Cleveland/Miles Award by the Columbia Lighthouse for the Blind in Washington, D.C., recognizing their activities in support of the visually impaired community; Medal of Merit, Garden Club of Palm Beach.

Sandra Gilston Hutzler: The Alumni Award of Merit from the University of Pennsylvania.

Carl C. Icahn: Ellis Island Medal of Honor in New York.

Paul and Angelica Ilyinsky: Above Self Award, Rotary Club.

D. Mead Johnson *(the late)*: An Honorary Doctor of Humane Letters degree from Johns Hopkins University.

Stanley and Marilyn Katz: Outstanding Benefactors Award, Albert Einstein College of Medicine.

William Koch: Business Leader Award, Northwood Institute.

Sidney Kohl: Alexis de Tocqueville Award; Outstanding Community Citizen Award, Community Chest/United Way.

Jo Carole and Ronald Lauder: Ballinger Award, Preservation Foundation.

Evelyn and Leonard Lauder: Ballinger Award, Preservation Foundation.

Rev. Francis Lechiara: Service Above Self Award, The Rotary Club.

Herb and Mildred Lee: National Human Relations Award, American Jewish Committee.

Paul Leone: Man of the Year, Il Circolo.

Robert List: Endowment Achievement Award, Council of Jewish Federation.

Ruth Mack: An Honorary Doctor of Humane Letters from Yeshiva University.

David Mahoney *(the late)*: The American Free Enterprise Medal from Palm Beach Atlantic College; also, Honorary Doctor of Humane Letters from Palm Beach Atlantic College; also the Mary Woodward Lasker Leadership in Philanthrophy Award.

Hillie Mahoney: Women of Distinction, Palm Beach Atlantic College.

Deedy Marix: Achievement Medal, Garden Club.

Cathleen McFarlane: Outstanding Volunteer Fund Raiser, National Society of Fund Raising Executives.

Norris B. McFarlane *(the late)*: David Ford McFarlane Award, Penn State University; Outstanding Business Leader Award, Northwood University.

John F. McGillicuddy: Leadership Award, American Ireland Fund.

Robert and Wendy Meister: Ballinger Award, Preservation Foundation.

Helen Messic: The Community Service Award from Hermes USA.

Gilbert S. Messing: The National Human Relations Award from the American Jewish Committee.

Sydell Miller: Outstanding Business Leader Award, Northwood University.

Robert M. Montgomery, Jr.: The Distinguished Community Service Award from the American Technion Society, Palm Beach Chapter, and the City of Hope Humanitarian Award; Haym Salomon Award, Anti-Defamation League.

James Nemec: The Williard Award at Stetson College of Law.

Melvin Nessell: Philanthropy Award, Community Foundation.

Elizabeth Newman: The Distinguished Service Award from the Jewish Guild for the Blind.

Jesse Newman: The Community Spirit Award from the Palm Beach Branch of the Cystic Fibrosis Foundation; Guardian of the Menorah

66

Award, B'nai B'rith Foundation.

Bill and Kit Pannill: Philanthropy Award, Community Foundation. **(Kit):** Women of Distinction, Palm Beach Atlantic College. **(Bill):** Royal Horticultural Society's Peter Bari Memorial Corp.

Elissa Landi Paparone: Woman of the Year, Il Circolo.

Mary Alice Pappas: Diamond Fundraising Award, Boys & Girls Clubs.

Lowell "Bud" Paxson: "American Free Enterprise" Award from Palm Beach Atlantic College.

George Petty: The "George Petty Park" in West Palm Beach, renamed in his honor by the Good Neighbor Council.

Martha Phillips (the late): The "Lifetime in the Field of Fashion" Award from her industry peers and the Bal Harbour Shops.

Ogden Phipps: The Eclipse Award from the Horse Breeding Association of America.

Jim Ponce: "Official Landmark" Award by the Historical Society of Palm Beach.

Dan Ponton: Years of Excellence Award, International Wine and Food Society.

Lois Pope: Honored by many organizations for her benevolence; especially honored by LIFE (Leaders in Furthering Education), an organization she founded; Distinguished Service Award, Citibank Private Bank of Florida; Ellis Island Medal of Honor, National Ethnic Coalition.

Michael Price: Ballinger Award, Preservation Foundation.

Connie Purcell: Child Advocate of the Year, Children's Home Society.

Pearl Resnick: An Honorary Doctoral Degree from Yeshiva University; Community Service Award, Wiesenthal Center.

John Rybovich Jr. *(the late)*: Lifetime Achievement Award, West Palm Beach Fishing Club.

Peter Sammartino: Ellis Island Medal of Honor in New York.

Lewis and Joyce Sang: Hermes Humanitarian Award

Arnold Scaasi: The "Man of the Year" Award from the Girl Scout Council of Greater New York.

Dr. Charles Schepens: Great Humanitarian Award, Schepens Eye Research Institute.

Mary Schott: Women of Distinction, Palm Beach Atlantic College.

Dorothy Schulman: Women of Distinction, Palm Beach Atlantic College.

Earl E.T. Smith *(the late)*: Palm Beach County Historical Society's James R. Knott Award for efforts to preserve Palm Beach County history.

Virginia and Philip Stein: Ballinger Award for Excellence in Architecture from the Preservation Foundation of Palm Beach.

Dorothy Sullivan: Child Advocate of the Year, The Friends of Abused Children.

Ann Summers: $100,000 Medallion, Animal Rescue League.

Pat Supper: Recognized by the Palm Beach Atlantic College for contributions to the College and achievement as a mother, and the Hermes Community Service Award.

Antonio Tambone: Distinguished Service Award from the National Italian American Foundation; "Man of the Year" Award from Il Circolo.

Stokes and Joan Von Pantz: "Friend of Planned Parenthood" Award.

Kathryn Vecellio: Women of Distinction, Palm Beach Atlantic College.

Etta and Arthur Wasserman: The "Citizens of the Year" Award from the Palm Beach Region of the American Committee for the Weizmann Institute of Science (Israel).

Morton and Hermine Wiener: The Distinguished Public Service Award from the Anti-Defamation League; ORT Honors (Hermine) Honoree, Brandeis University.

Judge Paul Williams: Several Scholarships in his name from the American Cancer Society of Palm Beach and the State of Florida Division of the Society; Certificate of Appreciation from Harvard Law School for the Paul W. Williams Endowment.

William Ylvisaker: Enshrined in the Polo Hall of Fame.

—CLAN ELAN—

*M*embers of these clans from across the country migrated to southern Florida over the last century and took roots. Their points of origin:

From **New York:** Auchincloss, Vanderbilt, Post, Cushing, McAllister, Van Rensselaer, Burden, Hutton, Randolph, Flagler, DePeyster, Bayard, Dana, Beekman, Read, Roosevelt, Lindsay, Buchanan, Murray, Tooker, Whitney, Van Alen, Rockefeller, Tiffany, Gurnee, Guest, Goelet, Allen, Bancroft, Baker, Belmont, Jennings, Livingston, Bouvier, Rogers, Gardiner, Munn, Delafield, Fish, Brokaw, Sloan, Tailer, Greer, Hewitt, Dodge and Harkness.

From **Boston:** Woodbury, Kennedy, Crowninshield, Conant, Thayer, James, Perry, Fiske, Clapp, Lawrence, Williams, Otis, Ames, Little, Pinchon, Aldrich, Eliot, Blodgett, Gardiner, Loring, Dudley, Robinson, Quincy, Phillips, Holmes, Parker, Crompton, Forbes, Lyman, Sargent and Sawyer.

From **Philadelphia**: Stotesbury, McLean, Drexel, Baldwin, Biddle, Wanamaker, du Pont, Bingham, Coates, Wood, Morris, Shippen, Cooke, Meade, McKean, Lewis, Dolan, Widener, Wheeler, Norris, Dorrance, Weightman, Wister and Clothier.

From **Washington/Virginia/South**: Kemp, Carter, Lloyd, Fairfax, Bacon, Izard, Bliss, Alston, Harrison, Fitzhugh, Hampton, Shippen, McLean, Cobb, Aiken, Pringle, Randolph, Blair, Brent, Rutledge, Patterson, Rhett, Warner, Marshall, Thornton, Ridgely, Porter, Bryan, Casey and Lanahan.

From **Chicago/Midwest:** Pulitzer, Shaw, King, Kettering, Pillsbury, Cudahy, Guest, Buhl, Knudsen, Dodge, Thorne, Ecclestone, Phipps, Chapin, Armour, Scherer, Mellon, Chrysler, Prentice, Firestone, Fisher, Patterson, Busch, Lovejoy, Montgomery, Paepcke, Hobbs, Muir, French, Trowbridge, Wyckoff, Preston, Brooks, Cooke, Butler, Irwin, Blossom, Chubb and Minor.

From **San Francisco**: Wallace, Baldwin, McAllister, Russell, Norris, Wilson, O'Brien, Ross, Hopkins, Hooper, Lyman, Livingston, Sanford, Cameron and Haas.

Demographers note that a new generation comes on line every 25 or so years. Since Palm Beach is barely 100 years old, only a few generations historically share the glories of the Island.

Among those with several generations of local family who constitute the great Palm Beach clans, are:

Anderson, Annenberg, Anthony, Amory, Appleton, Armour, Astor, Baker, Brokaw, Biddle, Blossom, Boardman, Bolton, Clarke, Cluett, Cowell, Cromwell, Cudahy, Cushing, Dayton, De Peyster, Dillman, Dodge, Drexel, Duke, Dunphy, du Pont, Emerson, Emery, Englehard, Folger, Fuller, Gubelmann, Guest, Hartford, Hitchcock, Hollingsworth, Hufty, Hutton, Kay, Kellogg, Kemble, Kendall, Lauder, Leas, Leidy, Maddock, Magowan, Mandel, Marston, Matthews, McLean, Melhado, Mellon, Merrill, Munn, Norris, Oakes, Obolensky, Phipps, Pillsbury, Post, Prentice, Pulitzer, Reynolds, Robinson, Rovensky, Rumbough, Sanford, Smith, Stotesbury, Strawbridge, Tailer, Vanderbilt, Van Rensselaer, Wanamaker, Warburton, Whitmore, Widener, Wrightsman, Woodward, Yates and **Young.**

—SOCIAL STARDOM—

*T*he *Social Index-Directory* has been, since 1933, the instrument by which prominent Palm Beachers (and residents of other Florida communities) are given their social validity. The 813-page book (5x7 in., 2 in. thick, black cover with gold embossing) has about 650 pages listing socially conscious residents in Palm Beach, Hobe Sound, Delray Beach, Boca Raton, Fort Lauderdale, Miami, The Treasure Coast, Gulf Coast, Central Florida and the Bahamas. Additionally, some 65 pages list officials of various clubs and civic organizations; 50 pages are devoted to advertising; and the final pages list Seasonal Guests, maiden names and owners of yachts and aircraft.

The *Social Index-Directory* is published in Palm Beach and according to the Preface... "Those listed in the *Social Index-Directory* have recognized social standing in their communities, both in Florida and their other residences." The book is sponsored by an Advisory Committee of prominent residents in each community; listees pay a fee of $100 for a listing and receive the *Social Index-Directory* at no charge each October. To the social climber, the book is indispensable; it is a credentials check, marital status source, phone book and "disclosure" informant, although many residents prefer not to be listed, simply because it publicizes/ categorizes them.

A sample (and fictitious) listing follows:

MORNINGSTAR, MR. AND MRS. JAMES J.
>(Sally O'Brien)
>1050 South Ocean Boulevard, Palm Beach 33480
>(561) 100-1000
>*Other Address:* Holly Lane, Remsenburg, NY 11960
>(516) 335-3242;
>29 Shady Lane, Chestnut Hill, MA 02167
>(617) 772-9080
>*Clubs:* Bath and Tennis, Everglades; Colony; ESU;
>Oyster Harbor (MA)
>*College:* Citadel, University of North Carolina '53 (Mr.);
>University of Chicago '55 (Mrs.)
>*Adults:* J. Donald Morningstar; Robin Hood Morningstar;
>Mrs. Elizabeth MacPherson
>(Elizabeth Mary Morningstar)
>*Yacht: Go For It* (60' Rybovich)
>*Airplane:* Cessna Citation II SP Jet

By way of contrast, the *National Social Register* (published by Forbes Enterprises) lists 28,000 names, addresses, phone numbers, alma maters, club memberships and yacht locations of leaders in 12 U.S. cities. It was founded in 1912 by Louis Keller and became the property of the late Malcolm Forbes in '76. It comes out each November at a cost of $100 a copy.

In Washington the "Green Book," officially called *The Social List of Washington, D.C.*, serves the same purpose. About 400 pages of Capitol Hill, Diplomatic Corps, Organizations of the American States, administration and federal officials and social personages are listed (some 5,200 names); 111 pages of advertising and miscellaneous dignitary listings, protocol procedures and maiden names flesh out the 511-page "Green Book" (it has a green suede cover) which is priced at $75 annually to subscribers (some 6,000 personages). Published by Thomas J. Murray in Kensington, MD, each fall, the "Green Book" identifies only names of listees, maiden name of spouse and children's names plus address and phone number.

The longest surname in the *Social Index-Directory* is **Heiligenstein, Mr. and Mrs. C.E.** (Eden Rd.) and **Hollingsworth, Mrs. James E.** (The Villas, Worth Avenue), with 13 letters each. The shortest names are **Cox**, Mr. and Mrs. Howard Ellis (Everglades Club); and **Fox**, Mrs. Harry V. (Woodbridge Rd.)

For the record, **John and William Theodoracopulos** (Dunbar Rd.) have the longest surname of any Island resident.

—PALM BEACH PHILOSOPHY—

*O*ur Island has a unique blend of Asian, European, South American and Middle Eastern cultures, coupled with historic American Indian-and-Anglo origins. Yet, somehow, when dealing with the esoteric side of life, **Latin** strikes a responsive chord. Often, a Latin idiom is used in matters of state or territorial imperatives. The following are some Latin phrases apropros to life-at-large in Palm Beach:

DUM VIVIMUS VIVAMUS: While we live, let us live. The motto of Epicureans who believed that pleasure is the goal of morality, but defined life as one of honor, prudence, and justice (later corrupted to suggest self-indulgence).

NON EST VIVERE SED VALERE VITA EST: Life is more than just being alive. A suitable motto for those who want the ultimate self-fulfillment; who "want it all."

BIS VIVIT QUI BENE VIVIT: He lives twice who lives well. Milton, in *Paradise Lost*, offered the same wisdom in these words: "Nor love they life, nor hate; but what thou liv'st live well, how long or short permit to Heaven."

CARPE DIEM, QUAM MINIMUM CREDULA POSTERO: Enjoy today, trusting little in tomorrow. From Horace's *Odes*.

GAUDEAMUS IGITUR: Let us therefore rejoice. The opening words of a student song of German origin; the melody to the lyrics is the *Brahms Academic Festival Overture*.

NUNC EST BIBENDUM: Break out the champagne. Horace's call to merrymaking, literally "Now it's time to drink," from the *Odes*.

PLURES CRAPULA QUAM GLADIUS: More people die partying than fighting wars. A subtle reminder that excessive champagne takes its toll; overindulgence is more lethal than the sword.

FACILIS DESCENSUS AVERNO: The descent to hell is easy. A grim caveat that too much enjoyment has its down side, too. From Virgil's *Aeneid*, this thought cautions that it is easy to fall, but difficult to make one's way back up.

ARS AMATORIA: *The Art of Love*, a work by Ovid on the amatory art with full accounts of how to find and keep a lover. The first "how-to" book on passion.

AMO, AMAS, AMAT: I love, you love, he/she/it loves. The beginning of the paradigm of a first conjugation Latin verb in the present indicative. An expression well known to man, an essential part of Everyman's verbal repertoire.

AMANTES SUNT ENTES: Lovers are lunatics. The foolish things lovers do are considered justification for this maxim. In *A Midsummer Night's Dream,* Shakespeare's Theseus put it this way: "The lunatic, the lover and the poet are of imagination all compact."

AMOR VINCIT OMNIA: Love conquers all. The famous line of Virgil, quoted by Chaucer in the prologue to *The Canterbury Tales*.

AMANTIUM IRAE AMORIS INTEGRATIO EST: Lovers' quarrels are the renewal of love. An old Roman proverb echoed by Robert Frost who chose as an epitaph: "I had a lover's quarrel with the world."

ALIS VOLAT PROPRIIS: She flies on her own wings. An independent spirit, she, who chooses her own destiny, pays her own way, and rejoices or suffers in her singularity.

QUO VADIS: Whither goest thou? The well-known and painful question from *John*. The universal conundrum.

JUDY TAUBMAN, F. WARRINGTON GILLET, JR. AND EMILIA FANJUL
animated, accomplished and amiable

PAULINE AND WILLIAM PITT
compatriots in many exalted events

ED AND RUTH HENNESSY WITH ELIZABETH DOLE (c)
perfect showcases for wit and wisdom

RICHARD AND JACKIE COWELL
amenable, active samaritans

NANCY BRINKER AND WARD LANDRIGAN
luminous and learned

RIDGLEY HARRISON AND JEAN TAILER
good vibrations, vogue and vitality

ANGELA AND BILL KOCH WITH KIM AND DR. ROLLA CAMPBELL
audacious and avid appreciators of life

ALEX AND NICOLE FANJUL AND JOHN LORING
mannered and marvelous

DIXON BOARDMAN AND HIS DAUGHTER, SAMANTHA
sparkling, smooth and skilled

BETTY SCRIPPS-HARVEY AND JEREMY HARVEY
active and ardent philanthropists

CHAPTER III

ANATOMY, APLOMB & ANTHROPOLOGY
(Martinets, Moguls & Mortals)

MICHAEL AND BETSY KAISER
cosmic, civilized and charismatic

83

PICK OF THE GLITTER

*P*alm Beach is distinguished in many ways, most of all in its citizenry! In no other 3.75 sq. mile island in the world is there such an impressive assembly of power, beauty, affluence, ego, wish-fulfillment, kinetic energy and meritorious conduct. The populace continues to peak the peak, performance-after-performance, conquest-after-conquest. Here are some of the notable players in the **Palm Beach Society Superbowl**.

Best at giving the Papal Blessing	**Helen Boehm**
Most vivid nostalgist	**Jim Ponce**
Most consecrated by the media	**Mary and Bob Montgomery**
Most enchanting & eleemosynary	**Lois Pope**
Loveliest first carriage demeanor	**Susan Partington**
Best at knowing time never sleeps	**Jeanne and Frank Habicht**
Most All-American apple pie	**Carol Hepburn**
Best at solving the Grand Quest	**Katie and Leo Vecellio**
Most effusive & indelible charm	**Celia Lipton Farris**
Loveliest Loretta Young look	**Cathleen McFarlane**
Best earth angels to animals	**Kim and Rolla Campbell**
Best unfailing silver tongue	**John Brogan**
Jauntiest jubilant look	**Janna Rumbough**
Frame her and she'd be a Botticelli	**Lisa Anderson**
Greatest at a show of sangfroid	**Pat and Richard Johnson**
Best at making one's cup runneth over	**Connie Nicolo**
Loveliest earlobes & nape	**Catherine Adler**
Swelegant Socialite	**Hillie Mahoney**
Most swanlike grace	**Betsy Kaiser**
Most successful social choreographer	**Brownie McLean**
Most intriguing Golden Girl	**Anita Hamilton**
Classiest chassis	**Susan Keenan**
Most beguiling laugh	**Barbara Berger**
Best spokesmen for whatever	**Ruth and Ed Hennessy**
Always, the One & Only	**Deedy Marix**
Most likely Aphrodite	**Audrey Gruss**
Ultimate Mrs. Conservative	**Helen Cluett**
Dishiest divine Dame	**Jackie Cowell**
Best at return engagements	**George Dempsey**
Liveliest baton twirler	**Cheryl Gowdy**
Most energetic hum & thrum	**Nicki Harris**
Fastest cut to the chase	**J. Ira Harris**

Best new faces/forces in Town	**Norma and Simon Fireman, Alicia and Bill Blodgett, Carolyn and Doug Regan**
Most made in heaven of peaches & cream	**Nancy Walsh**
Classic example of p&v	**Etonella Christlieb**
Choicest symphony for the taste buds	**Diane Millner**
Best aristocrat of the spirit	**Dick Cowell**
Champions of health & wealth	**Betty and David Scaff**
Most beautifully word perfect	**Alice Tarone**
Loveliest cheekbone definition	**Mary Schott**
Lightest walker on eggshells	**Lesly Smith**
Best at looking dashingly noir	**Bruce McAllister**
Grandee of Pop	**Bob Lappin**
Choicest & most contagious eclat	**Beverly Wilkes**
Sachem of the golf links	**Norman Grimard**
Can't possibly be improved by jewelry	**Kit Pannill**
Ultimate master of one-upmanship	**Alex Dreyfoos**
Prettiest exotic flowergirl	**Jasmine Horowitz**
Best at forecast & finesse	**Patrick Park**
Best eyes to hold you in thrall	**Terry Ebert**
Biggest collection of admirable qualities	**Candy Van Alen**
Gentlest of the gentlewomen	**Ann Keresey**
Best at smiling as sweetly as a convent acolyte	**Sandy Heine**
World-class style & fashion	**Arnold Scaasi**
Least complex, lovely hairstyle	**Suzette Wexner**
Best at living charmed lives	**Ruth and Ray Perelman**
Choicest cosmopolites	**Tina and Carlo Bilotti**
Best little pink tongue in Town	**Julie Efros**
Most adroit at working a party	**Mary Weiss**
Ladies with elan	**Elyse Rabin, Carmen de Mello, Nan Ourisman, Betty Lou Yaeger, Danielle Basil, Fran Feeney, Cindy Hoyt, Patti Travis, Maria Ponton, Diana Bell, Lucy Musso, Lori Stoll, Tori Baker, Courtnay Montgomery, Mary Baker, Sylvia James**
Best ad for the beauty and grit	**Pat Cooper**
Diplomat extraordinaire	**Jesse Newman**
Most magnificent mien	**Mosse Hvide**
Most Shangri-La like	**Chris Marden**

85

Best at playing both sides of the net nattily	**Susan and Michael Blank**
Master of all he surveys	**Bill Flaherty**
Best golden-blond halo	**Tina Flaherty**
Grandest golden-toned gift of gab	**Jim Morrissey**
Best star-spangled manner	**Kay Morrissey**
Bubbliest social worker	**Dorothy Sullivan**
Perennial Machoman Leader	**Stan Rumbough**
Most radiating gem-dandy	**Ron Viejo**
Most wonderful do-gooder	**Fanny Morgan**
Most active cerebellum	**J. Patterson Cooper**
Top society gastronomes	**Arlette and Bob Gordon**
Best at taking the road not taken	**Bill Brooks**
Most active new chariteers	**Sally and Dick Robinson**
Loveliest Leading ladies	**Paula and Pat Cook**
Jolliest English chap	**Alan Tremain**
Best dress extra	**Rex Ford**
Best at giving deeply approving glances	**Maura and Bill Benjamin**
Loveliest eyes that shoot fireworks	**Linda Rossback**
Most consistent soothsayers	**Marla and Bud Paxson**
Steadiest miracle workers	**Gerre and Curt Gowdy**
Most untouchable serenity and beauty	**Jean Tailer**
Most grace in any situation	**Ann Appleman**
Masters of the territorial imperative	**Joleen and Tom Martin**
Mr. Debonair role model	**Warry Gillet**
Best Blond Bombshell	**Gale Brophy**
Most charming arm twisters	**Leslie Claydon-White and David Veselsky**
Least likely CUBO (conduct unbecoming an officer)	**Simon Benson Offit**
Biggest legacy holder	**George Matthews**
Head honcho - caviar and civility	**Paul Ilyinsky**
Greatest at the Heimlich maneuver	**Jim Meany**
Most charitable smile	**Marianne Castle**
Best beauty queen looks	**Judy Grubman**
Women with *je ne sais quoi*	**Hope Annan, Fran Salisbury, Beth Summers, Pat Supper, Evalyn Swartz, Gio King, Kay Rybovich, Gay Gaines, June Rooney**
Loveliest green thumb	**C.Z. Guest**
Purest celestial appearance	**Joyce Vaughn**
Quietest self-assurance	**Bruce Bent**
Least in need of direction	**Judy Shepherd**

Top drawer doyenne of dish	**Patricia Kennedy**
Longest titian tresses	**Maureen Woodward**
Best at *scoop du jour*	**Shannon Donnelly**
Best brick & mortar mover	**Vera Swift**
Tannest leading man	**Jay Rossback**
Best at shooting a forefinger	**Reid Moore, Jr.**
Sauciest sylph-like silhouette	**Jill Rau**
Best dinner partner	**Nancy Brinker**
Most cupid-like Lady	**Denise Alexander**
Best at creating lore & legend	**Eileen and Joe Cornacchia**
Loveliest worldliness	**Herme de Wyman Miro**
Queen of Red Carnations	**Bea Tollman**
Most passion for fashion	**Lynn Manulis**
Best designated factotum	**Jim Nemec**
The Main Event	**Jeanne Ford**
Best at defying odds	**Helen Messic**
Loveliest Golden Girl	**Carolyn Buckley**
Most perpetually youthful couple	**Alma and Tony Tambone**
Most vivacious Venus	**Jean Van Waveren**
Most challenging literary lion's roar	**Parker Ladd**
Hippest mate to heppest gal	**Earl Hollis**
Most traveled Townies	**Pam and Peter Dupuis**
Best of the New Wave	**Mary Frances Turner, Gina and Scott Gordon, Susan and Lee Gordon, Louis Anthony, Lily Holt, Joanne Cutner, Samantha Boardman, Talbott and Jack Maxey, Merrilee Holt, Alana Henry, Heather and Lamont Harris, Celerie Kemble, Alexia Pickett, Tiffany Dubin, Marjorie and Bingo Gubelmann, Robin Grubman, Reid Boren, Jill Gladstone, J. P. Kelly, Liza Pulitzer, Joanne Cutner**
Loveliest blythe spirit	**Alma DuPuy**
Most dashing boulevardier & banker	**Chuck Ranson**
Most gracious & gorgeous	**Diann Scaravilli**
Best at tremense (tremendous & immense)	**Donald Trump**
Most full of charming electrolytes	**Florence Bonsuk**
Most ardent artsman	**James Borynack**

Best at beatific blandishment	**Ava Coleman**
Most effective as enhancers of life	**Christine and Alan Curtis**
The last word on style	**Robert Janjigian**
Most full of *spezzatura*	**Susan Bishop**
Best at sending delicious shivers	**Lore Dodge**
Best at mwah, mwah, kiss, kiss	**Ellie Goldberg**
Most perfectly coiffed	**Catherine Brister**
Least likely to play it safe	**Allan Scherer**
Best skin of unbreakable glass	**Kelly Brogan**
Best at creating rainbows	**Adele Siegel**
Best at going for the purple moon	**Joanie Goodman**
Most active truth-radar	**Al Taubman**
Best fonts of wisdom	**Betty and Herbert Swope**
Best at the Big Score	**Murray Goodman**
Best balletic sashay	**Peggy Rao**
Best reader between the lines	**Billy Cohen**
Most PB/DC frequent flyer miles	**Stephania and Don Conrad**
Most focused parliamentarian	**Mark Foley**
Choicest cover girl look	**Jacqueline Parker**
Most photogenic tennis jock	**Moira Wolofsky**
Most adroit verbal fancydancer	**Allen Manning**
Best marketers of dreams	**Shirley and Bob Wyner**
Prince of punctilio	**Jeff Bateman**
Most lilting loquacity	**Sharon Queeney Weintz**
Best at giving high-fives	**Michael Gibbons**
Most perfect Snow White look	**Madonna Coffman**
Most authentic living work of art	**Huldah Jeffe**
Best at living only once	**Rodney Dillard**
Best at playing flair	**Dixon Boardman**
Most stylishly sublime	**Betty Scripps Harvey**
Loftiest blond Wasp	**Mary Webster**
Most tantalizing sea nymph	**Judy Schrafft**
Most loved raconteur & *roue*	**Donald Bruce**
Best high wire walker	**Mel Shalek**
Loveliest stillness in the midst of chaos	**Jackie Crenshaw**
Most gifted at culinary seduction	**Dan Ponton**
Best at service with a smile	**Michael Brown**
Most vintage upper lip	**Bill Pitt**
Best at quenching curiosities	**Fran Scaife**
Loveliest society smacker	**Dolly Grimard**
Best at chic-to-cheek	**Wendy Meister**
Most always coming up roses	**Scott Snyder**
Most filled dance card	**Virginia and Bill Buckley**

Best at saying read my lips	David Berger
Best at making the sun shine for everyone	Phil Whitacre
Biggest believer in fortune favors the bold	Bob Harvey
Most Bountiful & Blissful	BJ and Bill Kemp
Best quiet Ladylike charm	Jane Volk
Most dazzling patrician beauty	Alyne Massey
Right up there with the Goddesses	Donna Shalek
Most anthropologically significant	Jane and Guilford Dudley
Greatest at ratiocination	Brad Greer
Best originator of seams & dreams	Alfred Fiandaca
Best chess-player look	Mason Phelps, Jr.
Best at vow & declare	Angie Ilyinsky
Best philosopher-poet-gunslinger	Lewis Schott
Most delicious crumpet	Samantha Boardman
Most admirable devil-may-care demeanor	Bert Sokol
Most perfectly scrubbed and clean shaven	John Mashek
Best at steepling his fingers	Bill Lickle
Best at *via vecchia* (Old World moves)	Franklyn de Marco Sr. *(the late)*
Best at *via nuova* (New World moves)	Franklyn de Marco Jr.
Most able at epiphanic moments	Bob Leidy
Best propensity for perfection	Paul Leone
Prettiest PP (Perfect Princess)	Pam Hoffpauer
Loveliest treasure from Saks	Norina Coursey
Most empyrean woman	Simone Karoff
Pulchritude & pizzazz personified	Bren Simon
Darlingest dancer & prancer	Mary Boykin
Best movements in sipping tea	Liz Schuler
Best at raising one eyebrow	Doyle Rogers
Most meticulously choreographed	Florence Bonsuk
Sweetest Duo about Town	Emilia and Pepe Fanjul
Best at knowing the mouse does not negotiate with the cat	Bob Gottfried
Loveliest eyes that widen and flash with humor	Eileen Berman
Best Joint Chiefs of Staff strategist	James Clark
Best at a fit of giggles	Carey O'Donnell
Highest altitude camaraderie	Patti and Perrin Blank
Best combo—lovely & stately	Dee and Tommy Cushing
For her, they'd fall on spears	Paivi Alperson
Most easy-going Bing Crosby-ish	Bill Pannill
Most full of bounce and promise	Patti Myura
Loveliest demure, iridescent sensuality	Nancy Simmons
Simply incomparable!	Bob Simmons

Biggest supply of deal-making moxie	**Abe Gosman**
Best Rainmakers	**Joyce and Dusty Sang**
Most timely and timeless	**Cora Mayne**
Hunkiest Hollywood looks	**Alfonso Landa**
Jolliest Jello-fellow	**Orator Woodward**
Best at great vibrations	**Sheila Haisfield**
Best symphony of splendor	**Jane O'Connell**
Most lilting & lovely	**Carol Ruhlman**
Creamiest *creme de la creme*	**Trish Donnelley**
Best come rain or come shine	**Joyce and Sam McLendon**
Best at instant gratification	**Bernd Lembcke**
Grandest Lady Legend	**Barton Gubelman**
Best performance record	**Gary Lickle**
Most glorious girl-next-door	**Angela Koch**
Loveliest accented swan	**Shelley Gubelmann**
Best sobriquet	**"Cookie" Callahan**
Most adroit at "showtime"	**Jan Willinger**
Most winsomely wonderful	**Jesse Araskog**
Best at make believe	**Fred Barr**
Greatest little scholarly soul	**Christina Orr-Cahall**
Loveliest retro elegance	**Pat Schmidlapp**
Most consummate southern belle	**Ashton Battle**
Best at handling the razor's edge	**Lowry Bell**
Masters of magnanimity	**Lori and Harold Corrigan**
Most sun-kissed & sensational	**Ellen Levy**
Best 5000-watt smile	**Suzi Goldsmith**
Least likely to be a spear carrier	**Leonard Sessa**
Best yawner, stretcher, purrer	**Cynthia Gibbons**
Most charming example of harmony	**Leigh and Chris Larmoyeux**
Greatest black velvet eye lashes	**Barbara Katz**
Least likely wannabee, needtobee, havetobee	**Carol Digges**
Lushest fall-into-these eyes look	**Eles Gillet**
Best glowing smiles & signals	**Eugenia and Bob Strauss**
Mistress of Win, Grace & Glow	**Pauline Boardman Pitt**
Consummate at creating new dimensions	**John Castle**
Sweetest little fox	**Laura Levine**
Bonniest bon vivants	**Nell and Jack Hight**
Loveliest Mona Lisa manners	**Carmel Quinn**
Best get it done achiever	**Kimberly Strauss**
Least pretentious princess	**Claude Rosinsky**
Most provocative *piece de resistance*	**Sunny Sessa**
Most all-around upbeat	**Susan and Dom Telesco**

Master of the Wasp code	**Fitz Eugene Dixon**
Big Time, Major Benefactors	**Sondra and David Mack,**
	Lorraine and Jack Friedman,
	Edie and Marvin Schur,
	Dorothy and Milton
	Schulman, Pat and Tom
	McCloskey, Dorothy and
	Sidney Kohl, Helen and Ted
	Persson, Helen and Harry
	Gray, Gladys and Sy Ziv
Best at getting table # 1	**Llwyd Ecclestone**
Best quintessential patina	**Chessy Patcevitch**
Most refined sex appeal	**Trish Hilton**
Most versatile chameleon	**Susan McAllister**
Paragon of fastidious manners	**Ann Anderson**
Biggest wheel on the Island	**Jack Campo**
Prettiest mistress of precious stones	**Vanessa Henry**
Highest eyebrows in Town	**Frank Shields**
Most able to handle a baton or a computer	**Laurence Levine**
Best recorder of life's rich pageantry	**Trudy and Gordon Brekus**
Best proof that the apple falls near the tree	**Warry Gillet, Jr.**
Leading Lady of Karma	**Brennan Cheshire**
Everybody's favorite Santa Claus	**Ray Friedman**
Most involved of the young social lions	**Cheryl and Homer Marshman**
Best head-turning effect	**Julia Koch**
Silkiest satin doll	**Maureen Basse**
Most cosmic gent	**Frank Butler**
Loveliest heart-throb	**Diana Ecclestone**
Priceless *avant garde* Lady	**Tiffany Boswell**
Most likely to have the Last Word	**Alexander Haig**

—PRE-PALM BEACH LIFE—

*E*verybody comes from somewhere, and some happy station in life. Here's some background on who was what before starring in Palm Beach:

Barbara Scofield Davidson	Champion tennis player (played at Wimbledon and in most major tournaments)
Cathy Duemler	Owner of *Traveling Trinkets* and *Jewels Fargo*, specializing in custom costume jewelry; developed marketing technique of "jewelry" parties as a sales channel in the USA

Celia Lipton Farris	Entertainer, recording star, actress; has garnered two gold records and is on the Grammy list; has had leading roles in NBC and CBS television series
Cathleen McFarlane	Actress appearing in TV "soaps" and off-Broadway plays; sang and danced in touring companies and had interior design firm in New York City
Cathy Barrett	Special editor of *Vogue* Magazine
Dee Cushing	Actress and Pepsi-Cola model
Pat Cook	Actress, singer
Arlene Dahl	Author, actress
Gregg Dodge	Author, actress
Carol Digges	TV talk show host
Dina Merrill Hartley	Actress
Alyne Massey	Society journalist
Hillie Mahoney	Miss Rheingold, TV commercials
Claudia Peltz	High fashion model
Judy Taubman	Miss Israel
Peter Broberg	Major league baseball pitcher
Enid Haupt	Magazine editor
Bob Lappin	Pepsi-Cola bottler
Lewis Fomon	Cosmetic entrepreneur, model
Audrey Gruss	Cosmetic firm CEO
Jeanne Habicht	City of Chicago Administration executive
Susan Keenan	TV anchor
Janna Rumbough	International equestrian champion (dressage)
Kathleen Ford	Model
Phyllis Ames Reed	Art dealer
Judy Grubman	Model, artist
Jackie Crenshaw	Jeweler
Jayne McConnell	V.P. Glenby, Int. Beauty Salons
Etonella Christlieb	Social worker in Nigeria
Elaine Flamm	Actress, dancer, producer
Robert M. Fomon	CEO, E.F. Hutton & Company
Camille Kassatly	Publisher/editor
Fran Salisbury	Nurse
Lana Marks	Tennis professional
John Groth	Baseball pitcher for American League
Cheryl Gowdy	Broadcast personality
Gale Brophy	Stock broker
Patrick Park	Concert pianist
Pam Dupuis	Journalist
Shelley Gubelmann	Airline executive
Lois Pope	Model, actress, singer
Inger Anderson	Fitness instructor
Lori Dodge	Resort owner/manager

Bren Simon	Interior designer
Carol Ruhlman	Fashion coordinator
Catherine Adler	Hotel executive
Barbara Berger	Public relations executive
Christine Curtis	Physiotherapist
Philip Rauch	Chairman, Parker Hannifan Corp.
William Brooks	Catholic priest
Richard Allison	Time, Inc, executive
Edward Hennessy	Chairman Allied Signal, Inc.
Joyce McLendon	Founder, auto museum
Bob Cuillo	Police officer and musician
Tina Flaherty	Corporate Vice President, Colgate-Palmolive
Nancy Brinker	Broadcast journalist
Betsy Kaiser	*Covergirl*, *Vogue*, *Harper's Bazaar*
Lin Gosman	Hospitality industry executive
Betty Scripps Harvey	Media executive
Alicia Como	Flight instructor, pilot
Mary Lou Watchman	Theater and business executive
Sharon Weintz	Special events executive
Leslie Claydon-White	Scenic designer, 20th Century Fox
Diann Scaravilli	Interior designer
George Cohon	Senior Chairman, McDonald's in Russia
Terry Kramer	Theater producer and journalist
Jim Ponce	Hotelier
Jan Willinger	Marketing, communications executive
Jackie Cowell	Private pilot
Dorothy Sullivan	Real estate broker
Kimberly Strauss	Composer, musician
Norma Fireman	Actress, model
Bunnie Stevens	Radio & TV personality, recording artist
Dorothy Lappin	Opera singer
Susanna Cutts	Model, fashion director
Andrea Dromm	Actress

—THE WRITE STUFF—

*O*ur Town also boasts a number of authors with considerable output in many literary categories; some are:

Hollis Baker	*Five Castles Are Enough*
Benjamin Balshone	*Determined*
Alicia Blodgett	*Just The Two Of Us*
Helen Boehm	*With A Little Luck*
Pat Booth	*Palm Beach Self Portraits*

	Palm Beach
	Sisters
	Beverly Hills
	Malibu
	Miami
Joella Cain	*The Venus Image*
Beatrice Cayzer	*The Royal World of Animals*
	Diane
George Cohon	*To Russia With Fries*
Arlene Dahl	Many Beauty Books
Ralph Demers	*The Circuit*
	The Island of the Goats
	Horses of the Night
	Sand Dollars
Felecia Elliot	*The Trusted*
Tom Feltenstein	*Uncommon Wisdom: Live a Joyful Life with Financial Success*
Simon C. Fireman	*No Justice*
Tina Flaherty	*The Savvy Woman's Success Bible*
	Talk Your Way to the Top
Eric Friedheim	*Fighters Up*
	The Travel Agent
	Music Critics
Terry Garrity	*Sensuous Woman*
Lou Gartner	*Needlepoint Design*
	More Needlepoint Design
	Seasons to Remember
Judith Green	*Sometimes Paradise*
	Winners
C.Z. Guest	*Garden Planner & Date Book*
	Tiny Green Thumbs
Kathryn Hall	*History of Bethesda-by-the-Sea*
Robert Haft	*How To Get a Better Job in This Crazy World*
Barbara Hoffstot	*Landmark Architecture of Palm Beach* (Three Editions)
Raymond C. Johnson	*The Achievers*
Thomas Kirkman	*Blessed On My Way*
Charles Klotsche	*Journeys*
	The Real Estate Revolution
	Real Estate Investing
	Real Estate Syndicator's Handbook

The Silent Victims
Color Medicine: The Secrets of Color/
   Vibrational Healing
Omega Point

**James R.
Knott** *(the late)*   *Palm Beach Revised I & II*
Brown Wrappers
The Mansion Builders

Estee Lauder   *Estee* - Biography
Estee Lauder: Beyond The Magic
   (By Lee Israel)

Laurence Leamer   *Three Chords and the Truth*
The Kennedy Women
*King of the Night—The Life of
   Johnny Carson*
*As Time Goes By—The Life of
   Ingrid Bergman*
*Make Believe—The Story of Ronald
   and Nancy Reagan*

Robert Lacey   *Grace*
Majesty: The House of Windsor
The Kingdom

David J. Mahoney
(the late)   *The Longevity Strategy* (with Richard
   Restak)
Confessions of a Street Smart Manager

Mia Martin   *Dog Heraldry*

Al McClane *(the late)*   *The Complete McClane*
New Standard Fishing Encyclopedia
Complete Book of Fish Cookery

Richard E. McConnell   *Hong Kong - Investments*

Joyce McLeary   *The Pocket Idiots Guide to the Portable
   Office* (with Susan Drake)

Kenny Miller   *Surviving Teenage Werewolves, Puppet
   People and Hollywood*

David Ramus   *Thief of Light*
The Gravity of Shadow
On Ice

Sugar Rautbord   *The Chamelion*
Sweet Revenge
Girls in High Places

Charles Dimick Reese
(the late)   *Palm Beach Roots & Recipes*

H.J. Roberts	*Princess Diana, The House of Windsor and Palm Beach*
Helen Rosburg	*Call of the Trumpet*
Jack Osborn *(the late)*	*Croquet: The Sport*
Jack Owen	*Palm Beach Scandals*
	Palm Beach - An Irreverent Guide
John H. Perry, Jr.	*Bridge to a Renewable Energy Future: Methanol*
Roxanne Pulitzer	*The Prize Pulitzer*
	Twins
	Facade
Lewis Sang	*Deadly Companions*
	The Right
	The Terror Chronicle
Leslie Aldrich Westoff	*Passionate Sex—Discover the Special Power in You*
	Corporate Romance
	Breaking Out of the Middle-Age Trap
	The Second Time Around
Zoe Shippin	*Cooking Can Be Fun*
Judy Schrafft	*Other Places*
	Places
Dr. Madeleine Singer	*Phenomenal Women—That's Us!*
Jesse Spaulding	*The Blue Nose Schooner*
Earl E.T. Smith	
(the late)	*The Fourth Floor*
Jacob Teshuva	*Alexander Calder —A Study*
Donald Trump	*The Art of the Deal*
	Surviving at the Top
	The America We Deserve
Gunilla von Post	*Love, Jack*
Natalie Pray	*Malcolm's French Mistress*
Brenda Starr	*101 Reasons to Read To Your Child*

Despite mergers of many top publishing firms, the industry continues to grow and present exciting new works from current and new authors. Prices of premium books have escalated to a level of almost $25 per copy and authors are raking in money from sales of hard and soft cover books, international rights, movies and first-run television films, mini-series and other outlets. Example: Globally, **Tom Clancy** made about $66 million from his geo-suspense novels last year, with Hollywood taking options on every word he writes. **John Grisham** sold 16 million copies of his 11 books last year and readers and moviegoers spent about

$1 billion on his works in the 1990s—his take $36 million. **Stephen King** gets 50% of the profits from his publisher and took in $65 million last year; **Dean Koontz**, who has been writing in a variety of genres for 30 years, made $34 million; and **Michael Crichton**, $33 million. Between huge advances to authors on their books and a percentage of the gross, plus film rights, writers have become major factors in the entertainment industry, and are expected to be significant forces as our economy turns more toward e-commerce.

Historical note. The top 20 books of the last century, based on opinion polls of major publishing firms and *The New York Times* are:

Ulysses, James Joyce; *The Great Gatsby*, F. Scott Fitzgerald; *A Portrait of the Artist as a Young Man*, James Joyce; *Lolita*, Vladimir Nabokov; *Brave New World*, Aldous Huxley; *The Sound and the Fury*, William Faulkner; *Catch-22*, Joseph Heller; *Darkness at Noon*, Arthur Koestler; *Sons and Lovers*, D.H. Lawrence; *The Grapes of Wrath*, John Steinbeck; *Under the Volcano*, Malcolm Lowry; *The Way of All Flesh*, Samuel Butler; *1984*, George Orwell; *I, Claudius*, Robert Graves; *To The Lighthouse*, Virginia Woolf; *An American Tragedy*, Theodore Dreiser, *The Heart Is A Lonely Hunter*, Carson McCullers; *Slaughterhouse Five*, Kurt Vonnegut; *Invisible Man*, Ralph Ellison, *Native Son*, Richard Wright

Final thought: If you wait long enough, books can appreciate immensely in value as collector's items. A four-volume work by American ornithologist John James Audubon, considered one of the greatest achievements of American intellectual history, recently set a world record for a printed book sold at auction when a private collector paid $8.8 million at Christie's for *The Birds of America.* Second biggest sale was for Chaucer's *The Canterbury Tales* at $7,565,396 at a Christie's auction in London, 1998.

—STEEL MAGNOLIAS—

*I*n a Town laden with beautiful women, most of whom could be model-or-trophy wives, many choose to be career/professional Ladies who rule their own domains and help perfect commerce in Palm Beach. The leading businesswomen are:

Art	**Helen F. Boehm** is Chairman of the Board of the Boehm Porcelain Studio in Trenton, NJ and Malvern, England. Established in 1950, Boehm Porcelain is exhibited in 130 museums and institutions around the world, including The White House, The Hermitage in Russia, Buckingham Palace, The Vatican Museum,

The Smithsonian Institute and The Metropolitan Museum of Art. Mrs. Boehm holds three Honorary Doctor degrees, has been honored by heads of state worldwide, and is a major force on the charity scene, having been chairperson of over a dozen balls and galas.

Finance　　**Mary E. Watkins** is Chairman and Chief Executive Officer of JP Morgan FSB and a managing director of JP Morgan Securities. Given these positions, she is the highest-ranking female financial executive on the Island. In her 26-year career at Morgan, she has managed a variety of businesses including the Global Loan Syndication and Private Placement Advisory. Further, she served on the firm's initial Diversity Steering Committee and led Morgan's firm-wide Diversity Initiative for a period of two years. Now in Palm Beach, Mrs. Watkins is responsible for Morgan's Private Client business in Florida. She currently serves on the Executive Committee of the Kravis Center's Corporate Partners Board.

Cosmetics　　**Estee Lauder**, of Estee Lauder Companies, is a long-time favorite of Palm Beachers. Although not active in day-to-day management of her international company (one of the largest private firms in the world), nor as active on the social scene as in former times, her spiriit prevails and she is always considered the "Leading Lady" in Palm Beach. Her son Leonard, and his wife Evelyn, have become involved with several local charities and are carrying on the philanthropic tradition of the Lauder Family. (Evelyn Lauder founded The Breast Cancer Research Foundation in 1993; since then the Foundation has given research grants of over $13.5 million.)

Philanthropy **Lois Pope** is one of the nation's leading philanthropists. She runs her foundation—LIFE (Leaders in Furthering Education), which "invests" in humanitarian efforts like a corporation and is fully accountable for each dollar spent. She serves on the board of many charities, holds an Honorary Doctor of Law Degree from Chestnut Hill College, was a recipient of the 1999

Ellis Island Medal of Honor (which she shared with Hillary Rodham Clinton, Senator John Glenn and Chief Justice William Rehnquist) and the City of Hope's Outstanding Woman of the Year Award, among many other honors. Her earlier career included work in the theater (one of her passions) and to sustain her interest she founded The Florida Stage in Manalapan. Currently she is helping to fund the first memorial in Washington, D.C., honoring the nation's more than 2.2 million disabled veterans.

Fashion

Lynn Manulis, and her boutique—Martha (named after her late mother—Martha Phillips) are synonymous with the finest in women's designer fashions and accessories. For some five decades the mother-daughter team unerringly introduced the latest designers (among them—Valentino, Halston, Randolph Duke) in a glittering array of mediums—fashion shows, galas, showcases and special events. Other top designers like Bill Blass, James Galanos, Gianfranco Ferre, Bob Mackie, Pauline Trigere and Norman Norrell were popularized due to the Martha connection. Recognizing and setting trends in the ephemeral fashion industry, Mrs. Manulis established a division—Martha International—to cater to the younger, stylish crowd. Designers for the new enterprise include Mark Badgley, James Mischka, Josie Natori, Zang Toi, Joanna Mastroianni and Christian Francis Roth.

Retail

Norina Coursey is Vice President and General Manager of Saks Fifth Avenue. She is a veteran of 22 years in management at various Saks stores around the country, and a highly visible presence in Palm Beach both professionally and philanthropically. She is Vice President of the Worth Avenue Association, Vice President of the Chamber of Commerce, and on the Board of Directors of the American Red Cross and the Hospice Guild.

Theater

Known as "Miss Broadway of Palm Beach," **Barbara H. Gault** has been associated with the Royal Poinciana Playhouse since its beginning—as production assistant, theater manager, special events director, director, producer, occasional actress and general factotum. She has been responsible for major productions like *Barefoot In The Park, Kiss Me Kate, 42nd Street, Evita, Phantom of the Opera, West Side Story* and more. A graduate of the College of St. Elizabeth in New Jersey, she has a long-standing love affair with Palm Beach and theater.

**Entertain-
ment**

Judith A. Shepherd is Chief Executive Officer of the Raymond F. Kravis Center for the Performing Arts; as such she supervises the overall operation of Palm Beach County's $64-million fine arts facility, overseeing a $12-million annual operating budget. She directs all functions related to programming, fundraising, marketing and administration. She is a member of many boards of Palm Beach organizations and recently was given the "Breaking the Glass Ceiling" Award by The National Association of Women Business Owners.

—BRASS RANK—

A number of the high-and-militarily-mighty live on the Island. Among them are (all retired): **Philip A. Whitacre** (Rear Adm., USNR), **Henry E. Bowes** (Brig. Gen., USAFR), **William C. Hushing** (Rear Adm., USN), **Leonard Snead** (Rear Adm., USN), **Alban Weber** (Rear Adm., USNR), **Alexander Haig** (Gen., USA), **Albin Irzykl** (Brig. Gen., USA), **Eugene Myers** (Col. USA), **Milton W. Arnold** (Brig. Gen., USA), **Richard P. Scott** (Brig. Gen., USA), **Leonard Holland** (Maj. Brig. Gen., USA), **Godfrey McHugh** (Brig. Gen., USA), **Raymond S. Goslee** (Rear Adm., USNR) and **Leland C. Shepard, Jr.** (Brig. Gen., USAF).

Much of a professional military officer's success is based on his performance during a war, actually being in combat. But in long periods of peace, an officer who graduated from West Point, the Air Force Academy or Annapolis and thereby started his "career" at age 18, can move up the ladder by (a) attending The Command and General Staff College at Fort Leavenworth (KS), (b) putting in some hard time at The Pentagon (especially at the Office of The Secretary of Defense) or The National Security Council (where Alexander Haig and Colin Powell made excellent impressions and contacts), (c) going on to higher education (Master's or Doctor's degrees) at a civilian university—most senior officers in the military today have one or more degrees, (d) attending

Defense Infomation School at Port Benjamin Harrison, (IN) where "media deportment" is taught (and where Norman Schwarzkopf, Colin Powell and Thomas Kelly polished TV perfomances before the Gulf War), and finally, (e) attending The National Defense University at Fort McNair in SW Washington, where global strategy and national security are the focus.

Officers in the military are graded by their seniors via OERs—Officer Efficiency Reports—which, in theory, reflect the overall perfomance of an officer. Top rating is a score of 200, and enough "outstanding" and "superior" comments by various grading officers through the years can position a subordinate for the ultimate ranking of General or Admiral. In peacetime, however, the process is long and debilitating, and if it happens, may take 20 or more years (from college to the first star).

The military is not a high-paying profession. A Brigadier General with 16 years of service is paid $5836.50/month as base salary; a Lieutenant General with 20 years makes $7280.40/month; and a four-star General with 26 years of service takes in $8842.20/month. Pay for all branches of service is comparable.

—HIGH FLYERS—

*O*ver 50 Islanders own their own planes (or have access to them via corporations they control). The aircraft inventory includes a 1984 Cessna, Cessna 185 Amphibean, Citation N57HC, Falcon 50, Cessna Citation V Ultra, Gulf Stream IV, Falcon 900, "161MM" Hawker Sidley 800, Falcon 900 N343MG, N711 Cessna 310, Learjet, Piper Aztec, Challenger 600, HS 125-700 Hawker Siddeley, Falcon 50, Gulf Stream III, Beechcraft King Air, Gulfstream 4, Cessna 402B and more.

Some of these high-flyers are: **John Kluge, Edgar Bronfman, Ken Langone, Donald Trump, Alex Dreyfoos, Max Fisher, Bernard Marden, William Flaherty, Kane Baker, Abe Gosman, the Lickle Family, the deVos Family, the Azqueta Family, the Fanjul Family, F. Lee Bailey, Stuart Subotnik, Murray Goodman, Sydell Miller, Sidney Kimmel, Anthony Baker, Fitz Eugene Dixon, Kenneth Adams, Melvin Simon, Stanley Tollman, the Cox Family, Ron Woods, James Lang Jr., Eugene Lynn, Robert O'Brien, Earl Powell, Wendell Ray, John Safer, Charles Shepherd, Carl Smith, Jeffrey Amling, Dr. Graham Whitfield, the Quick Family, Jimmy Buffett, Louis Hilton, Neil Boner, Thierry Pouille, James Clark, Paul Henry, Martin Gruss, Leighton Rosenthal, Nelson Peltz, the DeMoss Family, Ronald Perelman, Gerald Tsai, A. Alfred Taubman, the Kramer Family and the Lauder Family.**

101

—LAW & ORDER—

*T*he legal profession is on the ascendancy. About 40,000 law degress are awarded annually vs. some 15,500 medical degrees and 4,000 dental degrees. The big leap in new lawyers came in the early 1970s when there was a change in "ideological climate." Litigation was seen as the answer to social problems, and the limits of liability were expanded. Lawsuits against HMOs and other programs being funded by federal monies also gave rise to the need for more lawyers with specialties.

Fueling the legal profession, too, are the attractive salaries paid by top law firms. Example: the nation's top-ranking federal judge, **Chief Justice William Rehnquist** earns $181,400 for his duties heading The Supreme Court of the United States. It's not unusual for a very bright law school graduate to join prestigious firms like **Cravath, Swaine & Moore** (the most profitable firm in the country with 323 lawyers and 72 partners; and profits per partner at $1,515,000) at a salary of $125,000 plus a sign-on bonus of $25,000. After a few years of yearling work at other big firms like **Cahill Gordon & Reindel** (185 lawyers and 56 partners; profit per partner at $1,400,000) or **Wachtell, Lipton, Rosen & Katz** (126 lawyers, 64 partners and profts at $1,390,000 per partner), a young lawyer can routinely be making $500,000 annually. Partners of the major firms are in the $1,000,000 plus annual salary category. Rehnquist's Supreme Court colleagues earn $173,600; appeals court judges get $149,000 and district court trial judges earn $141,300. A federal judge can retire at full pay at age 65 after 15 years of service.

(Real injustice: Judy Sheindlin, *"Judge Judy"* on TV makes $7.8 million per year; Jerry Sheindlin of *"The People's Court"* checks in at $1.1 million and Mills Lane gets a yearly salary of $480,000 for his performance in *"Judge Mills Lane"*).

Forbes Magazine recently did a survey that named Palm Beacher **Bob Montgomery** (Montgomery and Larmoyeux) as one of the highest income lawyers in the country, with an annual take of more than several million dollars. Former partner **Christian Searcy** was in the million dollar category, too, as was controversial **Jack Scarola.**

Montgomery is high-profile in the Palm Beaches; he and his wife **Mary** are ballet, art and opera buffs and have donated considerable funds (minimum $500,000/year) in support of the cultural arts. The couple gifted the Armory Art Center in West Palm Beach with a record-breaking $1.2 milion several years ago (subsequently the center was renamed— The Robert and Mary Montgomery Armory Art Center); and recently invested more than $1.5 million in The Museum of Contemporary Art in Lake Worth (the museum was founded by the late J. Patrick Lannan in

1982 to showcase his considerable collection of art). Montgomery was also instumental in developing The Kravis Center for the Performing Arts, and served as vice chairman of the board for many years.

Some of his highly publicized legal cases have been: the infection with AIDS of Kimberly Bergalis (who later died) by dentist David Acer; the challenge by Henry Ford II's children against wife Kathleen DuRoss Ford over Ford's will; Mary Costa, opera singer, who sued Disney for residuals due. His firm recently served as lead counsel for the State of Florida in its $13.5 billion recovery against the tobacco industry. By arbitration, the team of lawyers was awarded $3.5 billion in attorney's fees, of which Montgomery's firm is due some $210 million, to be paid over a period of time. Wherever there is a legitimate case, and a tough one, Montgomery appears, and generally prevails. He has won numerous civic and professional awards and has the distinction of being the only non-Jewish member of the tony Palm Beach Country Club, where the initiation fee is in the six-figure range, with a commitment to the United Jewish Appeal for a matching amount.

Partners in leading Palm Beach law firms—**Alley, Maass, Rogers & Lindsay; Caldwell and Pacetti; Coe & Broberg; Edwards & Angell; Warwick & Banister; and Winthrop, Stimson, Putnam & Roberts**—based on performance can easily make a hefty six-figure income. Most firms require partners and associates to bill 1,800 hours/year. At anywhere from $150 to $350/hour, billing can generate up to $630,000/year. After expenses, individual lawyers receive about one-third of gross billing.

Some 50 law firms with several hundred partners and associates practice in Palm Beach; most are located on Royal Palm Way. Leading specialties are real estate; wills, trust and probate estates; and estate planning and administration.

Palm Beach County's largest law firm—**Gunster Yoakley & Stewart**, with 150 lawyers, has many specialties, among them trusts and estates; the firm's office (headed by **John Rau**) on Royal Palm Way represents a number of leading Palm Beach families. On a national basis, firms like: **Milbank, Tweed, Hadley & McCoy**, New York; **Sullivan & Cromwell**, New York; **Cadwalader, Wickersham & Taft**, New York; and **Morgan, Lewis & Bockius LLP**, Philadelphia are considered among the *creme de la creme* in estate planning.

But divorces are also very rewarding for Palm Beach lawyers. The cost of cutting loose continues to escalate as the chances of divorce increase (52 percent of new marriages end in divorce; of those marriages that last five years, 42 percent will terminate, and of those with enough endurance to last for 10 years, 30 percent will finally dissolve in the divorce courts), and thus divorce lawyers are both in demand and can demand very lofty fees. In the Palm Beaches, where last year there were some 5,580 divorces, these lawyer's fees dominate:

Lewis Kapner	$400 per hour
Donald Sasser	$400 per hour
Ronald Sales	$400 per hour
John Christiansen	$375 per hour
Mark Luttier	$350 per hour
Victoria Calabrese	$300 per hour

(Note: Fees vary based on emergency situations, after-hours/weekend work, travel, etc.; retainers range from $7,500 to $10,000.)

Although these fees are high, they suffer by comparison to those of top New York City attorneys like Raoul Lionel Feder, who has been practicing matrimonial law in Manhattan for three decades, and now gets $500/hour for his counsel. (They also are modest next to the $600/hour fee the Federal Deposit Insurance Corporation paid the law firm of Cravath, Swaine & Moore to handle the Government's litigation against Drexel Burnham Lambert, Michael R. Milken and others who traded high-risk "junk bonds" with savings and loans; or for the high-priced ethics probes conducted by the government in the last few years. Example: the cost of running the special independent counsel investigation of the Iran-Contra affair was over $47 million; for Whitewater, $27.3 million; for various lawsuits related to former President Clinton, the tab isn't in but it is likely the government will shell out over $50 million in the pursuit of justice). **Peter Bronstein**, who made a free woman of Mercedes Kellogg prior to her marriage to Texas magnate Sid Bass, earns upwards of $500/hour for his labors as do other leading divorce lawyers—**Robert Stephan Cohen** of New York (called by adversaries—*"Your Worst Nightmare"*) who has had roles in various Perelman, Trump and Kravis dramas; **Stephen Kolodny** of Beverly Hills (known as *"The Stealth Bomber"* because of his secrecy); **Donn Fullenweider** of Houston (*"The Big Gun"*) and Dallasite **Ike Vanden Eykel** (*"The Hired Gun"*). Yet, each of these attorneys agree that fees and court costs are small potatoes compared to the "equitable distribution" of marital property which is the largest, most painful cost for either party. Contested divorces of couples with children and property in common can take several years to settle and may cost each party as much as $300,000 in fees.

In the Palm Beaches, some 70 attorneys practice matrimonial law but only four are "boarded" (means they have 50 hours of additional education in matrimonial law, have handled a minimum of 25 contested divorce cases, have been practicing for at least five years, and have recommendations from two judges and three opposing attorneys) by the State of Florida to practice marital and family law. These board certified lawyers, who are Fellows of the American Academy of Matrimonial Lawyers, are **Martin H. Haines III, Lewis Kapner, Donald J. Sasser** and **Victoria Calebrese**.

The Florida Bar Board Certified Lawyers in Greater West Palm Beach are: **Katherine Beamer, Victoria Calebrese, Jorge Cestero, Melinda Gamot, Martin L. Haines, III, Lewis Kapner, Matthew Nugent, James Rich, Erskine Rogers, Peggy Rowe-Linn, Robert Shalhoub, Joel Weissman, Curtis Witters, Diane Kirigin, Stuart Manoff, James Maynor** and **Donald Sasser**.

Lawyers who are Fellows of the American Academy of Matrimonial Lawyers are: **Victoria Calebrese, Melinda Gamot, Lewis Kapner, Matthew Nugent** and **Donald Sasser**.

Those lawyers who are listed in *The Best Lawyers in America* are: **John Christiansen, Lewis Kapner** and **Donald Sasser**.

Prenuptual agreements are almost always mandated by marriage partners these days. Many of the super-rich have learned the hard way the true price of a divorce. Revlon billionaire and Palm Beacher **Ronald Perelman** allocated $8 million to divorce his first wife, Faith Golding, and $80 million to split from wife number two, Claudia Cohen. **Steven Spielberg** paid his ex, Amy Irving, over $100 million for his rights to walk. **Ann Bass** got a $99 million settlement; **Frances Lear** over $100 million; **Patricia Kluge** about $1 billion; and the late **Princess Diana** some $22.5 million.

But due to iron-clad prenups, big money earners like **Henry Kravis** and **Carl Icahn,** have escaped their marriages with their fortunes intact. High visibility divorces like those of **Burt Reynolds and Loni Anderson**, **Kevin and Cindy Costner**, **Lee and Darrien Iacocca** and **Marcia and Neil Diamond** almost always net the ex-wife a windfall (largely based on huge incomes for the male and a long marriage that finally turned sour).

Palm Beach has two law firms directed by father- and-progency management. Michael Small and his daughter Lisa, of the firm **Small & Small**. **Downey and Downey**, Attorneys, is a partnership between father Daniel and son Edward Downey.

—THE SPINNERS—

*P*ublic realtions has been a major factor in creating demand for about 125 years in this country; its originator, the "Father of Spin" was **Edward L. Bernays**, the nephew of Sigmund

Freud. It's said that Freud was interested in releasing the pent-up libido of the individual while Bernays engaged in directing the suppressed desires of the crowd. Bernays was most successful in getting his message across through a variety of strategems: flooding the media with an array of experts and opinion leaders, creating pseudo-trade associations to disseminate info favorable to a behind-the-scenes client, marrying PR campaigns to the purported public good, and staging special events or "photo ops." His method was to pinpoint as many constituencies as possible and work on each until the desired effect was achieved.

In Palm Beach, the spin isn't quite that elaborate. Time was when Leading Ladies in Palm Beach had a select few specialists in the business of "image" making; they would help choose top charities to support, assemble committee members, create themes and promotional materials, and generally function as alter egos to chairmen, all in the interest of drawing attention (hopefully, national media) to the charity events and underwriters.

The Town now has a hefty assemblage of experts at filtering the "write" stuff down through the ranks and into the media mainstream. It's a sophisticated business with high expectations and high pressures, often resulting in a revolving door for principals. But some publicity pros hang on to their sanity, present just the right supply of brio, get the job done and conclude each project with success and smiles-all-around. Among them are:

Kyle Zimmer (Waters * Pelton * Ostroff & Associates, Inc.): Represents a full-service communcations group involved in public and media relations, fundraising services, direct marketing, government grant writing, leadership awareness programs, event planning and management; active on the social and business scene on the Island, with corporate, charity and private "personality" clients.

Carey O'Donnell (Carey O'Donnell Public Relations Group): Long-term Palm Beacher with insider's view and connections. Handles corporate media relations and marketing, new product introductions, specializing in heathcare, travel and tourism, banking and real estate.

Kathy Adams (MediaReach, Inc.): Offers full-range of service to charities and corporations; capital campaign management, strategic planning, feasibility studies, and staff development.

Other top spinners (who prefer to be called communication consultants) are: **Jesse Newman** (a man of many careers, starting as a Worth Avenue merchant, then a real estate executive, President of the Palm Beach Chamber of Commerce for 29 years, and adding public relations and management consulting as current interests. Among clients are The Brazilian Court and Tourneau), **Peggy Rao** (vintage Palm Beacher, having represented many people and places over the years, notably the late

106

Aldo Gucci and his family and Club Colette; also handles Georgette Klinger), **Amy Krasker, Deirdre Sykes Shapiro, Maureen O'Sullivan, Mickey Spillane, Susan Reymond, Russell Turner (Sartory & O'Mara), Cheryl Crowley (Immediacy), Dale Carlson, Bobby Albre, Joella Cain, Ann Linvell, Jackie Slatkow, Amy Penn, Helen Turner, Y.A.Teitelbaum, Margaret Yansura (Wordsmith Communications), Jill Cooper, Kimberly McCarten, Joan Durante, Barbara Smart, Alison Pruitt, Karen Lustgarden, Brenda Star (Star Group International)** and **Maribel Alvarez**. Former WPBR radio station owner **Valerie Aspinwall** also handles special assignments for several clients.

A newcomer to Palm Beach may engage the services of any of these talents to help "launch" a social career, embellish a drab personality, or keep a prominent name **out** of the media. Retainer fees range from $1000 to $3000 (or more) per month for leaking names and photos to the press, securing invitations to the right parties, arranging memberships in private clubs and setting up liaisons and introductions that might abet the newcomer in the abstract, lovely arabesque of social success.

Among the biggest/best firms from NYC serving clients and causes in the Palm Beaches are: **Mitchell Manning Associates, Ltd.; Ufland Jannes Ltd.; Nixon Richman & Co.; Ober Onet & Associates, The Saxton Group Ltd., Gibbons & Morrow Communications, and Shuman Associates, Inc. Edelman PR Worldwide** and **Wragg & Casas PR Inc.**, in Miami also serve local clients.

(Note: **Waters * Pelton * Ostroff & Associates, Inc.**is the biggest full-service public relations agency in the Palm Beaches with estimated revenue at $10 million. Nationally, the biggest firms are: **Fleishman-Hillard** at $181 million; **Burson-Marsteller** at $165 million; **Shandwick** at $153 million; **Hill & Knowlton** at $138 million; and **Edelman PR Worldwide** at $128 million.)

Also filtering the word and adding to the spin are several top **advertising agencies** who represent charities, corporations, restaurants and hotels, retailers and attractions in the area. Among them: **Wilesmith Advertising & Design, The Boner Group Inc., Ray Advertising, Island Advertising, Lowe Associates, Inc., Fetterly & Associates, Dick Gruenwald Associates** and **McAlear & Beedle Advertising.**

—LILLY-LONGEVITY—

*L*illy Pulitzer, a former wife of Peter Pulitzer, began a line in the 60s, made in Key West, of brightly colored floral cotton sportswear. Originally created to disguise the occasional drop of spilled juice at her Worth Avenue fruit and juice shop, "Lilly" clothes soon became a summer wardrobe staple for fashionable women from Miami to the Hamptons.

After great success in the 70s, the line languished in the 80s but was recently reintroduced with Hollywood-type fanfare by Sugartown Worldwide, a Philadelphia-based manufacturing company. **The Lilly Pulitzer Collection** has been featured in *W* ("The Return of Lilly") and *Vogue* ("Pulitzer's Prize") and other national magazines.

During her "moment in the sun" Mrs. Pulitzer (now Mrs. Enrique Rousseau) added luster to the family that created the **Pulitzer Prize**. Lilly is the daughter of Mrs. Odgen Phipps (nee Lillian Bostwick) and the sister of "Dinny" Phipps, one of the legends in thoroughbred racing and breeding, and a former New York Jockey Club Chairman. Her stepfather, Ogden Phipps, is nephew to Ogden Mills (who became Secretary of Treasury under Herbert Hoover, succeeding Andrew Mellon).

Today, Mrs. Rousseau marvels at the staying power of her creations, while spending "quality time with her family"—daughters Liza Leidy and Minnie Leas and grandchildren Lilly and Rodman Leas and Jessie Pulitzer.

—THE VOICE—

*T*he elder statesman of sports broadcasting—**Curt Gowdy**—has the same cool, measured response to the vagaries of life, as he did to the celebrated moments in sport, which he reported, dating back more than a half-century to his first job, as sportscaster for KFBC Radio in Cheyenne. He fits the profile of "gentleman" perfectly, knowing when and what to say, how to listen politely and effectively, and above all, how to remain composed. Through decades of broadcasting for the New York Yankees, Boston Red Sox, ABC's Wide World of Sports, NBC's Baseball Game of the Week, the most popular outdoor show in TV history—*The American Sportsman*, World Series and Superbowls, "The Voice" has remained true to himself, and his profession. In the legend of sports, he is considered the pro's pro, an icon and an all-around good guy. His industry peers thought so well of him that he was given the Peabody Award, the first sportsman to receive the highest prize in broadcast journalism.

In Palm Beach, Gowdy is equally genteel, suporting many charities with his wife of 50 years, Gerre, and a close-knit family—two sons and a daughter, all in the communications business. His major pastime now is reminiscing about life-at-large with friends, giving a few speeches, trolling the waters of southern Florida for some choice pompano, and keeping the Voice in shape, just in case....

—THE PIPER—

*V*ic Damone is all about music, finesse, low-key happiness and dignity. With over 2,000 recorded songs, a 54-year career that is still active, a fifth wife who takes him places he's never been, a life of leisure and his youthful good looks, he's still wowing 'em wherever he goes.

Mostly he goes to the golf course from his Palm Beach home; and mostly he goes to charity events where after a brief introduction, he talks softly with chums and new acquaintances, who want to rub against him for good luck. His legendary "pipes" (well ballyhooed by Sinatra) are rarely used at informal events, but he can still put on a show—check out his SRO performances at The Kravis Center. And listen to his three-CD set on *Reader's Digest* Music, called *The Legendary Vic Damone*. His focus is on growing old gracefully and with pride. But the track record is there.

For a long time, Damone was a singer of American standards (*April in Paris, You Made Me Love You, On the Street Where You Live*), then a movie actor (*Kismet, Deep in My Heart, Hit the Deck*) and TV performer. A professional who wouldn't sing songs he disliked, didn't dig all the claptrap of the music industry, liked his relatively low nine handicap on the links, and particularly liked special ladies (fashion designer Rena Rowan is his fifth wife).

Whatever, his formula works! and there's no better proof than seeing him move about at high society social events, where he is, indeed, the Palm Beach Piper.

—THE GENERAL—

Alexander M. Haig Jr. has traveled the world extensively, serving in the highest echelons of government and business, and still, in his mid-seventies, is showing mastery at continuing the upward/onward pattern for which he is known.

A native of Philadelphia, schooled at Notre Dame, appointed to the U.S. Military Academy at West Point, commissioned as an officer, he advanced through various assignments in Japan, Korea, Europe and Vietnam to become a full general in 1972. He served as deputy to President Nixon's National Security Advisor Henry Kissinger in negotiating a cease- fire in Vietnam; as Chief of Staff for President Nixon, as coordinator for Gerald R. Ford's presidency, and as NATO Commander. In 1981 he became the 59th Secretary of State under President Ronald Reagan.

Haig resigned from government and became president of United Technologies Corp. before staring his own company—Worldwide Associates, Inc., venture capitalists in the biomedical and telecommunication fields. He serves on the board of America Online, MGM Grand and Metro-Goldwyn Mayer, and authored two books—*Caveat: Ronald Reagan and Foreign Policy*, and *Inner Circles: How America Changed the World.*

In Palm Beach, the General is a four-star personality at social events, is very active on the lecture circuit, helped launch the Drug Free Program in Florida and holds the distinction of being the most-sought after dignitary (by diplomats and statesman) at the annual International Red Cross Ball.

—THE COLLEGIATE—

*P*alm Beacher, **Dr. Arthur E. Turner,** is a co-founder of Northwood University (along with R. Gary Stauffer and Terry D. Carder), a private, independent, non-profit, co-educational college complex of four campuses (Midland, MI; Cedar Hill, TX; West Baden, IN; and West Palm Beach, FL) which specializes in business management programs. It was founded in1959 and now has some 12,000 full-time students. Dr. Turner has three Honorary Doctor Degrees (Law and the Humanities), has won many awards (Horatio Alger, Patti, Distinguished American Educator, Newcomen, Ten Outstanding Young Men of America), and is consistently listed in national and international biographical directories as a leading educator.

Each year Northwood hosts a dinner honoring Outstanding Business Leaders; recent recipients were Georgette Mosbacher, Jean Nidetch, Vince Scully, William Koch, Helen Boehm, Mary Kay Ash, John Brogan, Winton Blount, Jr., John Mack Carter, Alex Dreyfoos, Jr., E. Llwyd Ecclestone, Jr., Roger Penske, W. Clement Stone, Leo A. Vecellio, Jr., William Blodgett, Lowell Paxson, Muriel Siebert, Sydelle Miller and William T. Ylvisaker. David Fry is President of Northwood.

—THE ARCHITECT—

For the past 35 years, **Gene Lawrence** and his staff at The Lawrence Group have been active participants in the planning and design of Palm Beach, so much so that much of what has been built on the Island during that time span has been built to Lawrence Group's design. His extensive variety of architectural vernacular and building types range from posh shops on Worth Avenue to banks, office buildings, and trendy restaurants; from corporate headquarters to indoor tennis courts; and from oceanfront condominiums to exclusive private residences. In fact, Lawrence and his associates have been so successful at their craft that almost one of every four Palm Beachers live in a residence created by the group. Some are: The Palm Beach Hampton, Sun and Surf, L'Ermitage, Sloan's Curve, Ibis Island and currently the fashionably elite Il Lugano.

Recently, Lawrence has focused his efforts on the ocean block of Worth Avenue which is undergoing the most far-reaching growth in its history. The ocean block is now being beautified with the addition of Neiman Marcus, reconstruction of the facade of Esplanade Worth Avenue, and the enlargement of Saks Fifth Avenue, all of which have been designed by the Lawrence Group. Lawrence is convinced that "Any institution must renew and redefine itself to remain truly great." He contends that Worth Avenue is doing exactly that to remain one of the greatest retail streets in the world.

Now sixtyish, Lawrence still maintains his fast pace, continues to attend to his clientele personally, is active in civic affairs, and deals with Island matters on a daily basis. He is an avid boater who keeps up with the social scene and enjoys the arts. Lawrence recently compleeted the renovation of The Palm Beach Institute of Contemporary Art in Lake Worth.

—SUGAR DADDY—

*T*he demi-billionaire **Fanjul Family** (descendants of the Gomez-Mena and Rionda families, major sugar producers in Cuba for over 100 years), play an important role in the Florida Glades and the Dominican Republic in the production of sugar cane. Four brothers—**Alfonso** (Alfie) **Jr.**, **Jose** (Pepe), **Alexander** and **Andreas** (ages 40-60)—run the empire which accounts for 45 percent of our country's sugar cane production, and own 170,000 acres of land in Florida and some 240,000 acres in the Dominican Republic.

The Palm Beach Fanjuls are fourth-generation sugar barons and eminent emigres from Havana. The Fanjul home was usurped by Castro (as his domicile) during the overthrow of the Batista regime. They now own *Casa de Campo*, a far-flung 7000-acre Caribbean Resort (with two golf courses, 13 tennis courts, two polo fields and 150 polo ponies plus nine restaurants, art gallery, a fleet of fishing and sailing boats and many Spanish-style Villas for guests).

Pepe Fanjul is an officer of Flo-Sun, Inc. (a holding company for Fanjul Family assets) and a major fundraiser. He is an avid shooter and uses some of the vast acreage at the resort to sharpen his hunting skills. Alfonso Jr., an active investor, was the largest individual shareholder and chairman of the executive committee of the former Southeast Bank in Miami.

111

—THE TRUMPSTER—

When **Donald Trump** is in Town, there is always a buzz— what is he up to, what are his plans, any new deals, anything cataclysmic, what gives?

Since his arrival in Palm Beach in 1985, Mr. Trump has made many headlines and been the object of close scrutiny by peers, Town officals and society leaders, the media, and, in one way or another, by the resident population of the Island.

And he, overall, has scored well. Whatever the vicissitudes of his business and personal life through some turbulent years, Trump moves forward with panache. His attitude toward Palm Beach, which originally was simply the site of his investment in Mar-a-Lago, has improved; his pleas for fewer restrictions on his various properties have been answered with favor; and his image is definitely on the upswing.

With the birth of his daughter **Tiffany** (at St. Mary's Hospital), his frequent visibility in Palm Beach and his support of various charities (most notably the kickoff of a $10 million fundraising campaign for a new Salvation Army facility for the homeless in West Palm Beach—held at Mar-a-Lago and hosted with chair, Celia Lipton Farris and entertainers Vic Damone and Tony Bennett) Trump has gained a new credence in Town.

The most ambitious Trump plan, to convert Mar-a-Lago (which he bought in 1985 for $7 million) into a private social club, has been successful, and the concept is a milestone for Palm Beach. Since the 100+ room mansion was built by Marjorie Merriweather Post in 1926, only she and Trump have lived there—the property unoccupied most of its years.

Most Townies credit Trump for starting the trend towards "young, financial" types moving to Palm Beach. After his arrival, other high-visibility, youthful money managers like Gerald Tsai, Peter May, Ronald Perelman, Alan Curtis, Barry Wish and Nelson Peltz found the Island a perfect locus for exercising their social graces and financial leverage.

—NICKNAMES—

Appellations are important in our Town; often, as the name goes, so goes the person. Here are a few titillating designations: Martha **"Muffy"** Brooks; Mrs. Caleb **"Bunny"** Whitaker; Oliver **"Bus"** Reynolds; Laura **"La La"** Coffin; Mildred **"Brownie"** McLean; Yvelyne **"Deedy"** Marix; Elmer **"Bud"** Hansen; Charles **"Bud"** Huttig; Ogden **"Dinny"** Phipps; Henry **"Hap"** Perry; Lucy **"C.Z."** Guest;Lewis **"Dusty"** Sang; Dorothy **"Rusty"** Gulden; **"Sunny"** Sessa (Mrs. Leonard); **"Bunny"** Jones (Mrs. Gus); Mary Beth **"Cookie"** Callahan; **"Candy"** Van Alen

(Mrs. James); Mary Louise **"Loulie"** O'Sullivan; Rev. Ralph **"Hap"** Warren; Diane **"Gussie"** (Mrs. Wallace) Bostwick; Etonella **"E.T."** Christlieb; Alice **"Kit"** Pannill; Mrs. Pat **"Chessie"** Patcevitch; Amaru **"Mimi"** Landau Bolte; Sarah **"Babe"** Davidoff; Mildred **"Mac"** Warwick III; Charles **"Bud"** Warwick III; Paul **"Jay"**Maddock Jr.; Mrs. Ben **"Jo Jo"** Walton; Mrs. Harry **"Bunny"** Down Nelson; Hildegarde **"Hillie"** Mahoney; Arthur **"Pro"** Herbert; Linda **"Angel"** Rossbach; Harry **"Buster"** Mills; Ray **"Raky"** Friedman; Dorothy **"Dolly"** Grimard; Beverly Jo **"BJ"** Kemp; Diane **"Didi"** Shields; **"Bunny"** du Pont; Lowell **"Bud"** Paxson; Jean **"Baby Jean"** Van Waveren; Catherine **"Bunnie"** Stevens; George **"Laddie"** Merck; Donald **"The Donald"** Trump; F.N. **"Hap"** Solliday; Warren **"Mac"** McLaughlin and Edward **"Ned"** Cook.

—GRAND STRANDS—

*F*reshly scrubbed, spunky, brave and beautiful, with the smile of a convent acolyte and a mysterious way of wiggling without moving, these Palm Beach Women are known by the glow of their *grand strands*:

BRUNETTES

Catherine Adler, Lisa Anderson, Hope Annan, Ann Appleman, Vicki Bagley, Maureen Basse, Robin Bernstein, Mickey Beyer, Patti Blank, Alicia Blodgett, Nancy Brinker, Kelly Brogan, Becky Bruder, Rutilia Burck, Kim Campbell, Barbara Chevalard, Nancy Clark, Madonna Coffman, Stephania Conrad, Cheryl Crowley, Dale Coudert, Christine Curtis, Joanne Cutner, Susanna Cutts, Carol Digges, Margaret Donnelley, Diana Ecclestone, Emilia Fanjul, Marjorie Fisher, Cathy Flagg, Eva Forsyth, Cheryl Gowdy, Jerre Gowdy, Peggy Greenfield, Judy Grubman, Shelley Gubelmann, Helen Guest, Jeanne Habicht, Kim Haggin, Anne Hamilton, Lucia Harvey, Ruth Hennessy, Sally Higgins, Jasmine Horowitz, Betsy Kaiser, Hope Kent, Gio King, Julia Koch, Dorothy Kohl, Terry Kramer, Dorothy Lappin, Beverly LaTorra, Laura Levine, Sondra Mack, Hillie Mahoney, H.R.H. Maria Pia di Savoia, Jean Matthews, Jan McArt, Mary McFadden, Helen Messic, Mary Montgomery, Lucy Musso, Maria Ornelas, Nadia Oxenberg, Kit Pannill, Mary Alice Pappas, Sue Partington, Marla Paxson, Ruth Perelman, Natalie Pray, Dorothy Rautbord, Nancy Richter, Mary Robbins, Claude Rosinsky, Joyce Sang, Maggie Scherer, Judy Schrafft, Edie Schur, Doris Shaw, Bren Simon, Lori Stoll, Eugenia Strauss, Kimberly Strauss, Alice Tarone, Fran Todman, Pat Tracy, Jane Volk, Jo-Ann Wagner, Skira Watson, Sharon Weintz, Mary Weiss, Zoe White, Margaret Wilesmith, Casey Wright, Shirley Wyner and Betsy Ylvisaker.

REDHEADS
Jackie Abrams, Mercedes Cassidy, Beatrice Cayzer, Jackie Crenshaw, Arlene Dahl, Fern de Narvaez, Lore Dodge, PamDupuis, Terry Ebert, Jeanne Ford, Eunice Gardiner, Nadine House, Deedy Marix, Maggie McCloskey, Diane Millner, Linda Rossbach, Adele Siegel, Judie Tribby and Maureen Woodword.

BLONDES
Paivi Alperson, Jesse Araskog, Tori Baker, Mary Baker, Dede Ballinger, Cathy Barrett, Ashton Battle, Maura Benjamin, Cynthia Van Buren, Barbara Wainscott Berger, Eileen Berman, Tina Bilotti, Susan Bishop, Kathy Bleznak, Helen Boehm, Kathryn Bohannon, Ann Boutell, Jessica Boyajian, Mary Boykin, Jane Brown, Carolyn Buckley, Virginia Buckley, Ginny Burke, Eileen Burns, Lisa Carney, Carrie Cassidy, Marianne Castle, Brennan Cheshire, Etonella Christlieb, Barbara Claggett, Pat Cook, Paula Cook, Patricia Cooper, Eileen Cornacchia, Lori Corrigan, Jackie Cowell, Ashley Crystal, Jane Cummings, Darden Daves, Harriet De Rosiere, Susan Dearborn, Margo dePeyster, Herme deWyman Miro, Carol Digges, Trish Donnelley, Ann Downey, Petra Dresbach, Noreen Drexel, Roberta Drey, Jane Dudley, Shelley Ethel Jacobs, Kathy Fanjul, Nicole Fanjul, Anabelle von Falkenburg, Celia Lipton Farris, Holly Finch, Norma Fireman, Tina Flaherty, Linda Flower, Lewis Fomon, Gay Gaines, Barbara Gault, Sarah Gewirz, Cynthia Gibbons, Eles Gillet, Christina Goldsmith, Suzi Goldsmith, Joan Goodman, Arlette Gordon, Audrey Gruss, Marjorie Gubelmann, Anita Hamilton, Denise Hanley, Naoma Hanley, Mary Harper, Nicki Harris, Alexandra Harrison, Sue Hartigan, Betty Scripps Harvey, Betty Hassan, Donna Hearon, Sandy Heine, Pam Henderson, Marylou Whitney Henderickson, Vanessa Henry, Pam Hoffpauer, Claudia Holguin, Toni Hollis, Gloria Hollis, Diane Holmes, Cindy Hoyt, Mosse Hvide, Phyllis Jacknin, Sylvia James, Hulda Jeffe, Pat Johnson, Margie Kacoha, Barbara Katz, Susan Keenan, BJ Kemp, Patricia Kennedy, Ann Keresey, Michelle Kessler, Charlotte Kimelman, Angela Koch, Leigh Larmoyeux, Holly Lee, Jacquie Liggett, Andree Lindow, Dorothea Lorber, Kathlyn Maguire, Lynn Manulis, Chris Marden, Caroline Marston, Helga Marston, Alyne Massey, Betsy Matthews, Jayne McConnell, Cathleen McFarlane, Brownie McLean, Joyce McLendon, Wendy Meister, Elaine Merriman, Judy Messing, Debbie Meyer, Sydelle Meyer, Belle Miller, Jara Miller, Kathy Miller, Martina Moog, Faith Morford, Kay Morrissey, Laora Munder, Patricia Myura, Helene Newman, Connie Nicolo, Linda Olsson, Nan Ourisman, Maureen O'Sullivan, Jacqueline Parker, Sue Partington, Ruth Perelman, Bebe Pesenti, Pauline Pitt, Maria Ponton, Lois Pope, Kristy Posvar, Muffy Potter Aston, Connie Purcell, Carmel Quinn, Elyse Rabin, Peggy

Rao, Jill Rau, Joyce Reingold, Susan Reymond, Sally Robinson, Ava Roosevelt, Helen Rosburg, Bernis Rosenbloom, Carol Ross, Janna Rumbough, Frances Scaife, Diann Scaravilli, Mary Schott, Leslie Schram, Liz Schuler, Dorothy Schulman, Donna Shalek, Muriel Siebert, Nancy Simmons, Lesly Smith, Rita Stein, Bunnie Stevens, Dorothy Sullivan, Ann Summers, Pat Supper, Vera Swift, Alma Tambone, Judy Taubman, Susan Telesco, Cece Titcomb, Dyanne Tosi, Althea Toubail, Patti Travis Emrick, Ingrid Tremain, Jan Utterback, Jean Van Waveren, Joyce Vaughn, Katie Vecellio, Nancy Walsh, Mary Lou Watchman, Mary Webster, Beverly Wilkes, Jan Willinger, Mollie Wilmot, Oblio Wish, Heather Wyser-Pratte, Betty Lou Yaeger, Gladys Ziv and Paula Zukov.

SILVER GRAYFOXES
Ann Anderson, Iris Apfel, Dora Bak, Trudy Brekus, Claire Chalk, Helen Cluett, Jeanne Fogel, Joan Greer, Patricia Haig, Marie Hale, Evelyn Harrison, Carol Hepburn, Felice Lippert, Gertrude Maxwell, Susan McAllister, Joyce McLendon, Marjorie Meek, Paula Michel, Meredith Newton, Ronnie Roth, Kay Rybovich, Rose Sachs, Betty Swope and Anne Washburn.

—BEST TRESSED —

*U*tterly and always lovable, flawless experiments in woman-kind, are these grand ladies with grand strands placed with precision, creating an optimum image, almost like walking into a Cole Porter lyric: Gladyz Ziv, Helen Messic, Susan Lehrman Blank, Jillian Gilmore, Jeanne Habicht, Lori Corrigan, Hillie Mahoney, Susette Wexner, Simone Karoff, Lesly Smith, Helen Cluett, Helen Boehm, Ava Coleman, Norina Coursey, Celia Lipton Farris, Dorothy Lappin, Sydelle Meyer, Jeanne Ford, Pam Hoffpauer, Frances Scaife, Betty Scripps Harvey, Kathy Bleznak, Ruth Perelman, Kay Rybovich, Bunnie Stevens, Norma Fireman, Lois Pope, Dorothy Sullivan, Mary Harper, Herme Miro, Adele Siegel, Kay Morrissey, Mosse Hvide, Nikki Harris, Helen Bernstein, Pam Dupuis, Virginia Buckley, Mamie Walton, Patricia Kennedy and Carolyn Buckley.

—PRETTY WOMAN—
By any measurement, descriptive words for the Palm Beach Woman are hard to find. But here's a try:
• With her apricot-tanned shoulders and peachy complexion, she is a veritable **fruit salad of delight;** adding to the magic is her elegant jaunty look and all the right bona fides to make men hopeless victims of their glands.

- *Consummately, unforgettably the epitome of **feminine allure,** so alive as to stretch the meaning of effervescence; has dreams that take wings, a combo of startling beauty and nitroglycerine temper.*
- Her eyes are lovely, inviting. There is something about her that whispers inaudibly of silk sheets and lace negligees, some unarticulated hint of passion, motionless beneath the flawless **tranquility** of her silken appearance.
- *She knows that precautions will not conquer empires, nor build great cities, nor win fair men. A thing of beauty with a smile that would sell tons of toothpaste and a **lie-detecting mechanism** that allows her to skip over the con and get to the motive behind it.*
- When she cries, two large tears plop from her eyes and dribble down her flawless cheeks, merely enhancing her Edwardian beauty, that classic **Gibson Girl profile,** that lavish luster of radiant hair and brown eyes and alabaster white skin.
- *What Billie Holiday was to jazz; what Mae West was to an ample bosom; what a Rolls is to cars; what Seconal is to sleeping pills and King Kong is to brute strength, she is to **Answered Prayers.***
- Makes you feel Keatsian about her—that she's at an age more perfect than any other, that she should never have to change, grow old, grow pale or tired or bitter; that these things will come, but maybe, just this once, life could make an exception.
- *Projects the childish sexuality of **Monroe,** the flinty independence of **Hepburn;** has the Town's best little coos of pleasure, small kisses of greeting, and breathless exclamations of how maahhvelous you look.*
- A splendidly bejeweled woman of whom the world possesses perhaps several hundred; a shamelessly flirtatious manner, eyes that twinkle in wicked delight, a perfect "Fitter's Breast," always riding the lovely beast of love.
- *Whatever her name, she is there when you awaken, and when you go to sleep, and in between, and even when she isn't there, she's there. She is an overwhelming source of joy, inspiration, passion, balance. She can be a **Lady** or a **Tramp**, but always a **Regal.***
- With her lustrous silken blond hair, cheekbones as seductively ripe as in-season nectarines, icy blue eyes redolent of the Lord of the Manor's **mistress**, she glides through a chandeliered ballroom like crystals through the air; drawing eyes and proposals, mostly worship.
- *She is an engaging spirit, an **enhancer of life**. She covers herself with civility and her worshippers with affection. She is elan personified!*
- She has soft flawless skin, dark eyes that speak volumes and a haughtiness that devastates. She is a sea of silk, satin and velvet, an **Empress in waiting.**
- *She has a kind of luxurious abandon, urban, sleek, imperturbable.*

*She is modern opulance, effortless chic, an expert at breathless whispers. She is quintessential **DDG** - drop dead gorgeous.*

—MUSTACHE PANACHE—

*H*enry Morrison Flagler was an imposing figure, with tailor-perfect suits, handmade shoes and a discerning countenance, distinguished by a full and flowing white mustache. Through the years, many leading Palm Beach males have enhanced their looks via mustaches, notable among whom was **Frank Hale,** founder of the Royal Poinciana Playhouse in 1957, who brought theater and the drama of show business to Palm Beach. He was to legitimate theater in our area what **Dean Acheson** (another famous man-of-the-mustache) was to statesmanship around the world.

Noteworthy, now, are these handsome devils with: **Earl Hollis, "Pepe" Fanjul, Albert Ebert, Guilford Dudley, Thomas Walker, Jim Ponce, Leslie Claydon-White, William deGray, Dr. Zbigniew Schell, Judge Rex Ford, Matthias Radits, John Raimondi, James Nemec, Jr., Alan Tremain, Herbert Swope, Jr., Chip Wilson, Nicholas Porreca, Paul Leone, Ajit Asrani, David Prensky, "Mac" McLaughlin, Dom Telesco, Paul Chanin, Maurice Kazzi, Dr. Greg Boyajian, James Gilley, Dr. Vincent Dolce, Elliot Shaw, Julian Hipwood, Dr. Howard Berger, J. Richard Allison, Jim McNamara, Richard Greenfield, John Daniels, Bob Strauss, Doug McGlothin, Tom Tribby, Dana Thomas, Warren Tremain, Bob Doney, Charles Klotsche, Jeff Bateman, Ed Wignall, Dr. Edward Sandall, Butch Trucks** and **Wolf von Falkenberg.**

—TAKING THE FIFTH—

A number of Townies have homes in the Big Apple on its most prestigious street—**Fifth Avenue**: Donald Trump (751, Trump Tower); Rose Sachs (773); Mollie Wilmot (The Pierre); Mr. and Mrs. Eugene Goldberg (The Pierre); Mr. and Mrs. Edward Gropper (785); Mrs. Cornelius Vanderbilt Whitney (825); Mrs. Milton Petrie (834); Alma Slocum DuPuy (870); Mrs. Louis Yaeger (930); Edgar Bronfman (960); Mrs. Lewis Turner (912); Mrs. Lynn Manulis (800); Mr. and Mrs. Robert A. Harpenau (Sherry Netherlands); Mr. and Mrs. Eric Javits (800); Mrs. David Mahoney (800); Mr. and Mrs. Robert Peterson (860); Mr. and Mrs. William Ambrose Prendergrast, III (923); Mr. and Mrs. Wilmer Thomas (1020); Mr. and Mrs. George Abbott (1020); Helen F. Boehm (The Pierre); Mr. Geoffrey Neil Bradfield (781); Mrs. O. Roy Chalk (1010); Mrs. Thomas G. Chamberlain (870); Mr. and Mrs. Alexander W. Dreyfoos, Jr. (795); Mr. and Mrs. Murray H. Goodman (960); Mr. and Mrs. Bernard A. Marden (781); Lt. Cmdr. and Mrs. Robert K. Kaisler (910); Mr. and

Mrs. William W. Reese (910); Mr. and Mrs. William D. Roosevelt (880); Mr. and Mrs. Melvin Simon (641); Mr. and Mrs. Robert L. Sterling, Jr. (907); Mr. and Mrs. William E. Flaherty (1040).

Park Avenue also has many Palm Beachers: Ambassador and Mrs. Enriquillo del Rosario (550); Mrs. James Dorment (570); Mrs. Anne Hamilton (563); Mr. and Mrs. Edward A. Hansen (555); Mr. Thomas F. Leddy (1000); Mr. and Mrs. Wilson C. Lucom (530); Mr. and Mrs. Hunter S. Marston, Jr. (888); Mrs. Harry Mills (888); Mr. and Mrs. George C. Moore (875); Mr. and Mrs. Alfred Young Morgan III (850); Mr. and Mrs. Michael Gibbons (957); Mr. and Mrs. G. Keenan Morrow (470); Mrs. J. C. Penney (888); Mr. and Mrs. John O. Pickett, Jr. (770); Mrs. Stass Reed (465); Mrs. William Reese (910); Mrs. Anne Schuster (770); Mrs. Lawrence Snell (730); Mr. and Mrs. Humphrey Statter (521); Mrs. T. Suffern Tailer (475); Mr. and Mrs. Kentaro Ikeda (470); Mrs. Howard L. Ross (720); Mrs. Edward Van Pelt (465); Mrs. Barbara Berger (480); Mr. and Mrs. Melvin Shalek (700); Mr. and Mrs. Martin Gruss (720).

—CANADIAN CONNECTION—

A number of Canadians live in Palm Beach and are active in Island affairs; many come to escape the harsh winters in Canada, others like the tropical climate year-round.

The roster includes: distillery magnate **Charles Bronfman**; **George Mann**, Director of Unicor Energy Corp.; CEO **Donald Lowe** of Canadair; **Alec Rigby**, former owner of Ripley's Believe It Or Not; **Conrad Black**, CEO of Hollinger Inc.; **Paul Desmarais**, Chairman of Power Corp. of Canada, the Montreal-based financial giant; **S. Lyon Sachs**, owner of Ottawa-based Urbandale Realty Corp. Ltd. and The Four Seasons Resort in Palm Beach; **John Daniels** and **Ephriam Diamond**, founders of Cadillac Fairview Corp.; CEO **Gerald Schwartz** of Onex Corp.; Honorable **Charles Dubin**, former Chief Justice of Ontario; **Steven Stavro**, President of the Toronto Maple Leafs Hockey Club; the Honorable **Normand Grimard**, Q.C., Senator; and McDonald's Senior Chairman, **George Cohon**.

Former Prime Ministers **Pierre Trudeau** and **Brian Mulroney** are frequent visitors to the Island.

—PALM BEACH SCHADENFREUDE—

A **neighbor** who has recently been listed on the *Forbes 400* is tooling down South Ocean Boulevard in his Rolls, passes you and your Chevy with a flip nod, and is suddenly the focus of a police siren. As he's pulled over by our local gendarme, you wheel by majestically with a faint salute.

118

One of the more imperious Palm Beach chairmen, who has repeatedly ignored your good work at committee level, has her hair dyed to the latest rage-color of titian, but it turns out a sickly off-red, and can't be corrected for weeks because of a scalp problem. A **leading** Man in town who has been zealously courting a special and very rich friend of yours, makes the headlines via an indictment in New York for stock fraud. **The** biggest and most ostentatious house in Palm Beach is found to have life-threatening structural faults and is closed to its egotistical owner. **These** are the gleeful times and circumstances that give rise to **Schadenfreude**, that unyielding and limitless power we all have to bear the misfortune of others (with a quiet laugh, a deep sigh and a joyful lifting of the glass).

Throughout **history**, man has enjoyed a perverse appreciation of the failure of others; "The more my friends fail, the more success I feel" is the operative line. Schadenfreude is one of life's sweet consolation prizes.

For example, many of Manhattan's **queens of philanthropy** are the object of these feelings of pleasure derived from the humiliation of others. Toppled from the AAA society lists in the Big Apple was **Susan Gutfreund** for being too pushy and not pulling off her presumed knowledge of French well enough. **Gayfryd Steinberg** has been delisted for being tough and flashy, especially in arranging family birthday and wedding parties in the million dollar range. Many social elitists took secret pleasure at **Carolyne Roehm's** misadventure as a fashion designer ("Everybody knows her ex-husband **Henry Kravis** was indulging her by financing what was sure to be another business failure"). Other icons like **Milken, Boesky, Leona Helmsley, Khashoggi, Imelda Marcos, Noriega** or on the local scene, **Bissell, Sullivan, Norris, Paladino** and **Greyling** gave rise to many gleeful moments for millions of people via their misfortunes, misalliances and misfires. Life can often be a time of per-verse private joy produced by public comedowns of what-were-once-deemed world-class leaders.

Schadenfreude, from the German **schaden** - "damage" and **freude** - "joy," was (according to Freud) a form of humor based on juvenile impulses, a silly little good feeling we got when one of our peers who was always winning this-or-that had a monumental failure. Where we once envied that person in his success, we began to feel inferior with too much triumph outside of our own sphere, and an inverse human equation set in. Where we originally were just cynical about a friend's failure, in time, we become overjoyed.

Envy is universal, too. Think of the sleepless nights you've known because one of your companions was promoted over you, or won the country club golf tournament, or was elected to the board of CBS; you may feel some elation in another's upward mobility, but there's an undeniable envy, too. Having **envy** for a friend or someone in your peer group can be especially disturbing when you're constantly around that person; envy for a VIP or television celebrity carries less pressure because of remoteness. Same for schadenfreude; feelings are more intense if a friend is involved in the great gaffe.

Some people **set themselves up** as objects for schadenfreude. **Bill Gates, Bill and Hillary Clinton, Kathie Lee Gifford and Martha Stewart** position themselves as targets; **Barbara Bush, C. Z. Guest, Dina Merrill Hartley** and **Brooke Astor,** conversely, enjoy impunity. Even in their great and lasting success, people continue to root for them and are unfailingly supportive. That's largely a function of perception and an unassuming, lowkey personality.

Too much **excellence** in a given category is also a basis for schadenfreude; the *New York Times*, Harvard, Microsoft, the Vatican, *Washington Post*, NYC high society and Hollywood are so often credited with genius or sophistication that there's a natural turn-off. The public argues that no one can be that good and gloats over failure. Same for a dominant personality; when the long-time and thoroughly disliked head of Columbia Pictures, Harry Cohn, died, legions of entertainers breathed easier; and legions attended his burial services. Red Skelton commented on the massive crowd by saying: "That's show business, give the public what they want, and they really come out."

Although **schadenfreude** is a quiet, inner emotion, it often gets voiced at an embassy party, at a backgammon table or after a tennis match. People like to share the gratification they derive from the setbacks of leaders/winners/major players. But the wise voice their rapture **softly**; by being too vocal and overstating your case, it's easy to become an object of schadenfreude, thereby giving others the pleasure you once had. Instead of your rejoicing in them, they are titillated by you.

"**What goes around, comes around**" is a verity with schadenfreude, too; in Palm Beach the key to success is remembering that the greater the pride that precedes the fall, the less sympathy for the fallen.

Photo: Lucien Capehart

TOBY CALLAWAY, GARY LICKLE AND PATRICIA COOK
honored and honorable

ROBERT T. EIGELBERGER, INGER AND H. LOY ANDERSON
eminent and energetic

Photo: Lucien Capehart

LEONARD AND EVELYN LAUDER
colorful and captivating combo

Photo: Lucien Capehart

HARRY PLATT AND ALYNE MASSEY
vibrant and vivid, wise and worldly

**WILLIAM AND CHRISTINE STRAWBRIDGE,
MAGGY AND ALLAN SCHERER**
nobel, sanguine and stately

Photo: Lucien Capehart

LORE AND JOHN DODGE
poised and popular

JOHN AND LIZ SCHULER
classy and cosmopolitan

RUTH AND RAY PERLEMAN
big believers in benevolence

Photo: Lucien Capehart

BUD AND MARLA PAXSON
audacious and aglow allies

RAND AND JESSE ARASKOG
joie de vivre personified

CHAPTER IV

PATRICIANS & NOBLESSE OBLIGE
(Parties, Philanthropy & Panache)

Photo: Lucien Capehart

MARTIN AND AUDREY GRUSS
crusaders for countless civic and philanthropic activities

—GALA-MANIA—

*P*alm **Palm Beach philosophy**: What you do 9 a.m. to 5 p.m., should differ greatly from what you do 5 p.m. to 9 a.m.

Typically, the Palm Beach social day begins over cocktails at an oceanside mansion or ivory tower; fun is a secondary consideration in the social whirl. Amount of money raised, flags waved, contacts made, deals cut, connections advanced and affiliations secured are the major missions.

The social agenda in the City is set by the **chairman**; everything vital to one's success pivots around the workings of the charities, glad-handing and wordsmithing are only devices by which one climbs the social-charity pyramid. Although the elegant days of yore with roast beef and hovering servants and political idealism are gone, replaced by catered affairs, a cacophony of ambitious self-promoters, business tycoons and distrusting imports, the Law of the Jungle still suggests that nocturnal hours are prime for consummation (despite the majority of serious performers in bed by 11 p.m.)!

This is not to dismiss power-breakfasts and luncheons, as critical vehicles for making connections/deals. Both time periods are sure-fire means to an end, but are less formal and don't demand the same protocol as the evening hours.

There still are traces of the authentic party when people meet to discuss "issues" or to welcome new power-players or to honor work-well-done by peers. And although a privileged few (shrinking in quality and quantity) have preserved a semblance of the golden age, the Palm Beach of the 2000s is a result-oriented assemblage of human beings who somehow, in some way, make it through the days and nights with more than enough dignity to be considered elitist in the mix of humankind.

Since the **chairman** of a given charitable event has tremendous leverage in setting the stage, she can mix-and-match assignments and personnel to get top results, blending a little of the past with the present:

DAYS OF YORE	TODAY
calling cards	business cards
cottage in Newport	condo in Aspen
Martha's Vineyard	Martha Stewart
clipping coupons	putting it on the VISA
good work	network
country club	health club
Bentley with driver	XJ6 with three-year lease
at homes	office parties
polo at Wellington	Polo by Ralph Lauren

pheasant under glass	chicken anywhichway
Coco Chanel	St. John
utility bonds	dotcom
seated dinners	buffet or barbeque
anonymity	publicity
stationery with family crest	cell phone
equity	debt

Yes, parties and galas are important—vital, critical, the *sine qua non* of success in Palm Beach social circles.

—CAUSES CELEBRE—

*O*ver 100 charitable organizations held special events or fundraisers in the continuing effort to generate support for their causes. Among them are:

American Heart Association
Animal Rescue League of the Palm Beaches, Inc.
Palm Beach Community Chest/United Way
St. Mary's Hospital Foundation
Albert Einstein College of Medicine Yeshiva University
Palm Beach Chapter City of Hope
Angels of Charity
J.F.K. Medical Center
American Cancer Society
Jewish Federation of Palm Beach County, Inc.
Leukemia Society of America
Society of the Four Arts
Cystic Fibrosis Foundation
Henry Morrison Flagler Museum
Brandeis University
Anti-Defamation League
The Arthritis Foundation
Schepens Eye Research Institute
Palm Beach Rehabilitation Center, Inc.
Planned Parenthood of The Palm Beach and
    Treasure Coast Areas, Inc.
Garden Club of Palm Beach, Inc.
International Red Cross
Rehabilitation Center for Children & Adults, Inc.
Rosarian Academy
Palm Beach County Kidney Association, Inc.
American Society for Technion
Big Brothers-Big Sisters of Palm Beach County

Mental Health Association of Palm Beach County, Inc.
Ballet Arts Foundation, Inc.
Bascom Palmer Eye Institute
Visiting Nurses Association of Palm Beach County, Inc.
The Pheonix Foundation
Good Samaritan/St. Mary's Hospital (Intracoastal Health
  Systems, Inc.)
Preservation Foundation of Palm Beach, Inc.
Hospice of Palm Beach County/Hospice Guild of Palm Beach
Bascom Palmer Eye Institute
Croquet Foundation of America
Palm Beach County Community Foundation
Norton Museum of Art
Home Safe of Palm Beach County, Inc.
Easter Seals Florida
Magen David Adom
Stop The Violence/Face the Music
Save A Pet
The Lord's Place
Palm Beach Rotary Foundation
The International Society of Palm Beach
Zoological Society of the Palm Beaches
Ben Gurion University
International Children's Museum
Hanley Hazelden Foundation, Inc.
Juvenile Diabetes Foundation International
Kravis Center for the Performing Arts
Joseph L. Morse Geriatric Center
Palm Glades Girl Scout Council
Florida Conservation
Center for Family Services
March of Dimes Foundation
Bethesda Hospital Association, Inc.
Palm Beach County Food Pantry for People with AIDS
Food Relief International
The Armory Art Center
Palm Beach Pops
Beth Israel Hospital
Dana-Farber Cancer Institute
L.I.F.E (Leaders in Furthering Education)
Historical Society of Palm Beach County
The Auxiliary of Bethesda Memorial Hospital, Inc.
Edna Hibel Art Foundation

Palm Beach County Medical Society Auxiliary
National Italian American Foundation
The Jewish Arts Foundation
Hope House of the Palm Beaches, Inc.
The Jewish Guild for the Blind
Palm Beach County Chapter, American Red Cross
Jewish Theological Seminary
Muscular Dystrophy Association
United Jewish Appeal
Palm Beach Opera, Inc.
Boys and Girls Clubs of Palm Beach County, Inc.
Greater Palm Beach Symphony
Stop Children's Cancer, Palm Beach County
Junior League of the Palm Beaches, Inc.
Friends of Akim USA, Inc., Palm Beach Chapter
American Committee for Weizmann Institute of Science
Palm Beach Crime Watch
The Salvation Army
Ballet Florida
National Wheelchair Sports Fund, Palm Beach Chapter
American Ireland Fund
Crippled Children's Society
Israel Cancer Research Fund
United Cerebral Palsy of Palm Beach & Treasure Coast
Fraternal Order of Police, Lodge #19
Shaare Zedek Medical Center
American Association of Kidney Patients, Inc.
Alzheimer's Association
Nell Smith Residence for Girls, Inc.
Gilbert & Sullivan Society, Inc.
The Susan G. Komen Breast Cancer Foundation
Parent-Child Center of Palm Beach, Inc.
American Friends of Tel Aviv University

Collectively these charities raised approximately $34 million, up from the previous year by almost $3 million. Since tax legislation changes by the year, monies derived from various charities differ substantially. One factor is constant, however: the direct correlation between liberal laws and liberal donations. When charity-funding is allowable as a tax deduction, such funding is liberal; when the law is strict, so is the eleemosynary instinct.

On a national basis, the major charities (their headquarters and total revenues) are: **The Salvation Army**, Alexandria, VA.—$1.2 billion; **YMCA of the USA**, Chicago—$493.9 million; **American Red Cross**, Falls Church, VA.—$490.2 million; **American Cancer Society**, Atlanta —$488.5 million; **Fidelity Investments Charitable Gift Fund**, Boston —$456.2 million; **Catholic Charities USA**, Alexandria, VA.—$425.3 million; **Second Harvest**, Chicago—$400.6 million; **Boys & Girls Clubs of America**, Atlanta—$382.8 million.

The two largest charities in Palm Beach County are: **The Jewish Federation of South Palm Beach County** in Boca Raton, which raised $26.7 million; and **The Jewish Federation of Palm Beach County** in West Palm Beach, which raised $22.7 million

—SOCIALITE'S EVOLUTION—

*O*ne of Shakespeare's most brilliant passages, "All the world's a stage," traces, with poetic eloquence, the cycle of human endeavor through seven ages, from infancy to dotage. Using Palm Beach society as a stage, here are the **seven ages** through which a socialite lives/loves in a lifetime.

To pinpoint how/why one becomes "social" is difficult; it may be inherent or a function of ambition or a gregarious nature. But whatever the common characteristic, fledgling socialites can be spotted as soon as they can walk and talk. They listen to their elders, are curious about people and quick to comment, squirm in their seats when bored, are fastidious about clothing (even at age five), enjoy leafing through magazines, like chess and checkers vs. video games and have a gifted young tongue. That is the **first age**.

During the latter part of this greening, a budding socialite attaches to a **mentor**, usually of the grandfather-or-mother variety, or an elegant aunt or uncle. Whatever the strange alchemy, a vital bond is forged and the wisdom of age is passed on to absorbing ears. Gossip, small talk about money and rank, cars, fashions, the importance of fulfillment, the pecking order, wining and dining, dancing, etiquette and proper schooling, and personal grooming are all the focus of this **second age**, which initiates a lust for social recognition in the teenage years.

The **third age** is one of positioning on the social pyramid, and refinement. The socialite begins to perceive the **power structure**, and his/her placement; and, rather assiduously, develops skills and credentials that provide the right passport for upward mobility. This age is greatly enhanced by the mentor's introductions and coaching re social ploys, private clubs, cultural arts, party planning, the danger of misalliances, the potency of "consanguinity" and familial expectations, and the esoteric of subtle cannibalization! Having reached a point of "social validity" in the mid-20s, and given hard and smart work, and continued pressure to participate in the right social events, a lifetime as a successful socialite is on-line (if not assured).

As he/she becomes accomplished at the **social game** (and not merely a pretender) during their 30s and 40s, the fruitless hours of drab repartee at cocktail parties and unproductive social sorties are largely a thing of the past. In this **fourth age**, the socialite has reached a state of grace, where exposure and experience and just enough sophistication, have created a competent, competitive human being, values and standards in order, with no sign of selling-out on the horizon. Social/environmental conditioning is now a given, and proper behavior comes naturally.

The **trophy hunter** represents the **fifth age** in a socialite's development. Number of balls and galas chaired, amount of money raised, awards from gleeful non-profit organizations, peer recognition and prominent memberships, are the focus of life—the more plentiful, the more socially accomplished the person. Society is now international with a strong base in Newport, New York, Paris, Monaco and London. This is, perhaps, the socialite's **golden age** (45-65); one of supreme social skills and power, robust economic and personal health—the best of times, all that he/she has sought since childhood. It is also the beginning of the finale.

In the **sixth age**, the socialite assumes the role of **sage**, advocating the ways/means of social ascension, serving as welcome critic to the communal structuring of others, approving social connections and peerage and generally doling out benediction to the worthy. Yet, our sage is not quite so vigorous, not quite able to dance the night away nor handle all those sparkling flutes of Perignon, however, wise and magnanimous, and willing to be part of (versus leading) the scene.

The **seventh** and **final age** brings elysian memories; of tales and triumphs, tears of joy, glossy nights at Mar-a-Lago, the stunning dinner party for visiting royalty at Club Colette, soft music and star lit skies; yes, even the feeling of being in love, with someone, and with life; the exquisite gifts and the honest laughter, those smiling eyes and daffodils; prayers that are answered, promises that are kept, honor that is real, friends that last a lifetime. **Camelot.**

—THE CHAIRMAN—

*A*nyone who *has ever been an event chairman knows the rigors and pressures of the job; it is unrelenting hard work. Yet, each Chairman fantasizes a wonderful role, script, performance and resounding applause; and a **lifestyle and worship as presented in this fantasy version** of a Chairman.)*

The distinguished air, the regal hair, the unique flair. She's a Lady in search of excellence, an anthropologically significant entity; always prefers the pursuit of the best to the pursuit of the latest. Has 50 gowns and a cellular phone. She's a Palm Beach Queen. A CHAIRMAN.

She calls Her driver by his first name; knows all the hoteliers intimately, uses a jacuzzi for instant gratification. Thinks $200 for a private makeover by Olivier Echaudemaison is right on the money. Is surrounded by worshipers and totes an alligator briefcase in which crisp $100 bills are stashed for tipping.

Always has something to talk about other than Herself; is positively zealous about Her cause. Spends sleepless nights wondering about Her imperfections, yet gets up each morning expecting to win whatever confrontation might make Her day. Looks great on telly; slides into soft sell on radio like a virtuoso. Doesn't appreciate the bodyguard provided by Her beaming Husband. Wears provocative perfume and occasionally likes to slum in a leather bomber jacket and jeans. Knows that there are no draws in games of power, and that flatterers are lackeys. Drinks two (but no more) Bombay "silver bullets" a day; then on to the more mundane pourables like Perrier-Jouet. Loves Her Man to appear in an urbane satin-lapelled tux, with cummerbund and self-tied bow at collar, boutonniere and silk handkerchief; and adores bringing out the Astaire in this King of Hers. Gives Him gifts of gold, cashmere and silken nights.

Dances till dawn when the cause is good; has the masseuse in every other day. Prefers to write Her thank-you notes on Smythson stationery with a Mont Blanc pen. Knows computers and the new dotcom world, like the back of Her elegant hands, and isn't afraid to put those finely boned paws to work on table decorations and touch-ups.

She's turned Her charity around. This year, over $500,000 net. Applause. Smiles all around. Could be a corporate tycoon but is too humane. Heads turn when She walks into a room; She knows the jive of party-planners, fundraisers, banquet managers, caterers. She knows the bottom line, and baloney from a phony when She hears it. She doesn't mince words; they tumble from Her sensual mouth with legislative authority. She's a **cover girl** (in *Palm Beach Society*); a public relations expert who discusses the intricacies of hostile takeovers in the friendliest way. She can tell an off-color joke with the best of the Boys without a trace of vulgarity, and when protocol requires it, She can toast her comrades in French or Russian. She's impressed by people but not by titles or positions, and can always come up with a clever rejoiner.

The Chairman loves Her caviar from the Caspian Sea and thinks nothing of spending $1 million to build a greenhouse on Her oceanfront estate. She believes in the maxim—I may not have as much money as some people, but I've got as much *hubris* as anybody, and that's the next best thing to money. (Note: Her *hubris* is neatly and delightfully presented.)

138

She loves to turn the Boys on with Her luscious ruby red lips and a sleek, hip-hugging white Chanel gown. And She loves to go topless...in Her new XJS, V12 black Jag convertible. Drives it at full-throttle on full-moon nights. She can always find a way to be useful in an emergency and never hesitates to speak up, if She doesn't understand something. She never talks about Her considerable fortune and wouldn't dream of asking anyone about finances; She is a Master of the universe who handles Her own turf with great dexterity. Instant, and passing, friendships don't appeal to Her, and in consummating charitable deals, She knows the difference between teasing (She is a No. 10) and harassment.

She is an expert on the Testosterone Factor and hormonal puissance; will not tolerate those who engage in bang-the-drum posturing and free-floating self-anguish. She has never been a wannabe at anything; Her credo, in short, is "I'm gonnabe." And She is.

Our wondrous Palm Beach Chairman keeps Her promises and never promises what She can't deliver; She never stoops to gratuitous personal criticism of associates in their collective goal of making the world better, and stays in Her own lane. She is a walking think-tank, an advisor to presidents, a well-placed source for all data vital to the success of Her cause. Her reward for jobs well done are 10-day holidays in Her (really His) Gulfstream IV (She has a Golden Parachute) to Monte Carlo, Kathmandu, Rio. Or a $200,000 19-inch South Sea pearl necklace (Tiffany). Or buying a dozen suits for Her Man at H. Huntsman and Sons Ltd. in London (about $5,000 per copy). Her florist bill of $500 a week keeps Her in petals; She does all Her own arrangements (yes, She has a silver thumb).

We salute You, our Chairman of the Year. May You reign forever. And, in time, when the question—*Ou sont les neiges d'antan? Where are the snows of yesteryear?*—comes, may it evoke remembrance of the Brilliant Role You played in the Great Game of Life.

—INNER THOUGHTS—

*T*he first **fundraisers** probably go back to 150-200 B.C. when the likes of Caesar, Cicero, Epicurus, Marcus Aurelius and Petronius staged special events and debaucheries to entertain the populace and fleece them of tax money. Through the years, the **esoteric of generating monies** for good causes has been mastered over and over, and today is practiced with consummate skill in Washington.

Taking a little Latin from the Roman days, and combining it with the thoughts and quiet statements of a **Palm Beach Chairman**, these **considerations** come to mind...

* The opening sentence in the Chair's letter to Committee people:

"Adeste Fideles"— **O come, all ye faithful**.

* What every Chair seeks in a fundraising performance: *"Ne plus ultra"* —**Perfection!**

* The motto, invariably, of all Chairs: *"Mox nox in rem"*—**Let's get on with it.**

* The Chair of her detractors after a successful gala: *"Damnant quod non intelligent"*—**They condemn what they do not understand.**

* Note from the Chair on being told that Neiman Marcus would not be donating table gifts: *"Absit omen"*—**May this not be an omen.**

* The Chair knows this must be done occasionally: *"Asinus asinum fricat"*—**One fool rubs the other's back**.

* An integral part of every Chair's lexicon: *"Humanum est errare"*— **To err is human.**

* What every Chair knows and appreciates: *"Donec eris felix, multos numerabis amicos"*—**When you're successful, everybody wants to be your friend.**

* What a Chair may want after a particularly bruising Committee meeting: *"Consule Planco"*—**The good old days.**

* After a cancelled underwriting, the Chair accepts this homily: *"Ignis aurum probat, miseria fortes viros"*—**Life is not a bowl of cherries.**

* The philanthropist, according to a Chair, is: *"Amicus humani generis"*—**A friend of the human race.**

* The greatest need of a Chair: *"Amicus usque ad aras"*—**A friend to the end.**

* What a Chair is expected to be: *"Arbiter elegantiae"*—**An authority in matters of taste.**

* In certain situations, only the Chair knows the source of special underwriting; it is the *"Arcanum arcanorum"*—**Secret of secrets.**

* What a Chair says in developing a new idea: *"Audaces fortuna iuvat"*—**Fortune favors the bold.**

* What a Chair knows for certain: *"Aureo hamo piscari"*—**Money talks!**

* The Chair's pact with a recruit to the cause: *"Aut bibat aut abeat"* —**You're either for us or against us.**

* On hearing about the sell-out of a gala, the Chair can only think: *"Gaudeamus igitur"*—**Let us therefore rejoice.**

* How a Chair expresses happiness with a collective success: *"Non mihi, non tibi, sed nobis"*—**Not for you, not for me, but for us.**

* A Chair's perception of gala guests: *"Spectatum veniunt, veniunt spectentur ut ipsae"* —**They wish as much to be seen as to see.**

* After giving it everything, a Chair can only: *"Permitte divis cetera"* —**Leave the rest to the Gods.**

* What a Chair says of a newly rich and connected Committee leader: *"Felicitas habet multos amicos"*—**Prosperity has many friends.**

* A Chair understands how things get done: *"Argumentum ad crumenam"*—**An appeal based on money or the promise of profit.**

* One of the great appreciations of a Chair: *"Dis dat qui cito dat"* — **He gives twice who gives quickly.**

* A Chair knows motivation: *"Bonum vinum laetificat cor hominis"*— **Good wine gladdens a person's heart.**

* In joy, a Chair thinks this after a particularly successful benefit: *"Annuit coeptis"*—**He (God) has favored our undertaking.**

* For those who are indifferent, the Chair notes: *"Caeca invidia est"*—**Envy is blind.**

* In the matter of contracts, a sage Chair knows: *"Beati possidentes"*— **Possession is nine tenths of the law.**

* Only the most egomaniacal of Chairs would utter this: *"Exegi monumentum aere perennius"*—**I have raised a monument more durable than bronze.**

* What no Chair ever wants to experience: *"Ars moriendi"*—**The art of dying.**

* Of someone who abandons the Chair's cause, but picks up on another, it is said: *"Coelum non animum mutant qui trans mare currunt"*— **Those who cross the sea change the sky, not their spirits.**

* The Chair's understanding with staffers: *"Summa sedes non capit duos"*—**There's only room for one at the top.**

* What every Chair hopes for: *"Magnum opus"*—**One's crowning achievement.**

* Yet, what every Chair is ready to say (after a losing effort): *"Mea culpa"*—**I am to blame.**

* Said of a Chair who stared failure down, took the hits, did it graciously, and did it her way: *"Fluctuat nec megiture"*—**She is unsinkable.**

* The Chair knows the reality of life, and knows when it's time: *"Nunc est bibendum"*—**Break out the champagne.**

FINALLY, the Chair respects the three great maxims by which we live:

* *"Extinctus amabitur ideam"*—**How quickly they forget.**

* *"Fugaces labuntur anni"*—**You wake up one morning and find you are old.**

* *"Dei gratia"*—**By the grace of God, go I.**

—CHIC CHAIRS—

*T*hey are graceful, exciting, competent, peerless, radiant, indefatigible, elegant, breath-taking, visionary, tasteful and sanguine; they are **chairmen**. Some of the best in recent times: **Inger Anderson, Hope Annan, Ann Appleman, Tina Bilotti, Kathy Bleznak, Alicia Blodgett, Helen Boehm, Ann Boutell, Gale Brophy, Carolyn Buckley, Virginia Buckley, Kim Campbell, Caroline Cassidy, Etonella Christlieb, Nancy Clark, Helen Cluett, Stephania Conrad, Pat Cook, Paula Cook, Jackie Cowell, Christine Curtis, Carol Digges, Trish Donnelley, Margaret Donnelley, Pam Dupuis, Diana Ecclestone, Celia Lipton Farris, Catherine Flagg, Jeanne Ford, Gay Gaines, Eles Gillet, Arlette Gordon, Jerre Gowdy, Peggy Greenfield, Judy Grubman, Audrey Gruss, Shelley Gubelmann, Anita Hamilton, Heather Harris, Nicki Harris, Betty Scripps Harvey, Marylou Whitney Hendrickson, Trish Hilton, Wendy Isil, Susan Keenan, Dorothy Lappin, Estee Lauder, Jacquie Liggett, Rebekah Lowe, Hillie Mahoney, Betsy Matthews, Pat McCloskey, Cathleen McFarlane, Joyce McLendon, Herme Miro, Mary Montgomery, Nancy Myers, Patricia Myura, Nan Ourisman, Claire O'Keeffe, Kit Pannill, Mary Alice Pappas, Lois Pope, Carmel Quinn, Claude Daste-Rosinsky, Janna Rumbough, Betty Scaff, Diann Scaravilli, Mary Schott, Dorothy Schulman, Edie Schur, Jill Silverman, Bren Simon, Patt Sned, Dorothy Sullivan, Ann Summers, Jean Tailer, Alice Tarone, Susan Telesco, Cecie Titcomb, Betsy Turner, Mary Frances Turner, Jan Utterback, Joyce Vaughn, Katie Vecellio, Nancy Walsh and Mary Lou Watchman.**

—VINTAGE GIVING—

In the late 1920s, Marjorie Merriweather Hutton (at that time), opened Mar-a-Lago, hosting a tea to benefit the **Animal Rescue League**; it was the first local charity event on record. She continued to do this every year until her death. The **Red Cross** was another charity that she later supported with time and money. Mrs. Hutton was also responsible for a Palm Beach version of the *Ziegfeld Follies*—all in the interest of charity. Local "celebrities" of the time—Mrs. Dodge, Mrs. Phipps and Mrs. Stotesbury donned follies costumes and presented their own version of the celebrated Broadway extravaganza. Follies star Billie Burke often joined the locals in their production.

The **American Heart Association**, established locally, 45 years ago, holds a highly celebrated **Heart Ball** each year; it is the oldest continuing gala in Palm Beach; "Heart Affairs" have raised more than $6 million to date. The Ball is traditionally held on Valentine's Day; the first ball raised $40,840; last year's Ball and Auction netted over $1 million. Although heart research is a priority, many of the funds raised are used for local heart projects—CPR courses, "Heart Trails," diet counseling and Stroke Clubs. In honor of the second Heart Ball, Norman Rockwell dedicated his famous illustration entitled "The Family Doctor" to the Heart Fund.

—GRAND GALAS—

*T*he most prestigious charities in Town, usually presenting the grandest of galas, are: **American Cancer Society, American Heart Association, Bascom Palmer Eye Institute, Hospice Guild of Palm Beach, Intracoastal Health Systems** (Good Samaritan and St. Mary's in West Palm Beach), **International Red Cross, Juvenile Diabetes Foundation, Palm Beach County Community Foundation, Preservation Foundation of Palm Beach**.

The price of admission* for galas sponsored by these and other charities is:

Animal Rescue League	$250
Adam Walsh Children's Fund	$125
Albert Einstein College of Medicine	$550
American Cancer Society	$350
American Heart Association, Auction	$175
American Heart Association, Ball	$350
American Ireland Fund	$375
American Red Cross	$300
American Technion Society	$250
Angels of Charity	$250
The Arthritis Foundation	$250
Ballet Florida	$500
Bascom Palmer Eye Institute	$175
Big Band Hall of Fame	$200
Boys & Girls Clubs	$325
Center for Family Services	$200
The Children's Place at Home Safe Foundation	$500
Community Foundation of Palm Beach County	$350
Cystic Fibrosis Foundation	$300
Drug Free America	$500
Hanley-Hazelden Foundation	$100
The Historical Society of PB County	$125
Hospice Guild	$350

International Children's Museum	$350
Intracoastal Health Foundation	$650
International Red Cross	$750
International Society	$250
Israel Cancer Association	$250
Juvenile Diabetes Foundation	$500
Leukemia Society of America	$250
L.I.F.E. (Leaders in Furthering Education)	$100
The Lord's Place	$175
Magen David Adom (Israel Red Cross)	$300
Make-a-Wish Foundation	$175
March of Dimes	$195
Mental Health Association	$175
Northwood University	$250
Norton Museum of Art	$500
Planned Parenthood	$225
Preservation Society	$350
The Salvation Army	$200
Society of the Four Arts	$350
United States Equestrian Team	$250
Young Friends of the Red Cross	$300

(* All figures are per ticket.)

Generally, **fashion show** tickets start at $100. **Luncheon** tickets at $125. Dinners or cocktail parties for **political** candidates range in cost from $350 to $1000 per person. Tickets for **"juniors"** (interpreted to mean those under 30 years of age) are often $100 lower than prevailing prices. Tickets are just one medium for raising gala monies.

Balls or galas usually have glamous or historical names. Example: **The Renaissance Ball, The Emerald Ball, Glitz at The Ritz, A Night at El Mocambo, The Spirit of Mexico Bal Masque, Denim & Diamonds Gala, An Evening in Camelot, A Magical Evening, Black & White Ball, Gem of an Evening, Happily Ever After Gala, Evening of Vision, The Cinderella Ball.** Supporting the theme is an elaborate array of direct mail—pre-announcement cards, "save the date" mailers, the invitation itself (which often costs as much as $3 each, due to highly designed communiques featuring die-cuts, accordian folds, oversized four color work, stamped response cards and various inserts, plus post-event "thank you" cards. Usually a mailing list runs between 350 and 1,000 people. For a major ball, the invitation process in total can run as much as $10,000.

The Town of Palm Beach requires **accredidation** for charities. For each ball, gala or special event, the organizer must apply for a "Town of

Palm Beach Charitable Solicitation Permit." Info on name, address, title of event and goal is required. Figures on the amount of money raised by solicitation, amount of in-kind contributions and their value, amount expended in collecting funds (including cost of event, wages, fees, commissions, expenses paid to any person in connection with the solicitation costs), final disbursement of net proceeds collected and percentage of net proceeds applied directly to Charitable Organizations within the State of Florida and elsewhere, are required (and a Financial report must be available in the office of the Town Clerk). The actual cost "of the solicitation expressed as a percentage of the total amount raised" is also required, and usually falls in the range of—20% to 40%.

Highly efficient organizations like **The American Cancer Society** stage their galas with precision, leaving nothing untended and getting maximum output for dollars invested. The recent **"Roman Holiday"** Gala presented by ACS generated total income of $748,828 with costs at $133,180, creating a profit of $615,648. Income of $543,278 was provided by underwriting; $25,150 by donations; $104,000 from tickets; $60,350 from an auction; and $16,050 from program ads. Against that income, expenses of $20,692 went towards decorations; $1,830 for publicity photos; $3,900, for linen rentals; $6,775 for entertainment; $1,500 for valet parking; $3,080 for invitations; and $95,403 for dinner/reception. The result was substantial monies raised and a high efficiency ratio—1:7 (roughly $1 spent for every $7 raised which equals a 14% cost of solicitation). As flavor, guests got to meet Gina Lollobrigida, who was Guest of Honor, enhancing the magic of a "Roman Holiday."

—LENS FRIENDS—

*B*ased on frequency of appearance (in photos) in *Palm Beach Society* Magazine, the *Shiny Sheet* (*Palm Beach Daily News*), *Palm Beach Illustrated* and other local and national publications, over the last few years these were the most photographed partygoers:

Catherine Adler, Barbara and David Berger, Susan and Michael Blank, Inge Bowdre, Mary Boykin, Nancy Brinker, John Brogan, Gale Brophy, Carolyn Buckley, Etonella Christlieb, Helen Cluett, Patricia Cooper, Jackie Cowell, Vilda de Porro, Audrey Del Rosario, Margaret Donnelley, Peter and Pam Dupuis, Diana Ecclestone, Celia Lipton Farris, Norma and Simon Fireman, Tina and Bill Flaherty, Gay Gaines, Arlette and Bob Gordon, Abe and Lin Gosman, Judy Grubman, Martin and Audrey Gruss, Frank and Jeanne Habicht, Anita Hamilton, Nicki and Ira Harris, Betty Scripps Harvey, Ed and Ruth Hennessy, Pam Hoffpauer, Gloria Hollis, Jasmine Horowitz, Paul Ilyinsky, Susan Keenan, Jacquie Liggett, Bernie and

Chris Marden, Homer and Cheryl Marshman, John Mashek, Cathleen McFarlane, Brownie McLean, Herme Miro, Mary Montgomery, Christina Orr-Cahall, Kit Pannill, Patrick Park, Ray and Ruth Perelman, Pauline Boardman Pitt, Lois Pope, Mary Schott, Lesly Smith, Dorothy Sullivan, Pat Supper, Jean Tailer, Ted and Alice Tarone, Donald Trump, Joyce Vaughn, Ron Viejo, Jan Willinger and **Paula and Nikita Zukov.**

—DANCE MASTERS—

*R*ay Perelman moves with the utmost grace (he is also a great raconteur); so do antique impressario **Leslie Claydon-White**, philanthropist **Stanley Rumbough**, and gentlemen **Jim Nemec, John Brogan, Jack Fowler, Ron Viejo, Frank Butler** and **Alton O'Neil.**

Ladies whose graceful movements come easy are: **Jean Van Waveren, Etonella Christlieb, Jara Miller, Gale Brophy, Jayne McConnell, Diane Millner, Bunnie Stevens** and **Mary Schott.**

Couples: **Charlotte and Donald Miller, Pam and Peter Dupuis, Evalyn and Howard Swartz, Gay and Stanley Gaines, Joyce and Clother Vaughn, Nancy and Bob Simmons, Tina and Bill Flaherty, Trudi and Hans Behr, Barbara and Carlos San Damian, Audrey and Martin Gruss, Lori and Harold Corrigan, Linda and Jay Rossbach, Robin and Richard Bernstein, Marie and Zell Davis, Mary and Henri Barguirdjian, Stephania and Donald Conrad, Alice and Ted Tarone, Paulette and Ron Koch, Sally and Dick Robinson, Inger and H. Loy Anderson, Mary and Bob Montgomery, Joan and Brad Greer** and **Paivi Alperson and Alfonso Landa.**

—FUNDRAISING/PRAISING—

Few people know that the nonprofit sector of our society is by far America's **largest employer**—a total of 80 million people work as volunteers in raising monies for charity. Each puts in about five hours a week, which equals 10 million full-time jobs; were they paid, even at minimum wage, the payroll would amount to $150 billion, or about five percent of our Gross National Product. On a relative basis, each volunteer is highly effective. As an example, the Girl Scouts, which employs 730,000 volunteers and only 6,000 paid staff for 3.5 million members, generates more funds than corporations of comparable size, and is able to keep a greater percentage of them. Other highly cost-effective organizations are: Jewish Guild for the Blind, Catholic Relief Service, Legal Aid Society, National Council on the Aging, CARE, Project HOPE, United Cerebral Palsy Associations, American Diabetes Association and the

146

City of Hope.

Part of the success of these organizations is **manpower**; another part is the creative ways and means by which monies are generated. Since "donor fatigue" is a fact of life, and more people think twice about giving to a charity (based on tax and other economic considerations), fundraisers are introducing novelty as a means of raising interest. It's not uncommon to have a Las Vegas night, celebrity auction, bidding for bachelors night, fashion show, pink elephant sale, auction, murder mystery night or even a bingo night as part of the draw to a particular charity.

In Palm Beach, **celebrity entertainment** has arrived. Over the years guests have complained of "boredom," dancing to the same old tunes with the same people. A few years ago, Hanley-Hazelden broke the mold by importing **Liza Minnelli** for its first official fundraiser on the Island (proceeds to the Hanley Hazelden Alcohol and Drug Rehabilitation Center at St. Mary's Hospital). Another big event was the appearance of **Dustin Hoffman** and **Tom Cruise** at the "Rainman's Ball" to benefit Autism. **Neil Sedaka** gave a concert—The Good Times—to benefit the National Wheelchair Sports Fund; **Johnny Cash** later performed, as did **Harry Belafonte,** to raise monies for the Florida Atlantic University Foundation; **Ben Vereen** performed for the Palm Beach Albert Einstein College of Medicine of Yeshiva University, and singer **Frankie Valli** joined **Perry Como** at a recent National Italian American Foundation gala at The Breakers. Guests paid up to $500 to see **Dionne Warwick,** and to help raise monies for the Hanley Hazelden Center at St. Mary's Hospital; and **Luciano Pavarotti** performed in concert for the benefit of the Palm Beach Opera.

Debbie Reynolds, Tony Bennett, Shirley MacLaine, Victor Borge, Vic Damone, Bobby Short, Jimmy Buffett, Hal Linden, Celine Dion, Matt Lauer, Harrison Ford, Colin Powell, Tony Curtis, Newt Ginrich, Tippi Hedren, Tim Russert, Tom Brokaw, Mike Douglas, Martha Stewart and other mega-stars also appeared for various local charities.

Royalty, too, plays well in Palm Beach. Any true Duke or Duchess, Lord, Viscount, Prince or Princess can draw from the high & mighty; and if a cause is involved (as it usually is), donations can be very grand. Example: at a recent private party in the home of **David** and **Barbara Berger** for **Prince Philip**, at $75,000 per person, more than $1 million was raised for the Duke of Edinburgh's Awards Fellowship. All in a four-hour span! His Royal Highness, **Prince Edward** (H.R.H. Prince Edward Antony Richard Louis, the youngest son of Queen Elizabeth II and the Duke of Edinburgh) is a Palm Beach favorite who shows up every few years to chum with the younger set, and to generate a few pounds for the exchequer.

Americans, and Palm Beachers, are very **selective** about their donations and the types of charity they embrace. Over 52 percent favor religious causes; 24 percent favor human services; 23 percent prefer health services; 18 percent favor youth development causes; education is the preference of 15 percent of people and the environment, 10 percent. Art, culture and the humanities are favored by eight percent; and public and social benefits and international causes share the remains.

Rapidly emerging, are various environmental/conservation groups. International organizations like the African Wildlife Foundation (Washington, DC), Caribbean Conservation Corporation (Gainesville, FL), Cousteau Society (Norfolk, VA), Nature Conservancy (Arlington, VA), Rainforest Alliance (New York, NY) and Sierra Club (San Francisco, CA) have gained momentum in recent years and now receive substantial monies from philanthropic foundations and individuals. In Palm Beach, the American Friends of the Game Conservancy is being supported by the **F. Warrington Gillets** and will be visible in seasons to come.

—ADVANCEMENT JARGON—

*I*n 15th century Europe, **sumptuary laws** were created to limit the excesses of the rich; the tower of a castle could only be so high, the length of a jeweled train only so long. The size of a family was ordained, the amount of privilege clearly defined, even the expectation of monies given to "lessers" (as the poor were called) was charted. A master of the kingdom was expected to give at least 10 percent of his fortune each year to those in need; middle-level regals forked over a minimum of five percent of income yearly. Whoever ordained those laws probably escaped before he was targeted, or was exempt from the rule of the realm.

How easy it would be today if sumptuary laws applied to benevolence! There would be no need for **fundraisers, auctions, charities, donors, special events** and ploys to entice money from those in the upper brackets. It would all be programmed, gold would automatically trickle down from on high to those in need. In effect; tax the rich and mandate equitable distribution of wealth.

However, no such system is likely. We're all in a competitive get-it-while-you-can society and if funds are up for grabs, sharpen your elbows and get in the scrap. There's no easy way to solicit donations. Or to be solicited.

In fact, old **John D. Rockefeller** was so paranoid about parting with money, he advanced the cause of primogeniture, and in his late 70s, turned over his fortune to his only son—John D. Rockefeller, Jr. (the father of Abbey, John D. III, Nelson, Lawrence, Winthrop and David). Consequently, he no longer had to deal with fundraisers. Old John then lived off income only (today's equivalent of $100 million a year).

In contemporary jargon, **money-raising** is called **"advancement."** Meaning moving a cause or a university or a library or whatever forward by cash infusion. It's a nice word, but enacting it can be debilitating, deadly work. Here's some current terminology of the fund-seeker:

Target: potential donor, prospect, the "mark"—can also be used to define goals and specific levels of monies sought.

Capital Campaign: a multi-year advancement, usually of a high order, with major sponsorship from professionals, banks, law firms, corporations.

Nucleus: the early, formative stage of a campaign; often known to only a few staff members.

Case Statement: the rationale for advancement; a comprehensive document outlining goals, timing and responsibility.

Focus Campaign: a clearly defined, short-term project (example: air-conditioning the gym, enlarging the chapel).

Internal Audience: leaders within the organization—trustees, alumni, past officers, those who still have linkage to the cause.

External Audience: those outside the organization who may have an interest because of children, religion or social recognition.

Prospect: an alumnus or former-employee or officer who has a predisposition to further the cause.

Principal: a development staffer assigned to a specific project; the responsible person on whose desk the buck stops.

The Ask: the request for money; the moment of truth. There is also a **Double Ask** (money requested for an annual fund and a capital campaign) and **Triple Ask** (annual fund, capita campaign + bequest).

Friend-Raising: implementing The Ask on a friend or relative.

Window of Solicitation: parameter of the ask—who, how much, when, in what form?

Descriptors: words and images used to create fond recall of the organization or days gone by, or the future.

Lead Gift: an early, sizeable donation, a concrete signal that a campaign is underway. Will be followed by other gifts—**Major Gift** ($100,000);**Mega-Gift** ($1.5 million); **Preemptive Gift** (one that insures the giver against being asked for a larger gift); **Transforming Gift** (one that carries a physical significance—name on building, for example).

Multiplier: a large gift that induces others to join the cause; usually a highly motivated, dramatic effort.

Recognition Strategy: a memorial as incentive to give—names on large plaque or wall; sometimes required by corporations for tax purposes.

Bricks & Mortar: building projects, construction, additions. Big Time Stuff.

Donor Fatigue: the result of receiving too many Asks.

Volunteer Fatigue: the result of making too many Asks!

Whatever the situation, the cause, the technique, it's obvious that Asking is not a capricious endeavor. **It's big business**, carefully planned and executed. In the past it was often the work of unprofessional, unmotivated people who found themselves in "strange space" in life and wanted to keep busy. Today, Advancement is as competitive as the computer industry and uses all the scientific methodologies for gaining superiority—advertising, public and human relations, financial counsel, legal services, health and medical advice and on and on.

So if you find yourself on the giving end of The Ask, go along with it for the sake of humanity. It's estimated that several trillion dollars are meted out to educational, medical and charitable organizations each year, by over 100 million Americans. On that basis **it's easier to give** than not.

You don't have to get **Donor Fatigue**; just choose your Campaign wisely and well, make your pledge, and watch the future brighten by the day!

— THE NEW WAVE—

*A*s inevitable as those grim facts of life, death and taxes, is the emergence of a **younger set** of socialites who have gladly accepted the passing of the torch and assumed major roles in Palm Beach society. The Old Guard is simply a function of chronology—each generation playing its role on the revolving world stage. What we currently consider the Old Guard will soon be replaced by a younger set—**the New Wave**— who will enjoy about 20 years of leadership before being relegated to the role of Social Sage. Leadership, whether social, military, business or professional, usually has a life-expectancy of 20-40 years, which suggests that being a top social leader, or being considered the "Queen" of Palm Beach society is a role with clearly defined time limits.

Young socialites in Palm Beach have traditionally been reserved, preferring limited visibility, often moving to other cities to seek the brass ring. For many years, it was proper etiquette for young people, often heirs to dynastic fortunes, to stay in the shadow of their heritage, attend proper finishing schools and debutante balls, learn how to allocate trust-fund income to create a pleasant lifestyle, spend time as junior committee persons and await their moment of leadership. With the current climate of publicity, spin, celebrity in the USA, young socialites have emerged quicker and more visibly to show their considerable talents in careers, civic responsibility, and society. This potent Young Guard is destined to replace their predecessors in years to come, as surely as one generation succeeds the next; all part of the normal rotation of mankind.

As the demographics of Palm Beach have changed, so too has the Town. What was once a small, gracious, affluent resort community has become a robust town where ambition, money and power play a vital role. Whether the money comes from dotcom industries, Wall Street or hi-tech companies, it is evident everywhere, and with it has come the Age of More. The once quietly genteel sensibility of the aristocracy, enjoyed in Palm Beach for over a century, has been eclipsed by a "me first" style which befits a meritocracy. By and large, work ethic has replaced resort ethic and the Town hums and thrums with verve. The new energy is at once, alarming (to the Establishment) and welcome! With the More Generation, it's a matter of who you are, not who your parents were.

Among the New Wave in Palm Beach society are: **Louis Anthony, Brad and Denise Alexander, Paivi Alperson, Norberto Azqueta, Kane and Mary Baker, Anthony and Tori Baker, Tom Baldwin, Whitney Baldwin, David and Nancy Banner, Carey O'Donnell, Maureen Basse, Andreas Bessenroth, Florence Bonsuk, Reid Boren, Samantha Boardman, Serena Boardman, Beau and Jackie Breckenridge, Jane Brodsky, Jim Brodsky, William Castle, John Castle, James Castle, Mallory Cheatam, Jeff and Anne Cloninger, Cecelia Cochran, Jay Cochran, Mark and Paula Cook, Brian Cornacchia, Richard Cowell, Jr., Bob Crompton, Jay Crompton, Jill Crompton, David Chernoff, Owen and Victoria Colligan, Kelly Cushing, Ashton and Margo de Peyster, Patrick DeSantis, Vivien Dude, Sam Edelman, Amanda Essex, Lee Essex, Scott Essex, Emilia Fanjul, Pepe and Lourdes Fanjul, Andreas and Kathy Fanjul, James and Whitney Fairchild, Suzie Fairchild, Vanessa Fieve, Ashley Finch, April Finch, Steve Finch, Al Fisher, John Flanagan, Julie Franks, Caroline and Jim Freeney, Ralph Gaines, Mark Gilbertson, Warrington Gillet, Gina and Scott Gordon, Susan and Lee Gordon, Lindsay Grow, Max Gottschalk, Clay Grubman, Jimmy Grubman, Robin Grubman, Majorie Gubelmann, Tantivy Gubelmann, Phoebe Gubelmann, Winston Guest, Helene Guest, Marc and Lisa Haisfield, John and Holly Haynsworth, Alana Henry, Tom Henry, Henry Harris, Lamont and Heather Harris, Alexandra Harrison, Al Heisse, Danielle Hickox, Lily Holt, Merrilee Holt, Kenneth and Barbara Horowitz, Wendy Isil, Mike Jaffe, Steve Jaffe, Eric Javits, Jocelyn Javits, Stephanie Johnson, Christopher and Andrea Kaufmann, Celerie Kemble, Phoebe Kemble, Michaela Kennedy, Sam Kluge, J.P. Kelly, Hewlett and Sheree Kent, Amanda Kirkland, Elizabeth Kieselstein-Cord, Alex Kramer, Brad and Tina Kramer, Frederick Krueger, Chris and Leigh Larmoyeux, Alfonso Landa, Jane Lauder, Samantha Leas,**

Nanette Lepore, Bobby Leidy, Christopher Leidy, Paul and Kathy Leone, Garrison Lickle, Alex Lind, Liz Lind, Sloan Lindemann, Locke Maddock, Homer and Cheryl Marshman, Kelly Matthews, Jack and Talbott Maxey, Sarah and Jim McCann, James and Betsy Meany, Michael and Holly McCloskey, Elizabeth Meigher, Keith Meister, Todd Meister, Henry and Elizabeth Mellon, Ambrose Mondell, Carlos and Renee Morrison, Pedro and Carla Morrison, Christina Murphy, Mark Murphy, Norman Murphy, David and Polly Ober, Linda Olsson, Christopher Orthwein, Coleen Oricco, Tatianna Papock, Rachel Peters, Lily Phipps, Ogden Phipps, Samantha Phipps, Alexia Pickett, Dan Ponton, Trish Quick, Tom Quick, Andrew Quinn, Piper Quinn, T. Quinn, John and Jill Rau, Jon and Laurie Rapaport, Carter Redd, Doug and Carolyn Regan, Michaela de Reynal, Colt Robinson, Missy Robinson, Nicole Robinson, Cate Roessl, Rachel Rogers, Brian Rooney, Richard Sands, David and Betty Scaff, Alexandra Scaravilli, J.J. Scaravilli, Mitchell and Jill Silverman, Alex Snyder, Scott Snyder, Lori and John Stoll, Whitney Stroh, Dan Swanson, John Theodoracopolous, John and Isabele Tonelli, Patricia Travis, Mary Frances Turner, Wallace and Betsy Turner, Peter Van Ingen, Peter and Conway Van de Wolk, David Wassong, Frances and Catie Webster, Richard and Jodi Wentley, Karen Wertz, Winston Wren, Ashley Whittaker, Bill and Jane Williams, Aerin Lauder Zinterhofer and Eric Zinterhofer and Alexis Zoullas.

—CHAIRING & SHARING—

*A*mong those with great American style who share a new generation's perspective (which comes from many places), and express their vigor in every movement, are these New Wave chairpersons or officials of recent major Palm Beach/New York social events: **Marjorie Gubelmann** (Young Friends of the Society of the Four Arts, The Whitney Museum), **Heather Harris** (Young Friends of the Society of the Four Arts), **Lily Holt** (Young Friends of the Society of the Four Arts), **Kathy and Andreas Fanjul** (New Hope House), **Samantha Boardman** (The Whitney Museum), **Margo DePeyster** (Young Friends of the Society of the Four Arts), **Denise Alexander** (Red Cross), **Jill and John Rau** (American Cancer Society), **Diana Ecclestone** (Heart Ball), **Paula Cook** (Hospice Evening), **Mark Gilbertson** (The Winter Ball), **Betsy and Wallace Turner** (The Historical Society Antique Show), **Wendy Isil** (Young Friends of the Red Cross), **Mary Frances Turner** (Young Friends of the Red Cross), **Patrick Park** (benefactor of many charities), **Brian Cornacchia** (The Emerald Ball), **Michaela Kennedy** (The Emerald Ball), **Mitchell and Jill Silverman**

(Glitz at The Ritz), **Jill Gladstone** (Jewish Guild for the Blind), **Tom Quick** (The Winter Ball), **Whitney Fairchild** (Winter Wonderland Ball), **Trish Quick** (Susan G. Komen Benefit), **Jane Lauder** (The Whitney Museum), **Aerin Lauder** (Winter Wonderland Ball), **Shawn Donnelley** (Liberty Bell Gala), **Leigh and Chris Larmoyeux** (American Cancer Society), **Cheryl Gowdy** (American Cancer Society), **Gina and Scott Gordon** and **Susan and Lee Gordon** (American Cancer Society), **Paivi Alperson** and **Alfonso Landa** (Palm Beach Opera), **Karen Wertz** (Unicorn).

—YOUNG FRIENDS—

A number of major charities and institutions have auxiliaries or guilds which allow New Wavers an opportunity to grow through the ranks to prominent Chairmanships or the equivalent. Among them:

Art & Company—Junior Guild of the Norton Museum of Art. Hosts invitation-only opening cocktail receptions and lectures for exhibitions and other special events during the social season.

Maestro—Florida Philharmonic's young symphonic set, orchestrates mixers and cocktail receptions prior to performances. Also hosts special events throughout the social season.

New Directions—Benefiting the American Cancer Society, young professionals host cocktail parties to raise funds for this nonprofit organization. Major event hosted in the summer "Creative Black Tie" brings over 1,000 supporters.

Young Friends of the Kravis Center—Young professionals throughout Palm Beach County host monthly cocktail parties and special events throughout the year. Major springtime event, "Reach for the Stars," brings over 900 supporters and benefits art education programs for Palm Beach County school children.

Young Friends of the Opera—Junior Guild of the Palm Beach Opera, hosts dinner parties and pre-performance receptions during the social season. Special events raise funds for opera education in the school system and budding opera performers.

Young Friends of the Society of the Four Arts—Host bi-annual events to raise funds for the Society of the Four Arts building and education program.

Young Friends of the Red Cross—Junior set hosts annual invitation-only New Year's Eve gala, benefiting the American Red Cross.

—THE PERFECT YOUNG SOCIALITE—
(Part I)

HE was born in the Midwest, the second of three siblings.
SHE has an overbite and wore braces.

SHE studied ballet as a child.

SHE knows how to milk a cow.

SHE wanted to become a lawyer or lead an all-girl orchestra.

SHE was not the most popular girl in school... but

SHE was a cheerleader, and the sweetheart of Sigma Chi.

SHE likes cotton candy.

SHE enjoys aerobics, spinning and swimming.

SHE took fencing lessons; loves the riposte position.

SHE smokes occasionally—never on the street, before 6 p.m. or between courses.

HER favorite drink is pink lemonade.

SHE occasionally consumes several silver bullets, with olives and flair.

SHE is a respectable 35-24-35, 5'9" inches tall, weighs 120 pounds.

SHE has great fronts and an admirable bum.

SHE hates NKN (nobody knows nothing) situations.

SHE loves chocolates, avoids mayo, potato chips, french fries and dairy products.

SHE can be a non-stop giggler, when appropriate.

SHE gets a kick out of the high and low jinks of the uppercrust.

HER greatest upcoming challenge is competing in the Wellington Dressage.

SHE plays the harpsichord for amusement.

SHE likes baking cookies for friends; and can whip up a mean omelet.

SHE takes her expresso "neat."

SHE loves a snowy Christmas.

SHE wishes she could paint; collects modern art and vintage couture.

HER favorite nibble is Caviar Oscietre Royal sur glace oilee, at Salle des Etoiles - Sporting d'Ete, Monte Carlo. She can also handle a Big Mac.

HER favorite book is *Suzanne Valadon* by Jeanne Champion, the bio of a Toulouse-Lautrec model who became a painter and was the mother of Postimpressionist, Utrillo.

SHE enjoys listening to Miles Davis, Andrea Bocelli, Vivaldi and Prince; Gregorian chants and the sea.

HER favorite Broadway show is *Camelot*.

SHE applies her perfume sparingly.

SHE dislikes NM (newly minted), churlish Hi-Vis people.

HER major belief—it's a great gift when admiration is not soured by envy.

HER body, breasts, teeth and nails are real.

SHE believes in meritocracy.

SHE is a empathic, a lachrymal Lady, but only for the right reasons.

SHE has inexhaustible brio.

SHE adores the tango, and has been known to dance till dawn.

HER favorite holiday is a cruise, on which she can sharpen her skills at relaxation.

HER fantasy is to have her own calendar.

SHE is not sure what a Gen-Xer is.

SHE loves old black and white Hollywood movies.

SHE dislikes people who are "Hic in incorpore sed non spiritum"—here in body but not spirit.

SHE has the capacity to look primly sweet or icily imperious.

SHE can go anywhere in her little black dress.

SHE knows it's better to be alone than badly accompanied.

SHE never gilds the lilly.

SHE knows how to keep a secret.

SHE wouldn't dream of wearing panty hose.

SHE believes that style is what you are.

SHE abhors the belief that money is life's report card.

SHE loves to create something new, answer someone's prayers, give to those in need, obey her heart.

SHE is quite comfortable in a thong.

SHE knows that being proud and being lonely are mutually linked.

SHE understands that modesty has no place in the kitchen, or in the bullring.

SHE understands beauty—a cat with whiskers ten feet long may be pretty, but not functional.

SHE knows when the party is over.

SHE always hopes to have an hourglass figure.

SHE realizes that the only real values are the ones placed on herself.

—THE PERFECT YOUNG SOCIALITE—

(Part II)

*S*HE hates blind dates.

HER favorite flower is a long-stemmed rose.

SHE loves hayrides.

HER favorite sports figure is Michael Jordan.

SHE likes gruffly elegant, jolly old chaps who have a sense of destiny.

SHE loves running on the beach with her Irish setter.

SHE loves her blues down and dirty.

SHE loves long, hot bubble baths.

SHE believes mouton should not be dressed as lamb.

SHE gets a kick out of how the world wags.

SHE doesn't have to shout to be heard.

SHE loves tennis—has a killer serve.

SHE always write letters with a fountain pen.

SHE beats the guys at billiards, easily.

SHE would rather have the best than the biggest.

SHE adores Riguad candles.

SHE has a healthy relationship with food.

SHE is superb at dangling the olive branch.

SHE always creates the promise of possibility with her escorts.

SHE dislikes clannish laughter, that of cynical insiders.

SHE is genuinely interested in answers to her questions.

SHE knows that if you attempt to build a horse by committee, you end up with a camel.

SHE is aware that, often, more tears are shed over answered prayers than those unanswered.

HER favorite song is "Send In The Clowns."

SHE admires pianists who dig the bones out of a piece.

SHE often has a big pre-laugh smile on her face.

SHE wishes more of her peers had a well-scrubbed look.

SHE knows good taste never goes out of fashion.

SHE knows good manners are never out of place.

SHE has a superb hubris meter.

HER least favorite guys are the preening Lothario types.

SHE occasionally likes being an acupuncturist—giving others the needle.

SHE is constantly revising the upper limits of self-regard.

SHE can, at the right moment, project the childish sexuality of Monroe; or the flinty independence of Hepburn.

SHE knows that most people live more in their fiction than in their own fact.

SHE is torn between *la via vecchia*—the Old World, and *la via nuova* —the New World.

HER biggest fear is dying of irrelevance.

SHE knows that love is never enough the way it is; there is always more. Love has no boundaries.

SHE has come to be a gentlewoman at an early age.

SHE wants to be a person who walks through life lightly, but leaves a marked trail.

SHE knows that Nirvana isn't reached by holding on, but by letting go.

SHE is an aristocrat of the spirit—as sensitive for others as for herself. And..

SHE knows that to remain young and beautiful and resourceful, she must keep looking within, for it is there she will find her worth as a human being.

SHE is positively charming, devastatingly beautiful, brilliantly strategic in her thinking, wonderfully gifted at eliciting cooperation, facile

and frolicsome, articulate and ardent, the best of the best, the one &
only, the greatest, and **Palm Beach's** **unique and lovable national**
treasure. The Young Socialite, may **she reign forever.**

—JUNIOR POWER—

*A*t the turn of the last century, two lovely young ladies were
riding along Manhattan's Riverside Drive, in a snappy four-
wheeled carriage. While discussing plans for their respective
coming-out parties, they were struck by the notion that the parties
preceeding their Debutante Ball, had become a bit tiresome and con-
spicuously excessive. Heeding the preachment of their elders, they con-
cluded that, great wealth should walk hand-in-hand with civic responsibility.

The young ladies—**Miss Mary Harriman** and **Miss Nathalie
Henderson**—had impressive familial credentials as they approached their
senior teen years. Miss Harriman was the daughter of Edward H.
Harriman, a feared tycoon of the railroad industry with a fortune in the
range of $200 million; Miss Henderson's pater was a successful banker
and a master of one-upsmanship. On the basis of their genes, both ladies
had access to countless social players and a number of people in the
newly-developing profession of fundraising.

Miss Harriman suggested that although debs-to-be should have fun at
their various pre-and-post parties, a charitable focus should underlie the
main event. In this case, the Misses Harriman and Henderson chose the
College Settlement House on Rivington Street as beneficiary of their
largesse. And thus—The Junior League for the Promotion of Settlement
Houses—"for the benefit of the poor and the betterment of the city"—
was born. The nomenclature was later changed to, simply —**The Junior League.**

In those days, Settlement Houses were set up to **"Americanize"** immigrants who were pouring into New York Harbor by the tens of thousands; due to their overwhelming numbers, the houses could do little
more than delouse the newly-arrived and send them on their way, with
street directions and a welcome to the land of plenty. The Rivington
Street facility was particularly untidy, in the heart of the lower east side,
crawling with thieves and drunks. The prim young ladies were appalled
by the mistreatment of immigrants, and decided to attack the problem
with their considerable resources.

By putting in long hours at the settlement, embarrassing friends and
family into donating to the cause, and then seeking charitable monies at
their **Deb Cotillion**, enough loot was raised to repair the Rivington Street
facility and send a signal to affluent young ladies in other cities that

benevolence was an important avocation, and a perfect means of dispelling the image of debs being empty-headed social butterflies.

The concept of a **Junior League**, comprised of youthful men and women, affluent or not (usually the former) caught on quickly. Debutantes in Boston, Brooklyn, Baltimore, Philadelphia and Chicago formed their own chapters, and soon over 100,000 Junior League volunteers were restoring historic homes, singing Christmas carols for shut-ins, staging zoo parties for children, operating mobile museums, pushing book carts through hospital corridors and uplifting the imprisoned. No job was too menial, no cause unworthy. The Junior League was an idea whose time had come!

Naturally, the **Old Guard** frowned on the association of their offspring with such mundane activities. Even the originators of the concept—Miss Harriman and Miss Henderson—were off-put by the rapid expansion of their idea. Instead of the Junior League being comprised of debs only, the organization began accepting young ladies of ambition, given more to self advancement than social conscience. In time, barriers dropped and the League became a democratic group open to all young women—pedigree, breeding, credentials were only marginally important. Dedication to cause, and fundraising, were the keynotes.

Today, the Junior League remains a vital **organization**, albeit much transformed. In many cities, the Junior League stages a charity gala at which debs are presented. Ambitious parents can donate a prescribed amount of money to a league cause, and make their daughter a tax-deductible debutante. And a young woman can become a Junior Leaguer simply by being available, and putting in the requisite number of hours as a volunteer.

Some would say that the purity and prestige of the Junior League is now in question; and that it has opened up the private world of metropolitan **high society** to the masses—anybody with the price of admission can now become a socialite at the season's most glamorous gala!

Whatever the interpretation and social implication, the Junior League continues on its merry way, inspiring, benefitting, serving its many causes admirably.

Good example: The Junior League of the Palm Beaches and Wachovia Bank joined forces recently to present the first annual **Wachovia Woman Volunteer Award**, to recognize the dedication, importance and service of women volunteers. Leaders from charities, social service and not-for-profit organizations, hospitals and museums joined hands and hearts to honor their own and continue creating new dimensions for one of the most influential benefactors in the country—the century old **Junior League!**

MR. AND MRS. FRANK HABICHT AND CATHLEEN McFARLANE
gifted, giving and glowing

BILL FLAHERTY, COLIN O'DALY,
BISHOP ANTHONY J. O'CONNEL AND TINA FLAHERTY
peerless keepers of spirit

PATRICIA HIPWOOD, BILLY DAVID, ANITA HAMILTON AND JULIAN HIPWOOD
acknowledged affirmative actionaries

COLIN WRIGHT, DAVID VESELSKY, LESLIE CLAYDON-WHITE AND RON VIEJO
tasteful, talented and terrific

CELINE DION, DONALD TRUMP AND MARY WEISS
individual and inimitable

ANTHONY BOALT, SIMONE KAROFF, JIM MITCHELL AND TANYA VARTAN
onward/upward, charmingly

164

JOHN CASTLE, BARTON GUBELMANN AND MARIANNE CASTLE
all manner and variety of good

LEO AND KATE VECELLIO AND PAT AND RICHARD JOHNSON
zip, zest and walking tall

ARTHUR AND SYDELLE MEYER, LLWYD AND DIANA ECCLESTONE
exacting and enticing

RALPH DESTINO, LAUREL SAUER AND ABE GOSMAN
always on the cutting edge, with mastery

HARRY BELAFONTE, TINA AND CARLOS BILOTTI
admirable, adept and accomplished

DIANN AND VICTOR SCARAVILLI
cheerful, chivalrous chariteers

CHAPTER V

CHARACTERS, COMRADES & CHIEFS
(People, Personalities & Preferences)

Photo: Lucien Capehart

JANE AND THE HONORABLE GUILFORD DUDLEY
who could ask for anything more?

—DRESS CODES & MODES—

*O*ne of our Town's most sophisticated and gracious socialites, a decade younger than her peers on the gala committee, showed her style by attending a very prestigious ball wearing elegant black silk pants, a white blouse and gray dinner jacket. She was more than ravishing, and caught the eye of every attendee as she addressed the assembly on behalf of the cause. The evening proceeded with **deferent nods and salutations** to the fashionable women, with zero comments about her untraditional approach to gala dressing. The next morning her phone pulsed constantly—the media was on her case for daring to wear pants to a formal gala, perhaps the first time in history a charity official had been that audacious. Over the next few days, there was hyped-up verbiage about her dress code and enough headlines to get major publicity for the event/cause (and a few more donations and followers). In that regard, the event was successful; for the panted-one, however, there was extreme isolation and her ranking on party lists dropped to C. Her fashions may have escalated consciousness of the event, but de-escalated her social desirability. Just a matter of fashion protocol in a conservative community where propriety is sacred.

In a given lifetime, most people have gone through some of the psychological exercises of the era—**Zen, Iridology, Numerology, Hydrotherapy, Hypnosis, Psychoanalysis, EST, Psychic Readings, Regression Therapy** and the like. Many do it because of peer-pressure; some because of real need, many for the hell of it. These forms of therapy are to the mind what fashion is to the body. If engaging in intellectual revelation of this type raises eyebrows in Palm Beach, so do highly designed fashions. Balenciaga need never worry; he's safely tucked away in history and his gowns still fill the closets of the Old Guard. His fashions will live forever despite the fact that they aren't stylish in the obsessed-with-newness 2000s.

Having gone the route of formal pants at a ball (the act was never repeated), the next leap forward would have been miniskirts for evening wear or formal hot pants or some other **dazzling concoction** from the likes of Mackie, Scaasi or Oscar. But such a display of flesh won't hack it in Palm Beach, where the north side of breasts can occasionally be seen, but also, where low-cut is defined as skin showing beneath the Adam's apple. Quiet elegance continues to be the keynote of fashion in Town.

An **arriviste from LA or NY** may show up at a committee meeting in a leather mini and high heels and not cause a noticeable ripple; but her assignment will be modest and enthusiasm for her output limited. Her pizzazz may be too much for semi-Victorian associates and she may be taken for a Player—not really in it for the cause, but for self-aggrandizement. Being a genuine team member requires dressing down to a somewhat indistinguishable level, nonetheless being well turned out. It's not a contradiction—a Lady can be elegantly plebeian.

Much of the Palm Beach dress code revolves around **public-versus-private galas**, parties and outings. At a major fundraising event where the cause requires seriousness, supporters tend to adapt to the circumstance. Bland, twilight zone creations fill the ballroom. Women in hard working, dependable styles; no concern with power colors or cuts, just a blend of conformity. At a private party, glimpses of body-hugging designer dresses, arrogantly high heels, jeweled zebra pins and chic whateverhave-yous keep male eyes focused. Although the dialogue may be less than charity grave, it is not necessarily charitable, nor is it totally frivolous. Private party communication deals with universal subjects—the kids or grandchildren, golf, the market, new manager of the club and Republican politics. A few matronly types will always be present (as stabilizers and chaperones) but the general feeling is—glamour is allowable, enjoyable and should be pulled off sans guilt or explanation. Conversely, at a ball, too much glamour is often mistaken for vanity; and vanity has no place in fundraising, the apex of altruism. In short, those who are too aesthetically obsessed are hardly ever perceived as loyalists to the cause.

Unlike other cities—New York or Los Angeles—where men have most of the power, **Palm Beach is matriarchal**; women wield the social leverage and are the visible prime movers for most of the Town's action. The men dress Brooks Brothers and traditional black-tie, and manage quite separate lives, often on the phone, fax or in their library offices. They are supportive of their wives' work on charities, and willing enough to underwrite many activities, even high-priced (but not high-powered) gowns and gala accessories. An exotic bird as a wife works no better for her husband than she does for the cause. That ubiquitous tendency for understatement pervades lifestyle on all fronts.

Sensual, playful people are generally not drawn to fundraising as an outlet; helping generate research megabucks for a debilitating illness has none of the panache of getting backers for a Broadway play or feature film starring Julia, Kim or Warren. Yet, if they are so-drawn, by whatever circumstance, people assume a less-dazzling persona; they transfer what might be physical beauty to a more cerebral style, which simply translates to more work on behalf of the cause, less talk and party-party. Winning suddenly becomes the only thing in life; and whereas outside events dictated a life path before, now there's a higher calling which determines everything, even the number of martinis one enjoys each day. So, too, with the Gala Chairman, who dedicates a portion of her life to the serious business of running an event and being responsible for generating $$$. The playful and frivolous is out; replacing the frolic is **commitment**.

173

—HIGH TICKET TOGS—

*T*he average number of gowns owned by an active ball-goer is **eighteen.** An average of **two** are very feminine in the southern tradition—off the shoulders or pouf sleeves, fitted bodice with a full billowing skirt in a semi-stiff material such as silk taffeta or organza, maybe some glitter, reminiscent of Scarlett O'Hara and Tara. **One** in flamboyant colorings and **four** of traditional color such as black or white, perhaps a bead or two with a flower or velvet bow as accent. **One** "strapless" modest decollete in black or red, the fabric conforms to the body contours, cut velvet on chiffon, silk crepe or lame. (For variety one might have a very high neckline and long sleeves.) **Four** are "short" (something new to wear to the lesser balls or dinner dances). Lace, organza, satin and silk are desired fabrics. Necklines vary from strapless to jewel, maybe one with a high neckline and a very low back (the teaser). **One** must be in a fashionable designer pattern perhaps edged with sequins, rhinestones or gold braid. At least **one** beaded (top) dress is a must for the most elegant affair, some prefer one shade of beads while others select a beaded pattern in multi-colors. Something in velvet is very festive for the holidays and early January. The remaining gowns are old favorites and have been proven over the years—floating chiffons that were "in" then "out" and once again "in." **One** might even be a pleated Mary McFadden romantic creation that always seems to be *au courant*, or a glamorous Stavropoulos chiffon. Average price per gown $4,000.

Black and **red**, and **traditional** colors are always acceptable. In the last few years, more flamboyant gowns have been introduced, however, with brocade, cut velvet, gold lame, and rhinestones adorning more "glitzier" costuming. As Palm Beach is growing younger, the formal dress is reflective; with more "dynamics" built in, and a greater percentage of the human body presented (more provocatively). Long gowns take the lead at more elegant affairs, such as the Red Cross, Heart and Cancer Balls, but younger Palm Beach women opt for shorter lengths about half the time at other galas.

Leading men usually have three tuxedos. A very formal, elegant unit (by Brioni, Armani or Lanvin at $2,700) for the more playful parties; an orthodox-cut garment for the prosaic evening affairs; and a combination presentation for those "point-of-difference" galas. The traditional cut unit is the most actively worn.

Men usually have one white tie and tails (or access to same) for supremely formal occasions—state dinners, the Swan Ball in Nashville, opening night at the San Francisco Opera, the Al Smith Dinner at the Waldorf in NYC, or for special weddings.

Somewhat facetiously, fashion editors in various feature stories have indicated the high cost of being impeccably dressed, and the even higher cost of making the right connections and appearing at the right events, balls and functions, for possible placement on the International Best Dressed List. Some estimated expenses are:

Evening clothes
* 7 short couture dresses @ $10,000 and up;
* 2 long couture dresses @ $7,000 to $25,000 (and up) for the most formal affairs;
* 3 pairs of black shoes or sandals ($1,200);
* 3 pairs of metallic sandals ($1,400);
* 1 or 2 gold jeweled small metallic bags (Judith Leiber, $3,300).

Restaurant, cocktail parties, more informal dining
* 6 short evening dresses with the emphasis on pretty tops. For this season, at least one will be in chiffon; two will be bare with jackets or boleros to go over them. One of the jackets should be beaded and perhaps do double duty with other dresses ($30,000).

Dining at home
* 2 long hostess dresses for very glamorous nights ($5,400).

Cover-ups
* 1 long sable coat ($125,000);
* 1 long-haired fur coat (fox or chinchilla), to wear on really bad days or nights, cut so as to double for the country ($250,000);
* 1 long opera-cloak wrap, fur trimmed and in a rich color like red or burgundy so that it will go over every outfit ($9,500);
* 1 fur-lined raincoat ($8,000).

Daytime wear
* 6 suits—2 Chanel (one black-and-white, the other tweed); 1 dress-maker suit with peplum or other detail; 1 strictly tailored Yves Saint Laurent chic; 1 suit of the season (for fall, it would be in unmatched fabrics); 1 pants suit ($32,000);
* 5 silk dresses, some with matching jackets. If she likes prints she should stay with classics (dots, stripes and plaids)—that is the designer message ($18,000).

Accessories (this includes only the important pieces)
* 2 strands 13-mm pearls (up to $200,000);
* 1 jeweled compact, real ($1,500-$90,000) or Isabel Canovas ($350);

175

* 3 black alligator handbags of different sizes, one having a metallic clasp to show it is of jewel quality ($15,000);

20 pairs of handmade shoes ($20,000);

3 pairs of earrings—1 pearl, 1 black and gold, 1 gold and diamond ($35,000 for the lot);

* 1 gold cuff for day or evening ($8,500);

* 1 jeweled Indian maharani necklace to wear for informal evenings ($15,000-$20,000);

* 3 long, long dangling pairs of earrings for evening ($75,000 and up for the lot);

* 6 pairs of leather gloves in different colors—to hold if she can't be bothered putting them on ($4,500).

Based on one's motivation, needs/wants, desperation level, the cost of the couture life can easily be in the **high six-figure** category each and every year. For some of the more magnificent and munificent Ladies, a **cool million per annum** is just another household and lifestyle budget consideration.

To really escalate the cost of being fashionable, think about the price tag on some of the **most notable tiaras** worn in recent years to the International Red Cross Ball.

Marjorie Merriweather Post (when she was alive) wore the **"Empress Marie Louise"**—the Empress' gift from her husband Napoleon I (in 1811), celebrating the birth of their son, "King of Rome." Van Cleef & Arpels acquired the tiara in 1953, later selling it to Mrs. Post, who wore it annually at the Ball until 1966, when she donated it to the Smithsonian Institute. The predominant stones in the tiara were emeralds. Before selling the tiara to Mrs. Post, Van Cleef removed the emeralds (eventually selling them as separate pieces) and replaced them with Turquoise.

The **"Empress Josephine"** Tiara has adorned the heads of **Mrs. Guilford Dudley** and the late **Mrs. Harold P. Whitmore** at the Ball. This crown was presented to Josephine by Napoleon (in 1804), on the occasion of her coronation. Today, still in its original mounting, it contains 880 diamonds totaling 260 carats and is part of Van Cleef's collection of fine historical jewels; it was insured for $1 million when last worn at the Ball.

Mrs. Ann Light's name became synonymous with the **"Russian Royal Tiara,"** at the Red Cross Ball; it dates back to 1810-1830, and was originally a gift from the Czar to one of his daughters. Lost for many years, it resurfaced and was purchased by Van Cleef & Arpels; since the late Mrs. Light was a favorite customer in the salon, the store extended her the privilege of wearing this tiara.

Because the tiaras are historically priceless, it is impossible to determine exact value. An approximate value on the three pieces would be $4 million.

—MUSIC, MAESTRO, PLEASE—

*T*he true measure of a party's success is often how much **locomotion** it had, and how many people made their **statement** by dancing the night away. Being a social Town, Palm Beach has its share of society music.

Marshall Grant: the late grand old man of PB music, was at it since 1945, always in tune to the needs/wants of the audience; he was headquartered at The Breakers. **Billy Duke** (Entertainment Source) now serves many of the same clients.

Neal Smith: has played every venue in Town since the 50s; popular, uninhibited—sings, dances and plays the clarinet—a master at interpreting Cole Porter songs.

Lester Lanin: somewhat international but frequently in Palm Beach; played his first gig in Town at the kick-off of the Flagler Museum when the "area was all swamp land."`

Michael Carney: a steady date of groups, for over 40 years; quick to capitalize on musical trends and to "give the party what it wants."

Bob Hardwick: known as the "most danceable" sound, Hardwick leads his group from the piano; has great timing and ability to read the crowd.

Joe Ricardel: versatile orchestra leader, violinist and songwriter— *"The Palm Beach Woman," "Brooklyn Dodgers Jump"*— very much in demand.

Alex Donner: former attorney, now NYC and Palm Beach society band leader; good at judging moods and anticipating requests, also good singing voice.

Other orchestras under the baton of **Peter Duchin, Bobby S**wiadon (Palm Beach's resident piano "musicman"), **Michael Rose, Doug Verga** and **Richard Prentiss** fill the air with pleasant sounds in any given season.

—HIT PARADE—

The songs most frequently requested at galas are:

* **New York, New York** (to get the adrenalin flowing).

* **Bad Bad Leroy Brown** (usually played after the dinner entree giving party-goers an opportunity to "exercise" before indulging in a fattening dessert).

* **The Best of Times** (theme song from *La Cage Aux Folles*).

* **Memories**

* **Mack the Knife**

* **As Time Goes By** (you can just see Bogart and Bergman—a

romantic way to conclude a successful party).

* **All I Ask of You** (from *The Phantom of the Opera*).

* **String of Pearls, In the Mood, Pennsylvania 6-6500** (the Glenn Miller classics dating back to 1939).

* **Satin Doll** (the Duke Ellington all-time favorite).

* **Stardust** (Artie Shaw version, the most recorded song in history, along with *"White Christmas"*—about 2,600 artists have recorded it).

* **Chattanooga Choo Choo** (Glenn Miller treatment; the phrase "Golden Oldies" originated with this song).

* **I Left My Heart in San Francisco** (a giant hit by any measurement, with Tony Bennett and Count Basie).

National Public Radio recently compiled *The NPR 100*, a list of the most important American musical works of the 20th century. Some seem a bit esoteric for our gifted ear and may not fit the mood at a gala, but are truly national treasures:

(1) *Adagio for Strings*, Samuel Barber (1938); (2) *Ain't That a Shame,* Fats Domino (1955); (3) *Alexander's Ragtime Band*, Irving Berlin (1911); (4) *All or Nothing At All*, Frank Sinatra with Harry James and his orchestra (1939); (5) *Appalachian Spring*, Aaron Copeland (1944); (6) *As Time Goes By*, Herman Hupfeld (1931); (7) *Back in the Saddle Again,* Gene Autry (1939); (8) *Blowin' in the Wind*, Bob Dylan (1962), (9) *Blue Moon of Kentucky,* Bill Monroe and his Blue Grass Boys (1954); (10) *Blue Suede Shoes,* Carl Perkins (1955).

—FRAMERS & SHOOTERS—

*T*he leading society photographers in Palm Beach are **Mort Kaye, Bobby Davidoff** and **Lucien Capehart**. Each has a dedicated following and an encyclopedic knowledge of the players and pretenders in the social game, each can cut through a crowd lightning-like, to get their favorite subject, and each has built a relatively significant net worth, based on framing and shooting those who deserve their visage in print, those who detest publicity and the ever-growing category of those whose life is made (for the moment) by being blinded via a flashbulb.

Mort Kaye is considered the dean of social photography, although his competitors would disagree. His five decades in the area and his constant island-roaming, seeking subjects in all phases of the social dance, give him access to all but a few events and homes. He was a favorite of the Duke and Duchess of Windsor, Douglas Fairbanks, Jr., and other notables, who often seek him out to be straightened-away regarding the power structure in a given assembly. Kaye is the quintessential lens-aholic who will pass on, probably, with a last snap.

Bobby Davidoff is a long-termer on the Island too, having spent many years as the official photographer of The Breakers (a distinction he still has, along with The Mar-a-Lago Club) and as a kind of photojournalist on the subject of Palm Beach—1955 to today. He is writing a book on his experiences in the business and the ebb/flow of characters who seek pleasure or profit from the Island. His wife, **Babe**, the family matriarch, offers counsel and backup on photography shoots and helps direct the energies of three sons—**Daryl, Michael** and **Ken**—all active in some phase of the business, as is granddaughter, **Jennifer**. Father Bob suggests he has the only photographic "dynasty" going, and assures subjects there will be a Davidoff around for many generations, zooming in on Palm Beach.

Lucien Capehart is the youngest of the trio. He arrived on the Island in 1973 to do some underwater shots. Liking the atmosphere and the then-easy pace, he set up shop and soon became a favorite of the society crowd with his less-staged, more-spontaneous shots. He quips, that his is a power-job; he can tell a U.S. President to move left or right, smile, or stand up straight, and get his way. Not so, he notes with some of the Grandes Dames who expect a miracle from the camera. His favorite line—"They love me as much as they love their last picture." Off-season, Capehart is an adventurer, heading for Mt. Everest or Kathmandu or some exotic *locus* where he can "flex-muscle" and "ride-bike" with his wife Dina. His loyal following await each season to see if he'll return or be lost forever to the open trail. So far, he hasn't disappointed anyone.

Both Davidoff and Capehart began their Palm Beach careers working for Mr. Kaye; today there is a spirited rivalry among the threesome. Other photographers like **Maximilian Kaufmann** and **Michael Price** are actively flashing away each night and getting their share of shots, in an increasingly competitive world of photojournalism.

—PARTY PROS/PROSE—

*L*eading Palm Beach party experts, planners and promoters are: **The Breakers Catering, Ann 'Z, Gourmet Galley Catering, Palm Beach Catering, Savoir Faire Catering** and **C'est Si Bon Catering.**

Today, Palm Beach hostesses favor cocktail buffets and receptions over traditional sit-down dinners. The receptions range in price from $25 to $45 per person for food. More people can be entertained at a lower price, but importantly, people are quite health conscious today, and have lighter appetites. Cocktail receptions make up about 70 percent of catered affairs. In addition to traditional hot and cold hors d'oeuvres, Asian food and pasta dishes (currently replacing crepes in popularity) are very much in vogue. Palm Beach's favorite cookie "The Macaroon" and fresh fruit finish the buffet menu fare along with miniature french pastries.

For actual "sit-down" dinners, veal chop and rack of lamb are today's choice. Catered dinner parties range up to $125 (per person) including food (no liquor), staff and rentals.

All the caterers do extensive research in an attempt to locate new and exciting products—they utilize the finest caviar, baby vegetables, wild mushrooms and organically grown greens.

Buffet tables are now being decorated with displays of fresh fruits and vegetables, a return to the simple elegance of nature. **The Breakers'** culinary focus is, developing cuisines that utilize the freshest of locally available products: tropical fruits, fresh warm-water fish, organically grown greens and blossoms.

Jo's Restaurant (139 N. County Rd.) acquired a complete catering kitchen in West Palm Beach to better accommodate restaurant clients who want special culinary style in their homes. **Herbert's Lafayette Market** also offers complete gourmet meals to go; **C'est Si Bon** and **Piccolo Mondo** continue their "on-the-go" gourmet. Some of the most prestigious parties of the recent season have been coordinated by **The Breakers Catering** staff; a few were: The Good Samaritan Hospital Centennial Ball, The Norton Bal des Arts and Red Cross Luncheon at Palm Beach Polo & Country Club.

As for Party Planners, **Bruce Sutka,** of Sutka Productions International, is the most active with a large following; his work is avant garde, original, usually expensive and always provocative. His major party over the years, has been the New Year's Eve Party at the Flagler Museum, sponsored by the Young Friends of the American Red Cross, where French, Roaring 20s, Galactic and "007" themes have been well-executed. Entry to this affair is always one of the hottest tickets in Town.

Sutka also co-produced a recent Chanel Fashion Show, benefiting St. Mary's Hospital; over 300 people were involved in the production which was staged at a cost of $250,000 and included 14 models, seven hair-dressers, five seamstresses, 28 audio-visual technicians, 40 security guards and 18 musicians. Guy Lento, makeup director for Chanel, Julian d'Is, French hairdresser and several stand-ins for designer Karl Lagerfeld were part of the crew working to embellish the 112 outfits that were shown. Over 600 people attended the fashion bash, which was highlighted by the appearance of supermodel Claudia Schiffer.

Recently, Sutka produced a "Denim & Diamond" event for the Palm Beach Polo's Equestrian Center. He turned half of a 500-foot-long tent into New York City, complete with street scenes, skating rink, hansom cabs and vendors. The other half of the tent seated some

1,500 guests who heard Donna Summer warble. Sutka has also staged a weeklong show in Thailand for the Digital Equipment Corp.; the event cost about $2 million to produce.

Michael Ereshena Designs has served many causes, most recently the American Heart Association's annual Heart Ball at The Breakers. Themes like a Moroccan feast, Monet's Garden at Giverny and Old Havana, have kept the firm in the forefront, and delighted guests with their originality.

Ed Wignall of Grand Soiree is another heavy-hitter who always does innovative work; he handles many galas and private parties (even at the Everglades Club) and is a favorite of the "Ladies who lunch."

The **Gordian Group,** under the tutelage of **Stu Feinstein,** came to Palm Beach from NYC and quickly established a reputation for "cutting-edge" party planning. Feinstein's work features a full range of actors, mimes, musicians, off-the-wall themes and party games, videotaping and a general aura of excitement; the group also operates in NYC and the Hamptons.

Altima International, Inc. offers party planning (usually using well-known personalities as honorary chairmen or guests of honor) and a wide array of personalized services. The multilingual associates have staged special events in Geneva, Madrid, Lyford Key, as well as Palm Beach and Miami.

Although not considered professionals, a number of Palm Beachers are acknowledged as masters of gracious entertaining, and stage private parties with memorable themes like Pajama Party, Star Gazers Delight, Pie in the Sky, Swinging Taps, Rainbow's End and Sky-Caper. Tops at hosting are: **Alan Tremain, Audrey Gruss, Terry Kramer, Eles and Warry Gilett, Arlette and Bob Gordon** (who prefer "flavor" parties—Couscous in Marrakesh, Bouillabaisse in Marseilles, Rock oysters in Sydney), **Betty and Jeremy Harvey, Simone Karoff, Pat and Ned Cook, Scott Snyder, Marylou Whitney Hendrickson** and **Marianne and John Castle**.

There's a **floral arrangement** for everybody, and for every event, provided by the creative talents of these leading florists: **The Gazebo Plant Shop** (230 B. Sunrise Ave.); **The Potted Plant & Flower Shop** (235 S. County Rd.), **Olde Town Flower Shops, Inc.** (1930 N. Dixie Hwy., WPB) and **Extra Touch Flowers** (420 Clematis St., WPB).

Although party pricing defies logic and is highly subjective, based on the creative needs/wants of the committee, some average prices are (a gala at The Breakers):

Program Printing	$ 750
Photography	1,500
Orchestra	4,000
Wine	3,000
Reception	10,000
Decorations	3,000
Invitations/Postage	3,000
Valet Parking	1,500
Dinner	25,000

—TOP SPOT—

*T*he Breakers, with its three major ballrooms and numerous, smaller meeting areas, is the site of some 100 charity-inspired luncheons and 50 black-tie galas every year. Until The Ritz-Carlton opened (mid '91) with similar facilities, other hotels have attempted to tap this reservoir of revenue, but none have been able to match The Breakers' offerings of grandeur, service and the sheer size of its ballrooms. Charities can only charge so much per person, and the more bodies a facility can comfortably handle, the more tax deductible contributions go to the charity.

The Henry Morrison Flagler Museum is the site of about 20 charity functions per year; about 110 other functions (musical events, concerts, receptions, proms, etc.) are also held there each year. The Four Seasons Resort hosted many luncheons and affairs last year and is becoming very popular.

Smaller properties, each with a special appeal, vie for group business, too; although their physical limitations disallow large groups (several hundred people), they reach out and touch selective audiences. Among other party properties are private clubs—Palm Beach Country Club, Sailfish, Beach Club, Bath and Tennis, Everglades, Club Colette and the Governors Club, and hotels—Brazilian Court, The Chesterfield and The Colony with its new Pavilion—able to handle 250 people—and The Ritz-Carlton in Manalapan.

—BELLS ARE RINGING—

Palm Beach, a romantic garden spot by any estimation, attracts an unusual number of weddings each year; whether the private type, or a lavish affair at The Breakers, or an intimate family-only vow renewal, the affair is always lovely and lively and costly. Here's how our Town stacks up against the rest of the country in wedding-related costs:

	National Average	Palm Beach
Invitations (per 100) Thank-you cards	$286	$650 (Crane Stock and engraved)
Flowers	$478	$4,900 (one PB couple spent $89,000)
Photographs/videos	$908	$3,000
Music (ceremony /reception)	$882	$4,700 (Neal Smith)
Church/Clergy Donation	$166	$1,200
Limousine (8-hours)	$236	$400 ($50 per hour)
Wedding Rings (both)	$1,004	$2,700 (Cartier gold love bands)
Engagement Ring	$2,285	$20,000 ($150-200,000 top of scale and usually second marriage)
Attendant's Gifts	$286	$1,100 (Sterling picture frames)
Rehearsal Dinner	$500	$1,500 (20 @ $75 each)
Bride's Wedding Dress	$1,000	$6,500 (Vera Wang)
Bridal Attendant Gowns	$745 (5)	$2,500 (5 @ $500 each-(Kerr)
Bride's Mother's Gown	$236	$2,100
Groom's Formal Wear	$82	$1,500 (tails)
Groomsmen Attire	$333 (5)	$400 (5 rented @ $80 each)
Honeymoon Attire	$936	$5,100
Wedding Reception	$5,900	$18,750 (150 @ $125 each at The Breakers)
Honeymoon Costs	$3,200	$11,000 (Concorde to Europe)
Totals	**$16,143**	**$88,000**

• Last year, 210 **weddings** were performed in Palm Beach, in these locations:

Bethesda-by-the-Sea	38
Royal Poinciana Chapel	40
St. Edward's	22
Temple Emanu-El	5
The Breakers	85
The Brazilian Court	20

• On a national basis, the most **popular wedding gifts** were:
  —collectibles such as Lalique or other crystal art
  —art deco items
  —his and hers monogrammed robes
  —decorative clock
  —silver picture frames
  —Duvet comforters
  —barware, such as martini glasses by Baccarat
  —folk art
  —California sparkling wines
(Note: on a national basis, one of every three gifts is returned or exchanged.)

Palm Beachers preferred
  —clocks
  —silver picture frames
  —decorative planters
  —caviar bowls
  —white wicker bed trays
  —fine champagnes (cases)
• The **favorite patterns** of Palm Beach brides are:
  Silver—Christofles Aria Gold, silverplate trimmed in gold
  (Note: many Island brides inherit their silver)
  China—Festivity by Ceralene or Blue Garland by Herend
  Crystal—Montaigen Optic by Baccarat and Lismore by Waterford

• The preferred diamond **rings** are: brilliant (or round), oval, marquise, emerald, pear and oval. There is considerable variation in choice due to changing trends.

• The **first wedding** in Palm Beach was held at the Royal Poinciana Chapel: **Miss Belle Geer Dimick**, daughter of Captain E.N. Dimick (first Mayor of Palm Beach) married **Mr. Thomas Tipton Reese** on Dec. 18, 1895. Thomas Reese became our Town's second Mayor; and Belle and Thomas' son, Claude Reese, became our eighth Mayor.

For the record, more than 10 percent of this year's expected 2.4 million weddings will take place in June. The month's popularity among brides and grooms dates back to ancient Rome, which worshipped **Juno**, the protectress of women and marriages. In today's America, slightly more weddings occur in August.

Size of the US bridal market, $35 billion; average total spending for a formal wedding, $16,144; bride's gown, $1,000; groom's tuxedo (rental), $82; honeymoon, $3,200. Average number of **stores** a couple will visit before they decide on an engagement ring, 4.6. Average **age** in

1955 of a couple marrying for the first time, 21; average **age** today of a couple wedding for first time, 26. Chances a wedding is not the first for either the bride or groom, 1 in 3. Average **length** of a marriage ending in divorce, 7.1 years, 20 years ago, 6.6 years. Estimated number of marriage and family **therapists** in the US, 50,000; increase over the last decade, 50 percent. Marriages per week in **Las Vegas**, 1,700, as a portion of all American weddings, 4 percent; average **duration** of nuptial ceremony at Las Vegas's "Little White Chapel," home of the world's only drive-through wedding window, 7 minutes, cost $30.

—COCONUT CACHE—

*I*t's not a business reception or political fundraiser, not a pre-gala tasting or a mass market special event. **It's a payoff!** and it dates back to the early 1930s, when a group of bachelors felt obliged to reciprocate for the many invitations they received from married couples, by tossing a New Year's Eve party which would intermingle old and new friends, marrieds and singles, with a few internationals for flavor.

Today, the party flourishes and is considered the Mt. Everest of invitations for Social Climbers. A four-man committee of veteran **Coconuts** (the group has a fixed limit of 25 members; replacements are chosen only upon resignation or death) secretly select the 300 potential guests and forward a formal invitation. An entry in the Social Register, membership in the best clubs, even a Forbes 500 listing is no guarantee of an invitation. The reach-out is based on the sociochemical and comfort mix of the people involved, their long term friendships, and their acceptance as candidates for the "Coconuts Family." Anyone offering a gratuity for being invited is quickly rejected.

Earlier Coconut parties included such luminaries as **Harold Vanderbilt, Addison Mizner, Anthony Drexel Biddle, Florenz Ziegfeld, Maurice Fatio, Chris Dunphy** and **Charles Munn** (often called Mr. Palm Beach).

Mr. Munn was social leader on the Island in the 1930s. Each year he sent a Christmas card to his friends listing his favorite caterer, plumber, barber, taxi company, airline and the like. If, during the course of a subsequent social gathering, he found that his "advisory" had not been heeded, the nonconformist's name was dropped from the Christmas card list, and most other social lists. It was Munn's way of establishing a "power elite." The Christmas card list tradition is currently carried on by the Fanjul Family, although there is no penalty for noncompliance.

Many icons of Palm Beach, through the years, were Coconuts, but have since moved on to new elevations. Among them: **H. Loy Ander-**

son, Beverley A. Bogert Jr., Hon. Stanton Griffis, Albin Holder, Rodman A. Heeren, Edward B. McLean, John R. McLean, Hon. Earl E.T. Smith, Thomas Shevlin and W. Stanton Barbour.

Current members of The Coconuts are: **Guilford Dudley, Jr., D. Dixon Boardman, John W. Anderson, II, William Benjamin, J. Anthony Boalt, Edwin M. Burke, Rex D. Cross, Brownlee O. Currey, Jr., A. Alan Dayton, Rodney J. Dillard, Alexander Fanjul, William B. Hamilton, Ridgely W. Harrison, Jr., Paul R. Ilyinsky, Robert P. Leidy, William H. Mann, Allen F. Manning, John D. Mashek, Jr., S. Christopher Meigher, III, Frederick A. Melhado, George F. Merck, W. Blair Meyer, Jr., Felix A. Mirando, William Pitt, Allan D. Scherer, William J.C. Surtees** and **A. Alfred Taubman.**

Only three members of The Coconuts have been on board since 1970: **Guilford Dudley, Jr., J. Anthony Boalt** and **Robert P. Leidy**. An invitation from The Coconuts that year presented the list of "hosts" and a supper menu—Emincee de Volaille a la Ta-boo, Oufs Brouillees aux Saucisses Francaise, Petit Pains Assortis, Cafe Americaine and Cafe Expresso. Veuve Clicquot was the bubbly of choice for lively members, who danced to the music of Bobby Swiadon's Orchestra.

Among the striking ladies present that evening (many are still socially active) were: **Comtesse de la Valdene** (sister of Winston and Ambassador Raymond Guest), **Eleanor Cernadas, Lilly Pulitzer, Pat Schmidlapp, Lorraine Freimann, Alexandra Landa, Durie Shevlin, Ann Kunkel, Estee Lauder, Betty Blakemore, Jane Volk, Terese Anderson, Ruth Tankoos, Carola Mandel, Mrs. John Perry, Jr., Mary Donohue, Betty McMahon, Lesly Smith, Nadia Woodward, Julia Rousseau, Simone Karoff, Kappie Obolensky, Meg Fowler** and **Mary Sanford.**

The august group has no fixed *locus* for its annual event. The late Chris Dunphy hosted the first New Year's Eve party at his home and subsequent events have been held at Ta-boo, the late Marshall Grant's Restaurant, the Poinciana Club, the former Fairview Club of The Breakers, and the Pavilion in The Colony.

Dunphy was top gun in his time. His ongoing battle with the Everglades Club led him to found the Seminole Club, an exclusive hangout, which he ruled in Imperial style. Dunphy had the power to pick/choose members for both the Coconuts and Seminole Club, via his forceful personality.

—THE WORDSMITHS—

*O*nce upon a tongue there was Walter and Cholly and Louis and Dorothy and Leonard and Louella and Hedda—the good old days, when schmoozing in print was the reason people bought newspapers from coast to coast and everywhere in between. The word-smiths were as celebrated as their subject matter. Being a headliner in a top column, manufactured instant stardom, and although any given 24-hour period washes through the system of life quickly, even for a brief moment stardom makes the world a brighter place.

"I am not a gossip columnist. I try to convey a mood of what the fashionable and trendy people are doing."

"My column isn't really gossip. I consider it chitchat."

"I cover people, and people are what gossip is all about. You don't gossip about a computer or a helicopter, but you tell all you can about people, especially if they're in Society."

"Addison and Steele, Boswell and Saint-Simon may have considered themselves 'diarists' because they supposedly spoke the truth, but they were down-and-dirty gossipers."

"Anytime you talk about people, it's gossip. Pure and simple."

"A tipster with a good tattler can easily start a trend."

Over the years the gallery of gossips has had wide mode swings and varying degrees of impact on vicarious pleasure seekers, but where there are people, there are scribes (by whatever designation) who translate the mise-en-scene of the day. The high and mighty in the last 30 years have been (identified with the publication in which they gained their original fame):

Irv Kupcinet (*Chicago Sun-Times*), **Mary Strassmeyer** (*Cleveland Plain Dealer*), **Marilyn Beck** (*Chicago Tribune Syndicate*), **Taki** (*Esquire*), **John Fairchild** (*Women's Wear Daily*), **Nigel Dempster** (*London Daily Mail*), **Rona Barrett** (TV commentator), **Eugenia Sheppard** (*NY Post*), **James Brady** (*NY Post*), **Jody Jacobs** (*LA Times*), **Herb Caen** (*SF Chronicle*), **Liz Smith** (*NY Daily News*), **Suzy** (*NY Daily News* and *W*), **Maxine Mesinger** (*Houston Chronicle*) and **Shirley Eder** (*Detroit Free Press*).

The golden age of gossip began in 1929, when **Walter Winchell** parlayed his tip column in the *NY Daily Mirror,* into national celebrity, a $1 million annual salary and respectability. He was an occasional guest of FDR and Eisenhower, and during his tenure was considered—power out-of-control.

Maury Paul, the first Cholly Knickerbocker, was a man-about-society who filled the gossip gap for William Randolph Hearst; he coined the term "cafe society" as differentiated from the "Old Guard." His successor was **Igor Cassini**, a self-styled Russian nobleman and brother of designer, Oleg Cassini, best known for his designations—"snobility," "cafelegant" and "heir conditioned." Spielers like **Winchell** and **Cassini** abolished privacy and via radio shows and columns, created a whole new world of characters, real and unreal, who lived a lifestyle desired by most of the unwashed in America. **Doris Lilly, Louis Sobol, Ed Sullivan** and **Dorothy Kilgallen** perpetuated the frenzy, and when Hedda and Louella added their feed from the great studio machines, the average American newspaper reader had as many as 10 columns to peruse in one newspaper!

Though the era of the Studio is over, the Age of Hype isn't; the gossip net now includes fashion designers, cosmetic surgeons, TV celebrities, mineral water tycoons and any of the megabuckers. Almost anybody with a fortune (anything above $10 million) can become a celebrity, and gossip is the vehicle to the limelight.

Wordsmiths do "people stuff," says **Suzy** (a.k.a. Aileen Mehle, the undisputed doyenne of social gossipers, now at *W*): *"As long as they're flamboyant enough, rich enough, gifted enough, lively enough, powerful enough, they can get into the columns. If I have something to say about them, I say it. I can't imagine giving you a red-hot item about Robby Benson. But, then again, if he came into my sphere, if he married a Fernanda Wanamaker Wetherill, then that would be a different story."*

"Fame Eaters" must have good hard copy as a means of survival, and gossip columns serve the purpose. The question always asked by those in the business—If you went out for dinner last night and nobody wrote it up, would you still exist?—is not easily answered.

Currently serving the needs/wants of some of the highly visible affluentials in **Palm Beach** are:

• **Shannon Donnelly** (Society Editor, *Palm Beach Daily News*; three times per week during season; average length—600 words; number of top socialite/celeb mentions—80; no photos; number of hard-core readers—12,000 of estimated 24,000 readership)—upbeat blend of society and cultural coverage with skew towards Old Guard; occasionally has some wicked delights, sobriquets & epithets, sticks & stones. Great neurocepters!

Excerpt: It was sun and fun on the high seas as **Betty and AJ Fisher** hosted a luncheon cruise for some pals aboard their 95-foot yacht *Kingfisher* for nearlyweds **Mai Hallingby** and **Ridgley Harrison**.

Nearly 20 friends put on their boat shoes to wish the engaged couple—who just bought a house on South County Road—well, including **John and Liz Schuler, Joyce and Bob Sterling, Judy and Bunky Knudsen, John Bailey, Jack and Lisa Anderson, Maura Benjamin, Bill and Pauline Pitt, Frannie Scaife and Tom McCarter, Jesse and Rand Araskog**, and a few others who know their stems from their sterns.

Betty and AJ are soon off to the Anglers Club for a bit, then they're back in time to give a boat party for grandson **Ricky Grow**, who's graduating from the Palm Beach Day School. Then it's up north for a bit before returning to Palm Beach to see Ricky graduate, and then off for the summer.

AJ's so enamored with the sailor's life that they're skipping Ascot this year. "We've used the boat a lot," Betty said. "We've been to Lyford Cay for weeks at a time. All my husband wants to do is cruise." Betty said that AJ loves his boat so much that he's thinking of changing his name to Sinbad.

OK, not really.

Moon over Palm Beach... There was a big Palm Beach moon shining as **Lesly Smith** hosted 24 friends to dinner in her tropical casa. Among those dining on crab meat, filet and creme brulee in the moonlit garden were the **Duke and Duchess of Marlborough** (Rosita and Sonny to their friends), Rosita's sister **Elizabeth** and her husband **Prince Maximillian** of Bavaria (on their first visit to PB), **Pauline and Bill Pitt, Ginny** (recuperating nicely from a hip operation, thank you very much) **and Ned Burke, Bea and Stanley Tollman, Anabelle and Denis Coleman, Tina Fanjul, Jim Mitchell, Nicole and Derek Limbocher, Felix Miranda** and **James Walsh.**

Easter parade... **Durie Appleton** had 40 of her nearest and dearest for an Easter luncheon at her home. Durie's granddaughter **Melinda Bullough** was there, all the way from London. Also enjoying the luncheon of chicken curry, ham, ice cream and cookies were **Lotsie Busch Webster, Dysie and Buddy Davie, Paul and Angie Ilyinsky, Lulu Balcolm, Ann de Braganza, Robin and Donald Dial, Valarie Rooks and Jim Hanna, Helen Cluett**, and a few others who can still fill out an Easter bonnet.

Heard... that **Jo Carole Lauder** is the winner of the Philanthropy Award from Americans for the Arts. She was honored at Lincoln Center for her contributions to the Friends of Art and Preservation in Embassies.

Blind item of the week... Which media zillionaire and his much-younger wife are on their way to the Irrreconcilable Rodeo? He wants a more laid-back lifestyle, and she's already checking out new digs.

• **Thom Smith** (Columnist, *The Palm Beach Post*; three times per week; average length—600 words; number of socialite/celeb mentions—15; one headshot; number of hard-core readers—100,000 of estimated 180,000 circulation)—witty, fast-paced non-confrontational; highlights celeb arrivals with lots of namedrops of politicians and jocks, not into A-list social stuff, rather big believer in *Res ipsa loquitur*—Facts speak for themselves.

Excerpt: **Grace Kelly.** Great subject for a TV movie. But made in Palm Beach? Kelly had no Palm Beach links. She never lived here; if she paid a visit, no records of it exist. But the producer, **Larry Thompson,** doesn't want Palm Beach for Grace. He wants the look. "He wants to recreate some scenes from Newport in "*High Society,*" Thompson's publicist **Milton Kahn** said, "and Palm Beach has the homes." But Milton, doesn't Thompson know Palm Beach prohibits filming near homes? "He'll cross that bridge when he gets to it," Kahn said. "He also has a law degree and doesn't like to take no for an answer."

Sounds like battle lines are being drawn, even though production is months away. After all, Thompson acquired the rights only a few days ago to *Grace*, a biography by **Robert Lacey**, an English author who wrote much of the book while living in Wellington. Thompson still needs a network deal and a cast, but he'd like to have it ready for broadcast by early 2001.

As for casting, who knows? Hollywood scuttlebutt has **Sharon Stone, Ashley Judd** and **Gwyneth Paltrow,** who does have a Palm Beach hook —her grandparents live here. Thompson did produce one film that had Palm Beach connections—*The Woman He Loved,* about Island regulars the **Duke** and **Duchess of Windsor.** He also put out *And the Beat Goes On: The Sonny and Cher Story,* Lucy *and Desi: Before the Laughter,* and *Murder in the Mirror.* His TV films have received eight Emmy nominations and one Golden Globe nomination.

"He's a real player," Kahn said, "not some producer who blows a lot of smoke."

Stay tuned.

Who wants to be a... new mother?

What better place than Palm Beach for the new king of the world— and I don't mean **Elian Gonzalez**—to spend Easter. TV host extra-ordinaire **Regis Philbin** and wife **Joy** spent the weekend at Mar-a-Lago, schmoozing and enjoying the club's final weekend of the season. Bright and early Sunday, Reeg, who isn't a big Notre Dame fan for nothing, took a limo to St. Edward's Church for Easter Mass, slipping in and out the side door, leaving no chance for a final answer.

Spied coming from the second floor of a medical building on village Boulevard: **Celine Dion.** Significantly, the second floor contains only two offices—one for mammography, the other for obstetrics and gynecology.

• **Maureen O'Sullivan** ("Tales of Palm Beach," *Ocean Drive Magazine*; monthly; average length—800 words; number of socialite/celeb mentions—20; multiple photos; number of hard-core readers—100,000 of estimated 200,000 readership)—sophisticated name drops from in-formed sources; upbeat, far flung, lots of social topspin and inside A-list party stuff, good appraisals, approving nods, well received by large fan club.

Excerpt: No one starves for entertainment around here, especially during Season when the professionally famous start arriving in droves. Celebrated singer **Ray Charles** and three diverse divas—comedienne **Joan Rivers**, actress **Valerie Harper** and cosmetics magnate **Evelyn**

Lauder—were among the recent troupers.

Loquacious, audacious and outrageous, Rivers enjoys a measure of success that would exhaust most people. Coiffed within an inch of her life, the risque humorist packs a lot of power into her petite frame. The Emmy Award-winning Rivers was a guest speaker at the annual **YWCA Mary Rubloft Harmony House** luncheon, which benefits the emergency shelter that provides refuge for battered women and abused children. Rivers relied on her trademark coinage "Can we talk?" to set the tone for her subject list: plastic surgery and faked orgasms, not the usual commentary heard at The Breakers. Rivers' new book, ***Bouncing Back,*** is a quasi self-help book. Healthy, wealthy and wisecracking, Rivers has faced some tough times herself and suggests we should "identify the problem, wallow for a weekend, get out of bad relationships, get into therapy, keep a journal and appreciate your life."

Closely examining the life of novelist **Pearl S. Buck** was actress Valerie Harper, who recently did a run at The Royal Poinciana Playhouse of *All Under Heaven*, the one-woman play she co-wrote and stars in. The character of Buck is a definite departure from nasal New Yorker Rhoda Morgenstern, *The Mary Tyler Moore Show* character that made Harper a star. Recently, Harper and Moore reunited for the making of *Mary & Rhoda*, an ABC television movie that will air this month. Harper heartfully portrays 79-year-old Buck, who spent nearly 40 years living in China. In *All Under Heaven*, Buck is at home in her Vermont farmhouse awaiting a visa that will enable her to return to China.

Flashbacks and character changes during the play trace Buck's remarkable life: She pioneered global race relations, became an advocate for mixed-race children and was the first American woman to win the Nobel Prize for literature for *The Good Earth.*

Photography buff **Evelyn Lauder** finds the earth a good place to scour for inspiring images. She recently appeared at the newly completed, abundantly capitalized Chase Manhattan Bank on Royal Palm Way with her collection of photographs called **"Life Observed."** Proceeds from photo sales will benefit the **The Breast Cancer Research Foundation**, which Lauder founded in 1993.

American designer **Halston** dressed socialites by day and skulked behind the velvet ropes at Studio 54 by night. Credited with creating simple, architecturally ingenious clothes, his contribution to fashion is well documented in ***Halston: An American Original***, by **Elaine Gross** and **Fred Rottman**. Who better than Martha Phillips' owner **Lynn Manulis**, who put Halston on the map, to host the book signing? The party benefited Ballet Florida and featured a retrospective of original Halston designs.

191

• **James Jennings Sheeran** ("Tempo"—*Palm Beach Society Magazine*; weekly during season; average length—1,000 words; number of top socialite/celeb mentions—20; occasional photos; number of hardcore readers—12,000 of estimated 20,000 readership)—breezy, somewhat pontifical, essayish, crosses social spectrum past and present with great insight.

Excerpt: Ernest Hemingway fondly recalled: "The New Year's Eve action at the Paris Ritz is tops. It's a bright night. I knock back a couple of martinis in the bar, Cambon side. Then there's a wonderful dinner under an enormous chandelier, throwing off thousands of brain-bending patterns. After a few brandies I wander up to my room and slip into one of those huge Ritz beds. There's a bolster for my head the size of the Graf Zeppelin and four square pillows filled with real goose feathers—two for me, and two for my quite heavenly companion."

Well, to each his own. The Ritz may have its geese, but **Palm Beach** on New Year's Eve has its very own **Swans**. And its own panache. *Quel phenomene!*

And so our story begins. An invitation that simply reads—"The **Coconuts** request the pleasure of your company on New Year's Eve... The **Pavilion** at the **Colony... 10:30** p.m.—is entree to the Island's most distinguished event. For the better part of the 20th century, a group of bachelors who originally wanted to repay their chums for unusual hospitality, decided to underwrite a reciprocity party. Each year the event became more of a dazzler, and through the years included luminaries like **Harold Vanderbilt, Anthony Drexel Biddle, Florenze Ziegfeld, Chris Dunphy, Charles Munn** and **Ambassador Earl E. T. Smith.**

In recent years the group of derring-doers (mostly now house trained via multiple marriages) has been under the masterful tutelage of **Ambassador Guilford Dudley** and **D. Dixon Boardman.** But other seasoned Coconuts, the joint chiefs of staff, put on their jolly old chap faces and added to the merriment. Gents like **Bill "The Tower" Benjamin, Tony Boalt, Willie Surtees, Bill Pitt, Fred Melhado, Laddie Merck, Felix Mirando,** Bombay adman **Ridgely Harrison, Rodney Dillard,** cosmic **Bob Leidy, Allen Manning, Alex Fanjul, Brownlee Currey, Bill Mann, John Mashek, Blair Meyer, Rex Cross,** newly-ordained Coconut **Chris Meigher, Alan Dayton** and *papa gateau* **Al Taubman.** The well-laundered looks and dispositions of Townie couples like **Ann and Billy Hamilton, Betsy and Michael Kaiser, Kit and Bill Pannill, Eles and Warry Gillet,** the **Raymond Floyds,** the **Gerald Goldsmiths,** the **Robert Laceys, Betty and Herb Swope, Thomas McCarter,** Sir Galahad **John Brogan,** the **Rand Araskogs,** blond Venus **Jackie** and the gruffly elegant **Richard Cowell, Evelyn and Leonard Lauder,** lush **Mary** and kingly **Sam Boykin, Liz and John Schuler,** always-ready-to-tango **Lore and John Dodge, Angie** and His Most Humble Honor **Paul Ilyinsky,** Lady **Lisa** (frame her and she'd be a Renoir) and Gentleman **John Anderson** (perfect at giving Papal blessings), and the **Winston Guests** vied for Arthur Murray top honors on the dance floor, and gave sightseers a glimpse of how Givenchy, Dior, Blass, de la Renta and Armani make their fortunes.

There were glittering ruffles and royal ruffs and bows and puffs and status (frills and chic ribbons adorning lusty knockout ladies like **Jean Tailer, Hilary Geary,** captivating and cogent **Aerin Lauder, Gio King,** politically immaculate **Lesly Smith** in a breath depriving **Vera Wang** costume, **Mosse Hvide,** keeper of royals **Barbara Wainscott Berger, Nicole Fanjul,** always-effervescent, Fiandaca-clad **Jane Dudley, Lucy Musso, Pauline Boardman Pitt,** the redoubtable **Alyne Massey, Susan Bishop, Judy Taubman, Peggy Angevine, Liza Pulitzer,** gregarious and gracious **Kelly Brogan, Marjorie Gubelmann, Taylor Stein,** Oscar Wilde-garbed **Jill Young, Lisa Banes, Bebe Steinberg, Margo dePeyster** and the fairest one of all—Chessy Patcevitch.

Other star-quality leading ladies and men lovely—**Anita Hamilton and Billy David, James Lesher, Pam Surtees, Ann Anderson,** Susan and barrister **Bruce McAllister, Lady Burkley and Nelson Gunnell, Renate and John Franco, Frannie Scaife,** the regal **Ginny and Ned Burke, Karen and Richard Williams,** the **Alfred Fishers, Bobby Spencer, Barbara and Doyle Rogers, Tory and Chris Burch, Ambassador Francis Kellog,** chic and celebrated **Patricia Kennedy,** portraitist and international model **Diane Millner, George Dempsey, Linda and Jay Rossbach, Warren Scherer, John Baily,** Young Turks **Christopher** and **Richard Cowell, Jr., Samantha Boardman, Polly and Michael Fawcett,** bronco rider **Allan Scherer** and wife **Maggie,** and **Shelley and William Gubelmann** added to the trampoline effect of the room, people bouncing up and down from tables and on/off the lively dance floor (yes, **Neal Smith** at work with his licorice stick).

As with much of the action in Town, **Young Fogeys** were ubiquitous. The younger set bubbled with brilliance as the evening advanced toward—but never reached decadence. Many of the fledglings were new to Coconuts and their sprinkling of bounce and pounce, French perfume, little cherry cheeks, legs that start at their chins, and honey, lilac and hot chocolate scents added a nice cache to the **paaahhtee** and also gave credence to the passing of the torch, and the thought—it's a wonderful thing to reach the irresponsible age of 70, only it comes too late in life.

And so our story ends. The stars have given way and night brightens into predawn. Time speeds on and the hot Planet Earth spins on its axis and makes us dizzy with the wonder of it all. We circle each other in comfortable orbit, reach out, touch, draw back, caress, make love, never fully understanding why. All we know is that we care about our life and our bright and noble friends, and it's another new year, full of intrigue and promise... and, what the hell, **that's good enough!**

● ● ●

Most of Palm Beach's wordsmiths agree that only eternal life can be nastier than a boring life, and barrel through the days, giving good verbals, rubber necking, hanging out, dealing in olive branches or nut cracking as is appropriate, yet never really pulling wings off flies; and all the while, being the piper, playing the tune, overjoyed that readers **march to their beat.**

—SOCIETY WORDS & PHRASES—

*I*n any gathering there are invariably the talkers, listeners, advocates, affected ones, cheerleaders, teases, protagonists, crusaders, gossips, meek & milds, seducers, historians and toastmasters. Here's a sampling of dialogue from a recent cocktail party, and the meaning of some very special society words.

Party life is often verbally abbreviated. Note these acronyms and assorted forms of shortspeak:

NP = New people, the latest social arrivals, from wherever and whatever vicissitude; usually perfect at indiscriminately supporting causes and buying real estate and art.

NM = Newly minted, same as NPs but richer with dotcom money.

WUMP = used to difterentiate from WASP—means white, urban middle-class Protestant.

UIP = Unimportant person, a nothingburger.

FIP = Fairly important person, watch and see.

HI-VI = High visibility, a media pet, gets exposure.

LO-PRO = Low profile, avoids flashbulbs.

NOKD = Not our kind dear, not up to speed.

DDG = Drop dead gorgeous, a glam queen.

PPP = Practically perfect princess, about a 9.5.

PBR = Palm Beach Rumor.

PBF = Palm Beach Fact.

SIS = One who suffers in silence.

FUBAR = Fueled up beyond all reason, very drunk.

WOOF = Well-off older folks.

OINK = One income, no kids.

DINK= Double income, no kids.

MASP= Middle-aged, single parent.

SWORD = Single, widowed or divorced person.
SWELL = Single woman earning lots & lots.
SWAN = Single woman available nightly.
UMM = Unmarried, monied male.
SOCC = Social climber.
SLICK = Single lady with income, cache, a knockout.
PUSSY = Pretty, urbane, sexy single yenta.
REGAL = Royal elderly grandee with ancestry and loot.
TOAD = Terribly old and dreary.
YES = Young, eager and sexy.
SAM = Successfully avoiding matrimony.
GLAD = Great legs and derriere.
SOBB = Son of big bucks.
DOBB = Daughter of big bucks.
SWAP = Seeking wealth and power.

* **Angry and hungry** are the only two English words that end in **gry**—usually said by a woman to her date who has invited her to a very dull party.

* **Cygnet**—a beautiful young swan of a woman. What most senior Ladies would love to be (again).

* **"For heaven's sake"**—still the favored expression of WASPs.

* A **snoop** is one given to sulking around, gathering up all the latest superficial information about people.

* **Dicey reputation**—a fairly bleak and blemished past.

* Showing too much of **mother's milk**—dressing in a gown which displays a plentitude of breast.

* **To die**—something so great one would die for it. "The strawberries, to die."

* **If I don't print it, someone else will!**—typical society reporter **ploy** for getting inside info from one who denies everything.

* She's a **good seat**—ideal partner to be seated next to at a party; good spirited, flirtatious, knowledgeable.

* Typical conversation between **Old Guard** and **NP** prowler:

She: I haven't the vaguest idea of how much money I'm going to inherit. My family never fills me in on those things, but I live on a trust now and when grandfather dies, I'll get much more, same when Mummy goes.

He: Don't tell me all this, it's not important. I intend to pay the bills.

She: Music to my ears. I've always been warned to watch out for people after my money. It's an awful way to grow up distrusting everyone.

He: I've never understood that kind of thinking.

She: You know, you're the least suitable suitor in terms of my family and that kind of thing, but you're also the only man I've ever had who doesn't care about my money.

He: Well, maybe, I'm just your middle-class guy with real values.

She: Speaking of values, a couple of things. I don't like airy, windowy apartments and the minimal look.

He: And I don't dig gloomy rooms and cabbage-rose chintz.

She: Okay, a deal, but one thing more. I adore you and want you, but I'm not going to get up every morning and fry your eggs and make your juice when we can have a perfectly good maid to do that sort of thing.

He: Good. I hate being bothered in the morning, my mind is working too hard.

She: We're going to get along just great.

He: Here's to us, kid!

* **Alley cat**—a girl or guy who is obsessed with constant sexual prowling; has good intentions, weak spirit.

* Too much **dewlap**—loose skin hanging from neck.

* **Lentiginous**—usually means too many social freckles (liver spots) from too much Dewars.

* Blond **strumpet** is an attractive bimbo much younger than her date.

* A **once-only** person—lots of fun but misguided so that he gets invited once only to parties; is known for major gaffes.

* She had a **vomer** job—nose job on the septum, bone between nostrils.

* He gives me the **pip**—English way of saying one makes another angry.

* Oh **fugh** (foo)—exclamation of disgust used by the Ladies, shortened version of another commonly accepted word.

* **Tickitacky** is worse than tacky, the lowest in taste; saying fancy-schmancy, heavens to Betsy or hoity-toity is tickitacky.

* **Proprietary air**—supremely confident, arrogant, presumes to own everything in sight.

* You're an interesting guy. Have you ever written? No, just **checks** for my wife.

* You can say window treatment, but never say drapes when you mean **curtains.**

* My dear, it's **gauche** to stare with your opera glasses.

* He's with his **acolytes** tonight—usually a gay with his friends.

* He's on a **slip**—a recovering alcoholic who slipped a bit to celebrate; often with champagne.

* Your **lifeline** is showing—the thread that holds the lining of a tie is exposed.

* I read my **Edith Wharton**—I keep up with society, morals and propriety.

* A **marriage blanc**—a marriage of companionship and friendship, no passion.

* He's a **Nebuchadnezzar**—heavy drinking fellow (Nebuchadnezzar = 20 bottles of champagne).

* They call her **scattergood**—she spends, squanders, is unmerciful about blowing OP (other people's) money.

* A **beer drinker's finger**—only the most observant social critic can see the discoloration and swelling on one's finger from pulling too many pop-tops from beer cans; usually means someone with the curse of imbibing too much.

* From certain people, good wrapping means **cheap gift.**

* In delicate situations, it's better to **mouth** but not speak words : you don't say cancer, you mouth it; same for alcoholic, AIDS, lesbian, toupee, adopted, crazy, gay, suicide.

* Socialites, those who live by the etiquette code, remember **slights** far more than largesse.

* **Too marvelous**—great, unbearable, superior in every way.

* So proper, so **aboveboard**—too good to be true, not to be trusted.

* Friend to gay—No, after you. **AIDS** before beauty.

* **Frightfully**—used often by WASPs as an adjective.

* **WASP** talk about a wedding **ring**: If that rock is fake, it's silly; if it's real, it's ridiculous.

* **Anglophobe**—one who is bored by WASPs, dislikes the English.

* **Eth**—an ethnic, displays ethnicity to extreme.

* **Loyalty laughter**—forced gaiety by an underling for his date, ancestors, boss.

* **Ombibulous**—a guy who drinks any kind of distilled spirits; for effect not pleasure.

* He is about to celebrate his **plentieth** birthday; said of someone who is too old to count.

* She should have been a **visagiste**—spends so much time in preparation she could have been a professional makeup artist.

* **Punkaroo**—second-rate social player.

* **Punkling**—a young, promiscuous Lady on the move.

* Old **uxorious** guy—rich man excessively fond of his newly acquired trophy wife.

* It's a **piff**, forget it—a trifle, don't worry about it.

* He's in his **antology** stage—deep study of oneself.

* **OG** (Old Guard) on the NP: They **come and go**, these people. Last year everyone was talking about Count Courant. Now you never hear his name, or you hear it and people shudder. This year Mr. Cash is the name on every lip and his wife is here, there and everywhere, and only yesterday no one had ever heard of them. They're like leaves in the wind.

* **"Riveting"**—OG comment when listening to an NP pronouncement.

* Coffee, tea or **me?**—assertive waitress at a stag party.

* She has someone—a **publicist**, usually; not a lover.

* Life in **high society** may be boring as hell, but it spoils you for everything else.

* Their home has exactly the right amount of **shabby**. A nifty place.

* My **lips are sealed**; talking to me is like talking to the dead.

* He's NP, only gives to the **social advancement** charities like the ballet, opera, museum; he isn't into disease.

* **Placement emergency**—getting someone at the last minute to fill a cancellation at a major private party.

* **Ohhellohowareyou?**—Pyramid topper greeting a climber.

* **Down for the count**—socially ostracized (originally a term used in boxing to indicate a knock out).

* Live by the **place card**, die by the place card—social climber's credo.

* **Core** people—those who really run society.

* Observation—she has callouses on her hands from social **climbing**.

* Oh, the wickedness of it all, all that **swank**.

* In society, lifelong friends are always **not** speaking to each other.

* He's a very nice man, and certainly very rich, but he's not eligible for any of the **clubs.**

* Social women often need a **hairdresser** or a decorator in their lives; to tell them they're pretty and look good, the sort of things husbands often take for granted, or are too busy to mention.

* The **traditional wife** complaint—after all these years, you should know that I'm more than a mannequin. More than a hostess. You say you love me but I'm talking about love in the lovemaking sense of the word love.

* **Counter to an unpleasant** exchange—that's ludicrous and libelous.

* He acts like he's supposed to—he's a **bought-and-paid-for** husband.

* She's a bit **dim**, chews chlorophyll gum so her tongue is always green, moves her lips when she reads.

* He's got alligator skin—he's **uninsultable**.

* Society men often gives their wives gifts of **atonement**; the more unfaithful the husband, the greater the jewel collection.

* The best thing about having your own **jet** is that it won't leave without you.

* He made his fortune by knowing all the **right wrong** people.

* She's the most **fragile tough** girl you'll ever meet.

* His **IQ** hovers around room temperature.
* Oh, the **stories** I could tell you about her.
* He's just an old lion whose brains have turned to oatmeal, but his **libido** is still going bananas.
* She can **sleazify** even a Chanel dress.
* His money doesn't just talk, it **screams!**
* Society **women** go from beautiful to attractive to good looking to handsome to mustabeen.
* She's just **tart** enough to wear those go-to-hell white pants that are loose and floppy everywhere but in the crotch.
* One of the unwritten rules of **status conduct** is that when an inferior greets you with a how-are-you, you do not answer. You nod.
* He's gotten pretty high through the sheer power of his **wink.**
* His **nose** grows right in front of you when he's lying.
* He doesn't chew his **cabbage** twice; his bona fides are tops.
* Net worth and beluga for breakfast do not prevent **ignobility.**
* Treat a harlot like a lady; and a lady like a **harlot!**
* Use a long spoon when you eat with the **devil.**
* There's no point in lying & denying. They'll **believe** what they want to believe, and it usually isn't on the up side.
* From her eyes to her lips to her pips, she's able to drive a guy **bonzo.**
* With him, you feel like you're in a **blender**—being buffeted, sliced, diced, chopped, minced, ground and pureed.
* She stuck her **tongue** out at me—I thought it was more invitation than insult.
* The big **question** with them—who will end up the lion and who the lamb?
* She's one of those dames who has guys throwing themselves on **swords** for her.
* Everything she said was in a sort of half-childish lilt that implied **sexuality** the way an alto sax implies jazz.
* A gracious gentlemen always gets a shine before he kicks **butt.**
* He gets a little hammered and goes around telling everyone he's a naval architect! He designs **navels.**
* With her, when she says to slip into something comfortable, it means put on a **flak jacket** over a bullet-proof vest.
* The **cuisine** there is something less than *haute.*
* Her **rear** is in gear—she's sleek enough to be the hood ornament on a turbo-charged Bentley.
* She was wearing a state-of-the-tart **bikini.**
* If hate turns to love, it's **wedding bells** for sure.
* He's one of those guys who gives good **verbals**, but that's about it.
* They're the kind of people who are **highly therapized** and social and

199

will never deal with you in a direct manner.

* People who don't believe in God are stuck with believing in **mankind!**

* He's a **blade** around town. Why would he desert his wild, dissolute life and seek marital somnolence?

* If you can't be mean, nasty and cranky, what's the purpose of growing **old?**

* Too many people want the quick winner, no matter how tacky.

* The **lifts** on his shoes are so high, his ears would pop if he took them off.

* Oh darling, I have **oodles** to impart to you.

* He's a teensy, testy little **tse-tse fly.**

* He's famous for one **line**—"I dig you, little princess, I'll go and get you a rainbow."

* I like his **wit**—he always invites me to go out and roll in a few gutters with him.

* A good **plumber** does more for mankind than a bad TV ministry.

* She knows the **graves** on which she walks.

* With him, it's always the Year of the **Toad.**

* **Unhappiness** is his element—he believes he can't be happy without it.

* She gives good **lobotomies.**

* He's got the kind of face that belongs to a **cigar.**

* He's always looking into the past, trying to understand when it was that all the **laughter** died.

* She's one of those **Lemon Tarts**—a young blond fourth wife of an old man; he's stooped over, she's too thin for x-rays.

* She's **marvelous** at using puffs, flounces, pleats, ruffles, bibs, bows, battings, laces, scallops and darts to cover up all that baby fat.

* They throw **formula** parties, always the same mix: three titles, a ranking politician, four biggies in arts and letters, a major jock and the biggest anchor in town, two designers, three VIFs (very important fags), two billionaires, somebody from the White House, and three international types with heavy accents.

* He's a good **dress extra**—guy who dresses up the party.

* He's about as **tall** as a trash can.

* She is irresistibly **common**; not at all unattractive.

* He is stale, finished, out of date and too **light** in the loafers.

* He was just born **wrong.**

* What's she doing with a man who is taking her **nowhere?**

* He could be a page in the **Old Testament.**

* He's great at getting **horselaughs.**

* I dig you little princess—I'll go and get you a **star.**

* The only thing he wants from a woman is release from his **Oedipal** claustrophobia.

* I left him not because I didn't love him but because I had made him need me and his need was turning my love to **contempt.**

* Girls who don't give, don't **get.**

* She's got no **flint** in her.

* She has an elegance about her which she wears as **defiance.**

* **Life**—adjust, temper, modify; leave your pug mark and move onto the next check-point.

* He's always chortling at his own **cunning.**

* She's generally **versus** everything.

AND on and on; snide, catty remarks, sarcasm bespeaking attitudes, heritage, class prejudice, and a world not altogether perfect!

—SOCIETY MAXIMS—

*I*n any given group of more than two people, smart operators consider the maxims by which they live, before any type of engagement. Here are some Palm Beach specials.

* Life has **two** sides—your desire for fame, and your knowledge of the absurdity of it.

* Your **folks** gave you the face you're born with, but you earn the one you die with.

* When a man marries up, his wife almost always manages to **elevate** him to her level; when a man marries down, his wife drags him down to her level.

* **Charity** work is hard-slogging; lately it's become a blood sport.

* Self-preservation is all about **self-presentation**.

* We may pretend that class doesn't exist in our glorious **egalitarian** melting pot, but watch your flanks.

* **Old age** is what you call it—fogeyhood, pre-geezer, junior senior, oldest-old, mature, of a certain vintage, long of tooth, near-elderly, oldster.

* The growing gap between the merely rich and the truly rich is in the **air**—private jets.

* The **cat** does not negotiate with the mouse.

* The best lies are told face-to-face with a touch of **arrogance**.

* People get **assasinated** by long life, a bullet, scandal, or by the paparazzi.

* Tell me who you love and I'll tell you who you are.

* If you do **life right**, there isn't a second act—there's a mini-series.

* Fun is what life's all about, and the winner dies **broke**.

* People in **hell** just want a drink of water.

201

* Lover's **dream**—we were going to find an island and start our own country.

* No woman in America is allowed to have a healthy relationship with **food**.

* When dating a short girl be sure to clip your **nostril** hairs; don't worry about being bald.

* To have **sex** before dinner is very liberating because you can enjoy your date's conversation without motive.

* There should be a **law** about people's outsides matching their insides.

* With any couple, the rules are made by the person who loves **least**.

* **Need** is better than love; need is unchanging, love is fickle.

* A social invalid is prone to **paranoia**.

* You can only **carnally** love one person at a time.

* A person finds out what he wants by what he **does.**

* On these chairs have parked some of the most corrupt **behinds** in history.

* With **ambition,** town snobbery abounds, even block snobbery—lake vs. ocean, village vs. woods, northend vs. south, new construction vs. Mizner.

* Never shoot a drunken **Irishman** or you'll really make him mad.

* *Rex non potest peccare*—the king can do no wrong.

* When you build your social standing on a house of **cards**, sooner or later the joker will turn up.

* The fall from **grace** is a spectator sport, and those too meek to take risks watch from afar and cluck their tongues knowingly.

* New **money** always has to trumpet its bourgeois insecurity.

* When in doubt, **redecorate.**

* In society, beware of the Benihana chefs with their **clevers**.

* The only thing that **matters** are happily ever afters.

* **People** often seem closer when apart; and estranged when together.

* Style is **absolutism**—choosing and eliminating, knowing what is right for you.

* Sometimes a person who passes through life lightly leaves a **marked** trail.

* **I love you**—is a question not a statement, especially not the first time—it is said to see what response it gets.

* The fatter the guy, the more likely he is take a **toothpick.**

* An **aristocrat** of the spirit is a person who is as sensitive for others as he is for himself.

* **Wisdom** says the only true values are the ones placed on yourself.

* For the **soul** to be offended, it must first exist.

* When **birds** fly out of cages they sing and rejoice.

* Smart people look at life in the rearview **mirror**.
* Turn the **page**. It's over. Move on.
* Travel well, keep your arse to the **sunset**.
* **Firing** squads assemble at dawn.
* Stay still, be quiet, listen to your **heart**; then when it speaks, get up and follow it where it takes you.
* A **woman** should know how to look like a girl and act like a Lady.
* Beware the party with 500 **peacocks**.
* The **rich** form their own tight superior cosmos in which exceptional territorial rights are taken for granted.
* Most people live more in their own **fiction** than their own fact.
* **Avarice** is a passion doomed to be unconsummated.
* We must change to remain the same, but we must appear to be the same in order to change.
* Avoid tossing **grenades** in empty trenches.
* Every smart **woman** in the world knows if she had been born a man she would never marry!

—WAVE-OFFS—

*Y*ou're at an anniversary party, dressed to the nines, a flute of Dom in your hand, your attitude very up and your tongue more than ready to commence firing. You approach one of the town's finest and foremost couples and initiate smart-but-small cocktail talk, hoping to be anthropologically proper, and accepted.

You expect a rejoinder, but you get a **Disinterest Signal**, a definite reduction in the intensity of the expected friendly reaction, an aversion of the eyes and Mr. Finest actually turns his head away from you. If society wants to show its contempt or basic indifference to you, it first **ignores** you, then **laughs** or **snickers** at you, finally it **attacks** you. A good player picks up on the mood in the first 20 seconds and moves in-or-on accordingly.

The **Cut**, or cutting someone dead, is simply done by ignoring a proffered handshake or throwing off **Boredom Signals** (mock yawn, deep-sighing, a glazed far-away look or repeated examination of a wristwatch). None of these gestures suggest gentility, but they are all part of any social interaction (however sophisticated or exalted) since such functions are nothing more than human beings setting up a pecking order with one another.

A **Superiority Signal** really hurts; it's a special act which makes an insulter appear pompous or superior by simply tilting the head back a bit, combined with half-closed eyes, which gives rise to a "looked down upon" gesture. In reality, people with proper carriage often have their heads held high and are always looking down on someone because their noses are always up.

Let's say you're attending the premier charity cocktail party of the season. You're enjoying a pleasant conversation about the decorations with a charming couple, when two wannabes sidle up and intro themselves. The charming couple knows them from some other life and makes it known they're not quite comfortable; it's done with a **Deformed Compliment Signal**, which is simply distorting a compliment. Example: a friendly response is modified to make it unpleasant by using the **Tight Smile** (when you purse your lips while mouth-corners are pulled back in an ordinary smile), or the **Cheek Crease** (a pulling back of the mouth-corner). These are not fun smiles in that the recipient sees only a portion of a smile given gladly and fully to others.

Only in the more mundane social settings does one see real **Rejection Signals**, in which the insulter makes a gesture of mild rejection, like the **Thumb Jerk** (a get-lost signal) or the **Insect Flick**, where the flat hand flaps, flicks or pushes away the rejected person without touching him. More than a few drinks often bring on this type of behavior.

A form of insult can also take place at a performance where the talent is given a **Super-Slow Hand Clap**, a form of applause that is really negative. In Spanish-speaking countries, applause by tapping the back of one thumb nail against the other is an act of derision. There are endless ways to show one's superiority (or one's ignorance).

Since Palm Beach parties are so numerous and can go on for too many hours, you often see **Impatience Signals**—small movements that indicate an urge to get away from the present situation; strumming with the fingers, tapping the feet, a mild, but repeated slapping of the hand against the body, false-smiles and glances toward the door.

It's said that the speed of the impatience signal (how fast the fingers strum) roughly equals the speed with which one would exit, given the chance.

There are plenty of gestures which signal **appreciation** of a woman or man via the use of hands (with no insult intended). The Greeks were always great at the **Cheek Stroke**, in which the forefinger and thumb of one hand are placed on the gesturer's cheekbones and then stroked gently down to the chin—symbolic of the smooth roundness of a beautiful person.

The **Breast Curve** (and the **Waist Curve**) is simply a gesture where a man's hand describes the forward curve of female breasts or the exaggerated female trunk outline emphasizing a narrow waist and wide hips. What boulevardier has not used these gestures at least a million times in his robust and wicked lifetime?

The **Eye Touch**—where a person places a straight forefinger against the lower eyelid and may even pull it slightly downwards—signals that someone is an "eyeful." And the **Two-Handed Telescope**, where hands are curled and placed in front of the eyes like a telescope, suggests a closer look is in order.

The **Hand-On-Heart**—guy places his right hand over his heart— indicating the girl is so beautiful, she makes his heart beat too fast; we don't see much of this posturing in Town. It's a Brazilian manifestation.

Our Island is a proper setting for the **Fingertip Kiss**, where the guy kisses his fingertips and fans them toward the girl; the **Air Kiss** is also popular—a person simply makes a kissing movement with the lips in the direction of another person. It's a quick and effective way to bestow a subtle blessing on someone without getting rouged up from a painted cheek or abraded by a beard.

At the International Red Cross Ball, it's not unusual to see the **Cheek Screw**, where a straight forefinger is pressed into the middle of the cheek and rotated, to indicate the dimpling of a beautiful girl's cheek.

Naturally, it has to be done deftly by an Ambassador from a Latin country, and the object of his affection should be a 19-year-old waitress.

So much for propriety!

Coco Chanel and Fulco di Verdura (1937)

NICKI AND J. IRA HARRIS
original and innovative civic leaders

CARRIE AND TERRENCE CASSIDY
gracious, gregarious and generous

CAROLYN AND DOUG REGAN, MOSSE HVIDE AND JOHN BROGAN
lots of top spin and spirit

PATRICK PARK AND VICTORIA FARRIS
always up to speed on matters of humankind

MUFFIE POTTER-ASTON AND DR. SHERRELL ASTON, HOLLY AND MICHAEL McCLOSKEY
as sure and stunning as sunrise

WILLIAM AND MARTHA BROOKS
happily hospitable and helpful

BILL AND MAURA BENJAMIN
vigor, verve and values

HOMER AND CHERYL MARSHMAN AND BETTY AND DAVID SCAFF
quantum jump experts

213

PAIVI ALPERSON, ALFONS LANDA AND DIANE MILLNER
well-designed and dynamic doers

SIMON FIREMAN, TONY CURTIS AND NORMA FIREMAN
altruists, friends to the world

KELLY BROGAN AND JOHN MASHEK
limitless inspiration and initiative

CHAPTER VI

THAT'S ENTERTAINMENT
(Bars, Bistros and Bon Vivant)

Photo: Mort Kaye Studios

JANNA AND STANLEY RUMBOUGH
distinguished, dynamic and debonair

—BAR EXAM—

*A*s of this writing, **several dozen** bars, saloons, pubs, taverns and drinking establishments grace our Island; they run the gamut in terms of sociability, atmosphere, celebrity, royalty, old and new money, highhandedness, verbal jousting and joy and wassail:

AMICI — Right on the money for pleasurable moments; excellent taste (and tastes).

ACQUARIO — Tony setting for upscale conversation and libation.

BICE — Extensive selection of fine wines and dining specialties; very proper, continental and chic.

BRAZILIAN COURT — Celeb and social set hang out; great martinis to the tunes of various entertainers.

THE BREAKERS — (The Beach Club, Patio Bar, Cigar Bar, Henry's Place, Reef Bar, Tapestry and Seafood Bars and more). Something for everyone, a blend of natives, vacationers and conventioneers. Dancing in Seafood Bar.

CAFE L'EUROPE — Pure continental elegance and sophistication by any measurement. Caviar, vodka and champagne, specialties.

CASABLANCA — Mostly food but plenty of drink, too; trendy bistro, great wines and cuisine; impromptu entertainment.

CHARLEY'S CRAB — Top-of-the-line bar and restaurant, a favorite Palm Beach and tourist rendezvous. Piano music.

THE CHESTERFIELD — (Leopard Lounge). Sophisticated decor; rich wood bar with brass trim, tables topped with red tartan plaid prints; leopard trim completes ambiance; piano music. Very "in" spot.

218

CHEZ JEAN-PIERRE — Great French food and tempting drinks at a long, pleasant bar.

CHUCK & HAROLD'S — A main gathering place for the cocktail crowd; one of Town's longest and curviest bars; a good place to see and be seen. Music for dancing.

THE COLONY — Popular gathering spot; once a Town legend and still formidable. Great canapes, good drinks.

DEMPSEY'S — Cozy atmosphere in the Irish-like pub tradition; the current "in" place for casual times; piano music.

THE FOUR SEASONS RESORT — (The Living Room and Ocean Bistro Cafe and Bar). Gracious drinking amid the sun and ocean breeze outside; cozy with fireplace; piano music indoors; very upscale, very international. Dancing.

GALAXY — Ideal mid-town, expansive setting, showcase bar; lovely ladies and hip chatter.

HAWAIIAN OCEAN INN — Indoor cocktail lounge and patio bar adjacent to the ocean; comfortable and relaxing but not very Hawaiian.

HEART OF PALM — An intimate English Pub atmosphere offering full menu and good drink selection.

JANEIRO — Two bars in exotic, enticing Brazilian setting.

LUCIO'S — Some of the best liquor, food and atmosphere around; a native habitat. Colorful Capri appeal; piano bar.

PALM BEACH HILTON — (Sandcastle Bar). Great place to watch the glorious Atlantic with favorite drink in hand; mostly frequented by out-of-towners.

PALM BEACH TAVERN — Great friendly ambience, curving bar, over-brimming drinks. Lots of singles, desirables and availables. Super happy hour.

THE PLAZA INN — (Stray Fox Pub). Quaint, cozy bar hidden in intimate setting off lobby; snacks, big drinks, piano music.

RENATO'S — Authentic Italian decor, intimate, cozy, romantic and "in"—perfect for Worth Avenue shoppers and spenders and evening pre-dinner drinks.

TA-BOO — Long happy bar, perfect for peacocking, open view of Worth Avenue in front lounge; large drinks, good conversation, top bartenders. A must see/do for locals and visitors. Piano music, late night disco.

TESTA'S — Long time Palm Beach institution; prefers not to be considered a bar, but has good food and cocktail lounge, tropical dining garden and sidewalk cafe.

264 THE GRILL — Small, crowded, power players haunt; popular meeting place for socialites and business types alike.

OTHER — Places like **Jo's, Cafe Cellini, Cucina, Maxims, Echo, Toojay's, Pleasant Peasant, Garden Club Restaurant** and a few others are not bars in a true sense—they may have good spirits but do not cater to real drinkers (thus they have not been described in this section).

—Imbiber's Dictionary—

*F*estive lunches, the nightly give-and-take of balls or outings and afternoons at polo make the grape or the hop or the spirit (whatever it may be) an important factor; here are some of the terms used by the Town's expert imbibers as they make the social rounds:

Agrafes—the cage that holds a champagne cork in place (a French word, pronounced a-graph).

Barm—the froth on beer; sometimes called fob.

Beeswing—filmy tartar scales that form in some white wines after a long period of storage; so called because they look like the wings of bees.

BIB—short for Bottled in Bond.

Bottle Ticket—a small plaque hung around the neck of a bottle or decanter with the name of the beverage inside; often made of silver.

Bouge—the belly of a cask, the point where the circumference is the greatest.

Brimmer—a glass so full that the liquid touches the brim; although liquid has climbed to the brim, there is a slight depression in the center of the surface.

Bumper—a brimmer to which extra drops have been added to fill the hollow to a bump.

Depart—the final taste of wine in the mouth (French).

Dunder—the dregs left after distillation of rum; in some processes, dunder from one rum is added to the next for additional flavor.

Fliers—white, fluffy particles that float in white wine; most likely to appear when the wine is transported from a warm to a colder climate.

Hogen-mogen—said of strong booze; an explanation and a description.

Jirble—to pour out a drink unsteadily.

Katzenjammer— a cat's whining, literally, but most often applied to a hangover.

Legs—streaks that run down the side of a glass after wine has been swirled in it; wine with pronounced streaks is said to have "good legs."

Mini-petillances—light sparkle or crackle in a wine.

Muddler—the technical name for a swizzle stick, sometimes called a mosser.

Nebuchadnezzar—the largest champagne bottle (holds 104 glasses); it is larger than the 83-glass Balthazar, the 62-glass Salmanazar, the 41-glass Methuselah, the 31-glass Rehoboam, the 21-glass Jeroboam and the 10-glass Magnum (the standard bottle holds a mere five glasses).

Oenology—the art and science of wine making.

Peated—Scotch taster's term for the degree to which a particular

Scotch has a smoky or peaty character (a Scotch may be "well peated," "lightly peated," etc.).

Plonk—cheap ordinary table wine (British slang).

Pomace—the substance remaining after the juice has been extracted from apples, grapes, or whatever; often used as animal food.

Pony—half a jigger; three quarters of a shot, an ounce.

Pricked—wine that has turned to vinegar.

Shive—a circular wooden plug that is hammered into a hole in a cask after it has been filled.

Sling—synonym for cocktail, as in Singapore Sling.

Soda back—current bar talk for soda on the side.

Tastevin —the small silver saucer that is used for wine tasting; often hung around the neck of a wine steward as a symbol of authority.

V.S.O.—initialism associated with cognac for Very Special Old.

Worm—the business end of a corkscrew.

Worn—term for wine that has been too long in the bottle, or spirits too long in the cask.

"When men drink, then they are rich and successful and win lawsuits and are happy and help friends." So said the Greek philosopher Aristophanes some 2,000 years ago.

—THE MIXOLOGIST—

*Y*ou walk into the bar at Cafe L'Europe or Ta-boo and your favorite behind-the-mahogany person quietly signals you to the end of the bar and mouths, but doesn't say—avoid the character two seats away. He puts your napkin down, smiles, asks how you are and would you like your special? It all takes place in 20 seconds, and that little transaction speaks volumes and makes both parties quite happy. You've just waltzed into the theater to stage center, the director has greeted and given you some subtle wisdom, and the play is proceeding nicely. It's a territorial game at which a professional **bartender** (a female is not referred to as bartendress) can call most of the shots through eye contact and keen instinct.

Observe any of your favorite mixologists and you see how **technique** works; he looks you in the eye to see if you're in shape for booze, seats you where it's safest by napkin placement, sees if your mind is receptive by asking about your special drink, and makes you feel **known** by the whole treatment. Based on how you react, your favorite guy will schmooze with you, leave you alone, ask if you want the TV on, give you something to read, or just avoid you. Whatever your body language and mood, a good bartender will play against it so as to keep the harmony.

And it's not just to receive good **tips**. A typical eight-hour shift in a bad spirited bar (and occasionally, even a Palm Beach bar can be bewitched) is Vietnam all over; the quieter, the more graceful, the quicker a bartender can get a patron in and out via a pleasant experience, the better. The tip is incidental.

Some people hit a bar because of depression, others boredom or a sense of **belonging**, still others just want a good time. Invariably, exchanges between patrons are about money, sex, sports or nostalgia. Some sit for hours at a bar racking up memory points (*"I remember when this was the Parrot Bar just after the war. An old gypsy from West Palm Beach came in every Wednesday night and told fortunes, most of which were right on the money."*) and regaling guests with the history of the city. Others can quote batting averages of ball players for the last 20 years; for every expert on the past, there is a present tense listener. This is especially true about Palm Beach, say most bartenders, where the myth is so great visitors will gobble up any story.

One of the actions a mixologist dislikes most is when people at the bar surreptitiously look at him, thinking he's listening to their **conversation**. *"If asked, I'll participate with patrons talking about whatever. If not, my mind is elsewhere. Even if there's nobody at the bar, I have loads of work and I don't have time to eavesdrop. Besides, what am I going to hear I haven't heard a hundred times? Bar talk is all the same,"* says a long-standing bartender at one of the hotels.

Most of the men and women who serve you drinks have quite a **history,** impressive, usually. Many are college people who have served in the military, taught school, been in acting or broadcasting, have traveled extensively, are well read, and often have a meaningful avocation—following the stock market, competing in marathons, being a craftsman or designer, etc. Although many head out for a few hours of catch-up at a neighborhood bar after work (anywhere from midnight to 2 a.m.), most get their days going early and have accomplished goals by the time the evening shift begins. By comparing notes at these nocturnal get-togethers, bartenders get to know who the town hustlers are, the drug dealers, hookers, drunks and other perverse types. This avoids embarrassment when one of these characters walks into a bar; he's a known entity and is treated accordingly, mostly by a glacial look which tells him this is not the right place to practice any cunning. By dissuading bad news characters, a bar can move along merrily with everybody happy and safe.

Knowing the **tolerance** levels of patrons, and the process by which alcohol is assimilated into the system, also is requisite; each time a drink is consumed, in the mind's eye of a good barman this devastation takes place.

Ethyl alcohol and congeners and fusel oil are systematic killers, and when a drink is knocked down, trillions of alcohol molecules slip into the stomach and irritate the mucous membranes. Then that liquid hits the liver, where an enzyme transforms it into acid aldehyde and moves it into the blood stream. In seconds, arteries pump the stuff into the brain where the booze acts like a wrecking ball. In the cerebellum, the cells that control walking start to fade and alcohol pumps through the body, triggering the release of a stress hormone—epinephrine. Blood vessels dilate, giving off a warm, tingly, momentary feeling; blood pressure rises and heart rate jumps. Since the liver can only metabolize an ounce of liquor per hour, drinkers usually have several hundred milligrams of booze in every 100 milliliters of blood, creating a clear case of intoxication and potential disaster.

Legend has it that some of the most celebrated drinkers of our times like Brendan Behan and W.C. Fields and Bogey and Tracy at the Brown Derby and Cafe Trocadero and Mogambo always had several drinks going at one time; bartenders were instructed to keep at least one glass filled with a double so that the action wouldn't get cyclothymic. Heavy drinkers usually have a buddy with them, not to wave off their libation, but to steer them home or to a safe harbor. Most bartenders are cautious about serving excess amounts of booze to patrons, and turning down a W.C. Fields or equivalent requires the utmost diplomacy or cleverly diluted drinks.

Good bartenders, especially at places designed for travelers, are also **Chamber of Commerce** stringers advising guests on the best restaurants, theater, sightseeing, museums and Island attractions. Although this can set up a negative situation (if a guests does not like one of the recom-

mended restaurants, for example), most people are gracious enough to forgo comment and appreciate the effort. For the most part, bartenders refuse to direct people to illicit activities knowing that (1) it's not good business and (2) the arm of the law reaches far—grabbing anyone "party" to illegality.

In Palm Beach, the **biggest question** bartenders get—where are the moneyed people? Where are all these rich old guys I hear about? And, of course, the answer is—in places you'll never even know about, private clubs, private parties, private yachts, private mansions. The party line revolves around the word **private** which just happens to be the truth.

Cocktails have been around since the 18th century when hard-up tavern drinkers paid a pence to drink the leftovers from rum, wines, whiskies and ales—all mixed together with a cock feather as a swizzle stick. They enjoyed their mixtures and soon began asking for special leftovers mixed with other leftovers and from that sprang a series of drinks called cocktails. The most distinguished of old American drinks is the **Sazerac** (New Orleans, about 1800), developed by a Creole druggist who added bitters—a concoction of his own—to a French brandy called Sazerac, all of it as a medicinal.

Prohibition actually kicked off the cocktail spree in America; during the 1920-33 period, booze had to be smuggled into the country and modified, usually in a bathtub, to create something tasty. Gin, raw corn whiskey, smoke-flavored alcohol and beer became the rage of a whole generation, and loosened up the American psyche just in time for a depression and a world war. Through it all there were smiles-all-around, and an increasing level of sophistication in the raw product, the esoteric of making new and fancy drinks, and the professionalism of bartenders in the presentation.

—PALM BEACH COCKTAILESE—

*S*miling faces everywhere, beauty, brains, bosoms, some backbiting, some camaraderie, a great many hidden agendas, and, in some cosmic way, a touch of every part of the world at large.

The cocktail party. Palm Beach.

Listen.

*"She was **scrub-poor** when she came to town. He took her in and used Ivory."*

*"I envy him. He was bred, as they say of horses, in the **purple**; his money goes back to the 18th century, old money, ancient money, the best kind, the least destructive of all."*

*"He's like Khashoggi—they call him **'papa-gateau'** for the sugar daddy."*

*"God love you for a **liar**."*

*"He's a flake. He says his family is in **iron and steel**. He probably means his father steals and his mother irons."*

*"He thinks it's so cool to say—when you get on the **wrong train**, every stop is the wrong stop."*

*"It's likely that at death his **will**, will be—I have nothing. I owe a great deal. The rest I leave to the poor."*

"I've noticed there is nothing quite like the look of affectionate **contempt** the old and wise have for the young and foolish."

"She's one of those women who want to leave a little piece of the **hook** in your mouth, even after she's tossed you back in."

"They're a marked couple—if they didn't have any **bad luck**, they'd have no luck at all."

"Very few people ever really are **alive** and those who are, never die, no matter if they are gone."

"It's a wonderful thing to reach the **irresponsible** age of 70, only it comes too late in life."

"Darling, what's it like not to **matter** anymore?"

"He's had a few drinks. Now he'll go into his 'thanks for the mammaries' **routine**."

"She is one of those **rare women** who is not necessarily improved by jewelry."

"Discarded **mistresses** are very dangerous."

"Basically, he's a good man, but he's **unclubbable**."

"Oh, you don't know me. I'm just the '**dress extra**' here tonight. I'm the odd and extra man."

"Sorry, but you were **born wrong**, darling."

"Sweetheart, if you don't know your **jewels**, know your jeweler."

"We all have about two billion **heartbeats** in a lifetime; I've used up thousands of them just looking at you."

"He's not really boring, he's a kind of brilliant **raconteur** whose maniacal energy makes you numb and restless."

"She makes kind of a cheap **chic** presentation; has lovely little pecs."

"She is one absolute **winner**, upper crust all the way, has summit standards and a monopoly on taste."

"He was so damn **obsequious**, he was panting after her—she didn't return the panting but was very polite and primly sweet which made him pant all the more."

"Holly Golightly called them the 'mean reds.' **Hyper-anxiety**. She is loaded with it."

"Remember, my lovely, a **shark** is the only animal that never sleeps."

"Oh hell, she's so **Waspy**, she wears tweed brassieres."

"She has flawless **skin**; if her mind had been the equal of her skin, she would have been Einstein."

"He looks like he had a difficult **birth**."

"All she **wants** is all you got."

"Women are always dying to **forgive** you, you don't even need to apologize. Just give them any kind of opportunity to forgive you and the next thing is you'll be in bed together."

"I'd hate to end up with my immediate **peers** as my sole companions."

*"Listen love, if we **wait** all that happens is that we'll get older."*

*"I wasn't kissing her. I was **whispering** in her mouth."*

*"She's a darling, but she **spends** with both hands."*

*"He's one man in a **million**—a stud with brains."*

*"He's one of **those men** who is always doing the obligatory tap dance, always on the verge of another big deal, always about to ride high again, and always failing."*

*"I don't give a tiny **burp** what you think ducky."*

*"It's rough **waiting around** for all the in-between stuff when you know what's going to happen in the end."*

*"I've found out that if you have an **irrestible** urge to drag a person's name into every conversation for no good reason, you have a heavy love/hate going."*

*"Baby, you're a born **outsider**."*

*"She invariably wears a **diamond** big enough to receive cable TV."*

*"It's too bad—he married a blond, but he was looking for a **bluebird**."*

*"He's unbelievably **crude**—sniffing around like a truffle hound."*

*"She's very good at parties; she gets all **tarted up** and lets loose."*

*"He's one of those men who needs to **bed down** a woman to forget her; until he's done it, the power is all hers."*

*"Now after lots of practice, I believe—a **successful marriage** requires falling in love many times, always with the same person."*

*"I've been to parties where a Dalmatian can wolf down $200 of caviar and nobody will even notice. They're all too busy wishing they were young enough and beautiful enough and uninhibited enough to **skinny-dip**."*

*"Men always want women to **save** them from what they truly want to be."*

*"As a bosom tilter she's **world-class**, a master of the taunt."*

*"He's such a **loser**. . . he belongs in a runt museum. He swaggers into a room on his knees."*

*"He's always on the **grape**, can't stay off the jug."*

*"He's a baby looking for a **nipple**, so straight he could be a page out of the Old Testament."*

*"When she's not drinking, she's **lushing**."*

*"She's like the Christian trying to negotiate with a hungry **lion**."*

*"His only show of **erudition** is to reflect on Little Orphan Annie."*

*"His life is beating the other guy to the **buck**; and he has the force of a tidal wave about it."*

*"He pledges allegiance to the **fag**."*

*"He's a horizontal man, a cut rate **Rubirosa**—I'm a vertical woman."*

*"She's become a CAVE Jap = a proper Lady Brahmin who married a Jew and has become a **Princess**."*

227

*"She's being used as a **carrot**, social bait."*

*"His dream is to have a **position** named after him."*

*"She has a smile your dentist sees in his **dreams**."*

"He's got relatively few barnacles."

*"Dating him is like being handed the keys to a Rolls-Royce with **engine trouble**."*

*"She real **ready-to-wear**—all American face, clean style, casual."*

*"She's social **larva**—not quite a moth, certainly not a butterfly."*

*"She's one long running essay on elegant **bitchery**."*

*"She's got a wonderful **Waspiness** about her, but her Beverly Hills bumpers don't figure."*

*"She's one of those hi-heeled, hi-glam gals with **clankers** (big balls)."*

*"She's always so **cheerful**—"Mom, I got the part—something must be wrong."*

*"He has 21 personalities—only **one** is okay."*

*"She's class, has Ivy League pelt, a fine **kitten**."*

*"She has a world-class **keister** and a faux cutesy smile."*

*"She's a **fundie** (trust fund dollie); he's a **frivvie** (gold digger who pursues frivolous lawsuits)."*

*"When she walks, she makes sexy thigh **music**."*

*"She could be a thoroughbred, but doesn't want to be—won't **stoop** that low."*

*"She's queen of the **could-bes**, a real pumpkin butt."*

*"He's a true **lecher**—active, reactive, proactive, radioactive. He's also equal opportunity."*

*"She's like a **Serb**—forever at war with someone; it doesn't matter who, she likes the hostilities."*

*"He's got one of those deep, sexy voices that comes from his **scrotum**."*

*"She claims to be a journalist, but she doesn't write—she **cribs**."*

*"Most of the people here are studies in **taxidermy**."*

*"A **hard** man is good to find."*

*"His problem—he won't **genuflect** to anyone; he's perfect at the one-eyebrow lift."*

*"I got an invitation the other day that said—**don't dress**."*

*"Her voice is like an assault **weapon**."*

*"He just never came down out of the **trees**."*

*"She's an overnight **success**—a year ago she was pushing a cart down a TWA aisle, now she's living in a Park Avenue penthouse."*

*"She's either batting eyelashes or waving at Ben Franklin—she **gets** her way."*

*"He's smooth—could tap **dance** on a cream puff and not leave a footprint."*

*"He's a **leaf** that blows from one gutter to the next."*
*"She breathes **ambition** as if it were oxygen."*
*"He's very artful about **gaslighting**—you feel like you're the one going crazy."*
*"She's all **heir**—he's all air."*
*"She loves to push out her **rump** like someone about to play a croquet shot."*
*"He's one of those permanently **temporary** people."*
*"She's a unique combo—**buns and brains**."*
*"She's a woman who can **siphon** oxygen from male lungs."*
*"This room could be a **silicon** repository; every other woman is bumpered up."*
*"He's an **heir**, a puny caboose hitched to a long train."*
*"She's loaded with **spezzatura**—serenity of grace, to the manner born."*
*"Her social **strategy** could outdo the joint chiefs of staff."*
*"Her voice is full of **freon**—just another nouveau riche culture vulture."*
*"His **age**—somewhere between 40 and hell."*
*"She's a **disgusto bimby**; perfumes her knees in anticipation."*

Ah, yes, the **cocktail party**, with talk about life's song and dance, of soul-searching and impermeability, of divorce, abandonment, *ennui* filled with superficial bravado, the unacceptable and the unobtainable, uprootings, coups, desperate renewals, predictions, what will start and what will last and what will end, work and love, hidden forces unmasked, weaknesses discovered, the idle imagining of unreachable pleasures and the fact that there's no paying life in advance for what it will do for you, because generally, it won't do anything for you at all.

Finally, the **last** pronouncement: *"In life, the little roads that lead people up to and then away from one another, are the most maze-like of all."*

Verbal interplay is the key when one is going for the brass ring at a gathering, but so, too, are the PLOYS. Before the party, sagacious pyramid-climbers will check their inventory of DOs and DON'Ts; a whole shopping list of etiquette for a Palm Beach gala (ball, affair) which requires contemplation and a certain amount of staging, before the dramatist in a person emerges.

The social dance begins with **making an entrance**, at which time it's vital to move purposefully enough to be seen and photographed without appearing to have engineered mobility; then comes the verbal interplay at the **cocktail hour**, at which time much of the etiquette of **greeting** comes into play; as the trumpets blare, the rigor of **being seated** is acted out, as is subsequent movement during the actual process of **wining and dining**, sharing intimate thoughts with those seated to the right and left, and whatever flirtation is in order with those a bit distant, as well as any power playing with eyeballs and occasional snippets of conversation with the megamen at the table. It's all very stimulating and requires constant attention.

Facing the **music and dancing** is a vital segment of the evening— many a contract is inspired by the social dance and many an alliance is set up while moving to the sounds of **Neal Smith** or **Mike Carney**. At some point, testimonials, official pronouncements, tributes et al will occupy anywhere from five to 50 minutes, and it's important to be fully vertical during these dues-paying times. Occasionally something of real interest is said at toastmastering time, but basically much of the fluff of the event is acted out to keep principals and sponsors happy.

Once the main course is finito, **table-hopping** becomes *de rigueur*; again, many an active hopper has embellished his standing on the social pyramid, by judicious and well-timed drop-ins at the table of one of the high and mighty. The Anointed Ones don't have much recourse except to respond civilly to an approach from a wannabe. So a person with *hubris* can usually wedge a door open during the table-hopping sequence, and probably find some nuggets of info that can be parlayed favorably at a later date.

Throughout each stage of the party behavior, a sage climber choreographs movement, moods, embraces, strokes and **kisses** (hug, kiss, thrown kiss, air kiss, smile, nod, bow, curtsy); a show of sincerity is important but not to such a degree that lipstick gets smudged or guys walk off with tattoos on cheeks.

The final act, that of **egress,** calls for a stiff upper lip and the projection of an attitude that it was a great evening, we all served the cause well, and we look forward to a reprise. Sneaking out is *declasse*, and the exit should be as civil and comprehensive as the entrance. Brains may be a bit marbleized by 11 p.m. and the joys of life a bit diminished after having heard bizarre tales of family woe from dinner partners, but it's up, up and away. With aplomb.

Don't forget the bag of **party goods**—that small container with a great retail name emblazoned thereon is a payoff for rapt attention and toleration. It should be picked up casually, not examined (same for table gifts—let others open what the fairy godmother hath bestowed) and tucked underarm. Then erectly march from the ballroom, head high, smiles-all-around, another great night in the 30,000 evenings you spend on the **Hot Planet Earth**.

—COCKTAIL CHEER—

*C*ocktails and gimmick drinks come and go, and each year aggressive liquor marketers induce further consumption with novelty spirits, new recipes and socially "in" concoctions. But the favorites remain through the years and have long been sources of refreshment for Palm Beachers in these creations:

Brandy Alexander: The perfect cocktail for an afternoon rendez-vous—cognac and dark creme de cacao with some heavy creme. Always a favorite at The Colony.

Rob Roy: Scotch and sweet vermouth, perfect for the serious drinker. Goes down so easily at The Everglades.

Sidecar: Brandy or armagnac, Triple-Sec and lemon juice; created by a WWI officer who traveled to his favorite Paris bistro in the sidecar of his motorcycle. A legendary drink at Ta-boo for decades.

Stinger: An ounce and a half of any spirit (usually brandy) and either white creme de menthe or peppermint schnapps served on the rocks, in an old-fashioned glass. Popular at Galaxy Grille.

Cuba Libre: The El Morocco Special in NYC; a hit at Chuck & Harold's in Palm Beach. Coke and Bacardi (or Mount Gay) Rum. Hemingway liked the drink in his Havana days; Castro tried to ban it.

Old-fashioned: The ultimate whiskey cocktail; sugar cube, good whiskey, dash of bitters, soda and lemon peel. Then and now, a favorite at 264.

Martini: Gin or vodka with a touch of vermouth, either up or on the rocks. The gentleman's libation. Veddy civilized if done expertly. Perfect at the Palm Beach Tavern.

Incidentally, recent surveys have indicated that between the ages of 18-24, men like rum and Coke, women prefer Screwdrivers; between ages 25-44, men like gin and tonic, women Margaritas; from ages 45-54, it's martinis for the guys, Bloody Marys for the ladies. Some surveys show up to 80 percent of people order a cocktail before dinner (when eating out).

—BLISSFUL BREWS—

Beer dates back more than 8,000 years; it was a favorite of the Babylonians, Greeks, Chinese and Romans. Reputedly, it was even on Noah's Ark. The Pilgrims brought it to the USA; it was brewed by the English Colonists and the Dutch at New Amsterdam. William Penn was one of the early brewers in his Quaker settlement in Pennsylvania; Samuel Adams, George Washington and Thomas Jefferson were also pioneers in the beer business. Today, 500 brands of beer are available in this country; about half of them are imported. Here's how they rank with

231

Palm Beachers: the favorite domestic beers are **Budweiser, Miller Lite, Bud Lite, Coors Light, Busch, Miller High Life** and **Michelob**; tops among imports are Heineken (Netherlands), Corona (Mexico), Molson (Canada), Beck's (West Germany), Labatt (Canada) and Amstel Light (Netherlands). Non-alcoholic favorite beers are Moussey, O'Doul's and Sharps. For the record, Americans quaffed 192 million barrels of beer last year; on a per capita basis, that's about three-quarters of a barrel per person!

—RAVE RESTAURANTS—

*B*y the time a person reaches 70, he or she will have spent more than **126,700 hours eating**; it's a very pleasureable pastime, one that abounds on our Island. Every restaurant in Town is a winner in its own way; each has a defined image and caters to a specific market. Some atmospheres are light and informal, others traditional and quite formal. Some restaurants have extensive menus, others offer a few choice items. Yet, all provide real value and rank among the better eateries in the country. As of this writing, here's the line-up (B-Breakfast, L-Lunch, D-Dinner, B-Brunch):

AMICI RISTORANTE, 288 S. County Rd. (832-0201). Authentic Italian dishes, European charm, innovative daily specials. Sensible prices. L, D.

ACQUARIO RISTORANTE, 150 Worth Ave. (655-9999). Superb, Italian dishes served with sophistication in an extravagant atmosphere; mega-sized aquarium behind a handsome bar presents lovely tropical fish. All in all, a winner! Pricey. L, D.

AMBASSADOR GRILL, 2730 S. Ocean Blvd. (582-2511). Continental and mediterranean cuisine in ocean-view garden-like setting. Worth a trip, valet parking. A bit pricey. L, D, B.

BICE, 313-1/2 Worth Ave. (835-1600). A bravura eatery with new location, ambiance and quality all the way. Fresh fish, veal, steaks, scampi, people-watching, professional service—it's all there. Slightly on the costly side and above; casual attire. Very classy Italian. L, D.

BRAZILIAN COURT HOTEL, 301 Australian Ave. (655-7740). A landmark hotel, chic and versatile. Varied dining catering to every taste-bud. An authentic step back in time with today's panache. Flairish, pricey, informal enough. B, L, D, B.

THE BREAKERS, 1 S. County Rd. (655-6611). An international favorite, with menus for everybody. Innovative American cuisine served in a number of dining areas, from poolside to the fairways to elegant dinner/dancing. Bring a credit card and your semi-formal self. Classics: Circle and Florentine Dining Rooms, Flagler's Steakhouse, Seafood Bar, Henry's Place and Terrace Grill, The Pasta House. B, L, D, B.

CAFE CASABLANCA, 101 N. County Rd. (655-1115). Original American cuisine, pizza, shrimp and scallop cakes, a little of everything. No Bogie, but cool, slightly pricey. L, D.

CAFE CELLINI, 2505 S. Ocean Blvd. (588-1871). Excellent Northern Italian cuisine, pasta, fish and house specialities. Moderate price, casual attire. L, D.

CAFE L'EUROPE, 331 S. County Rd. (655-4020). Unique Continental-styled "in" place; a magnet for the elite; superb cuisine and impeccable service. Award winning in every way; elegant champagne/caviar bar and flowery decor. Expensive, but worth it. Proper attire. L, D.

CHARLEY'S CRAB, 456 S. Ocean Blvd. (659-1500). Only waterfront restaurant in town; specializes in seafood with Cajun and Mesquite selections. Sunday Brunch. A must in Palm Beach; see, be seen, enjoy, enjoy; charming and romantic. Moderate price; informal. L, D, B.

THE CHESTERFIELD HOTEL, 363 Cocoanut Row (659-5800). Traditional English and European menu; colorful "Leopard" lounge, music, generous cocktails. Moderate price, proper attire. B, L, D, B.

CHEZ JEAN-PIERRE, 132 N. County Rd. (833-1171). True French Bistro that is warm, friendly and relaxing. Homemade foie gras, fresh Dover Sole, baked snapper and homemade bread. Casual, elegant. Moderately priced. L, D.

CHUCK & HAROLD'S, 206 Royal Poinciana Way (659-1440). Offers outdoor cafe or garden room and dozens of specially prepared delicacies from seafood to pasta to grilled steaks. Superb bar for meeting/greeting; music for dancing. In the low-pricey range and casual. B, L, D.

THE COLONY HOTEL, 155 Hammon Ave. (655-5430). Stylish hotel setting for energetic people. Great service, a varied menu, and glamorous personalities. Lively bar activity and dancing. On the expensive side; proper attire. B, L, D, B.

CUCINA DELL 'ARTE, 257 Royal Poinciana Way (655-0770). Northern Italian with all the delicious favorites. Both classic and new specialties. Informal, moderately high. L, D.

DEMPSEY'S, Royal Poinciana Plaza, 50 Cocoanut Row (835-0400). Fabled English pub serving all the basics—fish, chicken, prime ribs, steaks and veal. Animated crowd, fun seekers, good age mix. Great for watching sports on TV. Middle-of-the-road prices and dress code. Recently served its "Millionth" meal. L, D, B.

ECHO, 230 Sunrise Ave., (802-4222). Offers diverse and distinctive foods of Asia in a stylish atmosphere; dishes from China, Thailand, Japan and Vietnam are specialties. Chefs are in full view at a theater-style sushi bar. Full service bar and private dining room. Reasonable. L, D.

FOUR SEASONS RESORT, 2800 S. Ocean Blvd. (582-2800). Imaginative Gold Coast cuisine at The Restaurant or The Bistro; magnificent surroundings, meticulous service. Slightly costly, but worth it. Dressy. Superb for B, L, D, B

GALAXY GRILLE, 350 S. County Rd. (833-9909). Spacious new format for fine Continental dining; great bar and views. Somewhat costly. L, D.

GREEN'S PHARMACY, 151 N. County Rd. (832-4443). A drop-in spot for most Palm Beachers; lively with chatter, personalities, auditioning, great inexpensive snacks. Very casual. B, L.

HAMBURGER HEAVEN, 314 S. County Rd. (655-5277). Excellent light menu—hamburgers, salads, special dinners. Versatile, airy, fast-paced. Makes desserts on premise. A perfect quick-take meal. Casual and reasonable (cash only). B, L, D.

HEART OF PALM BEACH HOTEL, 160 Royal Palm Way (655-5600). Intimate dining in the Pleasant Peasant; varied menu; also sunny atmosphere for snacks. A favorite for the quiet crowd. Inexpensive, informal. B, L, D.

JANEIRO, 191 Bradley Place (659-5223). American cuisine served in the tropics of Brazil. Extensive wine cellar. Original, provocative menu with many specials. Pricey. D.

JO'S, 139 N. County Rd. (659-6776). Family-operated eatery, superior in most ways. Features American Nouvelle cuisine and a wide range of Continental dishes. Expensive and semi-casual. L, D.

LUCIO'S, 375 S. County Rd. (655-6559). Italian cuisine in a great atmosphere, with indoor and outdoor eating. People-watcher hangout, superb bar. Reasonable. L, D.

MAXIM'S DE PARIS, 410 S. County Rd. (659-4349). Continental cuisine served in an intimate dining room with Art Deco bar. Gourmet take out available. Pricey. L, D.

PALM BEACH TAVERN, 251 Royal Poinciana Way (835-0385). Classic tavern ambiance with American/Continental cuisine; special cottage menu and entertainment. Superb-hangout for the in crowd. reasonable. L, D.

PALM BEACH GRILL, 336 Poinciana Way (835-1077). Casual atmosphere, open kitchen serving American cuisine. Rotisserie chicken, prime ribs and grilled fish. Moderate. D.

THE PASTA HOUSE, 45 Cocoanut Row (659-8488). Wide variety of pasta dishes with southern Italian specialties. Complimentary sampler-appetizer. reasonable. D.

PALM BEACH HILTON HOTEL, 2842 S. Ocean Blvd. (586-6542). Two oceanfront dining experiences—Sandcastle Dining Room and Beach Club Bar. Both praiseworthy with varied menus and innovative cocktails. From Continental to Campy. Up-and-down prices; same for dress code. B, L, D, B.

PLAZA INN, 215 Brazilian Ave. (832-8666). Superb cocktails and light snacks at the Stray Fox Pub. Moderate, casual. L, D.

RENATO'S, 87 Via Mizner (655-9745). Country-French environment, very Continental with Italian accent. Elegant, in-and-outdoor dining; great for seafood, pasta, veal. A superb experience, relaxing and socially-right. On the high $ side, semi-formal. L, D.

THE RITZ-CARLTON, 100 S. Ocean Blvd., Manalapan (540-4833). Stunning hotel with great eateries—Grill Room, The Restaurant and 100 South Ocean. Spectacular views and upscale menu. Pricey. L, D, B.

TA-BOO, 221 Worth Ave. (835-3500). Imaginative and contemporary cuisine. Superb selection, cocktails galore, inviting atmosphere. Dancing, chumming, mixing. A legend. Moderate, informal. L, D.

TESTA'S, 221 Royal Poinciana Way (832-0992). Palm Beach's oldest eatery. Sidewalk seating great for people watching. Popular breakfast spot, known for fresh Maine blueberry pancakes and strawberry pie. Continental and Italian dishes. Moderately priced, casual attire. B, L, D.

TOWERS RESTAURANT, 44 Cocoanut Row (659-3241). Continental cuisine, spacious, great Florida pompano. Pricey. L, D.

251 SUNRISE, 251 Sunrise (820-9777). American bistro fare with upscale bar menu. Late night spot for lively crowd. Costly. D.

TOOJAY'S, 313 Royal Poinciana Way (659-7232). Only true deli in Palm Beach. Eat-in or take-out. Huge omelets, French toast, tasty salads, lox and bagels, stir-fries and homemade breads. Killer cake truly kills. Very casual attire, reasonably priced. B, L, D.

264 THE GRILL, 264 S. County Rd. (833-3591). Festive hangout for all-age crowd; serves up tasty seafood; excellent steaks, sinful pies. Lots of spirit and flavor; mixed-but-mostly-casual dress. Cost on the moderate side. L, D.

(**Toojay's** is the largest restaurant group in the area with one facility on the Island; it employs some 464 people, has sales of $23 million and has a total of 11 eateries from Boca Raton to Orlando with six in Palm Beach County. In Palm Beach proper, The Breakers has sales of about $20 million from its food/beverage operation—its total sales are about $110 million, followed by Cafe L'Europe at $6 million and Ta-boo at $5 million.)

—MORSELS & MONUMENTS—

*T*he **oldest** restaurant in Town is **Testa's**, which recently celebrated its 78th season as a fixture in Palm Beach; it opened in 1921 as a 13-seat soda fountain in the Old Garden Theater and moved to its Royal Poinciana Way location in 1946. During season it serves breakfast, lunch and dinner and usually has a waiting line. Its strawberry pie and Italian dishes are Island favorites. The Testa family also owns a restaurant in Bar Harbor, Maine, which operates in the summer months. In our Town, Testa's is open year-round.

The **most honored** restaurant is **Cafe L'Europe** (331 S. County Road), a consistent winner of culinary awards; in recent years the elegant cafe has received the *Mobil Travel Guide* Four-Star Award, the Travel Holiday Award, the Golden Spoon, the Critics Award, the Readers Choice Award from *South Florida Magazine*, a Four-Star rating from *The Palm Beach Post* and the *Miami Herald*. **Norbert and Lydia Goldner**, owners of Cafe L'Europe, are known for their innovative food presentations, outstanding service and expert taste in giving customers a memorable dining experience. As stated in the *Mobil Travel Guide*, Cafe L'Europe is worthy of a Four-Star Award because of its "consistent commitment to excellence." The restaurant was recently inducted into the "Fine Dining Hall of Fame."

The Town's most **enduring** restaurant is **Ta-boo** (221 Worth Avenue), nestled between real estate firms and art galleries. It opened in 1941 and during its long and colorful history was considered by many to be one of the three major bars in the world (along with Harry's American Bar in Paris and "21" in Manhattan) catering to the likes of the Duke and Duchess of Windsor, Frank Sinatra, Peter Lawford, the Kennedy clan, Gary Cooper and Richard Nixon. Legend has it that during World War II, several German U-Boat officers snuck ashore and enjoyed a few pops at Ta-boo before heading back to their submarine and getting on with the dreary business of sinking American ships. The vicissitudes of life caused Ta-boo to shutter in 1987, thus ending one of the greatest nightlife love affairs of our times. The restaurant was re-opened in 1990 and still commands a prime audience of Townies, auditioners and social spinners.

It is owned by **Nancy Simmons** and **Franklyn deMarco** and was recently profiled in the book—*"The Season—Inside Palm Beach and America's Richest Society"* by **Ronald Kessler.**

Ta-boo is also reputedly the home of the **Bloody Mary**. In the mid-40s, one of the restaurant's regulars was Barbara Hutton, heiress to the Woolworth five-and-dime store fortune. One morning she dropped by Ta-boo looking pale and disoriented after a tough night on the Town. She asked the bartender to concoct something to relieve her headache and soften the blow of reality on a bright morning. He quickly threw some tomato juice in with vodka and sauces and as legend has it—the Bloody Mary was born. The formidable heiress spread the gospel instantly and Ta-boo became the locus for a drink that relieved hangovers while making music for the mind.

Islanders can have a "power breakfast" at **Green's Pharmacy** on North County Road, the morning *locus* for towntalk. Prior evening peccadillos, personal landscaping, hyperactive egos and lots of cogitation are manifest over ham and eggs and cups of coffee. Chauffeurs, weary socialites, executive types, laborers and public servants all come together for an exciting 30 minutes of news-and-views about our Island. For most, it's a rewarding A.M. ritual. Yet, as always, change is setting in; Green's has shared some of its panache. Many of the talented tonsils that performed the wake-up routines are now at Chuck & Harold's, the Brazilian Court and Testa's; and the dialogue is increasingly about international affairs, LBO's and the dreary business of making more and more money. Green's recently expanded their facilities to include an area for seven more tables or 28 more seats; the extra space provides storage area for walkers and wheelchairs for breakfast and luncheon patrons. Green's offers dinner until 7:30 p.m.

—KING CAVIAR—

*I*sland regulars seek out pleasure, wherever it is. They especially like the food of Kings, Czars, the rich and famous— **Caviar**. Expensive as it may be, with a fine ice-cold vodka, Caviar can produce the ultimate exhileration, a connoisseur's dream come true.

Townies can get their share of eggs from the Caspian Sea at **Maxim's, Cafe L'Europe, The Breakers (Florentine Room)** and the **Grill Room** at the **Ritz-Carlton**. Cafe L'Europe has the widest assortment with five varieties from salmon caviar at about $14.50 per one-ounce serving to beluga malossol at $59 per serving. A sampling of five caviars (total 2 ounces) at $79 is the beginners choice; a cache of 35 vodkas with Absolut, Finlandia and Stolichnaya encased in ice, help a novice enjoy the impact of these delicassies. **Maxim's** has an assortment of caviars—beluga, osetra and sevruga—to please most palates at reasonable prices.

(Note: high prices for caviar are largely due to scarcity. Caviar comes from 29 species of very slow-breeding sturgeon; beluga, for example,does not produce eggs until it is 18 years old, osetra produces at age 12, and sevruga at age eight. Caviar is harvested on ships where the sturgeon is netted, split open and the eggs sifted, washed in cold water and salted. Caviar is then packed in large cans and sent to importers all over the world, who repackage it to market in retail outlets.)

In the Palm Beaches, caviar can be purchased retail at Publix, Herbert's Lafayette Market, Maxim's, and C'est Si Bon Gourmet Foods.

—DINING ALFRESCO—

These restaurants offer some type of "outside dining" (open air, under assorted umbrellas or awnings):

BICE: in Via Bice under umbrellaed tables.

BRAZILIAN COURT HOTEL: Courtyard dining and drinking under individually covered tables.

THE BREAKERS: Poolside wining and dining at the Beach Club.
THE CHESTERFIELD HOTEL: Poolside and courtyard tables for wining and dining.
CHUCK & HAROLD'S: Covered sidewalk cafe outside, retractable roof inside.
THE COLONY HOTEL: Poolside tables.
CUCINA: Street tables and viewing.
LUCIO'S: Streetside gazing, drinking, dining.
FOUR SEASONS RESORT: Poolside potables and edibles.
PALM BEACH HILTON HOTEL: Outside tables overlooking ocean for eating and drinking.
RENATO'S: Tables under umbrellas in via.
TA-BOO: Offers windows/doors opening on Worth Avenue.
TESTA'S: Covered sidewalk cafe and retractable roof in garden room.

Most restaurants will accommodate take-out orders but those **specializing** in take-out include: **Herbert's Lafayette Market, Piccolo Mondo, Sprinkles** and **C'est Si Bon.**

—DANCING IN THE DARK—

*O*ur Town has a goodly number of dance places and parlors, and offers a danceophile a range of choice: **The Brazilian Court**; **The Breakers** (many varied options); **Chuck & Harold's**; **The Colony** (the legendary); **Palm Beach Hilton** (overlooking the ocean); **Ta-boo**; **251** (disco, late hours); **Four Seasons Resort; Janeiro;** and **The Chesterfield**.

—HANGOUTS—

Palm Beachers pursue their alliances with wholehearted, shockproof, unihibited enthusiasm, always seeking more and greater financial and social ascendancy, while building **comradeships** with their cronies and special interests. Here's where the troops cluster:

Pols: Palm Beach Tavern, Dempsey's, Cafe L'Europe
Singles: Ta-boo, Galaxy, Leopard Lounge (Chesterfield), Chuck & Harold's
Gourmets: Chez Jean-Pierre, Cafe L'Europe, The Restaurant (Four Seasons)
Socialites: Cafe L'Europe, Renato's, Brazilian Court, Ritz-Carlton
VIPs: Breakers, Bice, Cafe L'Europe, Brazilian Court, Maxim's
Stock Traders: Palm Beach Tavern, 264, Amici, Brazilian Court
Performers: Amici, Ta-boo, Janeiro, Lucio's, Ritz-Carlton, 251
Models: Cafe L'Europe, Galaxy, Acquario, Ta-boo, 251
Media: Dempsey's, Palm Beach Tavern, Amici

Jocks: Amici, Galaxy, Ta-boo, Dempsey's, Palm Beach Tavern plus the private clubs (golf, tennis, croquet)
Artists: Cucina dell 'Arte, Acquario, Casablanca
Internationalists: Chez Jean-Pierre, Bice, Maxim's
Adventurers: Ta-boo, The Colony, Bice, Charley's Crab, Palm Beach Grill

—CLUBS & SNUBS—

*T*hese are the original social clubs in Town:

The Everglades: Opened in 1919 with Paris Singer as owner; he became a social dictator as his club became the focal point of the Town. He issued club memberships for one-year periods; members were invited back depending on their friendship with Singer. He refused to admit anyone connected with a trade or commercial business.

Bradley Beach Club: Opened in 1910, it became famous for its gambling as well as its excellent food and impeccable service. People denied membership were Florida residents, those under 25 and those who became intoxicated. No one belonged at Bradley's if they ever asked about "price."

The Bath & Tennis Club: Opened in 1926 under the leadership of Edward F. Hutton and A.J. Drexel Biddle, who decided there was a need for another club on the Island. Founders memberships were sold at $10,000 each and as much as $250,000 had to be returned when memberships were filled.

The Sailfish Club: Originally founded in 1910 and first registered in Lloyd's Registry of Yachts in 1914 for the purpose of renewing the sport of angling for sailfish and other game fish. The original clubrooms were located at The Breakers Casino, then moved to Whitehall and finally (in 1928) to their permanent location on North Lake Way. The Sailfish Club became popular for its informality.

Club de Montmartre: Opened in the 1920s and became the Embassy Club; it was built by Colonel Bradley and was popular for its late night suppers and dancing.

Oasis Club: Opened in the 1920s; was an athletic club specializing in boxing with men only until 1928 when females were allowed (after 4:30 p.m.).

The Patio: A restaurant that operated as a club (on N. County Rd. and Sunrise Ave.); very popular for lunch and dinner. The finest chefs were brought to Palm Beach for the season. The Patio was known for its retractable roof that rolled back to expose tropical skies. Many famous bands played at the Patio; among them Meyer Davis and featured entertainers such as Joe E. Lewis and Sophie Tucker.

Between 1941 and the mid-50s, the Patio was the Island's most famous nightclub; it introduced a sliding roof that was copied all over the world. Palm Beachers in that era either began or ended their evening with popular tunes of the day like *"Florida, the Moon and You"* at the Patio; one could dance to top musicians, play backgammon or gin rummy, or dine on internationally famous cuisine. The demise of the Patio as a society watering hole began in the 50s when The Everglades Club introduced continuous dancing with two orchestras. The price for an evening of dancing at the Everglades (assuming membership dues were up to date) was less than what one had to tip the maitre d' at the Patio. Even then, the Old Guard wanted to get its "money's worth."

The **top private dinner clubs** in Town as we enter the 2000s:

Club Colette: In the late 1940s, a World War II French Resistance fighter emigrated to Palm Beach and set up a beauty salon at 211 Peruvian Avenue; her name, Colette Henry. Because of her international manner and expertise at turning lovely older dowagers into highly attractive beauties, the salon became a major social center as well as headquarters for the well-groomed set. Mary Duncan Sanford, then queen of Palm Beach society, spread the word of Colette's charm and soon the likes of Wallis Simpson, Jackie Kennedy, the Duchess of Windsor, Barbara Hutton, Marjorie Merriweather Post, Peggy Bancroft and Betty McMahon were regulars, each bringing their friends. Success is heady, and in the early 1960s, Colette was persuaded to buy the building next door and establish it as a world-class supper club. It immediately became top drawer, top ticket in the area.

The club flourished through the 1970s, and in 1980 Dr. Aldo Gucci, a Palm Beach champion, home owner and king of the far-flung Gucci Boutique empire, bought Club Colette; he fine tuned it, and ran it for a few years before returning to Italy to face tax evasion charges in 1986. He first leased, then sold the club to a young executive, **Dan Ponton**, and today Club Colette flourishes at an even higher level; it is considered the most elegant watering hole for the *creme-de-la-creme* with an international roster of top names. Initiation fee is $2,500, annual dues $1,000. Mr. Ponton is well-known for his generosity (often allowing charities to use the club for special events) and is considered among the top young professionals in the area. *Fame Magazine* described him as "an indispensable member of Palm Beach society."

Mr. Ponton opened a second Club Colette in Southampton in 1998; it is located on the site of the Old Post House, 136 Main Street, and is the oldest English Colonial building still commercially operated and privately owned in New York State.

Golf courses and private clubs represent a large source of recreation in Palm Beach. Included in this grouping are three 18-hole golf courses, 25 tennis courts, 78 boat slips and 4,730 feet of beach frontage. The very tony private clubs are:

Bath and Tennis Club, 1170 South Ocean Blvd. (10.5 acres)—$35,000 initiation fee, $3,500 annual dues; 750 members. Totally blueblood. Key members: Paul Ilyinsky, Fitz Eugene Dixon, William C. Lickle.

Beach Club, 755 North County Rd. (5.3 acres)—$8,500 initiation fee, $2,400 annual dues; 900 members. Semi-aristocratic. Key members: Curt Gowdy, John Weitz, J. Bradford Greer.

Breakers Beach and Golf Club, 1 South County Rd. (104 acres)—Initiation fee is $40,000; $5,000 dues annually. For the superior masses; golf, tennis, beach, dining, social. Key members are most of the Town's top professionals and their families.

Everglades Club, 356 Worth Ave. (86 acres)—Initiation fees begin at $35,000 (single, family, golf, tennis and/or social memberships), annual dues are $3,100-$4,200 depending on type of membership; 1,100 members. Nobility only. Key members:Byron Ramsing, Lesly Smith, John M. Reynolds, John R. Drexel, William Pannill.

Palm Beach Country Club, 760 North Ocean Blvd. (88 acres)—$100,000 initiation fee, $10,000 annual dues; 350 members. Super selective and pricey. Key members: Max Fisher, Abe Gosman, Bernard Marden.

Sailfish Club, 1338 North Lake Way (1.4 acres)—$10,000 initiation fee, $1,700 annual dues; 550 members. Upper middle-class. Key members: Alex Dreyfoos, Jr., Llwyd Ecclestone, Jr.

Mar-a-Lago Club, 1100 South Ocean Blvd. (16.98 acres)—$75,000 initiation fee; $3,000 annual dues; 500 members. Gaining popularity, upper-middle class. Key members: Lois Pope, Celia Lipton Farris, Michael Blank.

Many other Palm Beach area clubs vie for new members and provide a unique spectrum of friendship and special interest. Among the leaders: **Seminole Golf Club, Palm Beach Croquet Club, the 19th Hole Club of The American Cancer Society, Governors Club, The English Speaking Union, The Society of the Four Arts, Palm Beach Civic Association, Inc.; Palm Beach County Cultural Council, The Palm Beach Yacht Club, Old Guard Society of Palm Beach Golfers, West Palm Beach Fishing Club, Palm Beach Polo Golf and Country Club, Historical Society, Daughters of the American Revolution, Officers of the Society of Colonial Wars, The Florida Society - Colonial Dames XVII Century, Colonial Dames of America** and **Children of the American Revolution.**

Most private clubs have tradition, objectives and body-politic in order, and round out the selection of meeting places in Town. As in any other city, clubs are a personal matter and often are handy instruments for gaining the privilege of thin-air atmosphere. Private clubs are extremely fastidious about nominees for membership. An Admissions Committee sits in judgement and requires that a nominee be compatible with existing members (always noting that race, religion or national origin is not relevant to admission criteria). Membership is restricted to persons who are: of good moral character, financially responsible, 21 years of age or older, and have a backround, personality and interests similar to other members. The Admissions Committee requires multiple letters of reference, meets with the nominee several times in the screening process, and after tentatively approving the nominee, forwards a letter to current members asking for comments about the prospective new member. Once responses are accumulated, the Committee decides on the acceptance/rejection of the nominee. Accepted members are joyously received; those rejected often never hear from the Committee.

Regardless of admissions policies, on a national basis it is generally agreed that these are the leading clubs by category (city and founding date):

TOP CITY CLUBS:
DUQUESNE CLUB, PITTSBURG 1873
CALIFORNIA CLUB, LOS ANGELES 1888
METROPOLITAN CLUB, NEW YORK 1891
PACIFIC UNION CLUB, SAN FRANCISCO 1852
JONATHAN CLUB, LOS ANGELES 1895
CAPITAL CITY CLUB, ATLANTA 1883
UNION LEAGUE CLUB, CHICAGO 1879
CHICAGO CLUB, CHICAGO 1869
UNIVERSITY CLUB, CHICAGO 1887
MINNEAPOLIS CLUB, MINNEAPOLIS 1883

TOP COUNTRY CLUBS:
CHEROKEE TOWN & COUNTRY CLUB, ATLANTA 1956
LOS ANGELES COUNTRY CLUB, LOS ANGELES 1898
THE COUNTRY CLUB, BROOKLIN, MASS 1882
RIVER OAKS COUNTRY CLUB, HOUSTON 1923
HOUSTON COUNTRY CLUB, HOUSTON 1908
THE OLYMPIC CLUB, SAN FRANCISCO 1860
ONWENTSIA CLUB, LAKE FOREST, IL 1895
WOODMONT COUNTRY CLUB, ROCKVILLE, MD. 1913
GLEN VIEW CLUB, GOLF, IL 1897
WILMINGTON COUNTRY CLUB, WILMINGTON, DEL 1901

TOP GOLF CLUBS:
PINE VALLEY, CLEMENTON, NJ 1913
AUGUSTA NATIONAL, AUGUSTA, GA 1933
SHINNECOCK HILLS, SOUTHAMPTON, NY 1891
BALTUSROL, SPRINGFIELD, NJ 1895
WINGED FOOT, MAMARONECK, NY 1921

TOP ATHLETIC CLUBS:
ATLANTA ATHLETIC, DULUTH, GA 1898
DETROIT ATHLETIC CLUB, DETROIT 1914
MULTNOMAH ATHLETIC CLUB, PORTLAND, ORE 1891
NEW YORK ATHLETIC CLUB, NEW YORK 1868
WASHINGTON ATHLETIC CLUB, SEATTLE 1930

Private clubs have long been associated with seduction, of the mind or of the flesh. By any source of historical evidence, some of the first **mating grounds** were the hunting lodges and fishing camps maintained by royalty back in the days of the Crusades. Properly married royals may have projected a blissful image to the public but liaisons of many varieties occupied the private sanctuaries of their kingdoms. Who can forget the greatest of all love triangles and how it was played out— King Arthur, his spectacular wife Guenevere and his top knight Sir Lancelot? Lance and Ginny were simply doing what had been done for centuries; enjoying the simple pleasures of being non-throne for a while, and expressing passion in its most primitive way.

From the seclusion of a hunting lodge as a *locus* **for seduction** came the formation of more public but also more subtle enclaves to serve personal purposes. The **private club**. In his 18th century dictionary, Samuel Johnson defined a club as *"an assembly of good fellows, meeting under certain circumstances."* Assuming that definition, the first club in America was the **Fish House** in Philadelphia, founded in 1732, four years before White's was established in London (although the latter had been functioning for years without formal rules and a constitution). The club allowed the **men** of a family—businessmen or statesman or bachelors— to have a place to go, without question and need for elaboration. *"I'm going to my club"* was the complete declarative, rarely challenged.

Actually, the first formal club was the **Union Club** in NYC (1836)— it fit the specs as a "home away from home." Rather than being a place to conduct business, the club was a refuge from the deals and hazards of commerce, and its members used the facility for good food, congenial conversation and entertainment. No women were allowed in the **Union Club**, or the many similar organizations that followed in the 1850-1900 era: the **Somerset Club** in Boston, **Philadelphia Club, Union Pacific Club** in San Francisco, **Knickerbocker Club** (NYC) and the grandest of all—the **Metropolitan Club**, which was founded by J.P. Morgan when one of his friends was blackballed by the Union League. Half-a-century later the country flourished with clubs—the **Century** and **Player's Clubs** in NYC, **St. Botolph's** in Boston, the **Cosmos** in Washington, the **Cactus Club** in Denver and the famed **Bohemian Club** in San Francisco. All the clubs continued to be for **men only**; they served as a quasi-family for singles and a hideout for married men who were ill-equipped to deal with the propriety of an upper-class mid-Victorian home. Most of all, clubs functioned as a place where men could talk openly about their **extramarital affairs**, or their social aberrations or whatever business or human conquest would draw the interest of their peers. Importantly, the club served as a sound excuse for the **infidelities** of members, for the statement—"*I'm going to my club*" remained inviolate and covered many a dubious activity.

William B. Astor II, for example, belonged to several private clubs and often sought refuge in them as a means of expressing a love-void for his wife. During the Gilded Age, when Mrs. Astor was delighting society with her annual "400" Ball, Astor was consorting with the lowest level of streetwalker. Between his clubs and his tarts, he led a perfectly neurotic life, but it was better than facing the imperious Mrs. Astor (who didn't mind, her passion for William was very modest). Astor's proclivity for mundane women had a precedent—the **Duke of York's** penchant for ugly, questionable ladies led friends to agree that "*he chose his mistresses as a form of penance.*"

William Randolph Hearst used the Union Pacific Club in San Francisco as his hideout from a drab 15-year marriage to Millicent Wilson; it was also the place from which he launched a 33-year love affair with actress **Marion Davies** and faced the daily ridicule that accompanies romance with a woman 30 years his junior and hardly star-quality (by the standards of the fabled Hearst Organization, the most powerful media force in the country). Davies and Hearst never were able to marry legally, although their affair had all the conveniences of marriage; yet Hearst was a man's man and spent most of his "faithful" hours between his offices and private clubs.

Early **New York** and **Chicago** had a number of "Sporting Clubs" where the guys could toast one another, brag about their killing in the market, and enjoy the camaraderie of some "dolls." More than a few Grandees frequented these popular spots as a means of getting in touch with the common people and pressing some of the opposite sex's flesh. Most town leaders had a favorite Sporting Club and by whatever vicissitude, secrets were kept and privacy was privacy. No gossip columnists or photographers invaded their sporting moments.

Early day clubs were also "fraternal"—**The Chicago Club** in the late 1800s offered members ties, ribbons, suspenders, sweaters, hatbands and socks signaling their membership and glorifying club colors. But no women partook of the process since they were disallowed until the last decade. At the turn-of-the-century, a lady visited the club dining room and sized up the company with the comment—*"I know you let wives of members in, but I see you also allow mistresses."* She was advised, *"Yes, madam, but only if they are wives of members."*

The **Union League Club** of New York was actually anti-women in its formative days, and no woman even walked into the lobby for the first 20 years. Then, an irate wife pushed passed the doorman and stormed into the card room to find her husband. Though stunned, he acted with aplomb, introduced his wife politely and asked her to be seated until the rubber was finished. He then took her arm, bowed gravely to his friends, and left, never to set foot in the club again.

In the old days, club membership was **bonding** at a high level and members were animated about their ranks and prestige of membership. Things change, and role-playing often can't replace sheer productiveness. Those people on the move today use clubs basically to arrange intros to potential clients, patrons, contributors, business alliances. And in a business climate which favors the growth of women in top management, clubs take on a secondary position if women are uncomfortable in a predominately male club, and the possibilities of a deal suffer. So it's a matter of making clubs more available to women members and families, or being out of sync with the times.

Most clubs prefer perpetuating their multi-year heritage and bend with the breeze. **It's simply good manners!**

—GOURMET GROUPIES—

*T*he leading gourmet societies are:

CHEVALIER DU TASTEVIN: an international fraternity dedicated to fine dining and the wines of Burgundy. **Harrison K. Chauncey, Jr.** is Le Grand Senechal of the Palm Beach Chapter and hosts dinners for 35, in various restaurants and clubs in Town. A Tastevin is a small silver saucer that is used for wine tasting; often hung around the neck of a wine steward as a sign of authority. It is also the Society's symbol.

The fraternity recently inducted women as members of the Palm Beach Sous Commandierie. Key Tastevin members are **John Irish, John Brogan, Edwin Bussey, Edward Beneson, William Nutting, John Donnell, Jack Liggett, Normand Grimard, F. Lee Bailey, Robert Cuillo, John Stewart, Phil Whitacre, George Matthews, Ettore Barbatelli, Nikita Zukov, Reid Moore, Jr., Earl Hollis, Fred Brotherton, Alex Dreyfoos** and **Dr. Ray Tronzo.**

CONFRERIE DE LA CHAINE DES ROTISSEURS: a group dealing with the esoteric of food, wine and spirits. Bailli **Robert G. Gordon,** heads the Bailliage de Palm Beach (**Eugene Goldberg** is Vice Conseiller Gastronomique) and hosts a group of about 100 members and guests. The group is known for top entertainment and highly creative food preparation and presentation. A recent example: "Favorite Recipes of Famous Palm Beach Hostesses," was the theme for a recent Spring Dinner held at Club Colette (club owner Daniel E. Ponton is Vice Conseiller Culinare of the group). The favorite foods of Mrs. E.T. Stotesbury, Mrs. Guilford Dudley, Mrs. Walter Gubelmann, Mrs. Douglas Fairbanks, Jr., Mrs. Andrew Frazer and other notables were served with an annotated menu. *Example:* "Eva Stotesbury entertained elaborately. During season her guests would be asked to select their meals for the day from an engraved Cartier menu card brought in by the maid. Mr. Stotesbury, in 1916, tried to keep the house budget for the week at a mere $12,500. Large amounts of caviar were consumed, Russian, of course! Our first course is Russian Osetra Caviar, served in a natural Oyster Shell with bone spoons."

Mr. Gordon was recently voted Bailli of the Year by the National Chaines des Rotisseurs des Etats-Unis (in receiving his award, Gordon was called **"Mr. Hospitality"** by Doyle Rogers, Bailli of the U.S.; Gordon was selected from among 145 Baillis in the country). In Palm Beach, Gordon has built the organization to its current level of prestige over the years, and counts among members some of the most sophisticated food experts in Town. Among them are:

Wolfgang Baere (GM, The Ritz-Carlton); **Michael Brown** (GM, The Brazilian Court); **Matthias Radits** (Executive Chef, The Breakers); **Paul Leone** (President, The Breakers), **Kevin Walters** (Director of Food & Beverage, The Breakers); **Arlene Desiderio** (Owner, Renato's); **Nancy Simmons** (Co-Owner, Ta-boo); **Franklyn de Marco** (Co-Owner, Ta-boo); **Bernd Lembcke** (Managing Director, The Mar-a-Lago Club): **Anthony Damiano** (Executive Chef, The Mar-a-Lago Club); **Thomas Youchak** (Owner, Janeiro); **Alan Tremain** (Owner, Maxim's); **Hubert des Marais** (Executive Chef, Four Seasons Resort); **Lydia and Norbert Goldner** (Owners, Cafe L'Europe); **Sam Ioannidis** (Director of Food & Beverage, Four Seasons Resort).

Other notable members are: **Arlette B. Gordon** (who is also Vice Echanson of L' Ordre Mondial des Gourmets Degustateurs), **Scott M. Gordon, Danielle Basil, Edith and Howard Berger, Susan Lehrman Blank, John J. Brogan, Ray E. Friedman, Dolly Grimard, Alan Lebow, Melvin Nessel** and **Melvin Shalek.**

INTERNATIONAL WINE AND FOOD SOCIETY: also dedicated to the fine art of dining; group caters to about 35 members and guests at each outing. Headed by Thaddeus Trout for many years; now by **Alice Tarone**.

Each of the above societies holds about four dinners per year (half of them at The Breakers); up to $150 per person is spent on the dinner and accompanying wines and amenities.

—STEEP SLEEPS—

*T*he Island is loaded with pricey (and less pricey) hotels; they are: **Ambassador Hotel**, 2730 S. Ocean Blvd., 582-2511. No. of Bedrooms: 53. Recreation: pool; **The Beachcomber Sea Cay Apartments**, 3024 S. Ocean Blvd., 585-4646. No. of Bedrooms: 50. Recreation: pool; **Brazilian Court**, 301 Australian Ave., 655-7740. No. of Bedrooms: 134. Recreation: pool, restaurant and bar; **The Breakers**, 1 South County Rd., 655-6611. No. of Bedrooms: 528; Recreation: health club, pool, tennis, golf, restaurants; **Chesterfield Hotel**, 363 Cocoanut Row, 659-5800. No. of Bedrooms: 63. Recreation: pool, sauna, restaurant; **The Colony Hotel**, 155 Hammon Ave., 655-5430 or (800) 521-5525. No. of Bedrooms: 100. Recreation: pool, exercise room, restaurant, Polo Lounge Bar; **The Four Seasons Resort**, 2800 S. Ocean Blvd., 582-2800. No. of Bedrooms: 169. Recreation: pool, tennis, health spa, restaurants; **The Heart of Palm Beach Hotel**, 160 Royal Palm Way, 655-5600. No. of bedrooms: 88. Recreation: pool, restaurant; **Howard Johnson Motorlodge**, 2870 S. Ocean Blvd., 582-2581. No. of Bedrooms: 100. Recreation: pool, restaurant; **Palm Beach Hawaiian Ocean Inn**, 3550 S. Ocean Blvd., 582-5631. No. of Bedrooms: 58. Recreation: pool; **Palm Beach Hilton Oceanside Resort**, 2842 S. Ocean Blvd., 586-6542. No. of Bedrooms: 134. Recreation: pool, tennis, Jacuzzi, sauna, sailing, water sports, restaurant; **Palm Beach Historic Inn Bed & Breakfast**, 365 S. County Rd., 832-4009. No. of Rooms: 9 and 4 suites. Recreation: walking distance to Worth Avenue, beach, shopping, complimentary Florida breakfast; **Palm Beach Hotel**, 235 Sunrise Ave., 655-4705. No. of Bedrooms: 200. Recreation: pool, health club; **The Plaza Inn**, 215 Brazilian Ave., 832-8666. No. of Bedrooms: 50. Recreation: heated pool, Jacuzzi, Stray Fox Pub, complimentary full breakfast; **Sea Lord Hotel**, 2315 S. Ocean Blvd., 582-1461 or 800-638-6217. No. of Bedrooms: 40. Recreation: beach, shuffleboard. **The Ritz-Carlton** caters to the Palm Beach market but is located in Manalapan.

Despite the ever-growing and revolving number and types of hotels in Palm Beach, four properties remain symbolic of the glory years of the Island.

The Breakers, with its 140 acres of tropical setting and 528 rooms, is an ongoing legend and has been referred to many times in this book; it has served as a temporary home to every president since Calvin Coolidge and functioned as a winter residence for the likes of Andrew Carnegie, John D. Rockefeller, John Jacob Astor, J.P. Morgan, the Duchess of Marlborough and William Randolph Hearst. During World War II, the hotel served as Ream Army Hospital where wounded vets were rehabilitated.

In 1931, the apartment building at 301 Australian Ave. opened as the **Brazilian Court** and immediately caught the attention of Marjorie Merriweather Post, who was overseeing the construction of Mar-a-Lago and needed a place to stay. Soon, Hollywood discovered the B.C. (as it was called), and Gary Cooper, Errol Flynn, Howard Hughes, Cary Grant and others enjoyed their drinks in the courtyard. The 134-room property had the feeling of a country club and, in fact, has been referred to as a "country inn." The property has undergone a massive restoration and is positioning itself as a premier luxury hotel while marketing residential suites to an older, more affluent market.

Hammon Avenue is famous for **The Colony Hotel**, opened in 1929; through the years it fulfilled the fancies of an international set of royalty, investors, socialites and diplomats. With its 100 rooms and expansive bar, dining room, pool and outdoor gardens, The Colony was the place to meet-and-greet; it catered to the jet-set and to this day draws heavily from people in the fashion and communication industries. Its Polo Lounge is usually chock-a-block with colorful social players, and networking goes on with a passion.

The 1926 landmark **Chesterfield Hotel**, designed for Atwater Kent as a hotel and casino, has been the object of several take-overs and name changes over the last seven decades. It remains the smallest and most cosmopolitan of the hotels with an English taxi for transfers, 58 elegant sleeping chambers and a wood-paneled library with international newspapers and magazines and a tea room. It has a gemlike quality and attracts dignitaries like Margaret Thatcher, Mrs. Winston Churchill III, Bill Blass, Catherine Deneuve, Tony Bennett and Barbara Taylor Bradford. It is managed by Tollman-Huntley Hotels.

The 188-room **Heart of Palm Beach Motel** opened in 1961 and primarily serves transients; it, too, has changed hands several times, but remains popular and fills a travel need. The **Four Seasons Resort**, built in 1989, is a palatial property at 2800 S. Ocean Blvd. It can't yet be considered "historic"—but has attracted the high-and-mighty crowd very successfully in short order, both as guests and supporters of various charity affairs.

Based on a comparison of amenities and prices for a deluxe double room (per night), here's how our Town's lodging facilities score:

Brazilian Court	$295
The Breakers	$390
The Chesterfield	$290
Four Seasons Resort	$380
The Colony	$270
The Ritz-Carlton, Manalapan	$400
St. Regis, New York	$455
Plaza Athenee, New York	$425
Bel Air, Bel Air, CA	$450
The Ritz-Carlton, Boston	$365
Mandarin Oriental, San Francisco	$350

The most expensive suite on our Island is the *"Ritz-Carlton Suite"* at **The Ritz-Carlton** Hotel; $2,600 per night includes one-bedroom, ocean view, living room, dining room seating for 15, Venetian art collection enhancing gilded antique furniture, crystal chandeliers, marble floors, fireplace, service kitchen, state-of-the-art electronic systems and Jacuzzi tub—a cozy "home away from home."

On the other end of the scale, the least expensive hotel double in Palm Beach is at **The Plaza Inn**—for $97 per night (off season) guests can enjoy the same ocean and bike path as those staying at The Breakers or The Colony.

—"STAR-STRUCK"—

*T*he *Mobil Travel Guide* recently presented its prestigious Five-Star awards to **The Breakers, Four Seasons Resort** and **The Ritz-Carlton**.

As for restaurants, the **American Automobile Association**'s Five-Diamond award for overall excellence was given to the then **The Centennial** restaurant (The Breakers), **Cafe L'Europe** and **The Grill** (The Ritz-Carlton).

Only 24 USA properties are rated with five-stars by **Mobil**, three of them in Florida: The Boca Raton Resort & Club, The Grand Bay in Miami and The Ritz-Carlton in Naples. There are 36 **American Automobile Association** five-diamond properties, with two in Florida: the Doral Saturnia International Spa Resort in Miami and The Ritz-Carlton in Naples.

The Ritz-Carlton was voted "Best Resort in America" by *Conde Nast Traveler Magazine*.

—LOGISTICAL MIRACLE—

*A*lmost every other year the National Association of Drug Stores (NACDS) holds its annual convention at **The Breakers**. Some 2,500 guests show up for the four-day blowout and operate between cabanas, suites, private homes, restaurants, limos, golf courses, tennis courts **and** the 35,000 sq. foot tent (with 400 tons of air conditioning) that is erected on the parking lot. It's one of the biggest affairs in Southern Florida, and over the few-day period, these quantities of food are consumed:

3000 pounds, chicken breasts	800 pounds, pasta
60 cases of red grapes	400 turkey drumsticks
150 cases of berries	1500 pounds, sausages
1600 pounds, veal chops	400 candy apples
2000 pounds, rack of lamb	800 pounds, bacon
1000 pounds, beef tenderloin	25 cases potatoes *(80 per case)*
4000 edible blossoms	30,000 oranges
600 chicken kebabs	3000 clams
600 beef kebabs	5000 pounds, shrimp
1200 pounds, leg of lamb	3000 snow crab claws
16,000 rolls	700 stone crab claws
1600 sugar cones	10,000 oysters
50 gallons of ice cream	10,000 pieces, sushi
2400 hot dogs	36,000 eggs
3100 hamburgers	1000 pounds, sugar
500 pounds, chicken	2000 pounds, flour
300 pounds, ribs	*Bon appetit!*

The Breakers is a city unto itself, with provisions for practically any need/want. Some interesting facts/fancies about the property are:

* Total square feet: 850,000.
* Number of employees:1500.
* Number of full-time bellhops: 14.
* Number of limousines available: 11.
* Number of lost-and-found items handled annually: 6,200.
* Annual food and beverage budget: $30 million.
* Average number of meals served per day: 2,000.
* Number of bottles of wine in the hotel's wine cellar: 30,000.
* Cost of the most expensive bottle of wine in the wine cellar: $2,900.
* Amount of annual wine sales: $4 million.
* Most requested entree: Rack of lamb.
* Average number of charity events held annually: 75.
* Average number of hours to prepare for major charity events: 20.
* Number of bottles of champagne consumed annually at all catering functions: 8,000.

* Number of different pre-packaged catering menus available: 70, including breakfast, lunch and dinner.

* Number of centerpieces made annually for catering events: 4,500.

* Average number of sheets washed per day during the season: 3,000.

* Number of people in the room service department: 35.

* One of the most unusual room service requests during the last year: Three cases of Evian water because a guest said she would only bathe in Evian.

It is estimated that some **$1.6 million of fresh flowers** (at retail) are purchased each year by the more than 40 restaurants, hotels, bars and party facilities; another $200,000 is put in play by stores (boutiques, beauty salons, etc.) and banks. Private parties add another $150,000 to the total, making the fresh flower budget for the most visible social activites in Town a formidable figure of almost $2 million; The Breakers accounts for about 40% of this figure.

The Breakers is loaded with landscape lore, too:

Population: 34,000 annuals (17,000 planted twice yearly); 2,700 palm trees

Newcomers: 10,000 perennials added to grounds each year

Borders: 4 miles of formal hedges

Cultural Diversity: Palm Trees: 30 varieties

Interesting Tropical Perennials:

Aechmea	Lantana
Mexican Flame Vine	Bleeding Heart
Orange Geiger Tree	Copperleaf
Red Fountain Grass	Dune Sunflower
"Gold Dust" Croton	Crossandra
Chenille Plant	Blue Sage
Thryallis	Pentas
Golden Shrimp Plant	Spriral-Flag
Mexican Caesalpinia	Mandevilla
Jacobinia	Oleander
Purple Glory Tree	Hibiscus

Senior Citizenry: Four palms officially listed as "historical" and "specimen" (100 years old); Oldest 18-hole golf course in Florida.

STAR ATTRACTIONS:

• **Herb Garden:** Contents include 20 varieties, such as:

3 mints (including chocolate)	thyme
sweet tomatoes	3 basils
lemon grass	tarragon
hot and sweet peppers	cilantro
chives	oregano
rosemary	parsley

• **Children's Secret Garden:** Follow a red brick path from a resort entrance sidewalk to an arched doorway formed in a 10-foot high hedge of ligustrum trees and shrubs; proceed through a "plant tunnel" and discover:

　1,200 feet of hedge maze

　600 orange jasmine plants; produce small, white flowers which are fragrant in the spring and attract colorful butterflies

• **The Color Garden Walk:** 10,000 square feet of plant color blocks, comprised of 100 plant species that graduate from hue to hue as with a color scale.

—SLAVES & MAGICIANS—

*T*he word **concierge** comes from the Latin *servus*, meaning "slave." In Europe, the concierge has been the focal point of international travel for decades, but only recently has the concierge, the cultural ambassador and landholder, the magician at creating the right circumstance at the right time—become known and appreciated in the USA.

Palm Beach has three accredited concierges, members of an elite group called **Les Clefs d'Or** (The Golden Keys) who are dedicated to creating complete satisfaction for travelers staying in the grand hotels of the world. Committed to the development of the hotel industry and tourism in general, and to maintaining the highest possible standards of service for hotel guests, Les Clefs d'Or is a professional organization of hotel concierges exclusively. Chapters exist worldwide and all operate under the same "umbrella" organization of the Union Internationale des Clefs d'Or (UICO). Founded in 1929 by Ferdinand Gillet, the French association of Les Clefs d'Or was responsible for the creation of the European association in Cannes in 1952. In 1970, the association became international with over 4,000 members in 30 countries. Les Clefs d'Or USA is a not-for-profit, national association of professional hotel concierges and the only American member group recognized by UICO.

In Palm Beach, there are over 30 concierges serving guests in various hotels, but only three are members of the elite Les Clefs d'Or: **Jose Acevedo**, Four Seasons Resort; **Sam Garcia**, The Breakers; **John Aylward**, The Breakers.

Most concierges are fluent in several languages and can act as interpreters and negotiators for guests; calls to embassies and consulates are routine, and often a concierge will be the sole contact between an individual and his government in matters of policy, passports and currency. On the local scene, a concierge is expert on all matters relating to theater tickets, car rentals, limousines, sight-seeing, sports tickets, entree to private clubs and restaurants and even more unusual affairs, like securing belly dancers for a private party. Concierges also deal with special events —marriages, galas, fundraisers, teas, anniversaries, and other family or corporate lifestyle activities.

—ISLAND/BROADWAY—

*F*or almost three decades the **Royal Poinciana Playhouse** (in Royal Poinciana Plaza) has been packing the house with plays like *Amadeus, Oklahoma, Gypsy, Funny Girl, Tru, Lost in Yonkers, Clarence Darrow, 42nd Street, The Odd Couple, Annie Get Your Gun, Sunset Boulevard, West Side Story, Love Letters* and dozens of other classic productions. The Playhouse was founded in 1953 by producer Frank J. Hale and partners Jeremiah D. Maguire and Messmore Kendall, who opened the theater in the old slathouse of the Royal Poinciana Hotel. The trio were dedicated to bringing Broadway to Palm Beach, and the full-houses at any given performance during the season attest to their success.

The new Royal Poinciana Playhouse, completed in 1958, was credited as being the "poshest" in the South; it attracts the best performers and productions and has become a major contributor to the culture scene of Palm Beach. The Playhouse has been under the tutelage of **Barbara Gault** (director of special events) for many years; she is our Town's most ardent theater-goer, attending every performance and master-minding all details. In the summer, she retreats to her farmhouse in New England for well earned requiescence. **Nancy McDaniel** is house manager.

Most of the productions at the Playhouse are presented by the Florida Theatrical Association with the cooperation of PTG Florida, Inc. Depending on the projected audience, some plays are staged at the Raymond F. Kravis Center for the Performing Arts. Among them were: *Will Rogers Follies, Evita, Jesus Christ Superstar, Cats, Camelot, Tommy, Crazy for You, Guys & Dolls* and *Les Miserables*.

Due to the need for constant new presentations, there are no "long runs" at the Playhouse. But for the record, *The Fantastics* is the longest running show in history (40 years and almost 17,000 performances); *Cats* closed with 7,397 performances, a Broadway record; *A Chorus Line* ended with 6,137 performances. *The Fantastics* had 44 original backers; on average, each has earned more than $3 million on a $16,500 investment.

A number of impressive **cultural facilities and organizations** make their headquarters on our Island; they offer an extensive range of interests, exhibits, performing arts and forms of recreation. Among them are: **American Guild of Artists** (Harold Pysher, dean), musicians association; **Associated Artists of the Palm Beaches**, art interest association; **Bethesda-by-the-Sea** (Harold Pysher, music director), music series; **Big Band Hall of Fame** (Sally Bennett, chairman), music interest association; **Cuillo Center for the Arts** (Mark Schwartz, executive director), theatrical production; **Gilbert & Sullivan Light Opera Society** (Elwood Graves, executive director), community opera organization; **Greater Palm Beach Symphony** (Joan and John Tighe, general managers), professional orchestra; **Guild for International Piano Competition** (John Bryan, president), music competition; **Henry Morrison Flagler Museum** (John Blades, director), historical museum and exhibition center; **Hibel Museum of Art** (Mary Johnson, director), visual art museum; **Jewish Arts Foundation** (Toby Drucker, executive director), ethnic heritage education and festive organization; **Kravis Center for the Performing Arts** (Judith Shepherd, president), **Norton Gallery of Art** (Christina Orr-Cahall, director), major works of art and instruction; **Palm Beach Children's Theater Workshop** (Harriet Brier, director), community theater training organization; **Palm Beach Opera** (Ava Coleman, general director), professional opera company; **Palm Beach Pops** (Robert Lappin, director), pop music orchestra; **Palm Beach Recreation Department** (Leah Rockwell, supervisor), public recreation; **Poinciana Children's Theater Company** (Barbara Gault, president), theater training and performance organization; **Florida Stage** (Louis Tyrrell, producing manager), original theater productions; **Preservation Foundation of Palm Beach** (Polly Anne Earl, executive director), historic preservation organization; **Royal Poinciana Chapel** (Jack W. Jones, music director), music series; **Royal Poinciana Playhouse** (Nancy McDaniel, theater director), cultural facility; **Society of the Four Arts** (Robert W. Safrin, executive director), museum, sculpture exhibition center, library, music and lecture series; **Teen Music Theater** (Scott Pruit, program director), community theater and music training organization.

Regardless of the sophistication of any art or cultural group, cash flow is always paramount. Fundraising, or as it is sometimes called—**advancement**—through capital campaigns, endowments, pledges, annuities are always needed to augment operating income. Funding from contributions can amount to as much as 70 percent of the total budget, as is the case with the Historical Society of Palm Beach County. The Kravis Center has the highest operating budget at $12 million annually; 33 percent of the monies come from contributions. **Miami City Ballet** has a $9.7 million budget of which 48 percent is from contributions. **The Palm Beach Opera** gets 56 percent of its annual budget of $4.5 million from contributions; **The Society of the Four Arts** receives 50 percent of its $2.6 million budget from the largesse of a venerable group of supporters, while 29 percent of the $2.8 million budget for the **Flagler Museum** is from contributions. Most cultural groups try to build long-term relationships with patrons, and stage many lavish pre-and-post event parties and receptions for big donors; plaques and medallions, and seats, stages and halls named after the mega-donors, are all part of the solicitation process.

—GLOBAL GROUPS—

*S*even major international organizations are active in Town:

American Ireland Foundation

This charitable organization was originally started in Miami, later moving to Palm Beach; it is concerned with promoting international peace, charity and culture in **Ireland**. The Foundation was originated by President John F. Kennedy; Palm Beach Fund President and Founder is **John Brogan**. The group, about 90 members strong, donates $5,000 each, and assembles once a year, sometime around St. Patrick's Day, to eat, drink and be merry while noting their accomplishments and their care of those on the Emerald Isle. Nationally, in the past few years the 12,000 Foundation members have raised over $4 million.

English-Speaking Union

Founded 62 years ago, this non-profit educational organization, with 87 U.S. branches and affiliates in 26 countries, sponsors scholarships, fellowships, travel grants, books and literary programs promoting the English language and heritage.

The Palm Beach Chapter was founded by **Marshall B. Wood** in the late 1950s; currently there are over 500 members. They meet monthly from October through April for tea, lunch or black-tie dinners; a guest lecturer is featured at each meeting. In memory of the founder, the Marshall B. Wood Scholarship was recently established; it is to be given annually to an outstanding graduate student at Palm Beach Community College, for continuing education. Since 1960 the ESU has sent teachers from Palm Beach County to England to attend summer programs at British universities. Annually, the ESU sponsors an essay contest and a Shakespearean contest for local students; monetary prizes are presented as well as opportunities to participate in similar contests at state and national levels.

Il Circolo ("The Club")

The **Palm Beach Italian Society** is a non-profit cultural force in the community, founded in 1976 by **Father Nicholas Maestrini**, several prominent local families of Italian heritage, and Italophiles possessing a passion for Italy and Italian culture. Today there are approximately 200 members. In addition to celebrating the joy of being Italian at various social events throughout the season, the group has made it possible for 100 (to date) students to further their studies in Italian; it has also provided monies for Italian study programs at both Florida Atlantic University and Palm Beach Community College.

Members generally meet twice a month, when Italian lecturers, music, concerts and films are featured. Il Circolo has presented plays and operas in Italian with member participation; this helps the group hear and speak the Italian language. Once a year a dinner dance is held where the "Italian of the Year Award" is presented.

International Society

This non-profit Society was founded 19 years ago by **Rene deWyman** *(the late)* and **Herme deWyman Miro**. The 100-plus members meet several times during the season for luncheons, evening receptions and for one black-tie dinner dance (the Holiday Gala at the Beach Club). The purpose of the society is not totally social, as members also strive to do something worthwhile for this community; through personal contributions, yearly grants are distributed among the arts, education, medicine and research.

Le Cercle Francais de Palm Beach

A cultural organization dedicated to an appreciation of **French culture**, language and way of life. From November through May, Le Cercle holds monthly meetings featuring lectures, recitals, travelogues and movies, followed by refreshments and conversation, in French. A spring luncheon and a Bastille Day dinner are also featured, as well as a "Noel" party in December, all under the aegis of Mrs. John N. Morris, president.

A library of French books is available, as are French lessons. Le Cercle has a scholarship fund which enables students of French, as well as teachers, to go to school in France for one month, all expenses paid. The scholarship contest is held in the spring.

Le Cercle is a member of the International Alliance Francaise, headquartered in Paris, France. Speakers are provided by the Alliance; local talent, when available, is occasionally used. Le Cercle is open to anyone with a knowledge of French, regardless of age, religion, race.

Le Club InterContinental

Irene Schieman Porter was the founding president of this group in 1984; presently Le Club has 125 members, representing about 45 countries. During the season this group meets monthly for social gatherings of international flavor, musicals and lectures. The main purpose of this organization is to promote friendship and understanding among Palm Beachers with international backgrounds. Each year Le Club hosts a costume ball with a foreign theme. Last year was an Exotic Gala at Mar-a-Lago and this year a Moroccan Soiree at The Colony Pavilion.

Les Girls

Les Girls was founded over 25 years ago by **Giovanna Phillips**, a native of Italy. Today, the 50 multi-lingual foreign-born women members representing 42 different countries meet for lunch during the season as well as hosting two cocktail buffets per year, when "les boys"' are included. At the evening gatherings, native costumes are usually worn. Mrs. Phillips began the group to help newcomers adjust to the Palm Beach lifestyle; she states that members enjoy socializing with each other even though their countries have been (or are presently) at war with each other.

—ARTS X FOUR—

*T*he **Society of the Four Arts** was created by **Mrs. Lorenzo E. Woodhouse, Mrs. Maud Howe Elliott** and **Mrs. Frederick Johnson**—they helped form the Civic Arts Association in 1934, spearheading a drive that ultimately established what is now the artistic and cultural center of Palm Beach. Two years later, the group's name was changed to **The Society of the Four Arts**, and it took over the Embassy Club building, a Mizner-designed structure that had once been the home of Club de Montmartre (a hot nightclub during the early 20s). Society members used their considerable influence and connections to obtain works of art from important collectors, galleries and local residents. The most notable work in the group's first exhibition was Rembrandt's *"Aristotle Contemplating the Bust of Homer,"* which was lent by Lord Duveen and later sold to the Metropolitan Museum of Art for more than $2 million.

Today, the Society complex remains a non-profit organization which includes an art museum and auditorium-gallery (the site of many art exhibitions and film showings during the social season), a library facility (open year around), the Phillip Hulitar Sculpture Garden and a botanical garden. Membership is a status symbol in town; applicants may wait years for an opening due to membership limit, but for a nominal fee, the general public can view exhibitions and use the library. President of the Four Arts is **"Fitz" F. Eugene Dixon**; other officers include **Hollis Baker, Mrs. Robert M. Grace, Barry Hoyt, David Scaff, Wiley R. Reynolds, William S. Gubelmann, Henry P. McIntosh IV,** and **Robert W. Safrin,** former executive director.

Recent celebrity lecturers were Prince Albert of Monaco, Picasso biographer Arianna Stassinopoulos Huffington, Alistair Cooke, Desmond Guinness, Ambassador Selwa "Lucky" Roosevelt, Art Buchwald, Edward Albee, Bill Monroe, Prince Philip, Andy Rooney, Pierre Salinger, Mark Russell, David McCullough, Hon. Robert Bork, Sir David Frost and Dominic Dunne, Colin L. Powell, Senators Robert Dole and Bill Bradley, The Rt. Honorable The Barononess Thatcher, LG, OM, FRS, John Updike and Tom Wolfe (the series is now called the Esther B. O'Keeffe Speaker Series). Exhibits included the 52nd Annual National Exhibitions of Contemporary American Paintings, Victorian Paintings from the *Forbes Magazine* Collection and *"Empire of the Sultans, Ottoman Art from The Khalili Collection."*

Each season, the Four Arts Plaza in **The Society of the Four Arts** screens 10 to 12 "oldies but goodies" (*Out of Africa, The Red Shoes, The Whales of August, The Man in the Silk Hat,* etc.) on Friday afternoons and evenings. Members view "gratis" while non-members pay $2.50. Great way to reminisce; unfortunately no popcorn allowed.

—TALK, TALK, TALK—

*T*he Island's oldest lecture organization is the **Palm Beach Round Table**, originally fashioned after King Arthur's "circle of peace." It is one of the nation's most prestigious speaking forums, founded in 1932 by **Dr. and Mrs. Alexander Hadden**; after Dr. Hadden's death, Mrs. Hadden assumed leadership of the newly founded organization. For years she personally funded the group. The Round Table began as an intellectual discussion group with an occasional speaker; today it boasts over 1,000 members and brings in eight to 10 speakers per year. Dozens of internationally famous leaders have addressed the Round Table. For many years, **Frank Wright** presided over the group. Past presidents include Judge **Paul W. Williams, John J. Brogan, Mrs. Peter I. B. Lavan** and **Dorothy H. Rautbord, M. Eugene Cook** and **Dr. A. E. Turner. Thomas Martin** is President.

—ZOO DO—

Palm Beach's zoo—**The Palm Beach Zoo at Dreher Park** in West Palm Beach—recently received accreditation by the American Association of Zoological Parks and Aquariums; since its founding in the mid-60s, it has been a favorite of Palm Beachers, both as a place to enjoy leisure time and as a focus for charitable contributions. In 1969, the Zoological Society of the Palm Beaches, Inc. was chartered as a non-profit organization to run what was then called Dreher Park Zoo (named after **Paul Dreher**, former head of the West Palm Beach Parks and

Recreation Department); over the period of a decade the zoo suffered from too-much-or-too-little fame and cash flow; and not until *"Freddie the Alligator"* (a favorite zoo creature and mascot of the South Florida Water Management District) was killed by vandals, did the public really get involved with the zoo through contributions. Today, the zoo is a proud fixture in the culture of the Palm Beaches and a haven for those who want to see how another segment of our population lives and loves.

—SMART ART—

*F*ounded in 1941 by steel magnate Ralph Norton and his wife Elizabeth Calhoun Norton, the **Norton Museum of Art** is one of the finest museums of its size in the United States. The collection has more than 4,500 works of art including: French impressionist and post-impressionate art, American art from 1900 to present, Chinese art, contemporary art, photography and works on paper (Renaissance through Baroque). It's the largest museum in Florida, comparable in size to the Dallas Museum of Art and the Virginia Museum of Art in Richmond.

The museum is constantly expanding, adding new wings or exhibition galleries (it currently occupies about 77,500-square-feet of space), and is not only the *locus* for serious art aficionados, but also for the social crowd. Several major social galas are held at the Museum and dozens of luncheons and lectures, tours, workshops and special events fill out the calendar. Over 180,000 visitors tour the Museum annually.

The **Norton Library** has a collection of some 5,000 art books and periodicals; the Museum Store has a wide variety of art books, unusual greeting cards, interesting jewelry and unique gift items. Programs like *"Sundays at the Norton"* provide community members with a 12-month schedule of musical concerts, films, childrens and family programs. (1451 South Olive Ave, West Palm Beach).

—OVATIONS—

The Raymond F. Kravis Center for the Performing Arts is a monument to idealism, remarkable private sector financial support and community spirit. Set on 10.6 acres of property at the highest point in West Palm Beach, the Center includes three major venues—the 2,193-seat **Alexander W. Dreyfoos, Jr. Concert Hall**, the flexible 300-seat **Rinker Playhouse**, and the outdoor **Michael and Andrew Gosman Amphitheatre** with a capacity for 1,400 patrons. Additionally, the center facilities include the **Eunice and Julian Cohen Pavilion**, which houses a public restaurant and a meeting and banquet facility plus a five-level parking lot. Always in motion, the Center is now undergoing a $25 million expansion.

The Center hosts more than 800 events annually, with some 400,000 patrons in attendance. Many regionally based arts organizations consider Kravis Center as their home including Ballet Florida, Florida Philharmonic, Miami City Ballet, Palm Beach Broadway Series, the Palm Beach Opera and the Palm Beach Pops. Each season, the Center presents over 200 performances featuring top performers in every discipline (Bill Cosby, Vic Damone, Shirley Bassey, Ray Charles, Jimmy Buffett, Carol Channing, Celine Dion, Harrison Ford, Shirley MacLaine, Burt Reynolds, Kenny Rogers, Saludo Latino!, Jazz Fest).

Since its opening eight years ago, the Kravis Center has attracted over four million people, and is the site of the annual fundraiser—*Gala Night of Stars*, which recently presented the LIDO, Champs-Elysees Paris, La Tournee—raising over $1 million dollars. It is a major arts center in the Southeast with a growing national and international reputation. (701 Okeechobee Blvd., West Palm Beach).

—LIMO LARK—

*P*ark Limousine Service (in Paramount Center) is the oldest limo service in the State of Florida, having operated under the same name for 62 years. Its limos are Lincolns and Mercedes, with a variety of stretch and oversized units, plus a fleet of several vans; many have TV sets, moon roofs, bars, stereos and telephones. Park is a full-service operator, on call 24-hours a day. On voting days if a customer doesn't have transportation to and from the polls, Park will provide service *gratis*. According to **Jack Campo**, owner of the service, today's Townies prefer regular Lincoln Town Cars to the "stretch" variety—it's called inconspicuous consumption. Over the years, Park's 50 drivers (fleet is 60 vehicles) have lifted the likes of Elizabeth Taylor, Joan Collins, Prince Charles and Lady Di, Charlton Heston, Don Johnson, Jimmy Buffett, Liza Minelli and Kenny Rogers. Mr. Campo just inspected the world's largest ultra limo—104 feet, complete with swimming pool, putting green and aquarium, and price tag of $3 million and a $12,000 per day rental fee.

—PALM BEACH MISERS & SCROOGES—

Always entertaining and always right on the mark is the story about the rich old guy who asks his young paramour if she'd still love him if he lost all his money. "Oh, I'd still love you," she notes, "and I'd miss you, too!" So much for romance when challenged by money; so much for love when pitted against poverty.

Being without liquid funds is no fun; having the "shorts" is a sure way to social oblivion and generates castigation from presumed friends, foes, allies and associates. Maybe that's why so many people, even those in the mega-rich category, work their way through life with parsimony; always coveting small sums in the hopes of never being without huge sums for a grand lifestyle.

There are people in Town who never buy soap but simply accumulate dozens of bars at hotels; wash out zip-lock plastic bags for reuse; feel around the cushions of chairs trying to find coins; burn dinner candles down to the last fraction of an inch; eliminate costly telephone bills by calling late hours and speaking too fast for comprehension; buy small dogs or small horses to cut down on feeding bills; travel on airlines wearing several layers of clothes to avoid extra baggage charges; save rubber bands and paper clips and cigarette butts (for one or two more puffs) and all sorts of containers and used oversized envelopes and gift wrappings and tea bags and old socks (for rags) and on and on. There's even the frugal Lady who drives her Rolls on the inside of road curves thinking that she might save a gallon of petrol on a long trip. Such is the **spirit of the scrooge**.

There are also **extreme cases** of niggardliness: **Benjamin Altman**, the great retail merchant, died when he refused to pay the high price of a medical specialist for his case of pneumonia; and **William Vanderbilt** who was worth $194 million in 1883 (and said "I am the richest man in the world. I would not walk across the street to make a million dollars.") spent hundreds of thousands of dollars rearranging his various homes, but constantly endangered his world-class gardens by limiting the amount of water and electricity his gardeners could use.

John Paul Getty knew how to handle his guests with economy; he had a pay phone installed at Sutton Place, his stately English mansion, so that guests could chatter on at their own expense. He justified his position by suggesting that most of his friends saved the pins from new shirts, hoarded cocktail napkins from bars, and drank the lowest cost liquors. Getty once declared: "There are people who have been destroyed, physically and morally, by their wealth. The same people, born poor, would probably have become alcoholics or thieves." His philosophy was summed up as—"Waste not, want not."

The late comedian **Jack Benny** built a fortune via his showbiz image as a miser, yet he was extremely liberal in supporting charities and the less-fortunate. He once peeled off ten $100 bills for a down-and-out fellow comedian, whose skit mocked rich men who "poor mouth" it through life. Benny had compassion; after the donation, the needy comedian never mentioned Benny again in his routine.

William Randolph Hearst, who was the most powerful media mogul of his era, lavished money on his girlfriend Marion Davies, while scrimping on such things as razor blades, toothpaste and toiletries. He'd use blades dozens of times, washing and rewashing his face (with soap lifted from a hotel) to hopefully get a clean shave; then splash on an after-shave lotion he concocted from water and leftover lemons or limes. Like the late **Malcolm Forbes, Jr.** he refused to part with a tube of toothpaste until it was decimated. Twisting tubes to the point of total emptiness was the habit of many a capitalist and was, in fact, capitalized on by Tiffany & Co., which markets a sardine can-type sterling silver key ($50), that when engaged with toothpaste tube assures ingredients are fully expelled.

Palm Beach has its share of **scrooges**. Who hasn't seen those cuties who use the cocktail hour largesse of hotels and bars (comp hors d'oeuvres) to not only accommodate their drinking/dining needs of the day, but provide for breakfast in the morn, via a few rolls and leftovers? Or those who bike around Town in the interest of exercise, when, actually, their sportscar has been in the shop for years? Or those who attend funerals and ask for wreaths and assorted flowers after-the-fact, as a "memory" of the deceased? Same technique at balls where centerpieces are fought for quite competitively; a superb centerpiece can easily conserve $100 of the household budget.

After finishing a meal, many is the **doggie bag** that accompanies home a couple who abhor pets; and many is the unfinished bottle of Chablis that tends to walk out of a restaurant with its purchaser; napkins, cruets, salt/pepper shakers, envelopes of sugar and other spices have a tendency to vanish after the delights of a dinner. This miserly little larceny is all built into the price, suggest hoteliers and restaurateurs.

And you've seen the **scrooge** at work during a "Dutch treat" meal. He's calculating his share-of-cost throughout the feast, growing a little more paranoid with each course. He settles for his half of the food charges but will rarely pick up the tax portion or the tip. By the time that calculation comes into focus, he's already in the men's room. A scrooge is a scrooge even with best friends.

It's said that **preeminance** breeds **miserliness**; those who walk taller than others simply aren't expected to pay, they're guests wherever they go. The late **Averell Harriman** never paid for a meal, taxi or ticket; he'd simply excuse himself, walk straight out of the circumstance, assuming others would take care of the bill. And they always did!

The patrician who knows the **value of money**, spends it wisely—lavishly when expected, conservatively when required—and always makes it a source of **enjoyment** for you and those who have chosen to walk through the corridors of life with him/her, is the *rara avis* of our times!

MARIE AND HENRI BARGUIRDJIAN
persuasive and passionate

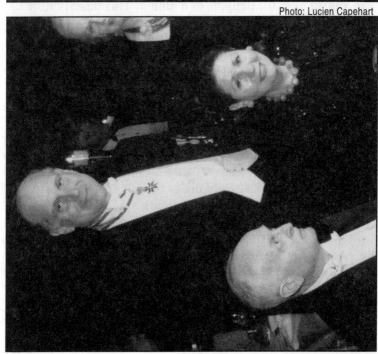

**AMBASSADOR OF ISRAEL DAVID IVRY,
RONALD AND JO CAROLE LAUDER**
protocol and propriety

LINDA AND JAY ROSSBACH AND JUDY GRUBMAN
smashing and superlative

CHRIS AND BERNARD MARDEN
light-hearted, heavy-hitting visionaries

SUSAN AND DOM TELESCO
dashing, daring and distinguished

CURT AND JERRE GOWDY
inventive, imaginative and informative

LADDY AND DEDE MERCK
enjoyable and effervescent

TONY AND MERRY NEWTON
charismatic and celebrated

JULIA AND DAVID KOCH
urbane and unbeatable

MILTON AND DOROTHY SCHULMAN
laudatory and lasting

Photo: Mort Kaye Studios

LIZ SMITH AND ARNOLD SCAASI
evolutionary, exhilerating and exalted

Photo: Lucien Capehart

**JOHN AND DOROTHY SULLIVAN
AND MASKED CHUM**
genial and gleeful

MEL AND DONNA SHALEK
high-spirited and frolicsome

CAROL DIGGES AND CHARLES McADAM
popular and purposeful

CHAPTER VII

PALM BEACH POTPOURRI
(Possessions, Passions & Perks)

Photo: Lucien Capehart

CELIA LIPTON FARRIS AND BERT SOKOL
elan personified

PALM BEACH/ USA EQUIVALENTS

*T*raveling to CapCity, City of Angels, Palm Beach or the Big Apple introduces many new people, places and things, but

CHICAGO	NEW YORK CITY	WASHINGTON
Gold Coast	Upper Fifth Avenue	Kalorama
Drake	Waldorf-Astoria	Willard
Steppenwolf Theater	Lincoln Center Pavilion	Kennedy Center
Magnificent Mile	Fifth Avenue	Connecticut Avenue
Grant Park	Central Park	Tidal Basin
Kennedy Expressway	Long Island Express Way	495
Art Institute	Whitney Museum of American Art	National Gallery
Chez Paul	The "21" Club	Jockey Club
Billy Goat	P. J. Clarke's	Billy Martin's
Michiana	The Hamptons	Rehoboth Beach
Chicago Magazine	*Avenue*	*Washingtonian Magazine*
312	212	202
Ricardo's	Sardi's	Palm
Black Tie	Tails	Black Tie
Fraternity	Anger	Diplomacy
Four Seasons	Carlyle Hotel	Ritz-Carlton
Treasure Island	Zabar's	Sutton Place
Pump Room Le Cirque	Laurent	Blackie's
Cadillac	Mercedes	Limo
David Mamet	Barbara Walters	Frankie Hewitt
Park	Bridge and Tunnel	Mall
Chicago Harbor Docks	South Street Seaport	Washington Harbor
Tower Place	Trump Tower Atrium	Georgetown Park
The Casino	Lotus Club	Cosmos Club

they're all basically "equivalents"—same game, different name. Here's the scorecard:

BEVERLY HILLS	PALM BEACH
Bel Air	South Ocean Boulevard
Beverly Wilshire	The Breakers
Dorothy Chandler Playhouse	Royal Poinciana Playhouse
Rodeo Drive	Worth Avenue
Venice Boardwalk	Phipps Park
San Diego Freeway	I-95
Museum of Contemporary Art	Society of the Four Arts
Chasen's	Cafe L'Europe
Fatburger	Palm Beach Tavern
Palm Springs	Bahamas
Los Angeles	*Palm Beach Society*
213	561
Musso & Frank	Amici
Sportscoat	Black Tie
Envy	Sociability
Beverly Hills Hotel	The Brazilian Court
Vincente Foods	C'est si Bon
Polo Lounge	Ta-boo
Bentley	Rolls Royce
Barbra Streisand	Barbara Gault
Valley	Beach
Santa Monica Pier	Australian Docks
Century City	Esplanade
Pacific Club	Club Colette

—Price Parity—

or the most part, there is parity in pricing for select products and services in Palm Beach and New York; since the Big Apple is many times larger than our Island, there is bound to be more variety in product/service selection there—but **Palm Beach** more than makes up for its less extensive inventory, with gentility and shopping convenience. Some items of comparison are: (A) Housing costs for four—estimate NYC costs for a three-bedroom condo at $750,000 to $2.5 million; in PB, a three-bedroom condo would cost $500,000 to $1.5 million. (B) Commuting time—from a suburb to NYC, about 65 minutes and $8.50 on a train; 20 minutes of driving to the center of PB with a fuel cost of $1.50. (C) Health Club membership—ranges from $500 to $2,000/year in NYC; about $1,200 at Island Fitness. (D) Monthly parking costs in NYC about $350; $75 in PB. (E) Baby sitting charges /hr.—$15 in NYC (if you're lucky); $10 in PB. (F) Initial visit to Internist—$80 in NYC; $50 in PB. (G) Dry Bombay Gin martini at a leading bar—$12 in the Big Apple; $9 on the Island. (H) A tennis lesson —$60/hr. in NYC; $50/hr. in PB. (I) Fifth-grade tuition—$10,500 at Trinity in NYC; $8,000 in PB at the Day School. (J) Night on the town—upwards of $200 for a NYC couple tapping all the right sources; in the $150 range for two in PB at Cafe L'Europe, after-dinner drink at Ta-boo. (K) Lady's hairstyle, shampoo and set—$65 in NYC; $55 in PB. For men, about $40 and $30 respectively for a haircut. (L) Taxes on the three-bedroom unit—about $7,500 in NYC; $4,500 in PB.

—Day of Fantasy—

Put it this way—it wouldn't be inexpensive! Especially in Palm Beach!

You and your loved one would have access to a cherry-red **Ferrari Testarossa** (which costs a healthy five-figures but leases to you for a mere $750/day, with up to 100 free miles) and you'd tool around the Island *sans souci*. You'd bunk at The **Four Seasons Resort** in the Presidential Suite at $850/day; breakfast via room service would feature strawberries, **Dom Perignon**, other wet-bar potables, and frolicsome stuff like caviar, truffles, smoked queen trout from Finland, imported chocolates and fresh foie gras, would start the day with a $350 tab. Tips for valet, concierge and doorman, all of whom know you're a man of means, would come in at $75.

Naturally, you'd shop **Worth Avenue**. For her the spree would rack up two **Valentino** suits (at $2,500 each), one **Leonardo** simple run-around dress ($2,000) at **Martha**, one polo outfit including scarf and boots ($3,000) at **Hermes**, a **Bob Mackie** evening gown, *tres charmant* and *tres cher* at $18,000 from **Saks**, several teddies and nighties ($900) at **Kassatly's**, an evening bag, scent and make-over ($2,000) from the good people at **Chanel**, a diamond trinket ($3,500) from **Van Cleef & Arpels** and lizard shoes ($900) from **Ferragamo**. His cache would include sports jacket, slacks and sweater (cashmere) at $2,500 from **Trillion**, a complete blactie ensemble (shirt, tux, etc.) from **Maus & Hoffman** at $2,750, and a money clip ($350) from the showcase at **Cartier**. Running total so far—$42,925.

Luncheon at **Club Colette**, accompanied by the proper wines, would add $210 to the expense account; and an afternoon at **Palm Beach Polo & Country Club**, where our man is sponsoring a tournament, escalates things by $30,000. Dinner for four at **Cafe L'Europe** (Sapphire martinis, nice wines, delectable entrees) tallies up to $525 (with tip). Add $100 for roses for the Ladies from the **Potted Plant**.

A quick jaunt down to Miami in a private **Gulfstream Jet** with a slew of friends, to catch Edward Villella and his **Miami City Ballet,** checks in at $8,500 which includes limos on both ends.

Back in Palm Beach, and a midnight cruise on a 125-ft. yacht designed by **Jack Hargrave**, with all the amenities (gifts for everyone, snacks from the **Gourmet Gallery** and mellifluous libations), music and entertainment, kicks in another $7,200 to the budget.

It's been a full day. **Fun and fantasy**. And all for a mere $89,460. Now for a peaceful sleep!

—MANSION MONEY—

M any of the wellborn who own mansions wish there was more fantasy in the brick & mortar of their lives, instead of the harsh reality of upkeep, improvement, code restrictions, etc. Here's a look at "mansioning."

Assuming the Mansion is endowed as follows—located on several acres of oceanfront property, 20 or more rooms, two heated swimming pools (one indoor), greenhouse, tennis court, five automobiles, a total staff of 17 full-time members (including six who live-in)—the monthly tab for staffing would be:

ITEM	PER MONTH TODAY	15 YEARS AGO
Head Gardener	$2,400	$1,000
Five Gardeners ($10 hr.)	6,400	2,500
Butler	2,600	1,000
Butler Valet	3,200+	1,000
Personal Maid	2,500	900

Parlor Maid	2,000	800
Chef	3,600+	1,500
Housekeepers	2,000	1,200
Laundress	2,000	1,000
Chauffeur (12 mths. Fla)	2,400	1,200
Masseur (daily)	900	300
French Tutor	1,000	500
Social Secretary	2,600	1,200
TOTAL	**$33,600**	**$14,100**

The most current trend in today's staffing is **the couple**, a live-in husband/wife team who do "double duty"; he's the inside man (butler/houseman/chauffeur), she is cook/housekeeper/personal maid. Their monthly salary totals approximately $4,500 including benefits (insurance, room, board, auto, etc.). In most cases additional staff is added to the household as needed. The average Palm Beach mansion has a live-in staff of 2-5 people; about two dozen local mansions maintain staffs of 12 or more.

EXTRA	**NOW**	**THEN**
Food	15,000	5,000
Liquor	2,000	800
Misc. (repairs)	2,500	1,000
Subtotal	19,500	6,800
GRAND TOTAL	**$53,100**	**$20,900**

Not included in these calculations are such things as taxes, club memberships (Everglades, B&T, Seminole, etc.), out-of-home entertainment, charitable contributions, maintenance on plane or yacht and assorted other toys of the rich. These costs could easily add another $20,000 to today's monthly ledger. The bottom line of all this social meandering/machination is that one's income (either via trust or a trusty family-owned corporation or sheer brilliance) must check in at a staggering level. Rich = responsibility, and responsibility is extremely costly; so much so, that many monied Palm Beachers are shedding homes, cars, commitments and superficial expenses in order to better afford a simple-yet-winning lifestyle.

—RIGHT WRITES—

*B*ic and Flair share honors as Palm Beach's most "popular pen" (Bic is also the largest manufacturer of over-the-counter pens in the United States). The most popular "status" pen is the **Cross**, with **Mont Blanc** gaining in popularity. In the past five years, fountain pens have become increasingly popular with consumer purchases totaling more than $126 million vs. $1.4 billion spent for ballpoint pens.

Palm Beachers also prefer Mont Blanc and Cross desk sets. The most expensive fountain pen in Palm Beach can be purchased at Cartier for $775. The most expensive new pen in the world is a solid gold Mont Blanc Diplomat retailing for $7,600.

Palm Beacher Donald Trump uses an inexpensive Berol Boldliner, while attorney Robert Montgomery, writes with whatever pen is available, often a fine-tip marker by Faber Castell. Townie Jesse Newman, prefers a Parker Duofold; and inveterate document signers like Bill Clinton, Tony Blair and Prince Charles, depend on Mont Blanc to give their John Henrys more panache.

On a note of miscellany, according to statistics, when writing love letters, 42 percent of the public prefer fountain pens, 24 percent ballpoints and one percent word processors.

—HAIR FARE—

In scissors-to-scissors combat with other markets, where vanity and a perfect personal presentation are keys to success, Palm Beach cuts a fine figure. Island prices for various beauty treatments are a shade below those of two other status-conscious metro areas—Beverly Hills and New York. Here's how we rate (based on average figures at a leading salon, women only):

Item	PB	BH	NY
Comb-out	$ 20	$ 30	$ 25
Shampoo/Dry	$ 30	$ 40	$ 40
Shampoo/Cut/Dry	$ 60	$ 80	$ 70
Permanent	$ 80	$ 100	$ 90
Basic Coloring	$ 40	$ 60	$ 45
Highlighting	$ 70	$ 90	$ 70
Facial	$ 60	$ 80	$ 60
Make-Up	$ 35	$ 50	$ 35
Manicure	$ 15	$ 20	$ 15
Pedicure	$ 30	$ 35	$ 30

Palm Beach salons have not declared war on each other, as leading hair gurus in other cities have. In New York, for example, when a salon employee reaches an income level of $100,000/year, he usually takes his Rolodex, rents posh space and hires his friends away to work on his new clientele. The most notable of these entrepreneurs was Mr. Kenneth, sixtyish silver eminence of the salon business, who left Lilly Dache in 1963 to set up shop in an elegant East 54th Street townhouse. Currently, in Manhattan, leading salons like The Spot, Vartali, Parallel and Thomas Morrissey are all owned and operated by former employees of well-known beauty emporiums. In Los Angeles, Jose Eber is a legend in his own time with a product line and a list of "Who's Who" clients; he worked for $150/week at the shampoo sink just 20 years ago.

—SAVOIR HAIR—

*B*lond is still the predominant hair color among women; golden tresses shimmer under soft illumination at galas, and a lighting technician from on high sees a sea of Rapunzels and Goldilocks as he scans the assemblage. Yet, Palm Beach blonds of the 2000s are more natural, with myriad blond streaks and highlights versus the "platinum" shading of years ago. Companies like L'Oreal, Revlon and Clairol find our Island a most unusual and attractive target market with per capita consumption of their tints, dyes and various hair coloring products, almost as high as that in Las Vegas and Hollywood.

For the record, according to a survey by *Allure*:

—16% of women have brown, black or auburn hair; 1% are redheads.

—27% of Mensa's 18,000 female members are blond.

—33% of Miss America contestants are blond.

—58% of *Playboy's* centerfolds are blond.

—64% of female anchors on network shows are blond.

—91% of blondes consider themselves popular with men; 74% of brunettes think the same, as do 64% of redheads.

—NIPS & TUCKS—

Approximately 99 percent of American women (and plenty of men) would change something about their looks if they could; approximately **38 percent** of Palm Beachers over 40, do so through cosmetic surgery of some kind (including collagen injections, liposuction and face peelings). The number is growing and includes many patients under 40. The number of cosmetic procedures performed last year rose to 4.6 million, based on info from the American Society for Aesthetic Plastic Surgery (ASAPS). The total represents a 66% increase over the previous year. There was a

16% increase in surgical procedures and a 98% increase in nonsurgical cosmetic procedures, in part reflecting the growing popularity of medically supervised skin care in plastic surgeons' offices. Chemical peel was the number one procedure, up 114%; Botox injections were second, rising 216%; laser hair removal was third, increasing 340%; Lipoplasty (liposuction), in sixth place overall, was the most popular surgical procedure; breast augmentation ranked second among surgical procedures; cosmetic eyelid surgery was third. Baby boomers between the ages of 35 and 50, accounted for 43% of the total number of cosmetic procedures—more than any other group. The top three procedures for boomers were those that require little "down time"—chemical peels, Botox and collagen injections. Over 11% of cosmetic procedures were performed on men.

According to **Dr. Fredric M. Barr**, Palm Beach Plastic and Reconstructive Surgeon, although the occasional "obvious" results from some cosmetic surgeries are unfortunately visible, the majority of results for most patients are noted as "pleasingly subtle changes." Locally, eyelid surgery followed by face and neck lift procedures, remain the most popular for male and female patients. There has also been a noted increase in facial skin care procedures. The cost varies for each procedure, depending on the surgeon's fee, facility charge, and type of anesthesia utilized. The goal of such "restorative" surgery is to provide a "well-rested, refreshed look." For the majority of patients who have undergone successful cosmetic procedures, only they and their Plastic Surgeons know for sure, since the desired effect is subtle enhancement.

Fees for the most popular surgical procedures are:
Liposuction: $750 - $4,000
Breast Enlargement: $2,000 - $4,000
Eyelid Tucks: $1,500 - $4,000
Nose Reshape: $2,000 - $6,000
Facelifts: $2,000 - $10,000
Chin Implants: $750 - $3,000
Tummy Tucks: $2,000 - $6,000

—SMELLS & SMILES—

*O*ver the years, Palm Beachers have tried every conceivable new fragrance. Most marketers favor Palm Beach as a point of product introduction because of the substantial influence a typical Resident has over family, friends and other potential fragrance users. Here's the scorecard since the 20s.

1920s—*Chanel No. 5* by Chanel (1923); *Shalimar* by Guerlain (1925); *Arpege* by Lanvin (1925); *L'Aimant* by Coty (1928); *No. 22* by Chanel (1928)

1930s—*Joy* by Jean Patou (1930); *Tabu* by Dana Perfumes (1932); *Je Reviens* by Parfum Worth (1932); *White Shoulders* by Evyan (1939)

1940s—*Chantilly* by Houbigant (1941); *Miss Dior* by Christian Dior (1947); *L'Air du Temps* by Nina Ricci (1948)

1950s—*Youth Dew* by Estee Lauder (1953); *L'Imterdot* by Givenchy (1957)

1960s—*Calandre* by Paco Rabanne (1969); *Azuree* by Estee Lauder (1969); *Estee* by Estee Lauder (1969); *Charmade* by Guerlain

1970s—*Givenchy 111* by Hubert De Givenchy (1970); *Aliage* by Estee Lauder (1972); *Private Collection* by Estee Lauder (1973); *Chloe* by Karl Lagerfeld (1975); *Opium* by Yves Saint Laurent (1977); *Oscar de la Renta* by Oscar de la Renta (1977); *Cinnabar* by Estee Lauder (1978); *White Linen* by Estee Lauder (1978); *No. 19* by Chanel (1970)

1980s—*Passion* by Annick Goutal (Elizabeth Taylor) (1980); *Armani* by Giorgio Armani (1982); *KL* by Karl Lagerfeld (1983); *Jardins de Bagatelle* by Guerlain (1983); *Diva* by Emanuel Ungaro (1984); *Ysatis* by Hubert De Givenchy (1985); *Fendi* by Fendi; *Poison* by Christian Dior (1985); *Obsession* by Calvin Klein (1985); *Beautiful* by Estee Lauder (1985); *Musk de Cartier* by Cartier (1981); *Coco* by Chanel (1985); *Red* by Giorgio (1989); *Knowing* by Estee Lauder (1988); *Tiffany* by Tiffany (1989); *Eternity* by Calvin Klein (1988); *Carolina Herrera* by Carolina Herrera (1988); *Panther* by Cartier (1989); *Misha* by Baryshnikov (1989); *Montana* by Montana (1989); *Alfred Sung* by Alfred Sung (1989).

In 1989, the most popular fragrances among Palm Beachers were: *Carolina Herrera* by Carolina Herrera; *Tiffany* by Tiffany; *Coco* by Chanel; *Musk de Cartier* by Cartier; *Panther* by Cartier; *Misha* by Baryshnikov (Saks exclusive); *Eternity* by Calvin Klein; *Red* by Giorgio; *Fendi* by Fendi; *Montana* by Montana.

1990s—Leading fragrances included scents making personal unique statements that seized upon current popular trends. La Prairie introduced *One Perfect Rose*—world's costliest scent at $1,500 per ounce, packed in Boehm procelain and decorated with 24-karat gold leaf. Of all the latest fragrances, the favorites include Bill Blass' *Black Magic*, *Cassini* by Oleg Cassini, *Escada Beaute*, *Romeo Gigli*, *Safari*, *Lacroix's C'est la vie*, *Byzance* by Rochas, Lagerfeld's *Photo* and Nina Ricci's *Ricci-Club*; enduring favorites include *Boucheron*, *Coco*, Gale Hayman's *Beverly Hills* and *273*, *Obsession*, *Opium*, Guerlain's *Samsara*, Sung's *Encore*, Lauder's *Knowing* and *Beautiful*, Klein's *Eternity*, *Parfum d'ete* by Kenzo, *Champagne* by Yves Saint Laurent, *Jaipur* by Boucheron, *Amarige* by Givenchy, *Angel* by Thierry Mugler, *Tuscany* by Estee Lauder, *CK One* by Calvin Klein, *St. John* by Marie Gray, *Parfums Van Cleef*, *White Diamonds* by Elizabeth Taylor, *Dune* by Dior, *Gio* by

Giorgio Armani, *Casmir* by Parfums Chopard, *Paloma Picasso Parfum*, *Sapphires* by Elizabeth Taylor.

It's interesting to note that in 1973, only 17 new fragrances were introduced; in 1999, 60 new fragrances were brought to market; the trend is eternally upward. Today there are approximately 800 fragrances on the market (almost every other major designer has a signature fragrance); one-third are for men. Further, despite all the competition, *Chanel No. 5, Shalimar* and *Joy* remain the most popular classic fragrances of all time.

For gentlemen, the most popular colognes recently were: *Bijan* by Bigan, *Fahrenheit* by Christian Dior, *Polo* by Ralph Lauren, *Armani* by Armani, *Aramis* by Estee Lauder, *Obsession* by Calvin Klein, *Hugo Boss* by Hugo Boss, *Jazz* by Yves Saint Laurent, *Imperiale* by Guerlain, *Lagerfeld* by Karl Lagerfeld, *Santos* by Cartier, *Eau Sauvage* by Dior, *Horizon* by Guy Laroche, *Eau de Rochas Christian* by Rochas, *Egoiste Platinum* by Chanel, *Wings* by Giorgio, *Herrera for Men, Escape* by Calvin Klein, *Polo Sport* by Ralph Lauren, *Tsar* by Van Cleef & Arpels, *Havana* by Aramis, *Rocabar* by Hermes, *Tiffany for Men, Desire* by Dunhill, *Kouros* by Yves Saint Laurent and *Very Valentino.*

—APHRODISIAC ALLURE—

*S*ome of our Town's most alluring sense-sations are:

Caviar: In addition to being nutritious (30 percent protein), caviar has been considered an aphrodisiac because of its obvious role in the reproductive process. All fish and their by-products have been linked to the myth of *Aphrodite*, the goddess of love who was born from the foam of the sea. Supposedly, fruits of the sea were endowed with *Aphrodite's* power. Try **Cafe L'Europe** for this winner.

Garlic: Both Eastern and Western cultures have long regarded garlic as an aphrodisiac. The Greeks and Romans sang its praises and oriental lovers claimed to be towers of strength due to ingestion of garlic. **Renato's** is a garlic-heaven.

Honey: Honey is highly nutritious and rich in minerals, amino acids, enzymes, and B-complex vitamins. Galen, Ovid and Sheikh Nefzawi, author of *The Perfumed Garden*, believed that honey has outstanding aphrodisiacal powers. Have a honey of time at **Testa's.**

Lobster: The lobster has been described as an amatory excitant by many writers, including Henry Fielding in *Tom Jones*. In addition, it shares the Aphrodite-derived power attributed to all seafood. **Charlie's Crab**=great lobster.

Oysters: Oysters are one of the most renowned aphrodisiacs; like other seafood, they are rich in phosphorus. Although they are not a high source of energy, oysters are easily digestible. Among the eminent lovers who have vouched for oysters was Casanova, who called them a "spur to the spirit and to love." Check out the oysters at **The Chesterfield**.

Peaches: (for those who enjoy their champagne embellished with slices of fresh peaches) "Venus owns this tree... the fruit provokes lust..." wrote herbalist Nicholas Culpeper. The Chinese considered the fruit's sweet juices symbolic of vaginal effluvia, and both the Chinese and Arabs regard its deep fur-edged cleft as symbolic of female genitalia. A "peach house" was once a common English slang term for a house of prostitution, and the term "peach" has been used universally to describe a pretty or sexually appealing girl. The **Brazilian Court** is a "peach-paradise."

Truffles: Used by Palm Beach gourmets, these precious underground fungi are similar to oysters, in that they are composed mostly of water, are rich in protein, and have similar effects on the indulgent. For something this special, try **Club Colette.**

Asparagus: A vegetable rich in potassium, phosphorus, and calcium, all necessary for maintenance of a high energy level. Catch this green delight with your high-level friends at **Galaxy.**

Some of the latest aphrodisiacs like Welbutrin or Viagra (a cure-all for reduced sexual drive), Yohimbine (for men with psychogenic impotence) and Papaverine (enhances the sexual appetite), are reaching the market with success; most require a prescription and use-supervision. On the other hand, not enough can be said about aphrodisiacs like **money** and **power** and **youth** and **success** and **good looks**... all of which play especially important roles in the Palm Beach lifestyle. Suffice it to say, that an individual possessing any two of those aphrodisiacs is already well-placed on the social pyramid.

—BEAUTY BITES—

*T*he ideal way for Ladies to get skin, nails and hair quite in order is not to overdo one nutrient and thereby undo the rest, but to have a balanced approach to nutrition. Here's what Palm Beachers consume for health maintenance: **watermelon** (plenty of water to flush toxins from the system); **olive oil** (lots of vitamin E to slow the skin's aging process); **mangos** (vitamin A, an important skin-nurturer; helps regulate sebaceous glands); **yogurt** (a generous supplier of calcium to help skin glow and strengthen bones and teeth); **lobster** (yields plenty of zinc, a great mineral for bolstering skin, hair, nails and eyes); **red peppers** (stocked with vitamin C; helps to maintain skin-plumping collagen); **pasta** (an American favorite—contains selenium to keep the immune system in order); **salmon** (plenty of body-building vitamin D for better muscletone and posture); **nuts** (peanuts, pecans, walnuts, almonds—the B family of vitamins for increased energy); **beefsteak** (has the iron required to form hemoglobin, the oxygen-carrying portion of red blood cells); and the most fundamental source of great nutrition—the **apple.**

There's been a modest preoccupation lately with the consumption (eating, that is) of flowers. Some safe and delectable Florida flowers-as-food are: geraniums—for tea and other beverages; chrysanthemum — quite edible and tasty; fuchsia—tart but tasteful; honeysuckle—sweet and bracing; marigolds—peppery and potent; and carnations—look great on cakes and have a pleasant after-taste.

—PALM BEACH CHARACTERS—

*T*he song and dance of Palm Beach creates a new cast of characters with great regularity; bourbon and bonbons, body-english, fun-worshipping are all part of their ploys as they swim in the Great Goldfish Bowl. Here are some types:

* **AGELAST:** One who never laughs; not much joy and wassail.
* **AMBIDEXTER:** A double-dealer; loves to run fancy patterns.
* **AMBIVERT:** One who is neither an in-or-extrovert.
* **CENTIMILLIONAIRE:** Millionaire with more than $100 million. A one-unit man in Texas.
* **CHASMOPHILE:** A lover of nooks and crannies, mostly in bars and restaurants.
* **COCKALORUM:** A very confident little man; usually with an identity crisis.
* **DEIPNOSOPHIST:** One who is good at dinner-table conversation; loves social steeplechase.
* **FANCYMONGER:** One who deals in tricks of the imagination; often good at tongue-tango.
* **GNOF**: A curmudgeon, frequently into autolatry (worship of self).
* **GRAMMATICASTER:** A verbal pedant; thinks that misuse of the word "hopefully" threatens Western civilization.
* **LYCHNOBITE:** One who lives by night and sleeps by day; not altogether uncommon in Town.

* MARPLOT: One who frustrates a plan by his/her officious interference.

* MINIMIFIDIAN: One who places the least possible faith in something; usually hates esoterica like astrology, tarot, the occult.

* MUMPSIMUS: A person who refuses to correct an error, habit or practice even though it has been shown to be wrong; often of the pip-pip, stiff upper-lip variety.

* MYRMIDON: Someone who carries out commands without hesitation or pity; has lots of life force and no scruples.

* MYTHOCLAST: A destroyer of myths; a high-stepper who loves standing ovations.

* ONCER: One who does something once and never again; has had a terrible experience and "once was enough."

* OPSIMATH: One who has learned late in life; has spent too much time in cognac and cogitation.

* PERPILOCUTIONIST: One who talks through his top hat; a superficial spieler with too much oom-pah-pah.

* PHILODOX: One who loves (and lives by) his/her own opinions.

* PICKMOTE: One who habitually points out and dwells on petty faults; a second-rate punkaroo.

* PYRRHONIST: An absolute sceptic.

* SALARIAT: A person with huge salary (income) and the security to go with it; quite in contrast to a proletariat.

* SPERMOLOGER: One who gathers seeds by extension, a triviamonger or gossip; enjoys the people-scape of life.

* THAUMATURGIST: One who works wonders; often the czars of charitable balls who with cool, classic equipoise and a primal passion for perfection, create the ultimate "mahvelous pahty dahling" and. . . **the concomitant currency.**

Photo: Lucien Capehart

BETSY AND WILLIAM YLVISAKER
power, purpose and performance-oriented

Photo: Lucien Capehart

ANNETTE ROQUE AND DAN PONTON
bright and bullish on life

Photo: Lucien Capehart

**SUSAN AND LEE, ARLETTE AND BOB,
GINA AND SCOTT GORDON**
a sextet for all seasons

Photo: Mort Kaye Studios

ELLIE AND GENE GOLDBERG
knockout socialites and servants of mankind

**MATTHIAS RADITS, LIDIA AND NORBERT GOLDNER
AND WOLFGANG BAERE**
jazzy, joyous and jaunty

HON. MARK FOLEY, JILL AND JOHN RAU
liberated and learned

Photo: Lucien Capehart

**JASMINE HOROWITZ, PRINCESS MICHAEL OF KENT
AND HELEN BOEHM**
civilized, charitable and commendable

Photo: Lucien Capehart

**JESSE AND HELENE NEWMAN, PAM HOFFPAUER
AND ROBERT GOTTFRIED**
at work, at play, always there when it counts

LORI AND HAROLD CORRIGAN
indisputable experts, driving forces

LOIS POPE AND GENERAL COLIN POWELL
all smiles and impressive achievements

289

PAUL LEONE AND MATT LAUER
effervescent and energetic

DICK AND SALLY ROBINSON
superb at the art of giving

CHAPTER VIII

PEERAGE & PERFORMERS
(Pleasures, Perfections & Phenomena)

Photo: Lucien Capehart

SUSAN AND JIM KEENAN
happy hosts and humanitarians

—Top Jobs—

*B*ased on occupational licenses granted to firms last year, the following professional endeavors were most popular:

OCCUPATION	# PRACTITIONERS
Real Estate Professionals	700*
Attorneys	163
Interior Decorators	54
Banks and Trust Companies	35
Jewelers	29
Beauty Shops/Operators	22
Architects	16
Masseurs	8
Dentists	7
Travel Bureaus	5
Barbers	4
Opticians	4
Medical Doctors	3
Veterinarians	3
Detectives	1
Artists	14

* Some 450 active, registered realtor associates and brokers belong to the Palm Beach Board of Realtors.

—Pop Wheels—

These are the most popular automobiles in Palm Beach:

Mercedes-Benz has the lead—the 500SL and convertible are very much in demand (the convertible is the favorite of women). There are more Rolls Royces in Palm Beach per square foot than in any other place in the world (except Hong Kong)—and black or white versions are frequently seen outside of bars, the Kennel Club, beauty salons and churches. **Jaguars** (about 200 on the Island) take third place and are increasing in popularity, as is the recently introduced **Turbo Bentley**. Of the American luxury cars, **Cadillac** is still the leader, with **Lincoln** close behind. The younger set has embraced the **Range Rover** as its status vehicle. (**BMW**s are also very popular.)

The five most-desired automobiles are:

1. **Ferrari Daytona Spyder**: red of course, clocking in at $650,000 (only 125 such convertibles built between 1969 and 1973).

2. **Rolls Royce Corniche**: convertible; favorite colors are black and white. (Only 100 shipped to the USA from Britain with a price tag of $200,000—among the most expensive imports anyone can buy).
3. **Lamborghini Countach**: red, 180 miles per hour is top speed; car is bold, loud, fast and expensive at $187,000. It is the widest and lowest auto ever built—referred to as a "sexy, space car."
4. **Mercedes AMG Hammer**: color red, top speed of 186 miles per hour. Price tag at $167,000.
5. **Aston-Martin Volante**: convertible in black, made famous by James Bond, attaining speeds of 168 miles per hour—only $167,000.

For the record, the most expensive car in the world is a recently sold vintage **Bugatti Royale** (made in Italy in 1931; cost then was $22,300)—selling price was $14 million to a group of Japanese businessmen. It was one of only six models made. Another recent top-seller was a 1963 **Ferrari GTO** that fetched $13 million.

Sotheby's recently held a vintage and classic car auction at The Breakers. Twenty-five cars from the collection of Rick Carroll were put up for sale; included in the group were eight classic Rolls-Royces, seven restored Duesenbergs, a 1902 Mercedes and a McLaren race car used by Johnny Rutherford to win the Indy 500 in 1974.

Several hundred Islanders attended the auction and put in appropriate bids for their favorite car; over $21 million was paid by car collectors from England, Switzerland and the USA.

The new trend toward roadsters is also apparent in Palm Beach. Two-seated convertible cars like the Mercedes SLK, BMW Z3, Porsche Boxster and Audi TT are showing their raffish stuff on the Island (average price about $40,000), usually driven by a member of the New Wave.

—THE SOUND OF MUSIC—

*T*he most **valuable** piano in Palm Beach is an "Erard" owned by Estee Lauder. This ornate 7-foot piano was built in 1900 in France. There were two Erards built at that time; one belonged to the King of France and the other found its way to our Island. The tone of the piano is not great in comparison to other pianos, but what it so valuable (insurance value $250,000) is the beautiful cabinetry. The case is handmade of inlaid (veneered) European walnut and rosewood with gold leaf embellishment.

The **best sounding** piano can be found at The Society of the Four Arts. It is a relatively new 9-foot Hamburg Steinway valued at approximately $60,000.

The most valuable **upright piano** is owned by the late Madame Alexander at the Biltmore; is approximately 150 years old, was built in France, and has an unusual gold leaf case.

Other **exceptional pianos** include Donald Trump's 5-foot 7-inch custom Steinway Model M. The piano was among the original home furnishings of Marjorie Merriweather Post; the scenic artwork painted on the case makes it unique and valuable. The Breakers has a classic Steinway duoart player piano, it has been there since the hotel was rebuilt in 1925.

Of the previous **"Stadivarious"** in existence, there is presently only one on the Island, and the owner wishes to remain anonymous.

There are two **pipe organs** (built-in) in Palm Beach residences today. One is located at the former Drucker home at 840 S. Ocean Blvd.; the only home with a full-size pipe organ built on three separate levels. When played, it effects the timbre of a cathedral organ. This home also houses the oldest piano on the Island—a Broadwood, built in England about 200 years ago.

The other pipe organ can be found in the **Flagler Museum**; it was built during construction of the mansion in 1901 by J.H. and C.S. Odell & Company of New York. Flagler liked music and always had an organist in residence, when he (and his wife) occupied the mansion. When the mansion was converted into a luxury hotel in 1925, the organ was sold to the Poinciana Chapel where it remained until 1963; in 1965 it was returned to its original location in the Louis XIV music room of the mansion. Walter Guzowski recently refurbished the organ.

Acoustically, the finest organ in a Palm Beach Church is the new **Austin** organ (cost: $1.5 million) located in the Bethesda-by-the-Sea Episcopal Church. Like the Poinciana Chapel's organ, it is really two organs in one. The main organ is housed in an ornate Gothic case located to the left of the chancel at the front; the other, and perhaps grandest organ in the area, resonates from the back and has a set of horizontal festival trumpet pipes which, when lighted, lend a note of high drama to services and concerts. The organ located in the Royal Poinciana Chapel was built by the **Austin Organ Company**; its cabinet blends with the Colonial style of the Chapel's interior. The Chapel's 91 Rank Austin Pipe Organ (largest in the county) has four keyboards and pipes as long as 32-feet high that produce sounds that are felt as much as heard. A separate organ called the antiphonal, is located on a gallery at the rear of the Chapel and features a magnificent horizontal festival trumpet spreading out from its center. Many famous organists have played on this organ (Virgil Fox and John Rose); Jack W. Jones, who holds a doctorate in Music from the Juilliard School, is the present organist. Harold Pysher, one of Florida's most respected musicians, is organist at Bethesda. St.

Edward's also has a historic organ; however, it is not played publicly.

A prominent Palm Beacher owns a rare Bruder **Monkey Grinder Organ** that was built around 1820 in the Black Forest region of Germany. The organ has traveled to Germany for restoration, soon to resume grinding out its original 12 programmed songs.

—GAME FAME—

*T*he prime mover of **backgammon** in Palm Beach was **Prince Alex Obolensky**, one of the many exiled Russian "royals" by that name; until his recent death, "Obie" taught backgammon at various clubs in Palm Beach and New York.

Many Palm Beachers are avid backgammon players; but their ranks are thinning due to a sudden interest in **croquet**, where the strategy is so vital, and the luck so minimal. Croquet also offers a healthier climate— fresh air, sun and a breeze versus a smoke-filled room.

A number of world-class **bridge** players live in town. Perhaps the most famous are **Benito Garozzo**, a Silver Life Master Bridge professional who has won numerous international bridge titles and spends six months each year traveling all over the world to attend tournaments (total international professional points 1,092.07), and **Samuel M. Stayman** *(the late)*, the "father" of the "Stayman Convention" known to bridge experts all over the world.

Other top local players include **William J. August** (also a great bridge teacher), **Lee Hazen, Jack Schwenke, Linda Perlman, Marty Bergen, Ellie Hanlon, Sterling Odos** and **Paula Ribner**. Well-known Life Masters in the area are: **Sally Campbell, Ann Goldfaden, Diane Holt, Carola Mandel, Richard Neff, George Phillips, Lloyd Ribner, Kay Rybovich** and **Tubby Stayman**. Noteworthy bridge experts: **Lesly Smith, Angie Ilyinsky, Judy Schrafft, Gloria Hamilton, Ellen Coates, Marjorie Rose, Nancy Glocke** and **Helen Cluett**.

The game of **contract bridge** was invented by the late **Harold "Mike" Vanderbilt**, a member of the Old Guard Vanderbilt clan and a world traveler who was active in many games of chance and was known to gamble on occasion. His dedication to bridge was to fuse the intellectual with chance and to give determined players an opportunity to show their prowess based on the degree to which they studied the game. He actually invented contract bridge in 1924 as a Palm Beacher; then moved on to Manalapan and became Mayor. At one time he was the country's leading yachtsman.

Our Town's top **marksmen**: **Barney Donnelley** has won so many awards for his skeet-shooting skills that he uses excess silver bowls (prizes) as serving platters for his dog. He learned the esoteric of shooting at his family's southern plantation. Overall, he is one of the world's top performers with a rifle and is an avid game hunter.

Sir Joseph Nickerson *(recently deceased)*, who wintered in Palm Beach, was also one of the best marksmen in the world. He was internationally known for hosting three of the best "shoots"—one in England, one in Scotland and one in Spain.

On the distaff side, **Carola Mandel**, a world-class marksman, holds more records for her unerring eye than any other woman; of late, however, she has traded her rifle for a new weapon—playing cards. An avid bridge player, she cruised around the world last summer with bona fide bridge professionals, winning in almost every port of call.

—JOCK FLOCK—

*N*ot surprisingly, **walking** is the favorite sport of our denizens; 50 percent of our residents walk as a physical activity. Swimming is next (favored by 32 percent of Palm Beachers), followed by tennis (24 percent), cycling (21 percent), golf (20 percent), jogging (12 percent), dancing (11 percent), boating and fishing (11 percent) and gymnastics/aerobics (10 percent). Croquet and playing polo are pursued by a select number of our residents, as is skiing off-season.

The number of athletic "courts" in town is impressive. **Swimming pools** make the biggest splash; about 1,100 on the island—kidney-shaped, heart-shaped, circular, rectangular, square, made to form initials, almost any design imaginable. The largest outdoor commercial pool is at **The Breakers:** 82 ft. x 72 ft. (The Breakers has three large pools). One of the largest private pools belongs to **Mollie Wilmot.** An average home pool holds 25,000 gallons of water; hers holds 90,000. Years ago her pool became famous when the freighter *"Mercedes"* beached on her property cracking not only her seawall, but the adjoining pool.

There are about **100 tennis courts**—a few at each of the major clubs, and on the premises of many private homes.

Seven croquet courts adorn our landscape; two at The Mar-a-Lago Club; three at the Beach Club, one at the Everglades Club, and one at The Breakers.

The Breakers also has lawn bowling, shuffleboard, scuba diving, snorkeling, 10 tennis courts and jogging trails.

Indoor athletics are pursued at The Breakers Health Club via Nautilus and other gym equipment; many women work their way to good health and trim figures at the Palm Beach Recreational Center where aerobics is the order of the day. New facilities have recently opened in the Palm Beach Hotel and the Royal Poinciana Plaza.

Of the 13,600 **golf courses** in the United States under supervision of the National Golf Foundation, Florida has a total of 932 (more courses than any other state); 101 of these courses are located in Palm Beach County and four are in Palm Beach:

1. **The Breakers**: 18-hole par 70 (6,200 yards) course located on 100 acres adjoining The Breakers; is the oldest golf course in Florida (dating back to the turn of the century, recently renovated by Brian Silva). It is a traditional golf course, short holes, big bunkers, water hazards and small greens. Important tournaments held at The Breakers annually include The Breakers Senior and the American Seniors, The Winter Golf League, and the Palm Beach Golf Classic sponsored by the American Cancer Society. A 32,000 sq. ft. clubhouse adjoins the course.

2. **The Everglades Club**: 18-hole par 71 (6,073 yards) located at the Club on Worth Avenue, a very picturesque course; many water hazards (13) and considered "short" for an 18-hole course. The front 9 holes were built in 1919 making this the first exclusive golf club in Palm Beach, and the back 9 in 1928. The 10th, 524-yard (par 5), hole is the most difficult because of its length. On this particular course women generally score better than men (as a group) because of the short fairways.

3. **Palm Beach Country Club**: Two miles north of The Breakers, it is considered to be the "youngest" of the "old" Palm Beach Clubs. Built (in 1953) on 88 acres bordered on the east by the Atlantic Ocean, this 18-hole par 68 (6,200 yards) course is perhaps the hilliest course in Palm Beach. The course was built in 1920; there are five water hazards and the 6th hole, 430-yard (par 4), is the most difficult. Last year some holes were redesigned to include a view of the ocean (Donald Ross designed the course). This course is hilly due to a coral reef located beneath the surface. When the course was redesigned, it was lengthened from 5,771 yards to just over 6,200 yards, with two par-3 holes converted to par-4 holes. Locally this is one of the hardest clubs to get into; initiation fees far surpass those of the other clubs, and in addition one must not only have money, but give multi-bucks continuously to charities each year.

4. **The Par-3 Golf Course** (South Ocean Boulevard): owned and operated by the Town of Palm Beach. Its 2,640 yard par-54 course ranks as one of the toughest of its kind in America. It is certainly the most scenic with views of both the Ocean and the Intracoastal (Lake Worth). A main thoroughfare (A1A) cuts through the middle of the course, producing an extra challenge for golfers. The most difficult hole is the 6th—167 yards running parallel to the ocean. The course was built in 1961 on 37 acres and purchased by the Town 17 years ago. Approximately 30 people each year make a hole-in-one. The course holds a pro-amateur tournament annually which features Women's Professional Golf Association players; proceeds are donated to three area hospitals.

Seminole Golf Club, just north of Palm Beach, is one of the country's 10 most difficult golf courses. Designed by Donald Ross and completed in 1929, it was the culmination of a dream of Edward F. Hutton, founder of the then brokerage firm of the same name. (Hutton was the second husband of Marjorie Merriweather Post.) Hutton and his friend Martin Sweeney wanted to have the best golf course in Florida; with the help of Donald Ross and Marion Wyeth (Ross did the golf course; Wyeth, who also designed Mar-a-Lago, created the salmon pink Mediterranean-style clubhouse), the course became a favorite of internationally known celebrities including the Duke of Windsor, presidents Dwight D. Eisenhower and John F. Kennedy and Ben Hogan. Through the years, Seminole has attracted top players and personalities and become one of the most exclusive clubs in the USA.

The **Old Guard Society** of Palm Beach Golfers is the area's oldest golfing organization (1918); it is headquartered in The Breakers Clubhouse.

Palm Beach Malleteers—**Barton Gubelmann, Libby Newell, Jack R. Osborn** *(the late)*, **Donald Degnan, Frederick** *(the late)* **and Patricia Supper, Herbert Bayard Swope, Jr., Catherine Tankoos Barrett** and **John Donnell** and **Michael Gibbons**—are **U.S. Croquet Hall of Fame** members. The Hall of Fame was inaugurated in 1979 by the Croquet Foundation of America, Inc. and has an impressive number of members including Paul Butler, Ned Skinner, "Teddy" Prentiss, S. Cortland Wood, Archie Peck, Moss Hart, Mrs. Ogden Phipps, John and Nelga Young, Darryl F. Zanuck, Richard Rogers, George Abbott, Louis Jordan, Alexander Woollcott, Harpo Marx and George S. Kaufman.

The Croquet Foundation, located in Wellington, FL, in conjunction with the U.S. Croquet Association, publishes the *U.S.C.A. Croquet News*, a quarterly magazine offering news and views of the croquet world.

Officers of the Foundation are: **Chuck Steuber**, President; **Bill Campbell**, First Vice President; **John R. Donnell**, Second Vice President; **Charles Evans**, Treasurer; **Norma Truman**, Secretary.

Board of Directors are: **Catherine Barrett, Diane Blow, Bob Chilton, Martha Clark Hunnewell, Eugene Goldberg, Charles Lazarus, Anne Frost Robinson, Andrew Sage** and **Patricia Supper**. **Johnny Osborn** is currently America's top-seeded player.

Games resembling **croquet** have been played for 500 years, but croquet was only introduced in the U.S. in about 1860 from England, where it is known to have been played since 1850. Croquet was quickly taken up by society from Newport to New York and soon gained popularity across the country.

The **Newport Croquet Club** published a set of rules as early as 1865. Lawn tennis was introduced at about the same time, but until the turn of the century, croquet enthusiasts outnumbered tennis players (Wimbledon was originally The All England Croquet Club). A croquet set was mandatory equipment for every estate, and civic leaders provided sets for public parks. Croquet was quite popular with women, and was one of the first games played in the U.S. by both sexes.

In 1904, croquet was introduced into the **Olympic games** (in St. Louis) where it was won by an American. The sport's huge popularity diminished with the outbreak of world hostilities in 1917.

Between World Wars, croquet reemerged as a favorite pastime of literary and entertainment people. East coast players, such as George S. Kaufman, Alexander Woollcott and W. Averell Harriman, developed a fierce rivalry with west coast players, such as Harpo Marx, Darryl Zanuck and Sam Goldwyn. These gentlemen are the over 50 inductees in the U.S. Croquet Hall of Fame.

To this day, it is one of the few sports in which **men and women** compete on equal terms. Croquet is played competitively in Great Britain, Australia and New Zealand, under the rules of the Croquet Association (English), where there are a large number of clubs, and open championships are eagerly contested, as well as the MacRobertson International Shield between these three countries dating back to 1925. The USA was invited to participate in this prestigious event for the first time in 1993. In 1986, the presidents of National Croquet Associations from England, Ireland, Scotland, Australia, New Zealand, Japan, South Africa and the U.S. met in London to organize the World Croquet Federation. The **United States Croquet Association** (USCA) is a charter member of the WCF. The first official World Croquet Championships were held in 1989.

Since 1981, the USCA has hosted teams of top **international champions** from all of these countries (except New Zealand and Japan) plus Canada and Bermuda in a series of U.S. International Challenge Cup Matches each spring in Florida.

"**Backyard**" croquet is played by millions of Americans at home. The USCA-level sport is played by a select group of people on finely manicured grass courts. Full-size association croquet courts are 105 x 84 feet in dimension, and matches usually last 90 minutes in tournaments, but can take longer informally. Croquet can be aptly described as a blend of chess on grass, golf, billiards and war.

Recently, after formative years in New York City, Wellington and Palm Beach Gardens, the USCA is opening new National Headquarters in West Palm Beach. The 10-acre croquet complex includes 12 courts, a 15,000-square-foot building with covered porches and balconies. Cost:

299

$4 million. It is among the largest croquet facilities in the Western Hemisphere. The USCA now has 6,000 registered members throughout North America and over 400 registered croquet clubs.

Palm Beach's most famous **polo** players (all are at the 9-10 goal level) are: **Winston Guest, Mike Phipps, Harry Payne Whitney, C.V. Whitney, Peter Bostwick, Stewart Iglehart, Raymond Guest, Stephen (Laddie) Sanford, Elbridge T. Gerry, Cecil Smith, Allan Scherer, Mario G. deMendoza III, Pepe and Eduardo Marcos, Nachi and Bautista Heguy, Carlos and Memo Gracida, Adolfo Cambiaso, Mike Azzaro** and **William T. Ylvisacker**, a visionary who used major corporate leverage (Gould Industries Inc.) to create the Palm Beach Polo and Country Club, one of the world's most sophisticated polo resources (now owned by Tri-State Group, Inc., Glen F. Straub, chairman). The always hard-charging Ylvisaker recently bought the Saratoga Polo Club and plans to perpetuate its illustrious past.

Palm Beach Polo is often the site of the oldest and most prestigious polo tournament in the USA—the **United States Open Championship** (begun in 1904 and, with the exception of breaks for the two World Wars, has been played ever since at various locations around the country).

Palm Beach County is an important equestrian center—Delray Beach has four thoroughbred farms and a standardbred training center; the Burt Reynolds Ranch in Jupiter breeds Arabian horses; and West Palm Beach has two large training centers for trotters. During the season, over 3,500 horses are gathered in the county.

An adjunct to Palm Beach Polo & Country Club is the new **Palm Beach Polo Equestrian Club**, situated on 125 acres with four permanent barns (64 stalls each); the facility caters to riders of all sorts and hosts the Winter Equestrian Festival, which runs four weeks, has four major events and over $100,000 in prize money; about 5,000 participants and spectators attend the event.

Cadillac, Cartier, Cellular One, Rolex, Ralph Lauren, Coca-Cola, Mega, Templeton Funds, Outback, Mirage Resorts and **Broward Yachts** all have major polo involvement and sponsor key tournaments. About 12 years ago, polo sponsorship was virtually zip; today companies spend up to $5 million for tournament sponsorship over a 12-month period. Ralph Destino (Cartier, Inc. former chairman, who brought polo ponies to Worth Avenue a few years back in celebration of the Cartier International Open at the Palm Beach Polo & Country Club) notes: "Polo is about style, quality, taste, beauty and elegance—the affinity appeals." Although the cost of sponsorship can be as little as $35,000 (for a single tournament), Cartier has spent more than $1 million for matches. Cadillac's role as official car (on the playing field) is very expensive and the Cadillac World Cup Tournament has been so successful that Toyota Motor Corporation has also picked up on tourney sponsorship. Rolex has a Gold Cup Tournament that has attracted the likes of Prince Charles. The Ralph Lauren image has benefited greatly from the famous silhouette of a horseman with mallet; and Lauren has participated in a series of polo tournaments to the satisfaction of the sales curve.

On an individual basis, polo playing is **very expensive**; an enthusiast should be prepared to spend about $15,000 to play polo twice a week for three months; maintaining the three required ponies costs at least $30,000 annually, and ground fees can add another $5,000 per year. As a pony stable grows, $5,000 to $10,000 each month is needed for 12-14 horses. Playing to win can easily cost $500,000 to $1 million per year (most costs go towards purchase and upkeep of horses; good horses can cost $40,000 plus; an average polo pony costs $20,000). Personal equipment adds up, too: mallet @ $30 to $70; ball @ $2; helmet @ $60 to $100; jersey @ $20 to $60; pants @ $65; knee guards @ $100; boots @ $200 to $600; spurs @ $50; bridle @ $150 to $300; saddle @ $400 to $1,000. The average replacement of these items for a rider and horse is $2,000 per year.

For the record, the U.S. National Polo Associaton suggests these polo facts:

* Average annual income of polo players: $174,000
* Average age of polo players: 40
* Number of registered players in the U.S.: 5,000
* Approximate number of unregistered polo players in the U.S.: 5,000
* Percentage of players who are male: 73
* Average annual income for grooms: $10,000-$15,000
* Cost of trained pony: $5,000-$50,000
* Number of trained ponies needed to be competitive: 6
* Cost to feed, groom, train and replace tack for horse: $1,000 per month
* Training for horse and rider: $350 per month
* Boarding for horse: $200-$250 per month

It's easy to see that if someone wants to be

301

the best of the best in polo, a budget of about $1 million is in order. Competition in the 60 countries and 255 clubs where polo is played is tough, and the fans (who have an average annual income of at least $100,000 and a net worth of $500,000) are very demanding.

Some top polo players who are also top social figures are **Martin Tarnapol**, Sr. VP, Bear, Stearns; **Martin Gruss**, CEO, Gruss & Co.; **Geoffrey Kent**, CEO, Abercrombie & Fitch; **Henryk de Kwiatkowski**, international aircraft merchant; the **Busch clan** (Adolphus, Billy, Andy, Peter), brewers; **George Haas**, CEO, Haas Financial Corp.; and **Guy de Wildenstein**, owner, Wildenstein Galleries; **Adam Lindeman**, Mega Music Company and Cellular One; **Neil Hirsch**, Blackwood Team; **Skeeter Johnson**, Coca-Cola, and **Pedro Morrison**.

For the first time in the 16-year history of the Palm Beach Polo & Country Club, women have competed in major tournaments; among them are **Phoebe Ingram, Sylvia Fine, Julie Boyle, Sunny Hale, Gillian Johnson, Vicki Armour** and **Alina Carta**, who hold their own in very aggressive play.

Although polo is a deadly serious game, with high-investment in assembling a team, high-risk in playing the sport, and high-stakes in the potential profitability of a team, it has plenty of **social cachet** and has support across a broad range of businessmen, socialites, entertainers.

Four polo clubs are headquartered in the Palm Beaches—the **Palm Beach Polo & Country Club** in Wellington; **Royal Palm Polo** in Boca Raton; **Gulfstream Polo Club** in Lake Worth; and **Windsor** in Vero Beach. The largest and glitziest club is Palm Beach Polo; the oldest Gulfstream; newest Windsor (where Prince Charles plays when in the area); and the only year-round activity is at Royal Palm

The major appeal of **Palm Beach Polo & Country Club** is its casual atmosphere (jeans and polo shirts) and youthfulness (active, successful 35-year-olds); although golf and tennis are popular sports in Wellington, horses are almost second-nature, and many children are taught to ride before age five. Unlike Palm Beach, where formality is the keynote, the "western" suburbs are given to a social freestyle.

On any given Sunday, when major matches are played, notables like **Calvin Klein, Susan Lucci, Dick Smothers, Gregg Allman, Jimmy Buffett, Mollie Wilmot, C.Z. Guest, Norman Brinker, Fitz Dixon, Tom Quick, Helen Boehm, Gale Brophy, Curt Gowdy** and **Orator Woodward** can be seen. The day usually starts with brunch, some light talk, the tournament at 2 or 3 p.m., either cocktails or dinner and a post-mortem on the day's score—about eight hours of playful and instructive fun.

Other chieftans in the world of horsemanship: **Bill Lickle**, owner of *Victorian Hill*, who won the National Steeplechase Association's Owner

Championship, and other major titles in recent years: **William Condren, Joe Cornacchia** and **Gale Brophy**, owners of Kentucky Derby winner *Strike the Gold* in 1991, and *Go for Gin* in 1994 (Condren and Cornacchia - owners); **Ogden and Dinny Phipps**, owners of many entries in various thoroughbred racing championships; **Peter Brant, Henryk de Kwiatkowski, Dee Conway, Jeanne Vance, Milton "Laddie" Lance** and **Fred De Mateis** are all top thoroughbred owners. Associated with the United States Equestrian Team, as riders or promoters of various events, are: **Mason Phelps, Jr.**, **Beverly Wilkes, Tim Grubb, Nancy Rutter Clark, Joanie and Murray Goodman** (whose daughter, **Marley**, is a distinguished rider in grand prix horse show-jumping competition), **Cornelia Guest, Bert and Diana Firestone, Sylvia Firestone, Alison Firestone, Renee and Bill Lickle, Joe Zada, D.D. Matz, Gene Mische, Neil Hirsch, Michelle Grubb, Susan Gubelmann, Ron Neal, Colleen and Bob Haas, Ronnie Beard, Kelly Klein, Nan Sexton, Stan and Janna Rumbough, Scott Snyder, Bruce and Elin Dixon Miller, Brownlee and Agneta Currey, Angela and Bill Koch** and **Marla and Bud Paxson.**

—YACHT YARN—

*T*he **Palm Beach Yacht Club** was founded in 1911; E.M. Brelsford was its first Commodore. Races were traditionally held on Washington's Birthday and visiting world-class yachts and their owners were the talk of the town. Commodore Clark succeeded Brelsford; he erected the first official clubhouse on his Intracoastal property. Later the club moved to West Palm Beach, where it is a popular attraction for boat people and some of Palm Beach's noteworthy citizens.

Changes in local yachting are evident; in the 30s the **Vanderbilts'** *Alva*, Solomon Guggenheim's *Frientze*, **Horace Dodge's** *Delfine*, and J.P. Morgan's *Corsair* (all ranging in length from 150 to 300 feet) were the biggest yachts; each carried a crew of 25 men. Actual costs for these ships topped $2 million. Because the maximum yacht the docks could accommodate then (and now) is 140 feet, these vessels were anchored in Lake Worth between the bridges. Over the years the waters in Lake Worth became shallower, making it impossible for the largest yachts to be docked locally.

Presently, these are among the more luxurious yachts in Palm Beach: *Blue Horizon Le Quatre* (100' sailboat) owned by Mrs. O. Roy Chalk; *Lady Caroline* (84' Burger) and the Silver Coud (100' Burger) owned by Mr. and Mrs. Alexander Dreyfoos; *Beth-A-Belle* (110' cruiser) owned by Mr. and Mrs. Edward Hennessy; *Enchantress* (118' Defoe) owned by Mr. and Mrs. Samuel duPont; *Golden Greek* (114' Bennetti) owned by Mr.

and Mrs. Alexander Gregory; *Inevitable* (93' M/Y) owned by Richard Hull; *Time To* (75' ketch) owned by Averell Harriman Fisk; *Keewaydin* (85' Ketch) owned by Mr. and Mrs. Joseph Fogg and *Solution* (67' Ketch) owned by Mr. and Mrs. Thor H. Ramsing. Over 150 Palm Beachers have their own yachts or sailing vessels.

Two of the most expensive ($5 million range) and luxurious boats for their size are the *Grindstone* and the *Buckpasser*, both carrying crews of five to six men. *Grindstone* owned by **Eugene Dixon Jr.** is a 100-foot aluminum Burger designed by Jack Hargrave; **Ogden Phipps'** *Buckpasser*, also all aluminum, was designed by Jack Hargrave and built in Japan.

The *Octopussy*, owned by **Abe Gosman** (recently sold to **Hans Behr** of Manalapan for $5 million) is considered a mega-yacht by any measurement (143-foot); in addition to being a state-of-the-art craft, it can speed up to 65 mph, which makes it among the swiftest vessels in the country (it is powered by three 3,500 horsepower, three-stage turbocharged MTU engines). It was featured in the James Bond movie—*Octopussy*.

There was a time when the Palm Beach docks were the winter home of some of the great names in the world. For example, as listed in the 1936 *Social Index*, these yachts/owners made the pilgrimage to Palm Beach: *Colmena*, **Jules S. Bache**; *Eagle Point*, **Bernard M. Baruch**; *Little Nourmahal*, **Vincent Astor**; *Onika*, **Edsel B. Ford**, *Sea Urchin*, **Henry F. duPont**; *Sonia*, **Henry Carnegie Phipps**. The 353-foot *Sea Cloud* (**Marjorie Merriweather Post's** wedding present from **E.F. Hutton**) was frequently in residence; at that time it was the largest sailing yacht ever built. Mrs. Post eventually sold the four-masted barque to **Rafael Trujillo**, dictator of the Dominican Republic, who armed it and made it a warship. The *Sea Cloud* is now a charter vessel in the Caribbean.

Today, it is common to see world-class yachts like *Bonheur 2* (39.60 metres in length with accommodations for 10 passengers renting for $62,500/week); *Emerald Isle* (38.40 metres, entertains eight guests via a crew of six, priced at $42,000/week); *Mirabella C* (40 metres, handles 12 guests with a crew of seven, leases at $50,000/week); *Safe Conduct II* (35.66 metres, entertains eight guests via a crew of six at the rate of $34,000/week); and the legendary *Octopussy*, cruising up and down the Intracoastal and docking at our basin.

The Other Woman, a 192-foot luxury motor yacht, often docks at the Brazilian Docks; it is worth $30 million, features state-of-the-art technology and engineering, massive horsepower powers its 550-tons by jet propulsion, and can hoist sail along twin 135-foot-tall masts. The "granddaddy" of yachts has accommodations for 12 crew members and 14 guests and houses some $4 million worth of paintings (Matisse, Chagall, Picasso, etc.); its owner—**Edward Cantor**—is a real estate and industrial developer from New Jersey, and with his wife **Jane**, hosts lavish parties for charities and friends aboard the Australian-built floating mansion. Other visiting yachts with names like *Chardonnay, Mikado* and *Fiffanella* add to the lore of the sea and conjure up delightful fantasies.

The **Town of Palm Beach** has operated the Municipal Docks since the late 40s; it was among the first marinas to accommodate yachts in the pioneering era of Flagler and the subsequent post WWII surge in yachting activity. Today, 78 slips for yachts ranging from 50 to 190-foot, fill the basin at the western end of **Australian, Brazilian** and **Peruvian** avenues. The docks handle over 400 transient yachts each year and act as home to some 60 yacht owners either during season or year-round.

Most dock residents are married, in their 60s, are retired and make yachting a career. Some 80 percent have homes elsewhere, and 5 percent own homes on the Island of Palm Beach. Merely having a yacht suggests status as a "millionaire"; and although few dock residents talk openly about their affluence, it's understood that most of them have significant seven-figure net worths.

Maintaining a yacht requires a **hefty net worth**. The annual costs of keeping a 125-foot yacht in top shape are: $115,000 for a four-person crew ($50,000 for the captain, the rest for the mate, engineer-deckhand and chef); fuel at about $65,000 based on 65 days at sea; dock rental at $65,000 (Palm Beach dock rental ranges from $7,700 to $15,400 yearly); routine maintenance at $10,000; food at $12,000 (doesn't include the Dom Perignon!); uniforms and flags at $25,000; insurance and miscellaneous at $60,000. A paint job can cost over $100,000; casual labor and replacement parts can tally up to $20,000 per year. So, any way it's measured, a yacht is an expensive mistress, with costs as high as $500,000 per year not out of line.

The primary **yacht broker** on the Island is **Camper & Nicholson USA, Inc.** (450 Royal Palm Way); with a staff of seven professionals and an international reputation (nine offices around the world, headquarters in Monaco), the firm specializes in large sailing yachts and exclusive motor yachts. Its staff has access to an inventory of hundreds of yachts for sale and provides yacht management and customized yacht construction for individual owners. The C&N world charter inventory is also extensive, with as many as 150 yachts for lease and prices ranging from $13,000 to $350,000/week.

Trends and trivia re yachts. New boat buyers on average are 48 years old and earn $50,000 per household; 27% are women. The sale of superyachts—80 feet or longer—has doubled the past five years from $2,700 to $5,000 a year. The 325-foot *Christina O.* where Grace Kelly and Prince Rainier celebrated their wedding and Aristotle Onassis wooed Jackie, sleeps 36 and is available for charter (for the recent Millenium

New Year's week, price was $2.8 million). *The Talitha*, owned by **Paul Getty**, goes for $393,000 per week. Palm Beacher and Netscape-Silicon Graphics founder **James Clark,** has placed an order for the largest privately-owned yacht, a 300-foot vessel that will take four years to build in the Netherlands. His current high-tech sloop, *Hyperion*, is so sophisticated it can be sailed from a keyboard at home.

Yacht owners who make their domicile at the **Palm Beach Docks** consider themselves among the favored few; life is upscale, tranquil and free of the normal hassles. They enjoy the best of company, can easily fulfill their travel dreams, pleasure in the camaraderie of fellow-yachtsmen or elect to be private, and generally reap the benefits of belonging to one of the most **exclusive clubs** in the world.

Palm Beach's most famous **yachtsman** and winner of the 1992 America's Cup is **William Koch**—a man for all seasons; in his 60s, he is a centi-millionaire with a Ph.D. in engineering from Massachusetts Institute of Technology. He owns the Oxbow Group, a complex of natural resource and energy companies (headquarters in the Centurion Building at Forum Place in West Palm Beach) and is chairman of Kendall Square Research, a successful computer manufacturer.

Koch is a larger-than-life figure who is a master at breaking rules and still winning; he put up $10 million of his own money (against a reputed $69 million total investment) to skipper *America 3* for the **San Diego Yacht Club** in the America's Cup competition, and supports the all-women team concept for Cup effort. Although he has created a financial empire, his $600 million inheritance (gained as settlement in a nasty lawsuit with his brothers over control of a $30 billion energy company—Koch Industries) gave him substantial leverage. Oxbow Group has sales of about $2.1 billion; Koch has a mansion on the ocean in Palm Beach, and he and his wife Angela are "socially active" in Town.

Another hi-vis yachtsman in Town is developer **Llwyd Ecclestone** who recently won the higly competitive 4 1/2 day Newport-to-Bermuda Race, one of ocean racing's most demanding tests. With a crew of 16 in a Concordia-built Frers 66-foot sloop—*Kodiak*—Ecclestone covered the treacherous course in 86 hours, 48 minutes and 21 seconds. His prize; the St. David's Lighthouse Trophy, one of yachting's most coveted symbols of victory. Ecclestone won the Chicago-Mackinac Race in 1990 and placed second in the Port Huron-Mackinac Race that year.

—WATER WALKER—

*W*ater skier **Dick Cowell** spends several hours a day skiing across the waters of the Palm Beaches. He credits his life to the sport; after undergoing a quadruple bypass operation, doctors advised that his daily skiing helped strengthen weakened heart muscles, helping him survive the serious surgery. A competitive skier for 45 years, he was a member of the United States Water Ski Team and competed in the first World Water Ski Championships. In 1960 he introduced the sport to the West Indies and in 1963 became the secretary general of the World Water Ski Union. In 1950, Cowell set a record for the longest time on water skis—6 hours and 14 minutes; the record stood for two years.

Cowell (70-ish) was named hospitality chairman for the 21st World Water Skiing Championships held in West Palm Beach (with closing ceremonies at The Breakers). Thirty-five nations were represented in the six-day water jamboree; the event marked the first time the world championship was held in the USA since 1961. Some 50,000 water enthusiasts watched the competition, including Cowell's wife **Jackie**, who is an avid participant. Cowell was recently inducted into the International Water Skiing Hall of Fame.

Cowell also holds the record as a competitor for 40 consecutive years in the Cresta Run—the oldest of all winter sports, and the fastest with downhill toboggan speeds of 120 mph. The sporting and social event is held annually at the St. Moritz Tobogganing Club in Switzerland. Cowell leads a group of Palm Beachers to the event each year, and is considered the "Honorary Mayor" of St. Moritz.

Incidentally, **Cowell was born in Palm Beach** at the family home on El Vedado; doctors from Johns Hopkins in Baltimore were transported in to assist in his delivery. He is one of a handful of Townies actually born on the Island.

—DANCE/ROMANCE—

*P*alm Beachers like most to do the **Fox Trot**, danced to a "society tempo." About 60 percent of music played at various balls is Fox Trot, followed by Tango and Rhumba, and a variety of modern-day rhythms. The Waltz is a perennial favorite.

In early Palm Beach, dances like the Jazz Ramble (1917), the Chicago Toddle and Hello Pal (1920s), the Charleston, Black Bottom and St. Louis Hoop (1930s) and the French Tango and Valencia (1940s) came and went but always proved popular to our Island's socialites. As far back as the turn-of-the-century the Cake Walk (originated by employees of the Old Poinciana Hotel who did an animated two-step as they served cakes and other food to guests) was the novelty of the times.

Through the years, Palm Beachers kept up with the tempo enjoying rock'n roll (in the late 60s, influenced by swiveling hipster Elvis Presley); the twist in the 60s (with the gyrations of Chubby Checker and the hullygully and the boogaloo); and even the hustle and the bump (spurred by the success of *Saturday Night Fever*). Recent years have seen a return

307

to sanity with ballroom dancing, cheek-to-cheek movements, and even a touch of dirty dancing.

The only professional dance company in Town is **Ballet Florida**; under the direction of **Marie Hale,** it began as a ballet school for children, but through the years has generated enough enthusiasm and support to expand dance programs to include a professional dance company. Each Christmas the company, assisted by youthful dance students in the school, present a production of *The Nutcracker* to local audiences.

A few years ago, Ballet Florida made a giant leap into Palm Beach Society by holding a major fundraiser "Le Grand Jete" at the Flagler Museum; the event has been annualized and is a major social activity in Town. Since then, Ballet Florida has implemented a national tour company under the direction of Columbia Artists Management and has purchased a building in WPB to house the offices/studio of the group.

Former president of the Ballet's board was **Leslie Claydon-White**, a highly successful antique collector and dealer (Mill House Antiques, Woodbury, CT) who, with associates **David Veselsky** and the late **Ferris P. Ellis**, has promoted the group tirelessly with inspiration and funding (including $200,000 for a new production of *The Nutcracker* and providing one-third of the money for the new building, amongst other forms of support). Current officials are: **Susan Telesco**, president; **Jan Willinger**, chairwoman; **Colin Wright**, chairman emeritus.

Although plagued by high costs and modest income from productions (like most other cultural arts in the area) **Ballet Florida** has a strong support group, impressive funding, commitments, highly creative programs, and the zeal to win.

—PET SET—

*D*ogs still have the honor of being the most **popular** of domestic creatures, but cats are not far behind. The most common small dog is the Poodle; among large dog fanciers the Black Labrador and Golden Retriever are most desired. The most common cat on the Island is the Alley Cat. In the USA there are 50 million dogs; 58 million cats.

The most **"in"** dog: although there are many Labrador Retrievers, Poodles and Cocker Spaniels on the Island, the **Chinese Shar-pei** is the current favorite. This species was brought from mainland China 11 years ago. Fully grown Shar-peis weigh about 60 pounds; they do not worry about their wrinkles (as do many Island residents), in fact, the more wrinkles, the better the dog. The dogs are highly intelligent, lovable and expensive which may be the reason they are considered so "in." One of the more famous Palm Beach Shar-peis (*Ko-Tu*), is owned by Mrs. Carola Mandel.

308

According to the American Kennel Club, across the USA the most popular dog is the **Cocker Spaniel** followed by the **Labrador, Poodle, Golden Retriever, German Shepherd, Chow, Rottweiler, Beagle, Dachshund** and **Miniature Schnauzer**. The Poodle holds the all-time record for being "top-dog" for the longest period of time (a 25-year span from 1959-84 when the Cocker ruled supreme).

Through the years, dogs have been popular with Palm Beachers, and with U.S. Presidents: Franklin Roosevelt had a Scottie; Coolidge, a White Collie; Kennedy, an assortment—Beagle, German Shepherd, Cocker Spaniel, Welsh Terrier, Irish and Russian Wolfhounds; Nixon, an Irish Setter; Ford, a Golden Retriever; Reagan, a Bouvier des Flandres. The First Dog in the Bush administration was an English Springer named *Millie; Buddy,* a Labrador was top dog in the Clinton White house.

The most **expensive** dog is a **Komodor,** valued at approximately $5,000; not surprisingly, the owner of the Komodor prefers not to be identified; although "animal" snatching is hardly big business in the Palm Beaches, it is a continuing threat. A pedigreed dog is something of value —not only emotionally, but, quite importantly, economically.

The most **unusual** pets owned by islanders are as follows: A **penguin** resided for a year with Mr. and Mrs. George Beckworth III *(now deceased)*; in addition, the family owned a monkey and two dogs. A **kangaroo,** *Joey,* lived for several years on Via Marila with Walter Brooks *(deceased)*; because of Town pressure (the kangaroo kept jumping out of its pen), the happy animal finally found a new home in a local zoo. (Kangaroos have been banned from the Island due to the Brooks experience—they're too hard to catch. Whereas most animals can only dart in four directions, a kangaroo can hop over you, too). One family owned **two wolves** (raised since they were six weeks old); they were walked regularly on a leash and looked like silver-gray German Shepherds; most people were unaware of their true identity—only their occasional "howl" was a giveaway. The late Mrs. Robert (Anita) Young, former *"Montsorrel"* owner, had a pet, 300-lb., **tortoise** that neighborhood children used to ride. Other small creatures owned by Islanders are **ferrets, leopards** and a **Florida otter**. In these very civilized times, most pets are quite normal, and having a baby panther, for example, as shock value, just doesn't generate much applause anymore.

—ART MART—

*T*he art aficionado can have an exciting time in Town surveying the various formats and techniques of artisans, ranging from tyros to the masters. The galleries on the Island cater to every whim and appreciation and present a magnificent panoply of creations. As of this writing, the galleries are:

Ambassador Galleries, 234 Worth Ave., 802-3377. Featuring wide range of contemporary artists, plus celebrity artists (Phyllis Diller, Tippi Hed-ren, Jack Palance).

Arij Gasiunasen Fine Art, Inc., 415 Hibiscus Ave., 820-8920. Showing works by modern and contemporary masters. (Also in Annex Gallery).

Collection Privee Gallery, 125 Worth Ave., 832-3233. Eclectic furniture by mark Brazier-Jones plus paintings by Picasso, Matisse and Rodin.

Findlay Galleries, 165 Worth Ave., 655-2090. Featuring landscapes, floral studies and Masters works.

Florence Gallery, 309 Worth Ave., 833-6660. Presents quality recreation of the Masters.

Galeria of Sculpture, 11 Via Parigi, 659-7557. Exhibiting American crafts by various artists and Italian sculpture.

Gallery Via Veneto (Prince Monyo), 226 Worth Ave., 835-1399. Exclusively showing paintings and sculpture by Prince Monyo of Romania. (Also Versailles Gallery).

Gallery 5, 325 Worth Ave., 366-9466. Contemporary works by Patricia Nix, Hugh O'Neill, Bruce Helander, Joanne Netting, Elyse Lucian Bernhard and others.

Grand Armee, 256 Worth Ave., 835-1958. Exhibiting unique military antiques—drums, decorations, uniforms, paintings, medals.

Irving Galleries, 332 Worth Ave., 659-6221. Featuring work by artists such as Helen Frankenthaler, Larry Rivers, Ben Shonzeit and William Barnet.

John Surovek Gallery, 349 Worth Ave., Via Parigi, 832-0422. Featuring American artists, including watercolors by Stephen Scott Young and paintings by William Glackens.

Palm Beach Society Gallery, 240 Worth Ave., 659-5555. Featuring modern "sculptured canvas" by Jennings.

Philips Galleries, 318 Worth Ave., 832-6311. Features the Masters and modern art.

Russeck Gallery, 203 Worth Ave., 832-4811. Featuring paintings, sculptures, drawings by modern and contemporary (20th century) Masters.

Select Fine Art, Inc., 339 Worth Ave., 655-6508. Featuring artforms of renowned artists.

Wright Gallery, 150 Worth Ave., 832-7724. Contemporary and modern masters, including Milton Avery, Ed Baynard and Donald Roller Wilson.

The Palm Beaches also offer a wide variety of art oriented museums and venues where some of the world's great art is displayed: **Ann Norton Sculpture Gardens** (832-5328)—brick and granite sculptures by Norton and special exhibits; **The Robert and Mary Montgomery Armory Art Center** (832-1776)—variety of showings in multi-media; **Flager Museum** (655-2833)—historical presentations, art and sculpture of high society; **Northwood University** (478-5555)—exhibitions, auctions of local artists; **Norton Museum of Art** (832-5196)—world-class collection of the Masters and revolving exhibitions of major international collections; **Palm Beach Institute of Contemporary Art** (582-0006)—contemporary presentations via film, slides, art, posters, usually emerging artists; **Palm Beach International Arts & Antique Fair/International Fine Arts Expositions** (220-2690)—several art fairs each year with outstanding creations from around the world; **Society of the Four Arts** (655-7226)—library of the arts, gardens, sculpture.

Among the highlights of recent exhibitions are: "Raoul Dufy: The Last of the Fauves," "The Invisible Made Visible: Angels From the Vatican," "Half Past Autumn; The Art of Gordon Parks" (all from The Norton Museum of Art); "The Cecil Family Collects: Four Centuries of Decorative Arts from Burghley House," and "Empire of the Sultans: Ottoman Art from The Khalili Collection" (from The Society of the Four Arts).

Our Town has a plenitude of **fine artists** with varying levels of skills and pedigrees; each offers a fascinating glimpse of life through his/her special prism:

Alfons Bach—award-winning celebrated Industrial Designer (Fellow and past president of Industrial Designers Society of America); coming to Palm Beach in 1960 he has become known for his colorful watercolors which have been exhibited around the world. He is listed in *Who's Who in American Art*; **R.W. Cowan**—portrait painter of royalty (King Hussein, Prince Rainier of Monaco) and show business personalities (Julio Iglesias); **Grace Forest**—does socially conscious work depicting world harmony and violence; **Alice Forster**—many types and styles, nature scenes; **Ouida George**—whimsical landscapes and domestic scenes; a

311

Palm Beacher since the mid-50s, collected by the rich and famous; **Cynthia Gibbons**—noted NYC and Palm Beach semi-impressionist artist with many exhibitions around the country; is also a fine art dealer (negotiated the sale of a Picasso and a Dali recently); **Judith Murat Grubman**—specializes in oils in whimsical style, also does ceramics and portraits (has donated designs for many ball program covers and invitations, posters and direct mail pieces) which have been exhibited widely in Palm Beach and NYC; **Bruce Helander**—artist and exhibitor, collector and writer; shows "cutting edge" art and creates superb, innovative collages; **Page Lee Hufty**—watercolorist with many credits, light and airy work but with a message (recently had a showing in Washington, D.C., to benefit Lighthouse for the Blind); **Huldah (Mrs. Ephraim F.) Jeffe**—award-winning impressionist specializing in LaBelle Epoque interpretations (also a major producer of reproductions sold through the NY Graphic Society), shows at Findlay Galleries; **Muriel S. Kaplan**—portrait sculptor with emphasis on famous personalities (Kennedy, Nixon, Reagan), has works in Columbia, Brandeis and Texas Universities; **Helmut Koller**—an acclaimed photographer of fashion and people, turned painter with objects that show motion, light and the "beingness" of people, also devotee of work about native Americans and animals; **Barbara Lawless**—romantic realist who creates in several media, shows at the Four Arts and Norton Gallery; **Norman LeBeau**—former jewelry designer, now sculpts bronze figures with "somebody inside them"; **Claire May**—sculptor of body works and dancers; exuberant, high-definition images; **Matthew McCarthy**—stressing that "art is the antidote for life," his work is versatile, abstract with pastoral feelings; **Thomas McKnight**—prolific painter who blends fantasy with reality in a colorful, highly detailed composition (also does silk-screen limited editions and posters), has shown around the world and authored a book exhibiting his works; **Daniel Meyer**—a sculptor for Absolut Vodka and multi-talented painter who goes for the highest form of creativity in all his work; **Diane Millner**—classic style in various mediums, considered the "Palm Beach Society" portraitist, also creates "dimensional" contemporary art; **Clemente Mimun**—figurative, abstract and floral images, vibrant, expressionistic; **Marsha Montoya**—massive sculptures in bronze, animate and inanimate objects; **Prince Monyo**—master bronze sculptor, huge figures, lifelike and overpowering; **Trudy Order**—combines semi-abstract elements in impressionist style; recognized by UNICEF as top interpreter of humanity; **Mary Louise O'Sullivan**—known for interpretations of Mediterranean moods in acrylics; realistic, brilliant use of color and reflections of sunlight on peaceful harbors. Recently she has been painting and photographing birds in the Everglades. Her works are represented in many museums and private collec-

312

tions throughout the world; locally she exhibits at Hobe Sound Galleries; **John Raimondi**—sculptor of massive images; deals with wildlife and the environment; **Evelyn Wallace Richter**—former art dealer, paints landscapes, still lifes, florals and animals; **Tomasz Rut**—grandiose oil paintings of larger-than-life mystical images in the style of Michelangelo, creates a patina of aging via a variety of transparent glazes yielding an illusionistic and expressive beauty in his figures; **James Jennings Sheeran**—creates sculptured canvas, combination wooden silhouettes with blazing color on canvas (won the Prix de l' Originalite in Paris recently); **Robert St. Croix**—oversized true-to-form sculptured bronze figures, also glass varieties, known as the "Renaissance Artist" since his work emcom-passes Greek era figures, children playing, sports figures, beautiful women.

In the last five years, the **art market** has been cyclothymic, but in the last few decades it has risen dramatically:

* The art market continues to outstrip the stock market, precious metals and interest rates; according to the Sotheby's Art Index, modern paintings showed an annual increase of 37.5 percent.

* Lithographs and serigraphs have consistently gone up in value, whatever their price range.

* A magnificent Original Miro Print worth $895 in '79 could fetch $10,000 in today's market.

* A Chagall lithograph could sell for $960 in '73, while Chagalls on the New York and London markets now sell anywhere from $15,000 to $25,000 U.S. (up to 2,500 percent and more).

* Jasper John's Screen Print, *Target,* jumped in value 285 percent in just six months.

* Eric Fischl's Print, *Year of the Ground Dog*, issued at $3,000 in '73, now sells anywhere from $26,400 to $41,000.

At the turn of the century, the typical salesroom price of a painting by **Vincent Van Gogh** was the equivalent of $829 in current dollars; however, in '95, the artist's *Portrait du Dr. Gatchet* fetched $82.5 million at auction, setting a new record for the sale of a painting.

Recent prices for classic art have been astronomical; *Irises* by Van Gogh went for $53.9 million; *Nature Morte: Rideau a fleur et fruits* by Cezanne, was sold to Ronald Lauder for $50 million; *Pierrette's Wedding* by Picasso sold for $48.9 million; *Yo Picasso* by Picasso at $47.8 million; *Sunflowers* by Van Gogh at $39.9 million, and *Acrobat; and Young Harlequin* by Picasso at $38.4 million.

Picasso was the most prolific of all painters. During a career that spanned 78 years, it has been estimated that he produced about 13,500 paintings or designs, 100,000 prints or engravings, 34,000 book illustrations and 300 sculptures and ceramics, plus drawings and tapestries. His lifetime work has been valued at well over $1.5 billion.

The highest price ever paid for an art work was $82.5 million for a Van Gogh, purchased in 1990 by the late Japanese paper tycoon, Ryoe Saito.

The record sale for an American artist is *Lost on the Grand Banks* by Winslow Homer—it went for $30 million to Microsoft Corp. chairman **Bill Gates** in 1998; next biggest sale was for *Polo Crowd*, a 1910 oil painting by George Bellows, which went for $27.5 million in 1999; third place is believed to be Edward Hopper's *Hotel Window* at $12 million (sold by Palm Beach art dealer Arij Gasiunasen for the *Forbes Magazine* Collection to an unnamed buyer in 2,000); and in fourth place, John Singer Sargent's *Cashmere*—sold at $11.1 million in 1996.

The highest price ever bid in a **public auction** for any painting was $6.4 million for *Juliet and Her Nurse*, painted by Joseph Mallard William Turner (1775-1851) in Venice in 1836, and sold in '80 at Sotheby's Parke Bernet, NYC, to an undisclosed collector. The previous owner was 82-year-old Flora Whitney Miller. The 3x4-foot canvas had been in Mrs. Miller's family since 1901 and had not been on public view until '66.

The highest price ever paid for a painting by a **female artist is** $1.1 million at Christie's, NYC in 1983, for *Reading Le Figaro* by Mary Cassatt (1844-1926).

The **John H. Surovek Gallery** (Via Parigi) has been specializing in 19th and 20th Century American Art for 20 years. The gallery recently sold two paintings for over $1 million each: a Van Gogh and a Childe Hassam; the gallery had the distinction of acquiring two paintings by Robert Henri (*Spanish Dancer* and *The Cigarette*) which had been seen only four times since 1904; the works are considered monuments in the career of Henri and very distinguished in the art world.

As for the most valuable painting of all time, the *Mona Lisa* (La Gioconda) by Leonardo da Vinci (1452-1519) in the Louvre, Paris, was assessed for insurance purposes at the highest figure ever ($100 million) for its move for exhibition in Washington, D.C. and NYC. It was painted in c. 1503-07 and measures 30.5 x 20.9 in. It is believed to portray Mona (short for Madonna) Lisa Gherardini, the wife of Francesco de Giocondo of Florence. The husband is said to have disliked it and refused to pay for it. Francis I, King of France, in 1517 bought the painting for his bathroom for 4,000 gold florins or 92 oz. of gold.

—PUNDITRY—

*T*he **Pundits** are a select group of 100 or so prominent Palm Beach businessmen who meet over lunch occasionally (once a month during the season, sometimes twice) to enjoy each other's company, and importantly, to listen to a featured speaker (who is usually the houseguest of a fellow Pundit). In the past, speakers have included Donald Trump, Alexander Haig, Ambassador Vernon Walters, Gerald Ford, Jeanne Kirkpatrick, George Schultz and other illustrious celebrities in politics, science and the arts. Meetings are usually held at The Colony and most gatherings are planned in advance; however, if a famous person just happens to be visiting Town and is available, meetings have been arranged with one day's notice to accommodate the speaker's schedule (the group is said to have the best telephone committee on the Island). Members are strictly male, but females are welcome on special "Ladies Days." Included in the organization are **Allen Manning**, unofficial "Head," assisted by **Wilson Lucom, Harrison Robertson, Reid Moore, Jr.** and **Robert L. Gardiner.**

—WAR BIRDS—

*T*he **War Birds** is an organization whose members are former or present **British pilots**; associate members are pilots from other countries who joined British fliers in World War II. The "Birds" meet a few times a year and recently have initiated a campaign to help raise funds to build the American Air Museum in Britain, in honor of American Airmen based in England during the war. Palm Beach members include John Fisher, George Frost, Donald Paton, Paul Rodzianko, Don Teel, Graham Whitfield, John Christlieb, Frederick Gibbons, Norman McDonald, Steve Middleton and the late Nigel Marix.

—VINE & WINE—

The Town's most impressive wine cellars: **The Robert Gordons** boast some 3,500 bottles of fine wines ranging from a Chateau Louis Latour '55 to a Chateau Lafite Rothschild '66, with dozens of varieties in inventory; among them are Montrachet, Clos de Mouches, Romanee Conti '69, La Tache '70, Krug and Dom Perignon Champagnes and Chateau d'Yquem '53. They are members of eight international wine organizations; including Eschanson de Chateauneuf du Pape, L'Ordre Mondial des Gourmets Degustateurs, Pairie des Vins a Arbois, Confrerie St. Vincent-Vigerons de Mercurey and Commanderie des Vinophiles du Canada.

Bob Cuillo probably has the most extensive cellar with over 5,500 bottles representing the best from every wine capital in the world. Some date back to the 1920s and were purchased from rare wine dealers; others are more contemporary from new sources such as Australia and Chile. The walk-in cellar is climate controlled with redwood racks; another 1,000 bottles are still in cases. Mr. Cuillo recently bought a vineyard in Italy and is producing his own wine under the label *Villa Casalvento*; it will be marketed in Europe and the USA.

315

Robert Gottfried has two separate cellars (the cellar for reds holds 500 bottles, and the white wine cellar has 1,500 bottles); they are state-of-the-art construction, concrete and steel with polyurethane-sprayed walls. The door weighs 471 lbs. (handmade, originally from an old European castle), there is an oak table and chairs for tastings, an alternate generator in case of power failure, and a computer chiller which keeps the cellar at 57 degrees.

Many Islanders are big-time wine collectors and consumers and maintain a wine cellar in the $25,000 range, as follows:

Quantity	Wine	Cost
1 case (12)	1985 Veuve Clicquot Vintage Reserve Champagne	$ 485
1 case	1985 Dom Perignon Champagne	900
1 case	1990 Domaine des Comtes Lafon Meursault-Charmes	1,200
1 case	1990 Domaine Leflaive Batard-Montrachet	1,400
1 case	1989 Louis Latour Corton-Charlemagne	900
1 case	1991 Kistler "Durrel Vineyard Sand Hill" Chardonnay	350
1 case	1991 Chalone Chardonnay	350
1 case	1990 Zind-Humbrecht Riesling—Brand Grand Cru	395
1 case	1990 Leonetti Cellar Cabernet Sauvignon	325
1 case	1989 Caymus "Special Selection" Cabernet Sauvignon	700
1 case	1989 Dunn "Howell Mountain" Cabernet Sauvignon	700
1 case	1987 Dominus Estate	540
1 case	1990 Chateau Margaux	950
1 case	1990 Chateau Leoville-Barton	320
1 case	1989 Chateau Lynch-Bages	480
1 case	1982 Chateau Mouton-Rothschild	2,400
1 case	1990 Domaine Leroy Romanee Saint-Vivant	2,800
1 case	1990 Jean Gros Richebourg	1,500
1 case	1990 Louis Jadot Gevrey Chambertin—Clos Saint-Jacques	575
1 case	1990 Comte Armand Pommard—Clos des Epeneaux	600
1 case	1991 Domaine Drouhin Pinot Noir	275
1 case	1990 Saintsbury Pinot Noir Reserve	325
1 case	1990 Chave Hermitage	825
1 case	1989 Domaine de la Nerthe Chateauneuf-du-Pape	250
1 case	1988 Guigal Cote Rotie—La Mouline	1,800
1 case	1989 Angelo Gaja Barbaresco "Sori Tilden"	1,300
1 case	1985 Monsanto Chianti Classico "Il Poggio"	375
1 case	1991 Duckhorn Merlot	250
1 case	1990 Matanzas Creek Merlot	250
1 case	1991 Ravenswood "Dickerson Vineyard" Zinfandel	185
1 case	1990 Storybook Mountain "Estate Reserve" Zinfandel	270
12 half bottles	1988 Chateau d'Yquem	1,000

TOTAL $24,975

—PALM BEACH NARCISSISM—

I never said—I want to be alone," noted Greta Garbo, "I only said I want to be **left** alone." The fabled actress was so notorious in her search for anonymity that she qualified as a masterful **Narcissist,** for she needed control over her life (to avoid criticism) and demanded-but-repudiated adulation in a way that kept her prominently in the press. Never has a person used the media so adroitly; in her absence she was constantly present, and feeding her ego without exposing it. **Image-makers** through the years have praised Garbo for her Machiavellian use of the media and her frequency of message. Whatever imperfections she might have had never came to light on the front page of *The National Enquirer*, a feat unto itself in this era of visible, electronic self-adulation. Typifying the narcissism of the 80s (and now the 2000s) was Warren Beatty's evaluation of Madonna: "She doesn't want to live off-camera."

Narcissism comes from success, hard-won or ill-gained. An 18-year-old model or actress who suddenly is cover girl to all the world gains entree to **mates, money, respect** almost too easily and too quickly. After a while it's difficult to separate her need for personal acceptance from the requisites of her profession; she's in the limelight whenever in public and soon becomes the petulant personality expected of her. If her image program goes well, she'll soon be the darling of the press for her **conspicuous self-indulgence** (a la Streisand and the late MM); whatever her public aberrations, they will add to her perception as a star, and feed her **narcissistic** needs, too.

A particularly disturbing aspect of narcissism can be the great divide between a warm, overindulgent **childhood** and a **real world** that never can match expectations—result is a tentative adult who searches for love indiscriminately, never finding it because to get love, one has to be capable of returning it. This is especially true when adulation is based on inherited physical beauty or wealth, and the **inheritor** feels that praise for her is false in that looks or money were bestowed on her and were not from personal accomplishments. Look to Barbara Hutton, Gloria Vanderbilt, Doris Duke (even Leona Helmsley who presumed infallibility) for proof of this vulnerability.

What makes **narcissism** even worse is the love of **publication**; all the world reveres a winner, and many people model their lives after a great public figure, a hero, icon, manipulator of the media. In contemporary America, there is nothing **worse** than **not** being talked about. Today's **narcissist** has little trouble getting adulation—he/she can spread the word about bouts with alcohol, AIDS, family mayhem, drugs, any perversity by talking to **Oprah**, or **Rosie**; the messiest divorces and legal hassles are on display in *Divorce Court*; and if Kitty Dukakis won't talk to the *Boston Globe*, she will tell **Barbara Walters** and millions of viewers about her booze addiction. **George Bernard Shaw** observed decades ago that "An American has no sense of privacy. He does not know what it means. There is no such thing in the country." By most standards, we enjoyed great privacy when that statement was made; today, privacy suggests isolation from the press, and thereby a kind of loser attitude. To be a winner = being the object of the media—exposed, examined, accepted or rejected.

Once upon a time there were honor and discretion in the **mass media**; when **FDR** was sworn in as President, the majority of his fellow Americans were unaware he was crippled; the drinking bouts of **William Holden** and **Spencer Tracy** were carefully guarded by Hollywood moguls (who controlled the lives of stars with uncanny success); **Joan Crawford** was the perfect mommy for several decades; and **JFK** was portrayed as the quintessential family man. The modus operandi of the press in that era wasn't motivated as much by the bottom line, but with more competition and a new rash of mergers/acquisitions, media companies had to dig deeper to come up with more provocative headlines and more exposure of members of the sacred society on TV. When a pair of junior reporters brought down the Nixon administration via Watergate, all barriers vanished; everybody was fair game for young journalists who found it easier to make their reputation by devastating an icon than by thoroughly investigating a story. With gravity on their side, totaling a person, company, or institution was relatively easy.

Nobody craves **negative publicity**, but plenty of society types want **media coverage**. No wonder high-powered social publicists can get fees up to $100,000 to launch a social career or hype a particular benefit. The Ladies who Lunch, chefs, restaurateurs, florists, designers, models, artists and writers all seek the media limelight as a way to enhance careers and add to their portfolios. For these mobile-and-visible media seekers, **privacy is death**; they are the antithesis of Howard Hughes who became so reclusive that upon his demise it was said: "It's a shame Hughes had to die to prove he was alive."

The media in Palm Beach, and the need for coverage, is subtler than in other cities; Scott Fitzgerald's line about the rich being different applies perfectly. Most dwellers here have had their fling with the press, felt the ecstasy of winning (and the agony of losing), have worn honors comfortably and then placed them on the mantel. Like J.P. Morgan, who so detested publicity that he never attended a public meeting or made a speech, most Islanders treasure privacy and the internalized life. There are certainly occasions when publicity of self-and-cause is welcomed—Chairing a Ball, for example—but once the function is over and the money is in the bank, a retiring but very self-assured personality re-emerges and carries on with the quotidian routines of life.

Invading privacy is big-buck stuff for the tabloids; a really inside story of the personal tragedy or perversity of a celebrated one can earn a reporter $50,000; and a tip about insider-trading and the attendant arrest of the offender, all live, on camera, in the trader's office, can make a TV journalist an overnight star, and launch him (and his hair spray) into the big time. Nothing is too mundane, nothing is sacred, there are no boundaries, and ethics-be-damned in the quest for hot copy. Wanting to be left alone almost guarantees that someone will come after you.

Even a **Narcissist** knows the danger of talking too much, revealing too much history, or being too chummy with the press. The loyalty of a reporter is to the story; **human interest** is the operative word; **human being** is just a means by which the story end is justified.

Photo: Davidoff Studios

**CHARLES, PRINCE OF WALES
AND DUKE OF CORNWALL**
during a visit to Palm Beach Polo & Country Club

319

JOAN RIVERS, CHRISTOPHER AND GALE BROPHY
plenty of panache

MELINDA AND BUTCH TRUCKS WITH HELEN AND JAMES ROSBURG
fun-loving in the grand manner

SUSAN AND MICHAEL, PATTI AND PERRIN BLANK
fully in harmony with the Universe

JAMES AND KAY MORRISSEY
friends, comrades, chums, whatever

321

SHARON (QUEENEY) AND ROBERT WEITZ
allies in action, great attitude

POLLY AND MICHAEL FAWCETT
smiles-all-around, consistently upbeat

REX AND JEANNE FORD
fresh, festive and faultless

**CHARLES RANSON, PATTI TRAVIS
AND JANE McCONNELL**
youthful, kinetic and result-oriented

ALICIA AND BILL BLODGETT
sparkling, smooth and skilled

GEORGE AND BETSY MATTHEWS
obliging and outgoing leaders

ROBERT AND DR. LUCIA HARVEY
affable, affirmative activists

TOM ROSSIN, JUDY SHEPHERD AND TOM PLEDGER
indefatigible and intrepid idealists

Photo: Lucien Capehart

HILLIE MAHONEY AND BILL PALMER
pluck, efficiency and vision

Photo: Lucien Capehart

CONSTANCE AND MARTIN PURCELL
alive and alert advocates

CHAPTER IX

PLUTOCRATS IN PARADISE
(Pundits, Practitioners & Promoters)

Photo: Lucien Capehart

LISA ANDERSON AND BILL BLASS
engaging, charming and genial

—POINT OF VIEW—

*P*alm Beach **architecture** has changed signficantly over the years. At the turn of the century (1900), homes tended to be box-like and shingled, New England-style. Before long, they began perking up with a nod towards the gracious mansions and plantations of the south. The breakthrough came with Flagler's **"Whitehall"** which was Spanish-mission in style (the work of design firm Carrere & Hastings); it set the stage for architectural derivatives. When **Addison Mizner** arrived in 1918, he compounded styles of the day by creating the Spanish/Moorish/Venetian/European look for The Everglades Club, which was then copied extensively around Town.

The 20s introduced Northern-style homes into our sunny environment; **Marion Sims Wyeth** debarked from New York and unloaded grandiose designs and sophisticated detailing. Then came **Maurice Fatio** (also from the Big Apple) who added a dash of flash to his homes but kept Wyeth's elegance. He embellished his homes with glass blocks and timber and cut coral stone. Not to be outdone, in the 30s and 40s, **Howard Major** introduced homes ranging in design from French neoclassical to Japanese; **John Volk** offered a Bahamian style with variations in the Norman, Polynesian and Chinese schools of architecture. By the 50s, the influence of **Frank Lloyd Wright** was evident with long, low svelte buildings; and the jet age ushered in curves, and angles and very mod silhouettes in the 60s and 70s.

In the 80s, there were moderate revivals of most types of architecture featured over the years, but the hit of the decade was the Regency-look, which can be credited to the French or English 18th Century, executed with severe styling, isolated elements of sculpture, square angles and white or gray coloration. Builder/developer **Robert Gottfried** has been responsible for "hundreds" of Regencys (although the originator of this type home is believed to be Clarence Mack from Ohio); Gottfried's most visible developments are the Regent Park and Parc-Monceau, both in the Regency style.

Examples of **Mizner-styled homes** can be seen at: 1095 N. Ocean Blvd. (the old Kennedy compound); 455 and 473 N. County Rd.; 280 N. Ocean Blvd.; 110 Dunbar Rd.; 112 Seminole Ave.; 135 Grace Trail; 150 S. Ocean Blvd.; and the Southeast Commercial Corner (239-247 S. County Rd.).

Some **Wyeth (Wyeth, King and Johnson) homes** are at: 1545 N. Ocean Way; 15 S. Ocean Drive; Bethesda-by-the-Sea at 165 Barton Ave.; and 172 S. Ocean Blvd.

Howard Major homes are at: 124 Via Bethesda; 334 N. Woods Rd. (Merrill's Landing); 756 N. Lake Way; 475 N. Lake Trail (The Vicarage); and Major Alley (411-417 Major Alley).

Some **Volk-created homes** are at: 250 Barton Ave.; 190 S. Ocean Blvd.; 116 Seabreeze Ave.; 598 S. County Rd.; and 134 El Vedado. **Addison Mizner** and **Paris Singer** had a major influence on Palm Beach; in 1917 they came to Palm Beach independently of each other. Singer came under the impression that he was dying; Mizner came without money and without a clear sense of purpose, also under the impression of impending doom. Singer, who was heir to the Singer Sewing Machine fortune, was an amateur architect; Mizner, a lover of antiquities was as much an architect as anything else. The two men whiled away their time with architectural fantasies that, as death seemed to come no closer, culminated in a determination to build. After the two adventurers talked themselves back to health, they began an architectural revolution in Palm Beach. Mizner compressed into 10 years the architectural history of Spain: he developed the workmen, crafts, kilns and shops that his structures required. All he needed was clients with money, to erect his fantasies. The result was—he reigned over his domain as architectural monarch. In the early days Flagler established the image of Palm Beach, but Mizner enlivened it with the spirit of the 20s, and with a boldness and originality rarely equalled in the development of an American town. In the 1920s the two men intented to build a veteran's hospital to be named The Touchstone Convalescent Club. Failing to attract disabled soldiers to Palm Beach, they converted their hospital to a club, named The Everglades Club; the building was a fulfillment of Mizner's romantic eclecticism in the Spanish mode and established the architectural prototype for a decade. The Club originally opened with 25 members.

Because of his successful design of The Everglades Club, Mizner received his first commission to build a house (*El Mirasol*) for the leading family of the time—**the Stotesburys.** Many other houses followed; probably his most satisfactory creation was the development of shops and apartments on Worth Avenue. With Singer's money, Mizner purchased Alligator Joe's Farm and on its location built **Via Mizner.** The following year he built a similar complex—**Via Parigi**—naming it in honor of Singer. As new architects came to Palm Beach, Mizner's popularity waned. Losing his money in the crash of 1929, he remained on the Island until his death in 1933—living off the generosity of his friends.

—MAX TAX—

*T*he largest plot of property in Palm Beach belongs to **Flagler Systems, Inc.**; the 130-acres are appraised at $139,100,404 and include **The Breakers** and adjoining apartments and condos plus the Golf Course. The 90 acres owned by Everglades Club, Inc. is second, appraised at $27,895,085.

329

Major landowners, based on recent annual taxes are:

Owner	Value	Taxes
Breakers Palm Beach, Inc.	$139,100,404	$2,985,092.49
JV Assoc.	44,000,000	939,822.80
Peltz Nelson & Claudia L.	36,763,969	765,721.80
Worth Avenue Assoc. Ltd.	32,900,000	694,374.31
Everglades Club Inc.	27,895,085	613,262.01
Kimmel Sidney	27,971,011	582,657.69
Gosman Abraham D.	23,251,285	484,507.80
Spiegel Sidney Tr.	21,586,747	476,729.53
Mar-A-Lago Club, Inc.	19,559,269	413,336.00
Thirty Eight East Corp	18,800,517	391,521.50
Palm V Assoc. Ltd.	17,000,000	358,137.84

—BRICK & MORTAR—

*P*roperty values in Town continue to escalate: nationwide, Los Angeles had the biggest gain at 31 percent; Washington, D.C., was next with a 25-percent gain; Palm Beach ranked third with an 18.5-percent gain; Chicago and Westchester County followed with 10-percent gains. Denver, Dallas and Anchorage had property value declines in the four-to-eight percent range.

* The Palm Beach real estate market is divided into **four areas**:
>   Area 1 — from Wells Rd. north to the inlet
>   2 — from Wells Rd. south to Worth Ave.
>   3 — Worth Ave. south to Sloan's Curve
>   4 — Sloan's Curve to South Palm Beach

* Last year, Palm Beach real estate firms sold about $450 million (500 property sales) in **residential** real estate; there are some 450 Realtors and Realtor associates who belong to the Palm Beach Board of Realtors (established in 1949 to ensure ethical practices among Realtors). Among officers of the board in recent years are: **Carol Hickman, John Pinson, Marlene Hayes, Ann Tierney, Jim McCann, Christine Franks, Mary Overall, Charles Romanoff, Barbara Whitford, Laura Coyner, Louis Anthony, J. Radcliff Ewing, Scott B. Gordon, Paulette Koch, Myra Mann, Zoe Anne White, Phil Smith, Zoe Stout, Anne Obolensky, Claire O'Keeffe, George M.D. Lewis Jr., William Hutton III, Carol Digges, Patricia Watts-Wearn, Barbara Shaffer, Carol Hickman, Detra Kay, Deborah Clark, Josephine DeFina Stetson, Marion Jones, Kim Nadeau** and **Richard Allison.**

* There are 65 real estate offices in Palm Beach ranging in size from a single person operation to firms with almost 100 sales associates. In each office there are a number of inactive ("license hangers"), licensed brokers who work part-time, referring sales and clients.

* There are about 5,000 condominiums on the Island; about 2,400 single-family homes. The assessed value of all Palm Beach real estate is $5.8 billion; and oceanfront property (land only) that sold for $1 a foot in 1940 now sells for $70,000/ft.

* Palm Beach's top producing (on an average) **real estate firms** are:
BARCLAY'S INTERNATIONAL REALTY, INC.
BROWN HARRIS STEVENS
(affiliated with Christie's Great Estates)
LINDA A. GARY REAL ESTATE
MARTHA A. GOTTFRIED, INC.
McCANN COYNER CLARK REAL ESTATE, INC.
LAWRENCE A. MOENS ASSOCIATES
SOTHEBY'S INTERNATIONAL REALTY, INC.
EARL A. HOLLIS, INC. (Commercial)

Eight Palm Beach brokerage firms are listed in the prestigious national publication—*"Who's Who in Luxury Real Estate."* They are: Barclay's International Realty, J. Richard Allison & Associates, Linda A. Gary Real Estate, Linda R. Olsson Inc., Martha A. Gottfried Inc., Patricia Watts-Wearn Real Estate, Paulette Koch Real Estate and Sotheby's International Realty.

The **average** selling price of homes is $1,750,000 (for condos, it's $500,000); most major sales are in cash.

In recent years, the **highest-priced** home sales were:

$19.2 million: **641 N. County Rd.**—former Ronald Perelman mansion, now owned by Oceanside Palms Estate Corp.

$18 million: **548 N. County Rd.**—Triarc Chairman Nelson Peltz's Montsorrel, plus acreage across street.

$16.5 million: **1290 S. Ocean Blvd.**—investment banker Bernard A. Marden mansion.

$14.4 million: **910 S. Ocean Blvd.**—Saudi Arabian Prince Khalid bin Sultan palace.

$14.3 million: **1300 S. Ocean Blvd.**—now owned by Ronald Perelman, formerly by developer Bud Hansen.

$13.2 million: **920 S. Ocean Blvd.**—Charles Becker owner, formerly the infamous home of James Sullivan.

The hi-tech people have also discovered Palm Beach. In the early '90s, Microsoft's **Bill Gates** tried to build a 35,000-square-foot home on the Island but couldn't find suitable land; he went on to erect a 45,000 square-foot palace in Medina, Washington. Talk.com founder **Boris Borislow** did find his place in the sun—a 10,000-square-foot house with a 2,200-bottle wine cellar at 830 S. Ocean Blvd. (price-$12.5 million). And Netscape co-founder **James Clark** and his journalist wife, **Nancy**, paid $11 million for one of the "gilded age" mansions at 1500 S. Ocean Blvd. (40,000-square-foot), once occupied by Jan Hooker (Annenberg family). The Clarks also own a large home on Middle Road. Cellular One's **George Lindemann** paid $13.1 million for Palm Beach terra firma where's he's building a 27,000-square-foot Bermuda- style house. Paxson Communications chairman and co-founder of Home Shopping Network, **"Bud" Paxson** and his wife **Marla**, paid $12 million for a manse at 780 S. Ocean Blvd., and recently opted to add more brick and mortar to their portfolio via an $8 million Mediterranean estate in Beverly Hills, CA.

Add to these impressive figures the homes (priced at $8 million or more) of **Martin Trust**, a 39,000-square-foot Palladian manse built by Robert Gottfried on N. Ocean Blvd.; nearby on the ocean is health care magnate **Abe Gosman's** 64,000-square-foot estate, with its 14-foot-tall bronze Fernando Botero statues guarding the entrance—annual taxes in the area of $450,000; **Sidney** (Jones New York) **Kimmel's** 26,000-square-foot contemporary south oceanfront estate; **Terry Kramer's** 37,000-square-foot Italian villa, with walk-in refrigerators and a 4,500-square-foot masterbedroom suite—twice as big as the average home; **Donald Trump's** *"Mar-a-Lago"* at 55,695-square-feet on almost 17-acres. (Note: most of these homes can be seen only limitedly; they are gate-enclosed or shrubbery-hidden, or have long driveways that disallow easy views—simply the privilege of the rich. "The best thing money can buy is privacy.")

Tops of the mega-mansions in cost is **Sydell Miller's** 37,000-square-foot linestone-clad manse at 1423 S. Ocean Blvd.; land cost at $26 million, total complex at about $50 million, designed by Palm Beach architect Jeff Smith.The home sits on 3.7- acres and some 334-feet of private beach (second only to the Peltz home—*"Montsorrel"* which has 600-feet of private beach).

Although these dwellings are impressive, they suffer by comparison to the great homes of Newport, R.I. **The Breakers**, built in 1895 for $5 million, and modeled after a Northern Italian Renaissance palace, has over 70,000 square-feet and 70 rooms, half of them for servants. **Marble House**, owned by Willie K. Vanderbilt (brother to Cornelius) has over 50,000 sq. ft. and used some 50 tons of marble in its construction. **Rosecliff**, built in 1900 for Mrs. Hermann Oelrich (gold and silver mining), and patterned after the *Grand Trianon* at Versailles, was used in several scenes in *"The Great Gatsby."* It has 80 rooms, and the largest ballroom in Newport.

These properties can't be priced because of their size, historical significance and practicality, but guesses are in the $50-75 million range.

For the record, according to *Worth Magazine*, Palm Beach is only the 35th most expensive community in America in which to buy real estate. **Aspen** rates #1 with a population of 5,049 and median home price of $1,512,500; **Jupiter Island** ranks second with a population of 601 robust citzens and median home price of $1,222,500. **Rolling Hills**, CA with 1,748 pop and median price of $1,165,000 is third.

Yet, another survey by the ***Robb Report*** lists Palm Beach second to Aspen in "top affluent communities." Greenwich, CT, Gross Pointe Farms, MI, and Kapalua, Hawaii are other leaders in the category.

Ocean front footage in Palm Beach (there are only 50 oceanfront homes) carries a high ticket. The former Manalapan home of **Lois Pope**, widow of *National Enquirer* publisher Generoso Pope, was sold for $15 million; with 305 feet along the ocean, the cost per oceanfront foot came to $49,180. By comparison, the 1-acre long and thin lot in Palm Beach on which the home of **Richard and Susan Smith** sits, is selling for $18.75 million, and has 240 feet along the ocean. That's equivalent to $78,125 per oceanfront foot. The premium is indicative of the price of admission to Palm Beach! As a general rule, the price for oceanfront land in Palm Beach is about $70,000 a foot; Manalapan is about $50,000. (Yet, Manalapan is expensive terrain—**Randolph Hearst** paid $35 million for the **Simon** estate!)

Real estate entrepreneur and developer **Frank McKinney** recently unveiled the most expensive "spec" house in the world—a $30 million, 72-room, 32,000-square-foot estate on three acres of oceanfront in Manalapan (1370 S. Ocean Blvd.). The massive home has 72 rooms, 18 luxurious bathrooms, eight bedroom suites including a 2,500 square-foot master bedroom suite with a 500-square-foot closet and oceanview bath, two elevators, six bars, two salt-water aquariums, glass enclosed private office with high-tech connections, fitness center, 2,000-bottle wine cellar and private humidor, movie theater, tennis court, seaside swimming pool with a swim-up bar and hot tub, six soaring windows made of the largest single panes of glass in a U.S. residence, a 12-car garage, access to the beach via a stairway that raises and lowers electronically on the dune, adjoining yacht dockage, and security cameras throughout the property. (It is the former home of Lois Pope.)

(Neighboring **West Palm Beach** real estate has also appreciated. Homes in the desireable El Cid area are now topping $300 a square-foot vs. $130 a square-foot last year. Homes that normally would sell for $300,000 are now in the $1 million range.)

The highest priced penthouse in Palm Beach is owned by **Robert Kanuth**, at 1 Via Mizner, once the personal residence of noted architect Addison Mizner; the elaborate four-story penthouse overlooks Worth Avenue and is listed at $6.5 million. Billionaire investor **Gerald Tsai** recently paid more than $6 million for the 6,000-square-foot penthouse at swanky lakeside *"Il Lugano,"* 190 Bradley Place. Other top-priced apartments are located at Two North Breakers Row, a luxury condo north of The Breakers. Large apartments go for $4 to $5 million; even an apartment with no oceanview can cost in the $3 million range. Next door is One North Breakers Row, a rental building, where six-room apartments come in at about $100,000 annually on a two-to-five year lease; they are difficult to come by (and when available, lease holders pass on improvement costs, usually around $500,000 to the next tenant). On the Intracoastal Waterway, the biggest sale was $2.9 for the largest condominium (6,230-square-feet, five bedrooms, five baths) in the Palm Beach Biltmore —the *Duke of Alba* suite, named after a Spanish Duke when the building originally opened in 1926. Buyers were **Seymore and Gladys Ziv.**

In comparison, the highest cost of a condo in New York City recently was $5.9 million for a 5,507-square-foot 10 room unit in Trump International Hotel and Tower, at Columbus Circle on Manhattan's west side. Other units in the same building run from $3.8 million to $4.7 million

The biggest mortgage held by a Palm Beacher is $25.8 million on the 46,700-square-foot oceanside mansion owned by **Nelson Peltz**. Called *Montsorrel*, the 13-acre parcel, mansion and accompanying 18,000-square-foot guest house (across the street), cost $18 million in '94 and is currently listed for sale at $75 million, the highest priced home in America. The complex sits on a 13-acre parcel and has an annual tax bill of around $765,000!

Overall, the relatively small Town of Palm Beach has 138 arteries for transportation, referred to by a myriad of names—streets, avenues, drives, roads, circles, rows, places, lanes,ways, plazas, trails, terraces, curves, vias and boulevards. There are some 1,851 businesses, 2,400 single family homes, 160 apartment buildings (housing about 5,000 apartment units). The number of **voting residents** is 9,155; number of people living in homes is 3,500, and those living in apartments = 6,500. The yacht owning population is around 100.

(This info changes often due to constant migration to and from the Island. Buying and selling of homes and apartments is something of a national pastime, and businesses are always on the move—thus these figures are only as accurate as the 1999 survey made by *Palm Beach Society* Magazine.)

—FINE DESIGN—

*N*obody dislikes a party with 500 peacocks wandering about more than an interior designer or decorator, who spend their lives trying to make "interiors" zing with flavor, bite, warmth, beauty, desirability. Peacocks on parade tend to look for connections, new chumships and assignations intently while ignoring the esoteric design or esthetics of a room. Yet, the work of interior designers is a vital part of any pleasure package and is often the *sine qua non* of social success in Palm Beach.

A key to interior designer status is membership in ASID (American Society of Interior Designers) which suggests that a practitioner has completed a course of accredited education, and/or practical work experience in interior design or a related field, and has been subject to rigorous national testing. These members have achieved the highest levels of accomplishment and knowledge in their field. The ASID appellation indicates the hallmark of professionalism.

In Palm Beach, ASID members are: **Astrid Baege, Tommy Camm, Dante Cerza, Leta Foster, Jennifer Garrigues, Claudio Guidi, Jeanine Heidtmann, Mars Jaffe, Ronn Jaffe, Sandra Johnson, Frederick Krueger, Phyllis Kuby, A. Jeanne Marks, Carol Munzenrieder, Monique Ogilvie, Bernice Parks, Eve Pomice, Janet Reynolds, John Rima, Theordore Simpson, Marilyn Stanley** and **William Wood Jr.**

Many other popular designers and decorators include: **Jack Fhipps, Bill Kopp, Pauline Pitt, Scott Snyder, Herbert Holzheimer Jr., Geoffrey Bradfield, Tui Pranich, Richard Plumer, Mimi Kemble, June Stehle Gara, Mary Lee Harper** and **Richard Himmel** *(the late)*.

The design community in Palm Beach is active on the charity scene. About 20 designers participate in the Norton Museum's **"Table Setting"** annual presentation, which showcases original and imaginative table settings. It is a major event, drawing several thousand guests. Many of the same designers contribute to the **Designer's Showhouse**, a major fundraising event for the Palm Beach Chapter of the American Red Cross. A group of interior designers and landscape designers show their stuff; each renovates or decorates one room (or the exterior) in a large home chosen for the event, thereby demonstrating individual style and skill. The activity draws upwards of 10,000 attendees over a two-week period, each paying $15 admittance fee (which goes to the Red Cross). The event appeals to consumers as well as professionals who get a chance to spy on their peers!

Robert Eigelberger is also a well-known local designer, who specializes in the restoration of architectural classics, old and revered homes almost ready for the demolition teams. Since his arrival in Palm Beach 25 years ago, he has restored about 20 homes, among them **Warden House**, a national landmark, and **Bienstar**, local sightseeing attraction. A member of the Landmarks Preservation Commission, the Preservation Society and the Historical Society of Palm Beach County, Eigelberger believes that "older is better," and his work in restoration has won him many plaudits.

—WORTH & MIRTH—

*S*ome background... **Addison Mizner** first designed a rehabilitation center for veterans at the far end of the main street, simply called the "Avenue" by Palm Beachers and the "Mink Mile" by others. The "center" was a rambling, stuccoed, poorly designed and constructed embarrassment. It went this-way-and-that-way with Moorish and Spanish eclecticism, and never rehabilitated anyone. Still, it became a legend and the home of the **Everglades Club**, a premier social club. Mizner designed other buildings along the Avenue. He predicted the Avenue would be a major commercial area; and was right on the money. Today, **Worth Avenue** is one of the most renowned shopping meccas in the world.

by Bill Olendorf

The legendary Avenue stretches from the **Atlantic Ocean to the Intracoastal** but as a shopping mecca its boundaries are from the Atlantic to Cocoanut Row—three blocks of the most varied and prestigious shops in the world. Worth Avenue is a tradition. A classic. And a thing of beauty.

The **rent** per sq. foot fluctuates wildly from a high of $513 to a low of $55; the average rental rate is about $150 (the average rental rate in Palm Beach County is $60 per sq. foot).

Worth Avenue rentals may be in the high-ticket classification, but they are not outlandish. Here's how the Avenue compares with other international commercial districts: (costs are per sq. ft.):

Madison Avenue, New York	$600
Causeway Bay, Hong Kong	$464
Champs Elysees, Paris	$460
Fifth Avenue, New York	$450
Oxford Street, London	$415
Apkujung, Seoul	$387
Pitt Street Mall, Sydney	$369
Ginza District, Tokyo	$350
Trade House Gum, Moscow	$279
Via Condotti, Rome	$225

(In terms of prestige, the most impressive **shopping arteries** in America are: Michigan Ave.—the Gold Coast in Chicago, Rodeo Dr., Madison Ave., Peachtree St., Rittenhouse Row and Union Square.)

The most expensive men's stores on Worth Avenue are **Trillion, Napoleon, Maus & Hoffman** and **Giorgio's**—items range from $75 to $40,000. Sales prices often dip 25% depending on the season.

Cartier and **Van Cleef & Arpels** are, undoubtedly, the highest-ticket jewelry retailers on the Avenue—it's no secret that you can invest $250,000 in minutes at either outlet. Cartier recently celebrated its 75th year in Palm Beach with the exhibition, *"Tiaras - Cartier's Crowning Glory"*—seven tiaras created during the 1902 - 1937 period, ranging in price from $500,000 to several million. During its 150-plus years, Cartier has created tiaras for many royals, including Princess Anastasia of Greece, the Queen Mother, and Queen Victoria Eugenie of Spain.

There's celebrity, too, a constant parade of top designers at Saks and Martha; Bill Blass, Scaasi, Oscar de la Renta, Randolph Duke, Pauline Trigere, Carolina Herrera.

The Esplanade at 150 Worth Ave. is a two-story shopping paradise with diverse salons and boutiques; it is not a shopping center as such, but an exclusive enclave of world-class shops.

In recent years, venerable names like St. Laurent, Elizabeth Arden, Sara Fredericks, Bonwit Teller, Delman Shoes and Stinchfield have vanished from Worth Avenue, only to be replaced with classics like Ferragamo, Gucci, Giorgio Armani, Escada, Pratesi, Ralph Lauren, Tiffany, MaxMara, St. John, Malo, Tourneau, and retail giant Neiman Marcus.

The types of stores on **Worth Avenue** are:

> 29 Women's specialty shops
> 18 Jewelry stores
> 10 Art galleries
> 8 Gifts and accessories
> 9 China and gift shops
> 9 Leather stores (handbags, luggage, shoes, clothing)
> 9 Antique stores
> 8 Beauty services
> 8 Food sources (restaurants and take-out)
> 5 Realtors
> 4 Men's apparel
> 3 Major retailers
> 3 Linens and lingerie
> 3 Children's apparel shops
> 1 Stationery store
> 1 Taxi service

Saks Fifth Avenue in the Esplanade is the largest store; it has 49,000 sq. ft. of selling space and a complete range of apparel, including a free-standing men's store. It is one of 60 Saks Fifth Avenue stores in the U.S. (owned by Saks, Inc., New York)

Pets can have a drink at the **"Dog Bar,"** a semi-circular trough in front of Philips Galleries (318 Worth Ave.). The "Dog Bar" was designed by architect John L. Volk in 1965 in memory of his giant schnauzer "Hans." The trough is decorated with colorful mosaic tiles topped with a silver spigot providing fresh running water. A pet can also quench his/her thirst at the "Dog Bar" in the Earl E.T. Smith Preservation Park on South County Rd.

The **oldest store** on the Avenue is **Kassatly's**—when Sam Kassatly (the late), a traveling linen and lingerie salesman from West Newark, NJ, first saw Palm Beach in 1922, he yelled: "This is God's Country!," and founded **Kassatly's Linen and Lingerie Shop.** Always an innovator, Kassatly immediately began to feature the latest European fashions and other merchandise from New York and California. The store is now run by sons Bob and Ed (who not only are bright merchandisers but also play a mean game of tennis).

The first building to be considered for involuntary designation by the Landmarks Preservation Commission is the **Gucci Building** (256 Worth Ave.), built in 1931. In the past the commission has not been able to convince Worth Avenue Merchants (owners) to apply for the voluntary designation of their properties as landmarks so the commission began an involuntary program that allows for the designation and protection of historically important buildings without the consent of the owners.

The jewelry design symbolizing early Palm Beach is the **Cartier Panther**, legendary symbol of the House of Cartier since 1917, captured in a whimsical collection of sleek and playfully posed panthers (crafted in white or yellow gold with emerald eyes and onyx noses—priced from $2,200 to $4,500). Panthers roamed the Island in the early 1900s and were the inspiration for the Cartier Panther.

The image of Worth Avenue as a haven for dowagers and white-gloved grandes dames with parasols, strolling langourously down the avenue with their chauffered-limos cruising alongside, has been displaced. The new magic is a mixture of hi-vis celeb, dotcom whiz, international socialite and confident, youthful case histories in success, who now live in Palm Beach and frequent the Avenue for whatever luxuries are requisite to their continued upward mobility. Small screen personalities like **Jay Leno, Matt Lauer, Rosie O'Donnell, Oprah Winfrey** and **Tom Brokaw** spiritedly pace the Avenue; big screen idols—**Paul Newman, Al Pacino, Kevin Spacey, Meryl Streep**—browse behind huge sunglasses. New Wave Palm Beachers like **Samantha Boardman, Tiffany Dubin, Jane and Aerin Lauder, Celerie Kemble, David and Polly Ober, Lamont and Heather Harris, Marjorie Gubelmann** and **Mary and Kane Baker** add distinctive verve to the Avenue. The tongues of Spain, Italy, Germany, France intermix with those of New York, Chicago and New Orleans. Dress is casual, attitude is relaxed, spending is often outrageous (compared to the fiscally conservative buying patterns of the Old Guard). It's a new era on Worth, as it is on the Island; and the freshness is both welcome and daunting. Evolution is inevitable.

Through the years, the **most influential** Worth Avenue merchants have been:

Sam and Alice Kassatly (the late): Kassatly's, Inc. (linens), more than seven decades on the Avenue.

Myers' Luggage: the late T.S. Myers and his new wife opened their Worth Avenue store in 1947 (they initially opened their leathery in the Alba Hotel—now the Biltmore, in 1924 before relocating on the Avenue). Mrs. Myers still actively works in her stores (another location in West Palm Beach) and is ably assisted by her two sons Ed and Richard, and daughter Jackie. In addition to a fine selection of the latest luggage, Myers' has become known for their gift items priced as low as $2.

Maus & Hoffman: Bill Maus Sr., opening his exclusive men's wear shop in 1961 on Worth Avenue, believed all his customers were personal friends and treated them accordingly. Although Bill Sr. died in 1980 (while on a buying trip to Portugal), his wife Gertrude remains as president of the corporation while sons Tom and John and other family members run the Maus & Hoffman stores in Florida. Only the finest men's wear is represented in their stores.

Findlay Galleries: opened by Walstein (Wally) Chester Findlay, Jr. on Worth Ave. in 1960. Wally Findlay (the late) is the third generation of Findlays to bring French Masters, European impressionists and post impressionists to the public. He became famous for establishing many public and private collections in America.

Richters of Palm Beach: was established in 1893 by founder Joseph Richter. Located in Miami for nearly a half-century, the store relocated to Palm Beach in 1969. Specializing in the purchase and sale of fine estate jewelry, the store in now owned by Stefan and Dudley Richter. Other Richters stores are located in Atlanta, Nashville and Hawaii.

Mariko: this mecca of baubles, bangles and beads has been an Island fixture for almost 15 years, and has been on New York's Madison Avenue for 18 years. Mme. Mariko, considered the doyenne of faux jewelry, and son Peter Kiyakawa offer a dazzling array of costume jewelry, Italian handbags, Majorica pearls, Faberge-inspired minaudieres, lockets, *objet de fantaisie* and assorted treasures.

There are a total of **eight vias** on Worth Avenue, as follows:

Via Mizner: Addison Mizner designed this shopping complex consisting of 19 buildings housing 40 small shops; topped off with his own five-story apartment (at 339 Worth; the tallest building on the Avenue). He designed a bridge that connected his living quarters with his architectural offices across the way; underneath the bridge was a little via which he named for himself—Via Mizner. After the completion of this Via, Paris Singer returned from a European trip, furious with Mizner (how dare a man whom he had personally financed name a via after himself). Mizner and Singer had a heated dispute over the matter, and Singer proceeded to build another group of shops on his own property located next to Via Mizner—the new via became Via Parigi.

Via Parigi: impressive but not up to Via Mizner's snuff.

Via Demario: traditional and well-maintained.

Via Encantada.

Via Garzo.

Via de Lela.

Via Marguery.

Via Bice: the newest Via on the Avenue—a complex of shops located near the award-winning restaurant, **Bice**.

There are **eight fountains** on the Avenue—one each in **Via Parigi** and **Via Mizner**; one at **240 Worth Avenue** (now flower-laden, in front of the offices of *Palm Beach Society* Magazine); one in the **Gucci** courtyard, one at **312 Worth Avenue** and one on the site of the former **Stagg Building**. The **Esplanade** has the distinction of two fountains. Without fail, the fountains that have not been made into flower beds are "coin collectors," and it is estimated that over $5,000 worth of miscellaneous change is dropped into the fountains each year.

The Worth Avenue **"wishing well"** is next to **Maus & Hoffman**. The well was built many years ago and until recently was used by the American Heart Association—monies found in the well were donated to the Heart Fund.

The Avenue has a number of different **parking** designations and space allocations designed to make life easier for visitors, shoppers and locals. From the ocean to Cocoanut Row, there are 127 one-hour parking spaces available; in the same area, there are 12 passenger loading/unloading lots, 29 commercial unloading areas, two taxi stands, 34 crosswalks (about four feet wide) and four fire hydrants.

Addison Mizner's pet monkey *Johnny Brown*, and Mortimer and Rose Sach's dog, *Laddie*—are buried on Via Mizner—original home of Addison Mizner and later the residence of Mr. and Mrs. Sachs. The tombstone over *Johnny Brown's* grave reads "Johnny Brown—The Human Monkey." *Johnny* was Mizner's constant companion and usually traveled wrapped around his neck. The tombstone over *Laddie's* grave reads "Our Laddie—We miss you so."

—BIG BUSINESS—

*B*anking is the largest, most diverse, most sophisticated and most competitive "industry" in the Palm Beaches. Dozens of major national banks (with branch operations) and many local banks and trust companies vie for the investment and discretionary income of residents (only 1.8 percent of USA households have incomes of $100,000/year or more; almost all Palm Beachers exceed that august level). Clients are wooed at country clubs and on golf courses and in conference rooms, with progressive intensity. With the remaining "old money" in Palm Beach and a plenitude of new funds from international investors and business-builders, the future of banking in the area is secure, but its shape and substance will probably change dramatically to meet the shifting composition of the marketplace on both a qualitative and quantitative basis.

Real estate is the Island's second biggest business category; it, too, is constantly undergoing changes in structure and format.

—BANK RANK—

*O*ur Town has a surfeit of great fortunes and more than enough institutions to service them. Due to the inexorable trend toward mergers and the big getting bigger (example: NationsBank bought Barnett Bank and Bank of America—three bank brands are now one), the number of bank brands in the area is actually decreasing while assets under administration/management and deposits are increasing substantially. Based on current deposits, in Palm Beach County, **First Union** is largest, followed by **Bank of America/NationsBank, Washington Mutual, AmTrust** and **Republic Security.**

A number of other major financial entities are represented by offices in Palm Beach:

Bank Julius Bar
BankersTrust Florida, N.A.
Bank of America/
    NationsBank
Chase Manhattan Private
    Bank, N.A.
Fidelity Federal Savings Bank
    of Florida
First National in Palm Beach (First
    Union's Private Bank)
First Union National Bank
Morgan, J.P., FSB
Northern Trust Bank
Palm Beach National Bank & Trust Company
Republic Security Bank
SunTrust Bank, South Florida, N.A.
U.S.Trust Company of Florida
Wachovia Bank, N.A.
Washington Mutual

Some of these banks have multiple capacity—as commercial banks for individual or corporate deposits with checking and savings accounts; others as trust companies for wealthy people or corporations who want financial advice and service.

Among the leading trust and investment service firms are (including those mentioned):

Bessemer Trust Co. of Florida
Brown Brothers Harriman

Citibank Private Bank
Cypress Trust Company
Crown Financial Associates
Cook International
Harmon Capital Management, Inc.
Harvey Capital Management, Inc.
Lehman Brothers
Merrill Lynch Trust Company
Munder Capital Management
Westcott Financial Planning Group, Inc.

The "Oldest Gold" in Palm Beach is **First National** (First Union's Private Bank), which recently celebrated its 72nd anniversary. It is also the largest bank (some 70,000 sq.ft. set on a seven acre plot) and maintains a 7,000 sq. ft. warehouse/vault for the storage of customers' furs, paintings, wine, antiques, coin collections and other irreplaceable valuables. First National also has the largest staff—some 80 professionals (at the "Yellow Bank" location on South County Road), many of whom have been associates for 30 or more years, and help care for over $5 billion of client investment assets in trust and brokerage (First Union Securities is the 6th largest broker/dealer in the USA). Opened in 1927, Francis A. Shaughnessy was the bank's first president; today the institution is headed by **David H. Scaff** (the bank's eighth president), and is a division of the First Union Corporation (the nation's 6th largest holding company with assets of about $253 billion).

Recently, the First National building was designated as a historic landmark; it was the third attempt to so designate the series of yellow buildings along South County Road (being "landmarked" often lowers the value of a property in that it can't be razed or substantially altered, thus diminishing its prospects for redevelopment).

Royal Palm Way is Money Row, or *"Rue de la banks"*—the locus of several dozen financial institutions, major banks or trust companies: J.P. Morgan, U.S. Trust Company, Wachovia Private Bank, First National in Palm Beach (First Union National Bank), Chase Manhattan Private Bank, N.A., Cypress Trust Company, Bessemer Trust Company of Florida, Lehman Brothers, Munder Funds, Brown Brothers Harriman Trust Company of Florida, Merrill Lynch & Co., Inc., Gabelli Asset Management, Electronic Trading group, LLC, Interunion Financial Corporation, Palm Beach Investment Advisors, Inc., Roxbury Capital Management, LLC., Peter Scholla Global Investments, Raymond Floyd Group, Westcott Financial Planning Group, Bank Julius Bar, Legg Mason Wood Walker, Inc., Morgan Keegan & Company, Inc. Deutsche Bank, Bankers Trust, Florida N.A., Bank of America/NationsBank Private Bank,

Citibank, FSB, Citibank, Citibank Trust, N.A., Harvey Capital Management, Northern Trust Bank, Morgan Stanley Dean Witter, PaineWebber, Inc., Palm Beach Capital Management.

Due to changing societal and economic patterns, financial institutions today are looking for wealth creators (entrepreneurs, entertainers, professional athletes) versus old money families where the wealth is shrinking as it is distributed among various clan members. A prime example is the new USA private banking unit at the New York branch of Banca della Svizzera Italiana (BSI), where only clients with a net worth in excess of $10 million are solicited—the money must be "developed," entrepreneurial style, not inherited.

In Palm Beach, the minimum account value (client's investable assets) for most institutions is high: BankersTrust ($2 million); Bank of America/NationsBank Private Bank ($1 million); Bessemer Trust Company ($5 million); Brown Brothers Harriman ($2 million); Chase Manhattan Private Bank, N.A. ($1 million); Bank Julius Bar ($1 million); Northern Trust Bank ($1 million); U.S. Trust Company ($1 million).

Royal Palm Way firsts:

• The Phipps Family established Bessemer Trust in Palm Beach in 1930, to manage the huge assets of the family, primarily from U.S. Steel; its private banking services have been available to the public since 1972.

• Citibank dates back to its founding in New York in 1812, almost 100 years before the incorporation of Palm Beach. It has been on the Island since 1974, 18 years on Money Row.

• Chicago residents who spend time in Palm Beach have their own Chicago-based trust company to give them a Windy City welcome—Northern Trust Company of Florida.

• The country's largest stock brokerage, Merrill Lynch, and its trust company, are among the major players on Money Row.

• First National in Palm Beach was Florida's first air-conditioned bank (1939), and the first to introduce drive-thru tellers (1945).

• Money Row is named after its "Royal Palms"—304 palm trees line the "Way" with a replacement cost of about $1 million.

Among the leading bankers in Palm Beach are: **H. Loy Anderson** (Palm Beach National Bank), **J. Patterson Cooper** (Bankers Trust), **William Helmly** (Bank of America/Nations Bank), **Frank Helsom** (Bessemer Trust Company), **Charles Ranson, Jr.** (Chase Manhattan), **Michael Blank** (Bank Julius Bar), **Douglas Regan** (Northern Trust Bank), **David Scaff** (First National), **Garrison Lickle** (U.S. Trust Company), **John Stewart** (Harris Trust), **Rebekah Lowe** (Wachovia Corp.), **Mary Watkins** (J.P. Morgan).

344

Each bank attempts to position itself in a unique way in **communications**, thereby to offer a special sales proposition to prospects/clients. These are the appeals:

Bank Julius Bar—"Since 1890, The Fine Art of Swiss Banking"
Bankers Trust—"Architects of Value"
Bessemer Trust—"Enhancing Private Fortunes for Generations"
Chase Manhattan—"The Right Relationship is Everything"
First National—"Service You Can Count On"
First Union—"Service. We guarantee it."
JP Morgan—"J.P. Morgan works for me"
Merrill Lynch—"A Tradition of Trust"
Bank of America/NationsBank—"The Power to Make a Difference"
Northern Trust—"The Private Bank"
Palm Beach National—"The Art of Banking"
SunTrust Bank—"Be Ready for Life"
U.S. Trust—"A Tradition of Growing Assets"
Wachovia—"Let's Get Started"

(Trivia note: the top ad themes or slogans of the century as selected by *Advertising Age Magazine* are: (1) "You deserve a break today" - McDonald's; (2) "Be all that you can be" - U.S. Army; (3) "Pepsi-Cola hits the spot" - Pepsi-Cola; (4) "Mmm good" - Campbell Soup; (5) "See the USA in your Chevrolet" - GM; (6) "I wish I were an Oscar Mayer wiener" - Oscar Mayer; (7) "Double your pleasure, double your fun" - Wrigley's Doublemint Gum; (8) "Winston tastes good like a cigarette should" - Winston; (9) "It's the real thing" - Coca-Cola; (10) "A little dab'll do ya" - Brylcreem.

For the record, most top economists agree that the 10 greatest investors of the 20th century are:

Warren Buffett (Bershire Hathaway)
Peter Lynch (Fidelity Funds)
John Templeton (Templeton Group)
Benjamin Graham and **David Dodd** (value investing analysts)
George Soros (Soros Fund)
John Neff (Vanguard Group)
John Bogle (Vanguard Group)
Michael Price (Franklin Mutual Funds)
Julian Robertson (Tiger Management)
Mark Mobius (Templeton Group).

And it is generally agreed that the most influential American businessmen in the last century are/were: Andrew Carnegie, steel and phi-

345

lanthropy; Alexander Graham Bell, Bell Telephone; David Sarnoff, RCA; J. Pierpont Morgan Sr.,banker; Henry Ford, automaker; John D. Rockefeller Sr., oil titan; William Bernbach, adman; Alfred Sloan Jr., General Motors Corp.; Bill Gates, Microsoft Corp.

—BONDING—

A number of financial trading houses are located on the Island, ranging from small to mega-sized, independent to branch office. It is estimated they invest some $10 billion in stocks and bonds each year for Palm Beachers.

The firms/locations are:
First Union Brokerage Service—255 S. County Rd.
Legg Mason Wood Walker, Inc.—324 Royal Palm Way
Merrill Lynch—249 Royal Palm Way
Morgan Stanley Dean Witter—440 Royal Palm Way
Muriel Siebert & Co., Inc.—240 S. County Rd.
Northern Trust Bank—440 Royal Palm Way
PaineWebber, Inc.—440 Royal Palm Way
Prudential Securities—50 Cocoanut Row
Quick & Reilly, Inc.—230 S. County Rd.

—FOUNDATION FINESSE—

Two major foundations are headquartered on the Island: **Lowe Foundation Inc.** on Royal Palm Way has total assets of $16.1 million, is run by Helen B. Hauben, favors arts, education and health funding and most recently gave $100,000 to the University of Miami School of Medicine; **Whitehall Foundation Inc.** (also on Royal Palm Way) has assets of $84 million, is presided over by George M. Moffett II, funds educational projects.

Other local foundations are the **O'Keeffe Foundation** (largely directs its largesse to medical causes, i.e., a Pavilion at Good Samaritan Hospital) and the **Lois B. Pope Foundation, Inc.** (developed and funds L.I.F.E.— Leadership in Furthering Education); the **Preservation Foundation** of Palm Beach, Inc. (356 S. County Road) largely spends its funds in "preserving" the architecture and beauty of Palm Beach.

Palm Beach County is headquarters for many top foundations, most of which have weighty buying or giving power. Listed by assets, they are:

FOUNDATION	ASSETS
Arthur S. DeMoss	$462 million
J. M. and Barbara Picower	$188 million
Carl and Ruth Shapiro Family	$ 95 million
Forrest C. Lattner	$ 90 million
Paul and Phyllis Fireman	$ 72 million
Theodore R. and Vivian M. Scholarship	$ 70 million
Janirve	$ 68 million
Frank Stanley Beveridge	$ 52 million
Community Foundation for Palm Beach & Martin Counties	$ 50 million

(Note: many of these foundations support local institutions in need of operating monies. Among the major recipients of foundation largesse or donations from the general public, and the amount of monies involved in a recent year, are: Florida Atlantic University Foundation Inc. at $10.1 million; Intracoastal Health Foundations Inc. at $9.8 million; Norton Museum of Art at $6.9 million; Kravis Center at $3.6 million and Hospice of Palm Beach County Inc. at $1.8 million.)

By way of comparison, top dynastic families like du Pont, Marriott, Pillsbury, Phipps and Firestone have foundations worth $250 million or more. And some of the great universities and institutions in the country are also very well funded:

Harvard University	$ 4.7 billion
University of Texas	$ 3.4 billion
Princeton University	$ 2.6 billion
Yale University	$ 2.6 billion
Stanford University	$ 2.0 billion
Smithsonian Institute	$ 314 million
National Gallery of Art	$ 186 million
Folger Shakespeare Library	$ 52 million
Kennedy Center	$ 39 million
Corcoran Gallery of Art	$ 13 million

(For the record, the individuals who shepherd and manage endowments are highly rewarded; Dave Mittleman got $1,237,874 for handling Harvard's endowment needs; Laurance Hoagland received $576,343 for his efforts at Stanford; Yale paid David Swensen about $200,000 for his professionalism; and Princeton rewarded Randall A. Hack with $208,000. These rewards are in the same range as presidents of major universities: New York University President L. Jay Oliva earns $528,000; Judith Rodin gets $529,677 as President of the University of Pennsylvania; Joe Wyatt gets $472,000 at Vanderbilt and George Rupp scores $452,500 at Columbia University.)

MR. AND MRS. SAM McLENDON
beautifully intoxicated with life

LEIGH AND CHRIS LARMOYEUX
enlightened and inspirational

PAT SCHMIDLAPP AND TRISH HILTON
lovely, lady look-alikes

GAY AND STANLEY GAINES
high and mighty, up for every contingency

MARY AND LEWIS SCHOTT
big believers in forward motion

BILL AND VIRGINIA BUCKLEY
incandescent insiders

GEN. ALEXANDER AND PATRICIA HAIG
professional and poised

FRED AND CATHERINE ADLER
magnetic, munificent and mirthful

351

BROWNIE McLEAN AND PHIL RAUSCH
compassionate, friendly and gentle

**VIC DAMONE, DOROTHY LAPPIN
AND SIMON BENSON OFFIT**
experienced with life's joys and toys

JIM PONCE AND KAY RYBOVICH
5,000 watt smiles and signals

BARCLAY AND AVA COLEMAN
openly operatic and obliging

PAT KENNEDY AND ALFRED FIANDACA
lots of life force

**CAROLYN BUCKLEY AND
MIKHAIL BARYSHNIKOV**
smiling supporters and social stars

CHAPTER X

MEMORABLE MILESTONES & MAXIMA
(Properties, Pinnacles & Panoramas)

Photo: Lucien Capehart

HRH PRINCE PHILIP AND ANN APPLEMAN
hearty, high-spirited and honorable

—SUBLIME SIGHTSEEING—

*P*alm Beach's top tourist attractions are:
 • **Worth Avenue**, Palm Beach's answer to Fifth Avenue and Rodeo Drive, boasts nearly 150 high-end businesses, offering everything from designer chocolates to designer jewelry. Its three blocks span the width of the island, from ocean to lake (it's a one-way street) and include an enclosed mall (Esplanade), eight shopping vias and several fountain-graced courtyards (Gucci's being the most visited). Without leaving Worth Avenue, the truly committed shopper can buy any article of clothing (or have it made), a gourmet meal, art (including your own portrait), books, antiques, eye wear, old or new jewelry, and toys—for children or adults. One can arrange to buy a mansion, or just another house. The truly discriminating can even have one designed. And, of course, one's physical needs/wants and necessities can be attended to, from head to toe.

 • Whether or not Henry Morrison Flagler would be pleased that **"Whitehall,"** the mansion he built in 1902 for wife Mary Lily Kenan, is now a popular museum, is open to debate. The fact remains that the Henry Morrison Flagler Museum is a top tourist attraction. Sold by his heirs in 1925, Whitehall was used as an elegant hotel residence until 1959, when Mrs. Jean Flagler Matthews purchased the property, painstakingly acquired as many of the mansion's original furnishings as possible, and opened the restored landmark to the public in 1960. Today, visitors are given a glimpse of Whitehall's former grandeur and a glimmer of local history. Noted for its architectural and historical significance, the museum is included on the National Register of Historic Places and was named a National Historic Landmark. The Museum recently underwent a multi-million-dollar remodeling job on the west wing (the former home of Flagler) and the lawn/parking area.

 • **The Breakers**, one of the Town's most famous attractions, is actually the third structure to stand on its garden-like, oceanside location. Henry Flagler first built "The Palm Beach Inn" in 1895, and its popularity required it to be enlarged three times. In 1903 it was destroyed by fire; rebuilt as an even larger and more luxurious hotel and renamed The Breakers, the structure became the centerpiece for beach cottages erected on either side. Seasonal cottage dwellers included John D. Rockefeller, John Jacob Astor, J.P. Morgan, President Warren G. Harding, William Randolph Hearst, the Duchess of Marlborough and Andrew Carnegie. In 1925, The Breakers was again razed by fire. The heirs of Flagler's third wife, Mary Lily Kenan, built the hotel once more, making The Breakers one of the finest resort hotels in the world. Waldorf Astoria designer Leonard Schultze was the architect. In 1927, after a year of construction and $6 million in costs, the new Breakers Hotel was completed. Inside, the hotel's walls and ceilings reflect Italian Renaissance artistry; the exterior was inspired by the Villa Medici in Florence.

The Breakers spends millions each year in renovation and is currently at its most impressive, with a wide range of wining and dining facilities, many new world-class shops, superb beach and athletic options and a professional staff that outnumbers guests by a ratio of two-to-one. The property is a regular winner of the coveted Mobil Five-Star and AAA Five-Diamond designations and consistently rates among the top resorts in the world. The Breakers is a key subsidiary of the Flagler System, a financial group that consists of resort operations, real estate development and management. On the 140-acre property, the corporation owns two exclusive complexes: Breakers Row apartments (rentals go for up to $200,000/year) and Breakers Row condominiums (purchasing prices in the $1.5 to $5 million range); all units have access to the services of the hotel. The Breakers is constantly undergoing up-grades and expansions and in recent years has added a new ballroom, several new swimming and sporting facilities, a variety of new food and beverage outlets and other amenities, all part of a $25 million capital improvement project. It has become a major meeting and convention venue, and has high occupancy year-around. Many conventioners tour the property via a lecture presented by Town Historian and long-term personality at The Breakers— Mr. James Ponce.

• Currently owned by Donald Trump, **Mar-a-Lago** remains Palm Beach's most lavish estate, with 16.98 acres of land from the ocean to Lake Worth. Breakfast cereal heiress Marjorie Merriweather Post literally crawled through undergrowth to find the perfect site for a mansion on an island that is occasionally threatened by hurricanes. When she found a coral reef under the property to which the house could be anchored, she told the somewhat startled real estate agent "sold." Construction of Mar-a-Lago took five years, $8 million, and two architects, Marion Sims Wyeth and Joseph Urban. In 1927, Mrs. Post moved into her 100+ room home with its lofty 75-foot tower. The grounds included a swimming pool, lakeside cottages, a nine-hole golf course, citrus groves, two greenhouses, three bomb shelters, and a private beach reached through an underground tunnel. Mrs. Post's will bequeathed the estate to the U.S. Government, and upon her death in 1973, it became government property. Designated a National Historic Site by Congress, it also became a historic expense with an annual upkeep of nearly $1 million. After several years, Mar-a-Lago was given back to the Post Foundation, and in

1985 was sold to Trump for $7 million—considered a real bargain by most Palm Beach Realtors. Not everyone, however, has been enamored with the mansion's aesthetics. Harry K. Thaw, who gunned down Stanford White in a long ago dispute over Evelyn Nesbit, looked at Mar-a-Lago and remarked, "My God, I may have killed the wrong architect."

Mr. Trump has converted the property into **The Mar-a-Lago Club**, an exclusive full-service facility with only 500 memberships (going for $50,000 to $100,000). The club offers a unique blend of historic preservation with modern comforts and services (overnight accommodations, spa and health club, several bars and restaurants, pool, major entertainment provided by the likes of Tony Bennett, Elton John, Neil Sedaka, Julio Iglesias, Diana Ross, the Beach Boys and Placido Domingo, tennis and any number of social activities). In terms of function, Mar-a-Lago has never been more effectively used, but many Palm Beachers feel that the commercialization of the historic mansion is not in keeping with the tradition and purity of Palm Beach.

The Mar-a-Lago Club is always in motion to further its "world-class" designation (it was recently honored with the coveted "Five-Star Diamond Award" from the Academy of Hospitality Sciences). Additionally, **Trump International Golf Club** (18-hole, 7,300 yards on a 215-acre plot in West Palm Beach, designed by Jim Fazio at a cost of $40 million—membership at $300,000) has opened to rave reviews and will be the locus for many Trump-related activities. The course has elevations up to 55 feet and numerous rock formations and waterfalls. At the 18th tee, a golfer stands higher than on any tee in Southern Florida, looking down the 15th fairway beside a flowing stream, then looking back up the 18th toward a huge Mediterranean-style clubhouse. The course has been given top ratings by most golf professionals.

—GRAND MANORS—

*T*raditionally, the most exclusive residential area in Palm Beach has been considered to run from **Hammon Avenue** to just north of Sloan's Curve; it boasts some of the largest houses on the island. The average home in this area is priced at $1.8 million and is taxed at approximately $17,000 per year. About 40 percent of the homes are used year-round and are owned by retired business people, who travel extensively during the off-season, but maintain a Palm Beach residence as their "home."

The "Greenwich Village of Palm Beach" is located on **Oleander Avenue, Park Avenue** and **Root Trail**, which have a residential mix of young professionals and retirees. Root Trail, as an example, has changed very little since Judge Enoch Root bought the ocean-to-lake property in the 1890s; some of the small wooden homes built on "Root Trail" (former homes of some of Palm Beach's first residences) are still standing or being renovated. Other homes in this area were built in the late 1920s for financially comfortable residents and to house employees of The Breakers. Today the houses may be slightly run down, but offer some of the most affordable rents in town and are in an area near the beach, restaurants, bars, the bike path, churches, a post office and grocery stores. For these residents, walking is easier than finding a parking space.

Back in the 20s when home building was the occupation or preoccupation for Islanders, Palm Beach was a small resort with big mansions, each given a very proper and lofty designation. Marjorie Merriweather Post did not live at 1100 South Ocean Boulevard; she lived in **Mar-a-Lago**. Forget 138 North Ocean Boulevard as an address for J. Leonard Replogle; his home was **Sunrise Villa**. In those days, few homes were known by addresses—most were identified by glorious names and designations, often conferred on the brick and mortar by designers. For example, at one time Addison Mizner had mansions by these names to his credit: **Kahlua, La Bellucia, Villa Flora, Casa del Ensuenos, Casa Nana, Villa del Sarmiento, El Castillo** and **Encantada**. Marion Sims Wyeth built homes with names like **Casa Juanita, Las Campanas, Qui-Si-Sana, Vita Serena** and **Casa de los Arcos**. Not to be outdone, Maurice Fatio built and helped name **Casa della Porta, Buenos Recuerdos, Il Palmetto, Casa Alva, Casa Eleda** and, in 1932, **Villa Today** (a major departure from the Italian and Spanish designations that were so common).

Among the most famous mansions of that era were: **Casa Bendita** (built for John S. Phipps and named after his son and wife—Ben and Dita); **Cielito Lindo** ("Taste of Honey"—built for James Donohue); **Croton Cottage** (built for Robert R. McCormick); **El Mirasol** ("The Sun Flower"—built for Eva Stotesbury, the first Mizner oceanfront manion); **Playa Riente** ("Laughing Beach"—Mizner's grandest mansion, built for Joshua Cosden and later owned by Anna Thompson Dodge Dillman); and **Reve d' Ete** ("Garden of Eden"—built for Charles Cragin).

In the early 90s, many homes and mansions still have poetic names. Among them are:

Casa Nana—780 South Ocean Boulevard

Casa Maria Marrone—480 Worth Avenue

Sin Cuidado—1800 South Ocean Boulevard

El Sarimento—150 South Ocean Boulevard

Amado—455 North County Road

Louwana—473 North County Road

La Bellucia—1200 South Ocean Boulevard
Costa Bella—111 Dunbar Road
El Solano—720 South Ocean Boulevard
La Guerida—1113 North Ocean Boulevard
Audita—582 South Ocean Boulevard
Conch A Marina—102 Jungle Road
Casa De Leoni—450 Worth Avenue
Villa Tranquilla—100 El Brillo Way
Lagomar—1560 South Ocean Boulevard
Collado Hueco—1820 South Ocean Boulevard
La Fontana—270 South Ocean Boulevard
Villa Flora—260 North Ocean Boulevard
Linda Vista—101 Wells Road
Villa Oiseau—152 Wells Road
Montsorrel—548 North County Road
Villa Artemis—656 North County Road
The Reef—702 North County Road
Plaisance—980 North Ocean Boulevard
Coeur Joie—1060 North Ocean Boulevard
Brisas Del Mar—350 Seabreeze Avenue
Sisobra—320 Seabreeze Avenue
Casa Catana—342 Seabreeze Avenue
Pelican Hall—159 Via Del Lago
Villa Maggiore—260 Via Bellaria
Villa Sol Y Mar—110 Chateaux Drive
La Favorite—120 Casa Bendita
Tree Tops—545 North Lake Way
Ashling—315 South Lake Trail
Beaumere—190 South Ocean Boulevard
Duck's Nest—561 North Lake Way
La Maison Du Sud—661 North Lake Way
Monte Fleur—710 Hi Mount Road
Feliz Ano—140 Hi Mount Road
Coucher Du Soleil—980 North Lake Way
La Salona—172 Clarke Avenue
La Casa Rosa—158 North Ocean Boulevard
Southways—130 Barton Avenue
Merrill's Landing—334 North Woods Road
Bellari—261 Via Bellaria
The Vicarage—475 North Lake Way
Bienstar—151 Grace Trail

Villa Bel Tramonto—241 Banyan Road
Maison de L'Amitie—513 North County Road
La Casita—200 North Ocean Boulevard
Villa Pompano—240 El Vedado Way
La Tour Carree—16 Golfview Road
Casa Alegre—105 Jungle Road
The Grey House—345 Pendleton Lane
Vue-Sur-Mer—101 Jungle Road
Chateau Cheverny—2160 Ibis Isle Road
Lowkey—577 South County Road
Villa Lyon—248 Sandpiper Drive
Derbe—631 Island Drive
Allegro—2 Via Los Incas
The Beachhouse—1125 South Ocean Boulevard
Villa Des Cygnes—456 Worth Avenue
Buenos Recuerdos—79 Middle Road
La Chosa—150 Banyan Road
Elvern House—770 South County Road
La Nid—248 Tradewind Drive
La Perla—214 Dunbar Road
La Folia—1295 South Ocean Bloulevard
The Riviera—455 Worth Avenue
Villa Banyan—217 Clark Avenue
Noble House—608 Island Drive
Villa Rideau—2175 Ibis Isle Drive
Qui-Si-Sana—101 El Brillo Way
Casa De Los Arcos—206 Phipps Plaza
Fernwood—109 Jungle Road
Mirabelle—129 Woodbridge Road
Le Maroc—272 Wells Road
La Ronda—444 North Lake Way
Whitehall—40 Cocoanut Row
Volk House—343 El Bravo
San Souci—1800 South Ocean Boulevard
Carstair—280 North Ocean Boulevard
Canterbury House—250 Sanford Avenue
Villa Vanilla—346 Seaspray Avenue
Villa Il Casteletto—1419 North Ocean Boulevard
Baur Au Lac—615 North Lake Way
Casa De Leoni—450 Worth Avenue
Nuestro Paradiso—860 South Ocean Boulevard

—PARK LARK—

A total of 11 parks and one plaza grace our Town, ranging in size from a hundred square feet to several acres. They are:

Bradley Park (Royal Poinciana Way)
Phipps Ocean Park (S. Ocean Blvd.)
Pan's Garden (Hibiscus Ave.)
Earl E.T. Smith Park (S. County Rd.)
Boyd Park (Bahama Lane)
Kreusler Park (S. Ocean Blvd.)
Lakeside Park (S. Lake Dr.)
Kaplan Park (S. Ocean Blvd.)
Mini-Park (Park Ave.)
Post Causeway Park (Southern Blvd. Bridge)
Memorial Park (S. County Rd.)
Phipps Plaza (S. County Rd.)

—MEGA-MEMORIALS—

The **Memorial Fountain,** located on South County Road just north of the Town Hall, designed by Addison Mizner and built in 1919, is the largest memorial in Town. The park extends down the center of South County Road; consists of a long narrow reflecting pool flanked by trimmed shrubs and cut coral stone pavement. Side alleys of flowers and palm trees border the walkway to the fountain plaza. The four corners of the plaza are cut coral stone piers with attached basins, animal heads and urns. The stucco fountain is composed of horses and three basins. The memorial was built at a cost of $25,000.

Additionally, there are six official statues in town: **The Memorial Fountain and Basin** statue; the **Henry Flagler** statue, the **Bicentennial Eagle** on Royal Poinciana Way; the statue of **Elisha Dimick** on Royal Palm Way, the statue in **Bradley Park**, and the statue of **Pan** in the Garden on Hibiscus and Peruvian. In addition to maintaining these statues, the Town provides landscaping for 47 different parcels of public land (parks, beaches, etc.) throughout the island.

The largest monumental sculpture in Town is the stainless steel internal mist fountain "**Intetra,**" recently moved from the entrance to the **Society of the Four Arts Gallery** (in Four Arts Plaza) to the lakeside. The sculpture by Isamu Noguchi (a gift from Ziuta and J. James Akston) was unveiled in 1976 (in honor of the U.S. Bicentennial); it stands 24 feet high.

—FOUNTAINS OF WISDOM—

*T*here are 19 fountains in Palm Beach: The **Mizner Fountain** and Memorial Park at Town Hall; the three-tiered florentine fountain in front of **The Breakers** with its elaborate sculptured accents patterned after the Boboli Gardens in Florence; the fountain located in the main courtyard of the **Brazilian Court** Hotel; the **Bradley Park** Fountain located just east of the Flagler Memorial Bridge; the **Volk** Fountain in Via Parigi off Worth Avenue; the **Intetra** mist fountain in the mall of The Society of the Four Arts; the **Kaplan** Fountain, donated by Mr. and Mrs. Harold Kaplan, next to Charley's Crab restaurant; the **Phipps Plaza** Fountain; the fountain with statue on the **Royal Palm Way** median strip; **Preservation Park** Fountain; and the **Pan's Garden** Fountain. The eight fountains on Worth Avenue are described in Chapter IX.

—POWER TOWERS—

The Breakers has two towers, each soaring 210 feet including the flag poles. **Mar-a-Lago** has the tallest tower at a private residence, standing 75 feet. For the record, the tallest buildings in the USA are: Sears Tower (110 stories) in Chicago; World Trade Center (110 stories) in New York; Empire State Building (102 stories) in New York; John Hancock Center (100 stories) in Chicago; and the Standard Oil/Indiana Building (80 stories) in Chicago.

—BIG BEN—

The largest and highest clock in Palm Beach can be found on the **First National Bank** building's upper-exterior—23 feet 4 inches from the ground. The clock itself measures 4 1/3 feet high by 5 feet wide. In the mid-60s the bank erected the clock so townspeople could note the time and temperature as they passed the bank. Unlike Big Ben, the movement of the clock is digital; it is not only Palm Beach's largest and highest clock, but also its only outside digital timepiece.

Another noteworthy timepiece is Palm Beach's first street clock; a cast-iron, double-faced freestanding unit located on the south side of **Town Hall**. The clock, a gift from resident Mary Alice Fortin in 1989 stands approximately 14 feet tall and is located in the traffic median in front of Town Hall. The $40,000 clock has Westminster chimes and sounds on the hour, half-hour and quarter-hour; it was the first of its kind in Palm Beach and is intended to be a reference point for travelers. On Worth Avenue, both **Tourneau** and **Tiffany** have impressive outdoor clocks.

363

—HOLY PLACES—

A church is defined as a "congregation" of people, not as a building. In 1883, Reverend Alexander Burrit Dilley made his way to the shores of Lake Worth. He was a Congregational missionary and preached to a small congregation living in the area. In 1884, Dilley successfully had his "church" officially recognized as the Lake Worth Congregational Church, and was influential in building the "Little Red Schoolhouse" in 1886. The schoolhouse was the first official building in Palm Beach used as a church edifice. In 1895 a chapel was built on a lot donated by Henry Flagler on Whitehall Way. Patterned after a New England meeting house, it was called the **Royal Poinciana Chapel** and seated 350 people. In 1900 due to internal conflicts, the congregation split, severing its bonds with the Congregational denomination. Henry Flagler paid the Chapel's debts and helped it become what it is today, non-denominational and "the freest pulpit in the world." A recent survey showed that 21 denominations are represented in the membership. The Chapel itself has been enlarged and moved three times —all within the area of a large city block; it was moved to its present location on Cocoanut Row in 1972, and has recently undergone an interior renovation.

In 1889, the Right Reverend E. Gardner Weed founded an Episcopal Church on the shores of Lake Worth; it became the first Episcopal Church on the Island, and the Town's second church. The chapel seating 100 people was built on the Maddock property on the North End of Palm Beach. The church building was the only such structure within a radius of 150 miles—most worshippers came by boat as there was no roadway to the church (which was bordered on the east by an extensive marsh). Mary Cluett Mulford, wife of the first rector, named the church **Bethesda-by-the-Sea** which meant "House of Healing by the Sea." In 1894 after the demise of the first Bethesda, a second Bethesda was built on an adjoining property and was completed in 1895 costing $13,485.71 to build. This structure, presently on the Maddock property has been converted into a private home. The location of the third Bethesda was the center of Town where it remains today—South County Road and Barton Avenue; it was completed in 1928 at a cost of $650,000.

Bethesda-by-the-Sea is perhaps the finest and most social church in Palm Beach today. The Episcopalian Church is Spanish Gothic in design and was completed with contributions from the Chicago McCormicks. It was constructed without regard to cost and remains one of the finest miniature Spanish Gothic Cathedrals in the world. Its inventory of liturgical art includes a Murillo, a Diepenbeeck (student of Rubens), and stained glass windows designed and fabricated in England and shipped during the war on three different freighters so that German submarines wouldn't destroy them.

A **columbarium** is located in the tranquil setting of Bethesda, and there rest the remains of many prominent Islanders. Some 370 crypts are assembled for church members only. On any given day, friends of the deceased can be seen paying their respects with flowers or quiet prayers. (Note: frequent visitor to Palm Beach, the late General Douglas MacArthur, in his latter years, would often visit the National Cemetary, United States Military Academy at West Point; there he would walk amid the gravestones reflecting on his heritage and the ebb and flow of life. When General Westmoreland was Superintendant of the Academy, they would walk together, remembering their fallen comrades. In a formal parting, MacArthur saluted Westmoreland in gratitude for allowing him to visit the best and most loyal friends he ever had.)

The third church built in Palm Beach was again a Spanish styled mini-cathedral, erected with the assistance of the Catholic elite who wintered in the resort. It was dedicated in 1927, and Colonel Bradley gave the first donation to break ground—after which the church was nicknamed "The Gambler's Church" because of Bradley's casino and the "flock" of worshippers he brought to **St. Edward's**. Other contributors to follow Bradley were the Joseph Kennedys and William Randolph Hearst who contributed the stained glass windows. (According to the Palm Beach County Historical Society, St. Edward's Church has the first complete set of stained glass windows in a Palm Beach church.) Anna Michna Curless is the organist and choir director and has the distinction of playing the organ longer at one church—35 years—than any other organist in Town. From the date of its inception, St. Edward's was a "mission" church. In 1941 the church was staffed by diocesan clergy and Father James Cloonan became the first resident pastor.

Of all the places of worship in Palm Beach, the finest modern design and appropriate simplicity is evident at the Jewish **Temple Emanu-El** which was completed in 1974 on North County Road—a modern, functional house of worship that many claim is the finest small synagogue in the world (it may have lost that distinction with the addition of a major wing in 1988).

Chronologically, our churches came on line as follows:

1884 — Lake Worth Congregational Church officially sanctioned.

1886 — Little Red School House built; Lake Worth Congregational Church services held there (Lake Worth became Royal Poinciana Chapel).

365

1889 — Bethesda-by-the-Sea built.
1895 — Royal Poinciana Chapel built.
1927 — St. Edward's completed.
1974 — Temple Emanu-El completed.

Of these places-of-worship, **Bethesda-by-the-Sea** Episcopal Church is the largest, with seating for 600-700 people, and has 1,000 confirmed members. **St. Edward's** Catholic Church can seat some 650 people, and has nearly 700 parishioners. **Royal Poinciana Chapel** seats 650, and has a congregation of 365 members. **Temple Emanu-El** has 365 members and seats 600.

Bethesda is led by the Very Reverend Ralph Warren, Jr.; St. Edward's by Father Francis J. Lechiara; the Chapel by Dr. Richard Cromie; and the Temple by Rabbi Leonid Feldman.

In recent years, the Palm Beach **Fellowship of Christians and Jews** has become a force in Town; it promotes understanding and respect among people in the community. It is fully supported by donations and pledges and has the sanction of leaders of all Town denominations.

Founded in 1994, the **Paramount Church** (non-denominational) holds services in The Paramount Building (which was recently purchased by the church). Its Minister is the Rev. Dwight Stevens.

—STREETS & AVENUES—

The Island is filled with fascinating byways:

* The corner of **North County Road** and **Royal Poinciana Way** is the busiest, with some 10,000 people, cars, trucks and other objects-in-motion passing by each day.

* **Wells Road** is lined with manicured Australian pine trees; the 40-foot beauties are maintained by the Town.

* **South Ocean Boulevard** is the longest street, running from Royal Palm Way to the most southern boundary of Palm Beach, spanning approximately seven miles.

* **North Lake Way** is the crookedest street, running between Wells Road to the most northern point of the Island; it curves through the "mountain" area and around the golf course which is part of the Palm Beach County Club. It has at least 15 sharp turns and requires constant vigilance to be properly navigated. It is best suited to a teetotaler.

* **Traver's Way** is the shortest public street in Palm Beach, running 350 feet, between El Brillo and El Bravo in the south end of the Island. **Lehman Lane**, in the north end, is the shortest privately owned street, measuring 190 feet in length.

* **Main Street**, just north of the Post Office (North Branch), is the

narrowest street, running east and west for several hundred feet and only 12 feet wide; there are a few small cottages on its northern side. **Grace Trail** is narrower but it is not a through street.

    * **Royal Poinciana Way** is the widest street, with a width of 200 feet.

    * The western section of **Ridgeview Road** has the steepest grade; it angles upward at 40 degrees, hardly a San Francisco, but no fun for joggers.

    * The 300 block of **Royal Poinciana Way**, where a heavy rainfall causes a lot of anxiety, has the lowest elevation.

    * Versatility: Running from Worth Avenue to the north end of Palm Beach, the street begins as **Cocoanut Row**, changes to **Bradley Place**, then as **Slope Trail**, and finally ends as **North Lake Way**.

    * **Hi-Mount Road** boasts the highest elevation; and some of the High and Mighty live there, among them Robert Gottfried—the prolific builder/real estate executive.

    * The newest streets are:

La Costa Way—named in honor of the late Paul LaCoste Maddock. Originally the Maddock Family owned a piece of property extending from North County Road to Lake Worth which became the Maddock "family compound." Following the death of Mr. Maddock years ago, the family subdivided the vacant acreage located between North County Road and North Lake Way. The "main" street in this "mini sub-division" was named in honor of owner Paul Maddock. The Maddock family roots go back to Henry Flagler's times when Sidney Maddock (Paul's father) was a major Palm Beach property owner; included in his holdings was the tract of land on which he built the Palm Beach Hotel. The hotel burned down in 1925 and was replaced with what is now The Biltmore. Before "young" Paul reached manhood, most of the property his father owned was lost or sold. Paul spent a good part of his life buying back and developing properties that originally belonged to his family.

Windsor Court—located on the site of the recently torn down Palm Beach Academy.

—SOCIAL STRIP—

*L*ake Trail, the long-time favorite of society walkers, cyclists and joggers, winds for more than five miles along (north and south) the Intracoastal from center city; on the north end of town the Trail runs from Lakeside Park at Brazilian Avenue to the Sailfish Club; in the south the Trail runs from Sloan's Curve (2000 S. Ocean Blvd.) to the southern border of Town. It is unique in that it cuts across private property most of the way. Residents with million dollar mansions are frequently enjoying their cognac and cogitation when a

367

group of runners or cyclists fly past (just 10 yards from their revelry).

Lake Trail (the oldest path/roadway in Palm Beach) is not only social; it is considered to be the favorite "walk" in the Palm Beaches, and one of America's 10 best walks (it ranks with walking areas in Pacific Palisades Park in Santa Monica, CA; Assateague Island in Virginia and Maryland; Steep Rock in Washington, CT; Long Trail, which runs through Vermont; Fifth Avenue in New York City; the Golden Gate Promenade in San Francisco; Gettysburg National Military Park in PA; the Historic District in Savannah; and Cascade Canyon Trail in Grand Teton National Park, WY). Lake Trail offers a clean and cool avenue for athletes, nature-lovers, romanticists and those looking for relaxation; its shores are beautiful (especially at dawn and dusk), lush tropical foliage makes Lake Trail a perfect outdoor sightseeing destination. In the 1880s this was the original path connecting all lake-front residences. Henry Flagler's edict prohibiting the use of motor vehicles or "horse drawn carts" stills stands with the exception of patroling police motorcycles.

—ISLAND CHUMS—

*T*hree islands adjoin Palm Beach: **Everglades Island** (formerly known as Cabbage Island, and one time home to a substantial shipyard), **Ibis Isle** and **Tarpon Island**—all residential.

The series of adjoining natural islands total approximately 39 acres and stretch from Everglades Island south to Ibis Isle; they are of limited usage. Some are owned by the Town and restricted to use by the "public," others are privately owned and have been leased for 99 years to the **National Audubon Society** to serve as bird sanctuaries.

The official sanctuary is located south of the Southern Boulevard Bridge. There, three Islands off the shoreline—**Fisherman's Island, Hunter's Island** and **Bingham Island**, are leased by the Audubon Society specifically as rookeries and bird sanctuaries. Native wetland areas along the shore of Lake Worth serve as roosting areas for birds in addition to providing natural habitat for a variety of small mammals.

—HEDGE HIGH—

Palm Beach is famous for hedges that seem to go up-up-and away with no particular limit to upward mobility. The natural height of hedges can reach **60 feet**, but 10 - 20 feet is the norm on our Island. Hedges must be trimmed several times a year, which is a costly process (up to $1,000 per haircut) and challenges the laddermanship of gardeners. If a hedge gets too high, the root system can be deadly to nearby plants as roots grow deeper and broader just to accommodate hedge height. Most tall hedges are of the ficus variety, evergreens with glossy foliage and graceful arches.

—FOND PONDS—

*O*riginally there was a continuous "**slew or swamp**" that ran from the center to the north end of the Island. There were several areas where the slew became very wide, and these areas were known as "ponds"—some reached a diameter of 150-200 feet. Most of the homes in early Palm Beach were built on the lakefront. In fact, through the early 1900s there were only two homes on the Ocean, both located in the south end. One was the Bingham Estate, the other the Croker Estate. Croker's fame was as "Chief" of Tammany Hall in New York. Both of these properties were south of Widener's Curve. In order for residents to get to the beach or the other side of the Island, individual car bridges had to be built over these ponds. There were approximately 15 individual bridges built between Clarke and Onondaga Avenues.

—GARDEN DELIGHTS—

The **Chinese Garden,** located in the gardens of The Society of the Four Arts, created by Mrs. Lorenzo E. Woodhouse in memory of her daughter, Marjorie Woodhouse Leidy, is a masterpiece. Built around a lily pond, the garden was inspired by Kwan Yin—Goddess of Mercy—in the style of the Tang Dynasty (A.D. 618-907). The artifacts in the garden were imported from China.

The Chinese Garden is part of the original demonstration Gardens created in 1938 at the Four Arts by the Garden Club of Palm Beach. Other gardens in this congerie include:

Tropical Fruit Gardens—Mrs. Alfred G. Kay, chairman
Fragrant Moonlight Gardens—Mrs. Joseph F. Gunster
Spanish Patio Garden—Mrs. John S. Phipps
British Colonial Garden—Mrs. Clifford V. Brokaw
Florida Jungle Garden—Dr. Edmund LeRoy Dow
Formal Rose Garden—Mr. Hugh Dillman

These gardens continue to be maintained (fiscally and physically) by Garden Club members. In order to raise monies for upkeep, the Club originally (in 1928) held annual flower shows; in the 50s the format changed to house and garden tours of local homes. Tours became so popular (more than 2,500 tickets sold per year) that they are now by invitation only.

369

Members responsible for maintenance of the 12 demonstration gardens include Joan Wilmott (committee chairman of garden maintenance); and "garden tenders" Betsy Matthews, Virginia Burke, Pat Mason, "Mac" Warwick, Bunny Nelson, Jo Jo Walton, Ginger Preston and Evelyn Harrison.

With the help of our God-given tropical climate, landscape architects, gardeners, green thumbs and tender loving care, Palm Beach gardens, in general, excel; there are, however, a few that have received special recognition for their beauty:

1. The formal gardens at the home of **Alan and Joanne Dayton** are exceptionally well kept with lush greenery and ferns abounding. A walkway separates various flower beds and the fern garden.

2. **Barton Gubelmann**'s well-maintained garden includes giant pots of geraniums surrounding patio areas, vine-covered doorways and windows, flower beds inconspicuously placed in strategic areas, rows of tall white lilies, nasturtiums, tuberoses, clumps of vibrant gold cosmos and pretty flower-lined paths. Natural ponds topped with lily pads add to the enchantment of the garden. Mrs. Gubelmann also raises herbs and vegetables.

3. The garden of **Paul and Angie Ilyinsky** also makes use of clay pots bearing orchids of many varieties; fruit trees hold attractive bird cages that house their feathered friends. Umbrella tables and ornate flower pots surround the pool; pretty, multi-colored impatiens line walkways around the lake-front property.

4. **Sam and Valerie Fleming**'s garden is a hidden treasure; lush and sensuous. Tall private walls are covered with climbing vines and topiaries; flower beds and herbs are sprinkled through the area. An aura of peace surrounds the still blue reflection pools; strategically placed benches provide sanctum for private reflection, all enhanced by the shade of tall green foliage.

5. **Warrington and Eles Gillet** used Richard Webel, a top landscape architect, to transform their tennis court into a lovely lily and fish pond. Three old iron benches are the focus of a semicircle shaded by a mango tree overhanging a selection of flowers. There are citrus trees, hundreds of species of ferns planted around a banyan tree in exotic patterns, small ficus hedges and a miniature flower pool, all yielding a lush intimate atmosphere.

6. **Mary and Bob Montgomery** have an eclectic mix of plantings — an Oriental garden, a child's all-green secret garden, vegetable and herb garden, rose garden, all terraced in a scenic lakeside setting, with two swimming pools, swans and lush folliage. Landscape consultant Brett Armstrong maintains the property.

Other noteworthy gardens are maintained by Kit and Bill Pannill (garden features an arrangement of lantana as spokes in a circular design), Mrs. William Lee Hanley, fomer mayor "Deedy" Marix, Serina and George Sanchez, Pat and Ned Cook, Page Lee Hufty, Dennis and Annabelle Coleman, Robert and Wendy Meister, Tina and Bill Flaherty, Winsome McIntosh, Bess Summers, Charles and Ziggy Berwind, and Didi Ballinger. Among others, Ken and Moira Wolofsky and Jill and John Rau have exotic gardens with Koi ponds. Many gardens have been designed by the Palm Beach firm of **Sanchez & Maddux**. **Mario Nievera Design, Inc.** has created landscapes for a number of Islanders, too; among them are David and Julia Koch, Terry Kramer, Pauline and Bill Pitt, Sandy and Leonard Heine, Edie and Marvin Schur and both Ronald and Leonard Lauder.

Mrs. William Lickle (granddaughter of Margaretta du Pont Carpenter) of Palm Beach keeps a magnificent garden which descends several levels to the banks of the Brandywine River in Montchanin, DE, where she and her husband **William** (former chairman of Morgan Trust Company of Florida, N.A.) have a home.

Many of the most attractive gardens use "ground cover"—low-growing, low-maintenance alternative to grass. They enhance a garden's beauty, only need minor pruning and limited fertilizer, and are perfect for filling ground space. Some of the best known are bromeliad (12-18 in. tall), false heath-grass (12 in.), purple queen (15 in.), mondo grass (6-12 in.), Wandering Jew (4-10 in.), artillery plant (12 in.) and philodendrons (6 in.)

The **Preservation Foundation** of Palm Beach recently created a magnificent botanical oasis called **Pan's Garden**—which showcases native Florida plants. Nestled on a 25,000-square-foot property at Hibiscus and Peruvian, the tranquil public park forms a welcome buffer zone between residential and commercial sectors.

The Garden features a wetlands and uplands area, a magnificent live 50-foot oak, an education pavilion and two gazebos, all interconnected by winding paths. Indigenous trees, shrubs, flowering bushes, grasses and flowers create a lush, colorful setting for relaxation and horticultural study. A turn-of-the-century bronze Pan graces the semi-circular pond inside the main wrought-iron gates. Architectural details include restored brick-wood and roof tiling, intricate iron gates and fencing, plus a patio wall and fountain recreated from historic tile walls.

The half-acre features a historic tile wall from the Casa Apava estate and a bronze statue of **Pan**, the Greek mythological god of shepherds, created by Frederick William MacMonnies and donated by Palm Beacher **Lydia Mann**, who also partially funded the garden.

—TREE GLEE—

*T*he **ficus mysorensis** (a rare example of the mysore fig), probably planted during the time of the Royal Poinciana Hotel, is our Town's most **beautiful** tree. It stands along the southern parking lot of the Royal Poinciana Plaza. Circumference at the base measures 33 feet 8 inches; the tree stands approximately 61 feet tall.

A **kapok tree** on the property of Mrs. Charles Davis (8 South Lake Trail) is the Town's **largest** tree; it is distinguished by its great buttresses and massive size measuring over 90 feet in height and 46 feet in base circumference. The second largest tree is also a kapok planted around 1890; it stands 80 feet tall and has a base circumference of 58 feet 10 inches. Palm Beach boasts the two largest kapok trees in the county.

The **oldest** tree is the **quercus virginiana**—very few examples of the mighty oak still remain on the Island. The largest and most likely the oldest of any tree in Palm Beach is located on the Maddock property at 545 North Lake Trail. The tree dates back to 1700. (The circumference at the base of the tree measures 9 feet.)

By comparison, the **most famous tree in America** is the Washington elm in front of the Senate entrance, believed to have shaded our first president when he laid the Capitol cornerstone. Some of the oldest trees are two English elms and a spreading American elm. The American elm, known as the Cameron elm, stands near the southwest corner of the House wing. The tree is named in honor of **Senator Simon Cameron**, who, in 1875, saw workers about to uproot it to put in a sidewalk; he hurried to the Senate floor, and pleaded that the tree be saved. His efforts were successful: instead of demolishing the tree, the workers laid the sidewalk around it.

Few people realize that when they visit the Capitol building, they walk through one of the finest arboretums in the world. Over 3,000 trees from 33 states, Europe, and Asia grow on the Capitol grounds. In addition to one of the most varied collections of trees in the country, the 155-acre grounds also boast 100 species of wooded plants.

The Japanese cherry trees by the Tidal Basin are also world-class and give joy to nature lovers. The early-April Cherry Blossom Festival showcases the 6,000 cherry trees each year and provides occasion for an annual parade and much merry-making.

The **Golden Shower Tree** is Palm Beach's **rarest** tree; it is part of the famous "Garden of Eden" of Charles Cragin during the early 1900s (located at 340 Garden Rd.; owned by Tye Matthews Lett, Jr.). The garden became famous at the turn of the century; and attracted thousands of visitors. The Cragin estate consisted of a two-story mansion surrounded by every plant, tree and flower to be found in the area.

Located at **Via Del Lago and South County Road**, the **Great Rubber** tree—60 feet high by 12 feet 5 inches in circumference with over 1,000 branches—is a favorite place for photo sessions. Still thriving, the tree was often the background for photos of Andrew Carnegie, Henry Flagler and the Henry Phipps family.

The **button-mangrove** tree on North Ocean Way was crowned a national **champion**, being the largest of its species, and placed in the National Register of Big Trees in Washington, D.C. There are 700 champion trees in the U.S., and Florida boasts 104 of them (more than any other state). This champion mangrove, commonly known as a green buttonwood, is 52 feet tall, with a 67 foot crown spread and a trunk circumference of 135 inches. It is difficult to tell the exact age of mangrove trees; however, the age estimates range from 80-800 years. (Originally the wood from button-mangroves was used to make buttons.)

There are actually over 100 trees in Palm Beach that are candidates for champion tree status; they will probably never be officially listed, as their owners want privacy and a listing in the national registry requires that addresses be made public.

—GARDEN MAIDENS—

*O*riginally organized in 1928 by 15 women including **Mrs. John S. Phipps, Mrs. Frederick E. Guest, Mrs. Alfred Kay, Mrs. Henry Phipps, Mrs. Edward T. Stotesbury** and **Mrs. Marion S. Wyeth**, the Garden Club had as its main purpose the preservation of Lake Trail, which was considered an important part of old Palm Beach. The first Town Plan of Palm Beach was financed by the Garden Club in 1929. In 1935 through funds raised from a flower show, the Club made possible the planting of three blocks on Royal Palm Way with royal palms. In 1938 the Club established "demonstration" gardens on the property of The Society of The Four Arts. During World War II, members worked on many defense projects. In 1947 the Garden Club campaigned against the pollution of Lake Worth by sewage from Palm Beach and Lake Worth; it continued to help beautify many community buildings through their plantings. In 1953 the club took over the renovation of the Gardens at the Four Arts. In 1960 through the efforts of members **Mr. and Mrs. Alfred G. Kay**, Pine Jog, an Environmental Science Center, was established. Through funds raised, the club in 1973 published a book identifying historic and specimen trees of Palm Beach. In 1978 projects included the beautification of six blocks on the ocean side of South Ocean Boulevard in addition to donating several thousands to Pine Jog, to beach beautification and for plantings on the Par-3 Golf Course and the Flagler Museum. The club received the Town's Beautification Award in 1979 and continues to work with the Town Council, Civic Association and Beautification Committee to help control zoning and lethal yellowing and to clean up the pollution of Lake Worth. In 1990, the club took on the responsibility of the entire renovation in front of Town Hall (sidewalks, plantings, sprinkler system). In 1998, the Club planted a demonstration xeriscape garden in Bradley Park.

Today, there are approximately 100 Garden Club members; last year they volunteered 4,000 hours to the club and raised $50,000 for civic projects. Current officers are: **Mrs. John T. Murray** (President), **Mrs. Dennis P. Coleman, Jr.** (1st Vice-President), **Mrs. George G. Matthews** (2nd Vice-President), **Mrs. Ronald F. Young** (3rd Vice-President), **Mrs. Anthony Thebaut** (Treasurer), **Mrs. Joseph P. Flanagan** (Recording Secretary), **Mrs. Bailey B. Sory III** (Corresponding Secretary).

The Garden Club recently held its annual flower show in the hothouse and gardens behind the Society of the Four Arts library. Themed *"Shakespeare in Bloom 2000,"* the event was chaired by **Mrs. William G. Pannill** and **Mrs. Joseph A. Webster III**. The Catherine Beattie Medal of the Garden Club was awarded to Mrs. Pannill, who also won the Club's Silver Cup, and the sweepstakes award for winner of the most blue ribbons. In recent years, the Club has published *Gardens by the Sea: Creating a Tropical Paradise*, featuring 300 color photographs and 200 pages of gardening tips (Joan Willmott, editor). The Garden Club was also the winner of the Historical Society of Palm Beach County's 11th annual Judge James R. Knott Award for the Club's preservation of the gardens at The Society of the Four Arts and its creation of educational programs.

The **Garden Club of America** was founded in 1913 in Philadelphia; it now has 194 member clubs and 16,000 members, and remains the blueblood of American gardening. **The Federated Garden Clubs**, a similar but not as "hotsy-totsy" organization, has 9,000 chapters with 275,000 members. Former First Lady Barbara Bush is GCA's most visible supporter, but through the years there was always a Taft, Hancock, Roosevelt, Wilson or other Old Guard gardener to add prestige to the group.

—FLOWER SHOWER—

*T*he flowers on Royal Palm and Royal Poinciana Ways are changed **twice** a year, using flowers specifically grown for that purpose at the Town's nursery on Palmo Way (north end of the Island). In 1989 the flowers were changed three times to commemorate the National Garden Club's annual meeting held at The Breakers.

Palm Beach generally spends **$14,500 annually** on flowers used to beautify these areas. In the summer, the Town mainly uses marigolds, periwinkles and portehulas. Winter flowers used include begonias, impatiens, geraniums and asgerium. Approximately 22,000 flowering plants are used each year; with three plantings in 1989 over 30,000 plants were used.

This year, Royal Palm Way's 12 flower beds will be surrounded by a single ring of Japanese boxwood; six of the eight beds on Royal Poinciana Way will have the usual flowers incorporated in a design of the boxwood.

In addition to these areas, the Town also provides the flowers at the Memorial Fountain at Town Square. Begonias are planted there in the winter, while periwinkles are used in the summertime.

—PINE WALK—

At the entryway to **The Breakers Golf and Beach Clubs**, the Australian pines and palms that line the roadway play home to hundreds of different varieties of wild parrots. The parrot "flock" began in the 1970s with the popularity of the *Baretta* TV show featuring a cockatoo; many Palm Beachers suddenly became parrot owners; unfortunately a few "pets" escaped and relocated in **Pine Walk**, where the birds interbred and the flock grew. Most birds are unable to survive when they escape captivity, but the conditions in Pine Walk are ideal for the Amazon variety of parrots. This population of parrots is an attraction for bird lovers who are awed not only by their brilliant plumage and entertaining treetop shows, but for the way they communicate with each other; having escaped from captivity, some parrots have acquired both English and Spanish vocabularies, and the result is a multi-lingual cacophony of jungle sounds peppered with spicy wolf whistles and common phraseology. The average life span of a parrot is approximately 50 years, so the parrots of Pine Walk will always be a tourist attraction.

Bird-watching is a popular form of recreation on the Island and at other locales. At the **Everglades National Park** in Homestead (FL), a vast park of 2,200 sq. miles of wetland awaits the visitor. A system of paved roads, trails and boardwalks allow access to marshes and patches of woods where herons, egrets, pelicans, bald eagles, barred owls, ospreys and woodpeckers are easy to observe. Other top places to spot birds are: Mount Desert Island in Maine, Central Park in NYC, Cape May Point in New Jersey, Dauphin Island in Alabama, Grand Teton National Park in Wyoming and Cave Creek Canyon in Arizona.

—WET ROLLS—

*N*ever to be outdone, Palm Beach has the most unusual Rolls Royce in the USA; it sits in waters off the beach providing excellent sight-seeing for scuba-diving enthusiasts; brilliantly colored coral formations, four species of large sea turtles, moray eels, nurse sharks and thousands of tropical and sports fish of all shapes and sizes give divers a fascinating underwater world. The 1965 vintage Rolls Royce was sunk offshore just south of the Lake Worth Inlet in 1965 by a Palm Beach businessman who wanted to demonstrate the need for artificial reefs. Although the sea has taken its toll on the classic car, divers can still sit behind the wheel and fantasize. The Rolls is part of the "Palm Beach Triangle" which harbors a barge and 120-foot freighter, both sunk to provide a home to schools of barracuda, grouper, amberjack and other fish found in the Caribbean Sea.

The Town of Palm Beach installed an artificial reef to fight beach erosion in the area from Hammon Avenue to Chilean Avenue; it's a 1,500-foot-long prefabricated strip of steel and reinforced concrete (at a cost of $600,000) that, in theory, is part of a beach renourishment project to keep sand at the Midtown Public Beach in place.

—RULING CLASS—

Palm Beach is a Town without a mortician, cemetary, hospital, public library, car dealership, dog catcher and neon signs. Yet it is a Town of extreme gentility, a very swift social merry-go-round, with the 27th degree of aloofness. And it works!

The Town is governed by a Town Council composed of five **Council Members** and the **Mayor**. Although the Council has elected officials, they are not politicians in the true sense (and are not paid); they campaign vigorously but usually avoid confrontations and emotional ping-pong. Political scandals, patronage or favoritism are not yet serious realities since Council Members are very professional and above-it-all (many are millionaires). In most towns with a population of 10,000 or more residents, the mayor is paid a salary and given certain amenities; not so in Palm Beach. The Mayor rules sans compensation, and, in fact, the rites of office may cost the Mayor up to $30,000 per year out-of-pocket expenses. The Mayor attends meetings of the Town Council, has the right to break a tie vote or veto ordinances, is recognized as the head of Town Government for all ceremonial purposes, and acts as Town Ombudsman.

The **ruling process** begins with citizens of Palm Beach electing the Mayor and Town Council (for two year terms), who, in turn, appoint a Town Manager. The Town Manager (six-figure salary), at the direction of the Town Council, manages the Town Attorney and eight departments —Finance, Fire-rescue, Human Resources, Planning/Zoning/Building, Police, Public Works, Recreation and Town Clerk. The Town's general operating budget is just under $40 million annually.

Although not directly involved in governing the Town, a number of civic clubs and associations have significant influence in resolving Town matters.

Among them:

Palm Beach Chamber of Commerce (600 members strong, with an appetite for accelerating-yet-controlling business ventures of the Town).

Palm Beach Civic Association (2,000 members devoted to addressing the Town's evolving needs in the 21st century via forums, educational programs, community-wide events).

The Preservation Foundation of Palm Beach (a nonprofit organization dedicated to preserving the unique environment of the Town and its special heritage; 1,200 members).

Citizen's Association of Palm Beach (1,500 members concerned with the growth and environment of the southern part of the Island).

Merchants Associations (Worth Avenue, South County Road, Peruvian Avenue, Royal Poinciana and Palm Beach Business Group—many members furthering their special professional interests).

Clubs (Garden, Kiwanis, Lions, Rotary—via educational programs, many members improving their lifestyles and interests).

In toto, the **Ruling Class** makes the Town pleasantly and gently functional; officials believe in Palm Beach as a world-class urban resort and labor around-the-clock to make the environment safe, secure and beautiful. They have preserved the past consummately, are preserving the present admirably, and will preserve the future with distinction. It is written in the wind!

MARGO AND ASHTON DE PEYSTER
distinctive and dazzling

BETSY AND WALLACE TURNER AND HELEN CLUETT
magnanimous champions of charity

GEORGE J. MICHEL AND ALEXANDER DREYFOOS
vim, vigor, vitality

**CLAIRE O'KEEFFE, MR. AND MRS. JOE JACK
MERRIMAN, DR. ARTHUR O'KEEFFE
AND CHRISTINA ORR-CAHALL**
motivated and marvelous

Photo: Mort Kaye Studios

JACK AND NELL HIGHT
kindly kindred spirits

Photo: Mort Kaye Studios

MARJORIE, WILLIAM AND SHELLY GUBELMANN
jovial, merry and matchless

Photo: Lucien Capehart

**MARK AND PAULA COOK WITH
JACK AND TALBOTT MAXEY**
summa cum laude, in everything

Photo: Lucien Capehart

JUNE, TIM AND CARA ROONEY
good vibrations, voque and vitality

BOB LEIDY AND CHERYL GOWDY
masters of treasures and pleasures

Photo: Lucien Capehart

BIL HAMILTON AND RODNEY DILLARD
agile, able, acclaimed

Photo: Lucien Capehart

Photo: Lucien Capehart

NANCY WALSH AND ORATOR WOODWARD
diligent, tireless, generous

EILEEN CORNACCHIA AND SUSAN LUCCI
testimonials to high style and standards

DEEDY MARIX
unboundedly special

CARLA AND PEDRO MORRISON
lively, involved and sparkling

Photo: Lucien Capehart

OBLIO WISH AND MITCHELL AND JILL SILVERMAN
betwitching, appealing, delightful

Photo: Lucien Capehart

KEVIN DELAHANY, WHITNEY AND TOM BALDWIN
exemplar, decorous and praiseworthy

FLORENCE BONSUK AND PAT MURPHY
exclusive and exceptional

HEATHER HARRIS AND LILY HOLT
heavenly and lovely

CHAPTER XI

PALM BEACH WIT & WISDOM
(Minds, Motives & Mandates)

Photo: Lucien Capehart

RENEE AND BILL LICKLE
gifted, giving and glowing

—Dukes Don't Emigrate—

*H*istory records that of the 23 male *Mayflower* passengers, not one used the title Gent. after his name, the equivalent of Esq., an indication that the man was a person of property, education or social standing. For the most part, *Mayflower* males were, according to author Charles M. Andrews, "...socially insignificant... their intellectual and material poverty, lack of business enterprise, unfavorable situation and defenseless position in the eyes of the law, rendered them an almost negative factor in the life of New England."

Yet, today, in terms of the quantitative impact of the 23 males, some 20,000 members of the **Society of Mayflower Descendants** flourish in America. They are mainstream professionals, business and political leaders, educators and athletes—a crosscut of desirable Americans of all ages.

The original 23 males were named: **Alden, Allerton, Billington, Bradford, Brewster, Brown, Chilton, Cooke, Doty, Eaton, Fuller, Hopkins, Howland, More, Priest, Rogers, Samson, Soule, Standish, Vaughn, Warren, White** and **Winslow.** (It should be noted that the full roster of the *Mayflower* ran to some 123 names of which 41 signed the *Mayflower Compact*—the 23 names celebrated through history were the "most important" personages.) A few of those names have been synonymous with American history but social historians have pointed out time and again that "the first permanent settlers— *Mayflower* passengers—were drawn from the middle and lower classes, from the aggressive, the dissenter, the ne'er-do-well, the underprivileged and the maladjusted." As has often been said—**Dukes don't emigrate!**

There are 126 hereditary societies in the USA today (including such diverse organizations as the Swedish Colonial Society, the Piscataqua Pioneers, the National Society of Colonial Dames of America and the New York Society of the Order of Founders and Patriots of America) but the two most prominent are the **General Society of Mayflower Descendants** and the **Order of the First Families of Virginia** (F.F.V.s).

The Mayflower Descendants was organized in Plymouth, MA in 1897 to celebrate the return to America of a masterful document entitled *Plymouth Plantation*; written by Governor William Bradford, the document had been stored at Fulham Palace in London and was welcomed home by the Puritans because it told the history of early Plymouth, detailing original families, inter-

388

ests, social interaction and comings and goings of families. It became the basis of a genealogical society.

The Society has never dealt with the quality of its members, nor has it ever suggested aristocratic lineage for any of them. Its interest is simply in **American history and genealogy** yet the society celebrates a number of distinguished citizens as proven descendants of *Mayflower* passengers. The list includes Boston's Adams family, Presidents Ulysses S. Grant and Zachary Taylor, both Roosevelt presidents, the Taft clan of Ohio, the five Rockefeller brothers—John D. III, Nelson, Winthrop, Laurance and David (because of John D. Rockefeller, Jr.'s marriage to the former Abby Aldrich), Henry Wadsworth Longfellow, J.P. Morgan, Mrs. Jefferson Davis and Grandma Moses. Even **Winston Churchill** had an ancestor who was a *Mayflower* passenger. The Society is particularly proud of the fact that from the original listees many great Americans have emerged and that the Society itself embodies the Horatio Alger concept of self-made men choosing their own destinies in a foreign country, and succeeding!

Those members of the Society who take their lineage very seriously are often the targets of Brahmins or members of the Old Guard who may rejoice in their heritage but don't cast about for acceptance. When one of Boston's grandes dames was asked if her ancestors had arrived on the *Mayflower*, she quipped—"Oh, no, we sent our servants on that. We came over on the second boat." (For the record, the second boat was the *Arabella* and it, in fact, transported a more distinguished roster of people including the first American member of the Whitney family and Sir Richard Saltonstall, a name closely linked to politics in New England—the Saltonstalls are the only American family having 11 unbroken generations of Harvard men and eight governors of Massachusetts.)

The **Order of First Families of Virginia** is restricted to individuals who are "lineal descendants of an ancestor who aided in the establishment of the first permanent English Colony, Virginia 1607-1624." F.F.Vs like to point out their forebears arrived on American shores 13 years prior to the landing of the *Mayflower*, and the quality of passenger was much better, noting that of the 105 men in the original Jamestown expedition of 1607, 35 had the all-important appellation of **Gent.** attached to their names. By and large, F.F.V.s reinforce their patrician heritage with impressive statistics that suggest their genteel breeding; but over the years questions have been asked about accuracy. Most historians agree that the First Families of Virginia are not descendants of the original colonists but of the first families who came to wealth and power—the **Lees, Randolphs, Fairfaxes** and **Peytons.**

Most of the smaller-yet-major cities (Savannah, Charlestown, New Orleans) have an unwritten genealogical code which basically ignores the

389

equivalent of a *Social Register* or *The Hereditary Register of the United States* (an annual 600-page volume that lists hereditary societies, their officers and bylaws, a "Revolutionary War Ancestors' Honor Roll," registered coats of arms, heraldic charges and symbolisms, and other ephemera of family-treedom) in favor of a philosophy that says—everybody knows who is socially acceptable or not—the **family name** is both a **symbol** and a **communique**—it tells all!

Heredity is presented in Washington, D.C. via the *Green Book*, *The Social List of Washington*. It carefully distinguishes between social and official Washington and is somewhat haughty about elected representatives of government. The late Supreme Court Justice **William O. Douglas** was dropped from the book when at age 67, he married a 23-year old woman, his fourth wife. And Major General **Harry H. Vaughn**, a Truman appointee, disappeared from listings because of his poor taste in clothing. An elusive board of governors makes these decisions and in private annotes pages of former books with initials describing potential entries—**BD**, for example, denotes a Bad Drunk; **OF** was applied to Douglas, Old Fool. **SC** is often used to categorize members of the house who are Sex Crazed or **FM** (Feather Merchants=lightweights).

The *Green Book* prefers listing **Cave Dwellers**—families who have been in the capital for generations, know the social scene and are woven into the city's fabric via economics or administrative clout. Since Washington is a one-industry city (government), people in positions of power are transitional and usually transplanted from other areas; that makes their entree to Cave Dweller society more difficult and suggests that even as they arrive, they should start packing. Few cities in America have greater turnover than Washington, where the average longevity for all arrivals (government, political, legal) is nine years.

Yet, even the sanctity of the *Green Book* is being eroded; some of the **NP** (New People)—wealthy contractors, real estate developers, auto dealers, electronic media moguls—have made the pages of the book and rub shoulders casually with the real power brokers. By having a nice home (on Foxhall Road, for example) and being a generous host, a flow of ambassadors, cabinet members, under-secretaries and justices is assured. This further isolates Cave Dwellers, who are often hos-tile to the passing parade, knowing all too well that the headlines these people make are usually short-lived and negative. Yet, like any other city, Washington is in transition itself, and a new tier of **Cafe Society** is displacing tradition.

Surprisingly, the oldest city in the USA—St. Augustine, FL (founded in 1565)—has no hereditary society or **First Family** fixation. It stands alone, pristine, ever-evolving without tracing its roots back some 440 years. Maybe it's the place where pure democracy, an egalitarian society, truly exists and all the flourish of social stardom and status seeking is simply presented as—**living out your destiny!**

—SOCIETY. THE WAYS & MEANS—

*J*n 1931, **Joseph and Permelia Reed** enjoyed a holiday on the jungle-choked island of Hobe Sound; they were impressed, built a home for themselves, bought extra land and sold it to friends from Greenwich, bought more land (1,500 acres), and donated it to the US Fish and Wildlife Service and when the big real estate crash hit, for about $25,000 they had themselves a 2.9 square mile enclave (called Jupiter Island) serving residents with world-class names—Ford, Mellon, Doubleday, Whitney, Heinz, Armour, Field, Vanderbilt, Hamm, Searle and Stroh—and a tight little fraternity that became one of the most controlled and affluent social jewels in the world (Palm Beach was *arriviste* by comparison). Even today, not much has changed, although the Reeds have gone on to another life.

A twice divorced Baltimore woman with a convieniently absent husband, found herself adrift in London. When a friend cancelled an invitation to a weekend in the country, she was asked to substitute. Knowing the Prince of Wales (Edward VIII) would be there, **Wallis Warfield Simpson** elected to go and thus became the woman who caused a king to renounce his throne. For the next 50 years the Duke and Duchess of Windsor traveled the world, their tarnished royal luster serving as passport to a hedonistic international society. From a humble beginning to world-class celebrity in less than 18 months.

It's said there are **three ways** to gain entry to society; you're born into it, you **earn** it or you **marry** it. The Reeds earned their titular leadership of Hobe Sound; Mrs. Simpson vowed via marriage to share a royal life; and the **Puritans** of the Massachusetts Bay Colony didn't plan to form a society (their mission was to survive) yet were first among equals, and in their respective roles (shipping, manufacturing, real estate) gained

Louis Lacy, Winston and Raymond Guest and Thomas Hitchcock

391

prominence which engendered prosperity and social leadership. The New York Knickerbocker Greys and the Pennsylvania Quakers didn't plan roles as social leaders, either, but their positions mandated leadership. With their names and fortunes, came the beginnings of American society.

London society was the model from which Americans took their cue. Aristocratic families—Beekman, Livingston, Astor, Van Rensselaer, Roosevelt, Rhinelander, Whitney—modeled their efforts after the Brits but unlike English society where title and position determined the rank of the male, American society was primarily moved by women. And it was a strenuous job, built around balls and extravaganzas and conspicuous consumption, trips to the Continent to snare a titled son or daughter-in-law and whatever culture could be bought. Said Mrs. Oliver Hazard Perry Belmont, one of society's sentinels: "I know of no other profession, art, or trade that women are working in today as taxing on mental resources as being a leader of society."

When Cave Dweller **Cissy Patterson**, who for a time was a powerful media magnate in Washington (owning the *Times-Herald*) attended a gala at the mansion of Evalyn Walsh McLean (one time owner of the Hope diamond), she would spend hours in preparation. From a loose-leaf notebook she'd select her clothes; every item in her wardrobe was catalogued and numbered. Rather than try on, she'd simply pick and choose her evening wear by the numbers. A maid in white-lace and dove gray uniform would take instructions; as Mrs. Patterson leafed through her catalog, she might select dress 105, belt 17, scarf 39 and shoes 28. The maid would collect each item from a green silk-padded hanger, make sure it was pressed and deliver it to Mrs. Patterson at the appointed time. With all the fuss and motion, several hours were consumed in what Mrs. Patterson considered the most efficient way to party prep. Once immaculately dressed, she would proceed to one of the Walshes' famous Sunday night dinners featuring dance orchestra, movies, caterers (who were cued as to which china went on what table and what silverware was to be used where, by marked tapes placed in the appropriate matching locations) and some of Washington's richest, most famous and powerful people. It, too, was a taxing process.

Just how taxing? Banker John Jacob Astor at age 46 married an 18-year-old non-pedigreed woman and was virtually disowned by society, despite his millions and power. The Astors retreated to London where his social standing was unimpaired. Chancing a return in 1912, the couple choose the *Titanic* for their trans-Atlantic trip. Astor perished (as did Washington Augustus Roebling, the steel heir, Henry Sleeper Harper of the publishing empire and banker Washington Dodge) but Madeline, his five-month pregnant wife was saved and gave birth to John Jacob Astor VI a few months later, thereby perpetuating the dynasty.

The Astors had a strange fling with society. **John Jacob Astor** was a German who emigrated from Frankfurt to America in 1783; within a 20-year period he parlayed a fur pelt business into one of the largest and most diverse fortunes in the country. But the family was not fully accepted by Mayflower society and his great-grandson William Waldorf Astor moved a sizeable portion of the fortune to England where he bought his way into the aristocracy; after renovating Hever Castle to the tune of $13 million in 1903 he was given the title **Viscount Astor**. The family thereafter exploited its English "nobility" effectively in America.

Entree to society can come through **social fakery**, too. Using a title to gain acceptance, however acquired, is nothing more than good marketing. But the title must have value. Ladies who married **Russian Prince Romanoff** found he was a superb restaurateur in Hollywood but hardly a nobleman under the Tzar; and Sir Francis Alexander Richard de Merveilleux Wunderlich may be a mouthful but it's only a bogus title valued at zero. Yet, having even a questionable title may attract a game player—Prince Alexis Mdivani was attracted to Barbara Hutton's money; she to his title. A not uncommon situation.

You can also buy titles outright. **Prince Frederic Von Anhalt** (husband of Zsa Zsa Gabor) functions as a royal title broker and can arrange a transfer of title from Europeans who are willing to sell. For fees ranging from $10,000 to $150,000 titles can be secured through adoption (the royal one adopts you, bestowing rank by name) or marriage (a quickie that makes everything legal, then a divorce). In seriously titled countries like Austria, Germany, England and Switzerland, not much stock is placed in these "dime store" ranks. (The Catholic Church bestows the title **Papal Count** or **Countess** on Catholics who are extremely generous in their philanthropy toward the church; the title is bestowed in person by the Pope at Vatican City and carries weight in Europe.)

And you can flaunt social status to extreme, too. Wall Street lawyer Bradley Martin and his Mrs. made it big in old NY society, moved to London, married their daughter to a Lord and returned to toss a lavish costume party heralding their new status. Five thousand orchids were placed about the Waldorf ballroom, a 50-piece regimental band played, Mrs. Martin wore a necklace formerly owned by **Marie Antoinette**, society guru August Belmont was garbed in a $10,000 gold inlaid suit of armor, and 400 carriages were hired to move guests about. Since the country was poor (1897) outside of this small clique, the press pilloried the Martins for their excesses, they were denounced from pulpits across the country, their real estate taxes were doubled and club memberships cancelled; in short, they had overplayed their hand. Too much show. They packed off to London, never to return.

Title and power today are best associated with ownership of a major Hollywood studio, a network, cable system or some highly visible means of communication. **Kirk Kerkorian, Edgar Bronfman, Jr.** and **Ted Turner** have become household names and society leaders via their splurging for various causes and power to command the presence of top TV or screen stars. Part of the draw for an event is a stellar personality— and that star's boss is a key player, and usually a key funder.

But through it all, one fact remains: **money is the root of all society**. As much as one of the high-and-mighty may huff and puff and denigrate the ploys of peers in the golden circle, money got them there and only money will keep them there. When donations slow to a trickle so do invitations; when the lineage is still in place but the cash flow has been cut in half by a nasty stock market, so will the ooohs and aaaahs accompanying a rich (or formerly so) couple. Life may be unfair; it is also perverse and demands a *quid pro quo* in all cases and regardless of circumstance. As they say—it's Darwinian out there: only the fittest survive!

Cinderella put her best foot forward and parlayed a few white mice and a pumpkin into a **happily-ever-after**, and Prince Charming enjoyed a similar success. But fantasy doesn't have much of a part in the current play of social life. Ascendancy in society is grueling hard work, requires brilliant strategy and oodles of money.

So it's simply a matter of accumulating acceptance through cash, then using it to stoke all the right people in the right places and with the right finesse! Toil = spoils!

—PALM BEACH WASPINESS—

*Y*ou've probably been to a **Wasp party** where everything was so patrician and so proper that it wasn't very real. The guests locution carried an air of arrogance pronouncing their purebred Yankee heritage; all the young ladies wore Peck and Peck dresses, pageboy hairstyles and gold barrettes; and there was the usual quota of "dress extras"—those tidy chaps who fill out the seating arrangement and make chatty conversation while clenching their cigarette holders at a jaunty angle.

These little affairs are something out of *Gatsby*, well-intentioned but not crude enough to be real. At **real parties**, guys get drunk, insults are hurled with gay abandon, smoke is blown in faces, drinks are spilled, derogatory comments are made about old bosoms or broad derrieres or wrinkled brows—it's showtime and everybody who is anybody enjoys the right to misbehave as long as it's done gracefully.

Take the party when **chain-reaction** took over and almost defiled a family reputation. Guest A spills some wine at the dinner table. Guest B, seated next to him, sprinkles salt on the wine spot so it won't stain the tablecloth. In an effort to ward off bad luck, Guest A throws some salt over his shoulder which goes directly into the eye of a waiter about to serve him chicken. The waiter drops the platter, which is immediately pounced on by an 80-pound Labrador who tears the chicken apart and chokes on a bone. The guest of honor, gallantly, grabs the dog and tries to dislodge the bone, only to be bitten by the dog, and the finger has to be amputated. All over a little **spilled wine**.

Each time you engage in any form of social intercourse, strange and nasty things can happen; but if you want to be a player in the world of social interaction, that's a **chance** you take.

Social cynics suggest that the **ideal party** is quick, quiet and occasional. Ralph Waldo Emerson was once invited to dine with Thomas Carlyle; the two intellectuals sat by the fire smoking pipes for an entire evening, only voicing their pleasure at being with each other. Upon departing, they thanked one another for a most "stimulating" evening; by actual count, only 27 words were spoken.

Compare that event with the typical party of the 2000s where a full **life-repertoire** is poured out to any responsive ear; since we can articulate at 180 words per minute with some deft tongue movements, in any given three-minute session, a good listener can learn of the life plot, ambitions, concerns, expectations and frustrations of an out-of-control talker. And based on the Great American Eagerness to entertain, please, persuade and befriend people (even those you don't know), this scenario is played out regularly at parties in Palm Beach and elsewhere. It's the norm.

Today's norm is lightmiles distant from the behavior of the eminent Wasp families of **New England**. The Otises and Quincys, Faneuils and Boylstons, Hutchinsons and Gores, Royals and Cabots, Dudleys and Lodges were all bluebloods who prospered through mercantile interests, often involving shipping. Through generations of intermarriage and interbreeding, the families became dynastic, the supreme Wasps of the era, a hierarchy which prevailed up until a few decades ago.

As recently as 1950-59, for example, there was a *Mayflower*-descended Robert Fiske Bradford as Governor of Massachusetts, Sinclair Weeks as the Secretary of Commerce, Robert Cutler as special assistant to then President Eisenhower, Christian Herter who replaced the late John Foster Dulles as Secretary of State, Henry Cabot Lodge as Governor of Connecticut and later Ambassador to Spain, John Cabot as Ambassador to Brazil, Robert Moors Cabot as the top authority on the Marshall Plan, Leverett Saltonstall as US Senator, William Gurdon Saltonstall as principal of Exeter Academy, Charles Francis Adams as head of Raytheon, and a Pulitzer Prize poet by the name of Robert Trail Spence Lowell, Jr.

Such eminence created a Wasp Aristocracy which was known for proper behavior, mostly, and a zeal for leadership. In much the way of any organized group of people, a pecking order developed, and that order had its own manifesto of Dos & Don'ts, Rights & Wrongs, Haves & Have Nots and Ins & Outs.

In Palm Beach, social **INS** and **OUTS** have to be seen and heard to be acknowledged, to be a personage; one must be photographed, serve on committees and be fashionable. Going to dinner is a must for the elitist who equates media visibility with success. The **nouvelles** go to **Ta-boo**; **Dempsey's** is a **Wasp** bastion; the **quiet powers** go to the **B & T**; **Cafe L'Europe** is for the **affluententials** who want some modicum of peace; **Bice** caters to the **fashion** establishment; and the private clubs, all the private **inner sanctums**, gather up all those who want to remain privately visible. Even today, the likes of the Dixons or the Lickles or the Drexels don't hang out in public places, unless in their own wings of museums. They enjoy the camaraderie of private clubs where they are assured of dealing with peers who are "altogether correct."

It's said that with enough **money and stamina**, and the right long-term strategy, a nouvelle can become an overnight attraction for society and gossip columns. But in the long run, these people probably won't be "clubbable" nor will they get the right invitations to dinner. What you aren't born into, often, will never be attainable. It's the Law of the Jungle.

There are party players who relish in being **spoilers**. Like the well-dressed and rehearsed gent who writes a little note and has the waiter discreetly place it in front of a ranking guest. Says the note: *"You are drunk, please leave at once."* Or the spoiler who purposely doubles up on the vodka of the hostess, assuming he'll be called in to take command of a deteriorating situation. Or the cygnet who creates movement under the table with older less energetic men and then complains about their raging libidos. All party players, each in his/her own element in an attempt for recognition and, perhaps, social ascendancy.

Winston Churchill, noted for his sanguine and substantial speeches, always reverted to the **counterpunch** role at parties. Rarely would he volunteer information on any subject; he'd wait until something was said, then, usually sarcastically, make a comment of correction. His assumed knowledge and wit on any subject gave him the right to edit the words and thoughts of most other peers, and he did so with enough charm to make the correction pleasing. In the process, he said precious few words during a party. Many people accept a sadistic sense of humor as witty and wise; the more important the personage, the more likely he is to get away with what is really a social gaffe.

When your broker has called your margin in, or your daughter announces she's running away with the gym instructor, or your company is bought by a Japanese toymaker, the pressures of normal living move in and wreck an otherwise good day. Wasps say: a collision at sea can spoil your day. It may take less.

Yet, when all is said and done, and you realize that we're in the mix together, and each of us shares, by some **eternal rotation**, the joys and glories of our times as well as the troubles and tribulations, there does seem to be logic to it all. The chain reaction of life is simply part of the dynamics of social intercourse. For better or for worse, things lead to other things, and the game gets played out in one way or another.

Oscar Levant, late composer and wit, said to his wife after having dinner at the White House with the Harry Trumans—*"I suppose we have to invite them to our house now."*

That's the story of life.

—WASP/CODES—

*T*he English make few concessions to people of other nationalities. They are neither hostile nor friendly and certainly don't make small talk as a kindly gesture, as we do in the USA. Speaking to strangers is regarded as challenging in England; it means entering a minefield of verbal and social distinctions, and thus the great preoccupation with silence. The English are tolerant in the sense that they are willing to turn a blind eye to anything that might embarrass them— they are humane but also shy, and oh so rigid in their social etiquette. The Wasp code is derived from this English sensibility.

Let's say that the necklace once owned by the Duchess of Windsor sold at auction (directly from the Windsor estate) for just over $605,000 10 years ago; one year ago, the necklace fetched only $154,000. The pedigree was tarnished along the way, resulting in a 500% drop in value. Wasps call this **"marring."**

When little Erin, a delightful, flirtatious lass of 16 who kept her uncles and their chums in a state of constant arousal simply by prancing through the great room in a DKNY sweater, was banished to a prep school in Connecticut, the act was called **"yondering."** Erin is yonder this year—serving time in an environment where heart attacks aren't so likely.

"Securing" the fortress, whether it be the club, the social circle, the bridge group or the well-handicapped foursome, simply is Wasp code for setting tighter membership rules, thereby securing the primacy of the peer group.

And when a member of the club becomes a bit overbearing or flashy, he is given special treatment called **"embaying."** Along the southern shores of England, the tide is so unpredictable one can easily be caught between it rising and falling and be **embayed**—isolated on a small rock formation for hours. In an uppity club, the isolation can be much longer, and one gets more than a few splashes from the Irish Sea.

Andy Warhol in a moment of usual irrationality bought a ceramic cookie jar with a value of $5; a few years ago it sold for $7,700. It was part of Andy's stash and part of the frenzy and fantasy of obtaining any of his possessions. Not many Wasps went for the hype—they engaged in one of their favorite ploys—**"renunciating."**

When the kids finally discover genitalia, they get into **"bundling"**— "The young people were bundling on the beach." It's one of those inevitable passages in life; not even the sternest Yankee can thwart its arrival, but bundling can be discouraged by the "yondering" threat—one is sent off to finishing school (where the headmaster, probably, supervises any/all bundling).

When the late **Gianni Versace** bought a $2.7 million Italianate villa on Ocean Drive in Miami Beach, then bought the building next door (for $3.7 million) and tore it down to make room for his pool and garage, Wasps forlornly categorized this economic perversity as **"ornamenting."**

If one of the well-offs asks you—what are you **"doing?"**—It means what kind of work are you involved in and do you have an impressive title and, roughly, how much money do you make??

"Sweatering" translates to—some of the well-endowed girls at the beach club who flaunt their neatly-toned bikini-clad (or cladless) bods need to be covered up!

At the recent auction of Jackie O's personal property, there was a fetish for **"credentialing"**—the simple act of paying many times too much for an item just to be accorded ownership speaking rights. Frank Sinatra's metal mailbox recently sold for $13,800 at Christie's to a young computer wizard who promptly made it the focus of the hallway in his home.

When a definitely B-list couple commissions a pricey decorator to charm up an expensive home, thereby befriending the decorator and his friends/clients/associates, Wasps consider this an overt act of **"linking."**

It's said that one of the most flamboyant chevaliers around the globe is Saudi construction ace **Nasir Al Rashid** (he's also tight with King Fahd); he revels in coasting along the Cote d' Azur on his newly acquired yacht—sevens decks, six cars in the hold, helicopter, squash court, disco, crew of 60—costing about $80,000/day to maintain; its annual paint job comes in at a cool million. His wife **Mouna** buys 30 Chanel gowns each season, to be worn under her chador. In the words of a tweedy Wasp, this is outright **"drenching."**

In the one-plus mile of NYC's **Madison Avenue** between 59th and 72nd Streets, the great names of fashion, style, the new luxe stand side-by-side, testament to money-begetting-money. Valentino, Vuitton, Prada, Armani, Ferragamo, Piaget, Calvin and Ralph, Versace and on and on invite self-indulgence under the guise of "being fashionable." Wasps prefer the soulful minimal to the statusy maximal in any confrontation with the latest & greatest commercial efforts, and people who flaunt & flash their luxe lifestyle are **"emblazoning."**

Jet compulsion really vexates a Wasp. Those corporate lords, billionaires and monarchs who pony up anywhere from $10-35 million for a Gulfstream V or the Bombardier Global Express, there-by to enter the rarefied world of privileged flight, really meet the specs for "flauntatious" by whatever Wasp code. Forget that those birds can fly at 500 mph from Dallas to Cairo, Chicago to Taipai or New York to Tokyo without re-fueling, and in an emerging global economy can make the difference between getting the contract or not—to one of the Brahmins/Old Guard/ Gentry/Cave Dwellers, a high-flying jet just isn't requisite. At luncheons when a jet-setter talks about the shower in his aircraft and the peaceful stratospheric sleep he enjoys, the stiff upper lips grow thin and grim, and via a few har-rumps, the subject is changed. One is **"kiting"** by owning a jet, creating an air of lofty self-majesty.

When a Wasp is compelled to **end** a relationship (with anyone from a domestic servant to a financial confidant), regardless of vicissitude, the event is one of **"expiring."** The former associate has expired and nothing more can ever come from that source. *Finis. Finale. Terminus.*

Finally, **"forswearing"** is a particularly loaded Wasp word. It suggests a satisfaction in the certainty of death, because dying is a way of avoiding the indignity of what one imagines will be a grim future. The favorite expression is—"I'm glad I won't be around to see it." In effect, forswearing is rejecting longevity—if you're vain enough to wish for a long life, you deserve to suffer!

—THE GENTLEMAN—

*W*ay back when definitions were being issued and integrated with our everyday language, the word GENTLE-MAN was born. "Gentle" in its original meaning did not mean soft, honorable or gracious; it comes from the Latin word *gens* which means clan or family. So, by translation, a man from an assumed good family became a gentleman. In European history, someone who came from a family that was respectable and well-behaved was, perforce, a gentleman and conducted himself in a tradition which maintained the integrity of his clan.

England begat the quintessential concept of a gentleman; one thinks of the old aristocrats with their understatement, stiff demeanors and parlor-perfect manners—a cross between David Niven as Phileas Fogg and Jeremy Brett as Sherlock Holmes. But the English were foreshadowed by the Italians who back in the days of royal courts, were dressing in silk and drinking wine from silver goblets and pronouncing themselves as "gentiluomini"—proper men of bearing.

Callow by any comparison, gentility became a function of **heritage** in America. The noted British lawyer John Selden, who dates back to the Pilgrims, suggested that *"gentility. . . is ancient riches."* He meant that what it took to make a gent was old money—but cynics knew better and were aware that in a formative country like the USA, title from another land had some significance, but brains, hard work, a political sense, and opportunism really made the man; and given enough success, that man became a gentleman—usually a social leader, member of the right clubs (often a founder) and churches, and patriarch of one of the great families in the land.

As far back as 1777 John Adams went on record with this admonition: *"People in all nations are naturally divided into two sorts, the gentlemen and the simplemen. The gentlemen are generally those who are rich and descended from families in public life."*

As with the Aristocrat, in the old days a gentleman was a man of property, usually not engaged in any business and often not in a profession. In Virginia, 1673, a York County tailor raced his mare against a horse owned by one of the gentry but never collected his winnings. The county court judged the race illegal, *"it being contrary to Law for a Laborer to make a race, being only a sport for Gentlemen."* The court went further and fined the tailor 100 pounds of tobacco and cash for his insolence.

A more contemporary example of good breeding was the late **General George Catlett Marshall** who refused to write his memoirs of World War II because he felt it unworthy of his gentility. Those close to him knew his decision was primarily due to the example set by General Lee; his veneration for his fellow Virginian and his desire to emulate him was primarily responsible for the fact that

General Marshall alone of all World War II leaders best exemplified a "Gentleman" in the tradition of Lee. (After the Civil War, Lee declined many top posts in the business and political worlds and settled into the relative obscurity of being a college president at $1,500 per year; the college later became Washington and Lee—now a venerable institution.) In England, a **coat of arms** often distinguished a genteel family. One could pay a heraldist to dig back in the archives to find (or invent) a coat of arms, and as questionable as the process might have been, you were not a gentleman without your coat of arms. Even the ultimate cynic and master of the language, who himself invented many of the ploys and policies of the English, **William Shakespeare** had a coat of arms developed for his father, so that he could be considered a second-generation gentleman.

In the definitive book on heraldry titled *Your Family Tree* (by David Starr Jordan and Sarah Louise Kimball), it was conclusively proved that Lincoln, Grover Cleveland and John D. Rockefeller were descended from King Henry I of France, that Ulysses S. Grant was descended from William the Conqueror, and that Calvin Coolidge was a descendant of Charlemagne, while William Howard Taft and J.P. Morgan were descended from King David of Scotland. Since such tracking of family origins dates back to antiquity and is so subject to interpretation and "word-of-mouth" through the ages, not much credence is given to this sort of ancestral heralday.

The **American gentleman** was a clone of an upper-class English gent for five decades following the Declaration of Independence. We followed the patterns and practices of class structure, all within the framework of a democracy, until our gents figured out what really constituted a honorable way of life. For a long time, the surest sign of gentility was quietude, the ability to know when words are appropriate, when the esoteric of amused silence was the right response, and when a call to arms seemed in order. History has recorded the success of men of few words, the strong and silent ones who conquered in their own subtle ways. Andrew Mellon, a Pittsburgh banker, was the richest man in America (after John D. Rockefeller) in 1921 at 66 years of age, but spoke few words and abhorred publicity. His visibility was so modest that when he was proposed for Secretary of the Treasury in the Harding Administration, the reaction was *"Who is he?"* At the time, his various enterprises employed over 200,000 Americans, and his gentle but competitive style was the benchmark of industry for years.

From the 1850s on, in parts of New England and on plantations in the South, the role of lord of the manor was perpetuated with large homes, servants, libraries, family conclaves, and a genteel lifestyle, enhanced by a female equivalent—the **matriarch** of the family—who kept everything in order. But this was not an idle time for gentlemen—they worked hard to produce their fortunes and only had momentary reprieves from the great opportunities inherent in steel and railroads, mining and land ownership.

In short, men of this era became "professional gentlemen," with the amenities of one born to the manor, but a more pragmatic outlook—that suggested a rich lifestyle predicated on hard work.

Teddy Roosevelt was the father of a latter day school of rough and ready gentlemen who could drink with the best of the saloon crowd, throw a few sledgehammer blows if required to defend their policies, yet could retreat into Thackeray or Sir Thomas More or Homer with unexpected grace. They were versatile, worldly, ambitious men who knew how to crack the social code while maintaining their masculinity.

The greatest of all the "professional gentlemen" was Teddy's cousin **Franklin Delano Roosevelt**. Educated at Groton in the Wasp tradition, and a natural upper-crustman by sheer instinct (as well as family breeding), FDR can be singled out as the greatest and most successful **contradiction** in history—he was frivolous and deadly earnest, debonair and arrogant, courageous and courteous while demeaning his adversaries, adroit at mental abuse while generous to a fault. Through these qualities, a smile from Dame Fortune and good timing in history, he dominated the world scene for 20 years and may well be the bearer of the best-known name in the world.

In America today, remaining a gentleman is progressively more **difficult**. The pace of society, the many ignoble players in the game, the loopholes in most structured arrangements (business, taxes, politics) and the peer pressure to be successful mandate a format of self-expression that often disallows gentility. Very few CEOs of top corporations can be considered "gentlemen"; the title doesn't go with the job. Stockholders want a ruthless, bottom-line executive who makes money, not friends. And in politics, it's an absolute contradiction to equate winning candidates with "gentlemen"—there is little honor in politics (simply because political leadership demands a flexible demeanor, and therefore little conviction about right vs. wrong, honor vs. achievement); and there is dwindling space for a real gentleman. The facade may be that of gentility but actions speak something quite to the contrary. No big deal—politicians simply should not position themselves as gentlemen.

Stanley Rumbough, Edwin Burke, John M. Reynolds, William Claggett, Sam Boykin, Byron Ramsing, John Drexel, William Lickle, William Pannill, Doyle Rogers, Warrington Gillett, Fitz Eugene Dixon, John Schuler, Henry McIntosh and **John Dodge** are quintessential PALM BEACH gentlemen.

402

Slightly on the facetious side, the **Palm Beach Gentleman** is a different breed; he practices his genteel art with mastery.

HE:

• Accepts with grace any condemnation that arrives because of his behavior; he offers a vague kind of regret when he is in one of those no-win situations. Smiles throughout.

• Does not sweat. If he must perspire, he does so with his own kind at the athletic club. He never sweats in public because he never does anything that requires complete exertion.

• Buys only combinations of clothes, never suits, jackets or trousers; all his "stuff" works in tandem and with five issues of each item, he has hundreds of appropriate combinations. And each is neither new or old—everything is equally unpretentious and understated.

• Does not run for public office since at one-time-or-another he has ignored the laws of morality and has been seen on a yacht with a bimbo, or some equally compromising escapade that will, invariably, become a headline once his candidacy is announced.

• Never discusses money in public, and never, never accepts the largesse of a rich friend. Possibly after being offered a small stipend to buy a hot dog at a football game, for example, he might take the dollar and engage in a modest eating frenzy. But it should be anticipated that the giver of the largesse will probably say—*"A true gentleman would not have accepted that money."*

• Accepts with resignation and a certain stoicism the cadet honor code at West Point: *"A Cadet does not lie, cheat or steal, nor will he tolerate those who do."* Perhaps that's why gentlemen are often seen alone.

• Will not allow his home to be photographed for a national design magazine, under any circumstances; does not want the old ballroom chairs and the moth-eaten rugs and the bump and grind sofa to become a spectacle to an adoring public.

One of the most remarkable examples of gentlemanly conduct took place at **The Breakers** during the fire of 1925. Local businessmen sat about and toasted their defiance of the destruction of their businesses with champagne. Then, when the fire roared into the bar itself, the gents hastily filled their pockets with cigars and liquor bottles, picked up the red-satin sofas from the lobby and took them to the shore where they sat and watched the skyline diminish while finishing their libations.

The *Oxford English Dictionary* defines a gentleman as "*one of genteel but not noble birth. . . a socially respected person."* Really great men take that definition further by adding. . . with age comes a **certain grace** that is, unto itself, undefinable—but it's always there, in manners, acts, deeds, any form of human contact.

And it is the ultimate **point-of-difference.**

—Walkers & Talkers, Wheelers & Spielers—

*A*s in many cities where there is a social crust, the relationship between *homme* and *femme* is vital; although the single status is quite acceptable, society is still centered on the couple, preferably the happily married couple of many years.

But nature takes its toll, and an offshoot of the natural process is the widow or dowager, a formidable Lady with enough sophistication and money to be held by her peers in high esteem. Whatever her circumstance during the years when her husband was breathing in/out with the nonchalance of a Grandee, the widow becomes a person in need if she is to remain in the mainstream of society. And thus emerges a for-real phenomenon—**The Walker** or **The Escort.**

Over the years, Kept Women were always evident; although they may have been filtered out of most conversation and were rarely presented in public, they had a unique niche and completed the male cycle of need/want nicely. In recent years, Kept Women have become too commonplace to be of interest and have been subordinated to **The Walkers**, as societal fixtures.

Walkers are most visible in places like Saratoga, Palm Springs and Newport, but they are all-pervasive, and Palm Beach has a select number of these handsome, adroit gents who function quite normally as carriage tradesmen.

The Walker is generally seen in the right places; he is impeccably tailored, sports a George Hamilton level of tan, moves with nimbleness through the ranks, bows and curtsies with the skill of a courtesan, can be very voluble but practices the art of listening as a means of sustaining himself and actually learning a great deal (about a life he was not born into). He can be middle-aged or older and often travels as one member of a team of men kept by a dowager. Since sex, and any serious dalliance is out of the question, **The Walker** has little jealousy about favoritism and plays his role with aplomb, as long as his needs are met. He amuses and flatters his Lady, makes a fuss about her dress, inquires about her dog and children, watches her handbag and fur, and performs some of the check signing and tipping; in short, he services her emotionally to whatever degree is possible and generally is a proper companion. For this he may collect modest wages, usually a place to stay (although he also has his own little apartment and regroups there after a night of being **"kept"**), and, of course, invitations to all the right parties with the right people. By association, he becomes a member of the social aristocracy; whatever his sexual proclivities, they are consummated quite outside of the ring of society.

The Walker became an entity around the turn of the century when upward mobility was the major thrust of the newly-minted. Some were hairdressers, florists or decorators who played *Pygmalion* to social ladies, dressing them and choosing fabrics for their beach homes. Though not gigolos, much of what they did was for money, power and acceptance. It is not uncommon today for a Walker to be on a first-name basis with semiroyals, grandees and the *creme*, largely due to a transference of clout via his sponsoring Lady.

Not surprisingly, in sophisticated families, married couples often have a **Walker** at their disposal. Many is the husband who abhors social functions and is delighted to send his supernumerary with the Mrs. to a function, while he contentedly sips bourbon in the quietude of his den. Walkers carry on about antiques and shopping and the *lobster bisque* far more adroitly than a disgruntled husband—and in that regard, he becomes an extension who complements the family perfectly.

A Walker can travel with his dowager, sit comfortably with her if she's hospitalized, watch her during massage, carry her shopping bags, cheer her, take her to the hair-dresser, advise on new fashions (and even accompany her to Paris for the Spring Collections). He may entertain her, dance the night away with her, be preposterous with her, even propose a permanent alliance with her. One of Palm Beach's most adored Socialites in the 60s married her Walker when she was widowed, and lived happily ever after. So for every rule there is an exception.

Palm Beach **Walkers** are often of European descent—Italian, Greek or English. Many have titles, more have faux titles. Most have some vague occupation: interior designer, consultant, historian, author or artist, photographer. They live in a nether world and are more of the flesh than of intellect. They are seen at Club Colette in a tux by Brioni, at the B&T sipping tea on the veranda with the ladies, at opera and symphony, antique, fashion and art outings, and are always perfect gentlemen, happy partners to their protectresses and functional members of high society.

For a **dowager**, life is simply easier when escorted to an event by a man (forget his credentials). Seating arrangements, limousine containment (two couples per limo; one couple on the jump seat, the other, older couple in the back seat), covers at a banquet, even the final addition of funds raised are all easier for twosomes.

Some of the most exalted Walkers are: **Boaz Mazor, Kenneth Jay Lane, Alexis Gregory, John Galliher** and **John Richardson**; designers **Bill Blass** and **Arnold Scaasi** are well-regarded as escorts to top-drawer walkees like **Brooke Astor, Nan Kempner, Jayne Wrightsman, Kay Meehan** and **Anne Cox Chambers.**

Whatever the rationale, the Palm Beach **Walker** is a fixture in society, and when all is said and done, a very welcome member of the fringe that surrounds the Ruling Class.

405

—LES DAMES QUI MANGENT—
(THE LUNCH BUNCH)

*O*ne of the best ways to get into the columns today is to have a **name-designer** on your guest list; having the likes of Scaasi, Lagerfeld or de la Renta turn up at your very special and very own charity function is sure to get ink in the media. Up until about 1960, members of the designer-fraternity were taboo—they were only seen in white frocks with pins in their mouths; but when Jackie O (then First lady) started hanging around with Oleg Cassini, and Halston designed her famous pillbox hat for the inauguration, designers emerged from salons and took their dutiful positions in all the finest places. They dined with their client-Ladies at La Grenouille, La Cote Basque and Le Cirque, explored fine art at Findlay Galleries and the Met Museum, danced the night away at whatever disco was in at the moment, and **lunched** over heavy discussions about hemlines, flared pants and the state-of-the-art. Today, class-acts like Lynn Wyatt won't be seen without Bill Blass; Ivana makes headlines with costume jewelry mogul Kenny Lane; Barbara Bush put Arnold Scaasi on her AAA invite list; and Bunny Mellon jets about with her good friend Hubert de Givenchy. If image is vital, the image-maker is king.

Through the years, **clothes** have been a symbol of **identity**. In the 19th century, the Wasp **old rich**—those that would not acknowledge a Gould, Fisk or Kennedy—were either abundantly fancy dressers or so fearful of being ostentatious that their clothes were threadbare. Since clothes often were an **insignia** of leisure, most mega-rich dressed down in public so the masses wouldn't be alienated, but dressed up in private moments. In the 2000s, fashionable clothes intimate success and respect-for-self and a forward position in the pecking order. Finely rendered dresses and jackets and pants are a mark of the Lady, and the perfect *locus* for showcasing them is, of all places, the **Lunch**.

There are several categories of women engaged in the rituals of luncheons. (1) Ladies who **do lunch** are a special breed; usually on a diet, slim, lean, meaning well but mean, devoid of interest in anything that has calories or fat content or the potential of creating adipose tissue. Yet, they gather at Cafe L'Europe, Chez Jean-Pierre or Maxim's to show their fastidious manners and the latest from the collections of Yves or Geoffrey or Calvin. It's a wonderful world. All the while conducting serious business.

These **do lunch** Ladies are fearsome, ferocious performers who must do something to justify their lovely lives; they are beaverish in plotting, executing, analyzing, conspiring and organizing charitable and business affairs, if not empires. They can be seen in two-three-and-foursomes talking with animation, nodding agreement almost always and being very discreet about scanning the room. They are immaculately turned out and do present an image of assertive perfection.

(2) Ladies who **have lunch** are a different breed; they are more internalized, purely social and motiveless in their acceptance of food. They reign, have reigned or will reign (through marriage, inheritance, circumstance, chronology, anything but work) and are all atwitter, usually about larger issues—their families, grandchildren, Armageddon, ozone layers, the rain forest, how noisy jets still are or membership policies at The Everglades.

(3) Another category of diner is Ladies who **meet for lunch**. Quite well presented, proper, but a little overweight and tacky, these wholesome beings accept an occasional date as a means of getting away from domestic duties and seeing how the rest of this admirable world is getting on. There are modest constraints on the amount of money and time being spent on the outing and the degree to which one must listen to the endless problems (or the passionate affairs) another member has. Feminism plays a big role in these discussions. The clothes are from Lord & Taylor, a glass of house wine is the beverage, Cobb Salad is the entree and desserts are allowed. There is much bill-scrutinizing and doling out of dollars and quarters to pay Caesar for what he has rendered. Tips are **invisible** according to waiters who wonder why meet-for-lunch Ladies aren't at Sizzler's.

As to **availability**, Ladies who **have lunch** usually have their dance-card-of-life filled (at least temporarily); they flash their security via Cartier and Winston, Chanel and Galanos, and it's automatically assumed that their "man" is powerful, more than affluent, part of the Old Boys network, and thereby, possibly even dangerous. **Do lunch** women prefer quick but elegant outings, with arrangements made by secretaries (even down to the mineral water being consumed). They are wrapped in a power-dress (having just come from an hour of inspired aerobics), are clear-eyed, quick-witted (freshly-shaven legs always) and desirous of getting the matter resolved. They invariably attract males, and as a courtesy do a little eye-flirting; it's likely that their names and *curriculum vitae* will be requested from the maitre d' after their departure by some husky hormonal gent. They are not impressed with big Texas business-men talking loudly, with cigar-smoking, multi-dialed watch-wearing politicos, and they hardly fall head-over-heels with all things English; they are a kind of All-American Sweetheart of Sigma Chi who often speak to men as puppies, and still retain power and aplomb. **Meet for lunch** women scrutinize the men in the room as closely as the bill, but their circumstance in life usually disallows any serious dalliance. They enjoy major desserts, take their time in ordering, don't turn anybody on and use the occasion as the "dream of an everyday housewife." For them, it's show-time—escape from reality.

Since **clothing** signifies rank and breeding, it's natural that women can be pre-classified as they enter a restaurant. Owners and managers can discern a **do luncher** from a **lunch meeter** or **lunch haver** in seconds, and know just how to handle each species. They fear most, long-term, the **have lunch** type who can spoil things permanently if they're not pleased with the service, level of deference and presentation of the lunch; although subtle and unassuming, Ladies who **have lunch** expect perfection, and anything less can bring forth unexpected wrath. The **lunch meeters** accept mediocre performance without much ado; they're living out an illusion and don't notice untidy things. In between is the **do lunch** Lady who demands a top performance, enjoys it, comments on it, and becomes a press agent for the restaurant if satisfied; anything too mundane will rate a rebuke but usually not disenfranchisement. Being in a power-restaurant is often more important than the food, and it's not uncommon for a **do luncher** to note that the food was only satisfactory and the portions were small yet the **ambiance** was superb.

It's said that **you are where you eat.** BON APPETIT!

—MONEY - OLD & NEW—

*A*t any given party, the subject of money always has a priority—whether it's donated, LBO'd, inherited, gleaned from divorce, won in a lotto, or even earned. There's a fascination with **gelt** that seems to pervade all aspects of society and commands the attention of the indigent along with the affluent. Money talks, and talk of money demands listeners.

Invariably, chatter about lettuce relates to its **origin**—where did it come from, how old it is, is it appreciating or in decline, earned or picked up via generations, tainted or clean, used properly or flaunted? Usually money is given an omnipotence it doesn't really possess—that it **rules the world**. Granted, it may be influential, but only when combined with language and religion is it a basis for the architecture of mankind.

Money was at first perceived as a **utilitarian** means of helping a new society grow; the first generation of Americans actually resented the privileges bestowed on the colonial aristocracy and played money down. The landed gentry were replaced over time by New England shipping magnates, then fur traders, cotton planters, gold and silver miners, cattle barons and rail tycoons—growth in those endeavors brought on further expansion and the intro of Wall Street moneymen, organizers of trusts, auto, oil and agriculture experts, then dealers in religion, liquor, movies, and on into high-tech. **Money and power** were linked in these forward moves.

Old money people tend to huddle together for a major reason—privacy. Most suggest that the best thing money can buy is exclusiveness or the means of being private. Big money huddles in the dens of Southampton, Grosse Point or Lake Forest and feels safe with its own kind from what it often regards as envy by the **less fortunate**. Because many old-monied types realize their inheritance is a fixed object which over time will be chipped away and depreciated, they are justifiably protective of their turf, knowing that if the fortune was somehow dissipated, they, personally, would have little capacity to build another fortune (no experience at making money one-on-one).

That leaves the field of **making money** open to **arrivistes** who take full advantage of the opportunity. And in the typical sequence of life, as one generation of the newly ordained acquires the means to buy the indicia of success, it looks down upon the next generation of **arrivistes** and an air of condescension sets in. Thus, the eternal merry-go-round of pleasure, profits and image projection. If you listen to an octogenarian about society in Palm Beach in the 40s, for example, you get the flavor of what a pristine world was all about. Everything was proper, comfortable, void of an obvious pecking order, genteel, honorable and private. What scandals occurred were quiet, hidden from the media, and tucked away in solitary vaults.

The question of how **old vs. new money** operates is always a viable subject for conversation. Whereas old money is niggardly and defensive—it is paranoid and perceives the slums and the IRS and foreign governments and all manner of treasure hunter moving inevitably toward its territory—new money loves to blow it in bizarre ways—sending the driver out for pizza at midnight, taking a table at some fancy benefit and leaving early, doing things with panache, generally promoting magnitudes of movement and color and noise.

Old money might revere the works of Picasso; new money says *"I like it, I'll take two of the blue ones."* Sinatra, Bennett, Mathis were part of an era favored by oldsters; newsters want to hear Whitney Houston and Mariah Carey. It's a time and cultural difference that is also seen in the way people greet each other—old rich give off faint and subtle signals via tone of voice and talk of friends, golf courses, summering, schools in common, whereas the **arriviste** compares possessions, specifies capacity of cars, length of yacht, square footage of the new wing and extensiveness of the wine collection.

As for **servants**, old money treats them as family and often allows them to become part of the dynasty; they are concerned about the helps' children, schooling and general welfare, in a way assuming responsibility for their achievement as human beings. Newer types treat servants as servants—they do the things that make life easier and allow more freedom.

409

An **unusual aspect** of the old rich is constant concern about what he could have been, had he no money. *"I might have written a great novel, if I was born poor"* is the operative concept. It haunts those old rich who don't get involved in some kind of philanthropy or productive endeavor, whereas new money feels that it could have written a *magnus opus* had it only had time away from amassing money.

It's natural for new money to take the **most expensive suite** at the Hassler in Rome, while old money settles for something less expensive, less comfortable, in an effort to see how the less fortunate live. Old money deals with moral virtue—horses, corn fields, happiness of employees— while new money goes straight to power, position, connections, image. In effect, old money supports the theory of William James (1906): *"The moral flabbiness born of the exclusive worship of the bitch-goddess Success. That—with the squalid cash interpretation put on the word 'success'—is our national disease."* New money sees it differently: *"It is better to live rich, than to die rich."* (Samuel Johnson, 1778).

Old Money tends to deal life with more **civility**, propriety and sensitivity. The concept of **civility** comes from England, where those born to nobility had a responsibility to conduct themselves (at least publicly) with propriety and finesse; they governed a colony or a fiefdom and were positioned to be role models for the populace. But Dale Carnegie didn't offer courses in "winning friends" in those days, so learning the esoteric of civility became the function of **parenting**, with an assist from institutions (private schools, convents, military academies) where manners were bred. Between stern parents dedicated to protecting their royal lineage, regimented bastions of knowledge, peer pressure and the desire to sustain the family tradition, a sibling had every expectation of being civilized.

There are **professional gentlemen** like Franklin Roosevelt or David Rockefeller, William Webster or Warren Christopher; and there are **made gentlemen** like former Senator Bill Bradley and Rupert Murdoch. The palaver may be similar, the movements graceful, the whole *modus operandi* out of a textbook, but the difference lies in the **spirit**. When a municipal bond loses its tax-free status, or a broker makes a margin call, an authentic gentleman doesn't miss a stroke, just keeps propelling forward with hardly a frown. The other type manufactures pretense as a means of maintaining resolve and momentum.

Civility is often confused with **snobbery**, a word coined by and practiced with relish by the British. In the 50s, Labour Prime Minister Clement Attlee's cabinet included three ministers who had been to Eton; a decade later Prime Minister Harold MacMillan's cabinet had six Etonians, and therefore was *"twice as good."* The business of replenishing snobbery is smoothly carried out in cloakrooms and private clubs where the undercurrent is decidedly uppish; the joke about three officers—one British, one Belgian and one French who see an attractive women riding by on a horse and remark: the Belgian, *"what a fine horse;"* the Frenchman, *"what a fine woman;"* and the Englishman, *"I wonder who her family is?"*—still is told over pints in bars. It's simply a matter of maintaining stiff upper lips and class structure as the pivotal measure of rank.

In England, speech reveals from which **social class** a person comes; in America, speech suggests the **region** of origin. Margaret Thatcher, whose mastery of the English language and all the proper inflections was most impressive, took elocution lessons to remove all traces of a white-collar background from her speech; in her role as Prime Minister she helped define social divisions and a pecking order reminiscent of Britain before World War II. And much of what she instilled as civility in her country was translated into gentility in the USA.

Ancestry plays a major role in success, here, too. It's called birthright, and in a way, it's a contradiction to democracy. A southern Baptist with a degree from a state university will not meet with the same level of acceptance as a job candidate at Brown Brothers Harriman, as a Waspy, ivy league-educated, affluent, family-oriented youth. A subtle form of discrimination opens/closes doors with a fierce finality, and by whatever definition (snobbery, prejudice, civility) there are precise formats for the **haves** and **have nots**. Such delineation is endemic to any ordered society despite pretenses to the contrary.

Whatever. **Life is a cycle**, for the rich and the less rich. Its purpose is happiness; however found, it's the key to a good life. Sophie Tucker observed: *"From birth to age 18, a girl needs good parents. From 18 to 35, she needs good looks. From 35 to 55, she needs a good personality. From 55 on, she needs good cash."*

Maybe that's what it's all about!

—FUNDING & FAME—

*C*hances are that about five of the people you see next time you dine at the Chesterfield, Renato's or Cafe L'Europe are enjoying themselves on what is known as **"ancestral funding."** That's simply trust and estate money passed down for generations past, and to come. These fortunate imbibers and diners have been **selected by genes** to receive monies from the bulky fortunes built up by their ancestors—and the fortunes are enormous, in the area of **$100 trillion** in the USA alone.

To better understand the significance of that number, observe:

```
        1,000,000      = one million
    1,000,000,000      = one billion
1,000,000,000,000      = one trillion
```

It doesn't take much arithmetic to note that one trillion is the equivalent of **one million million**; major money any way you take it. *(Note: there is no zillion, although reference to a zillionaire is often heard—it simply means major bucks.)*

It's estimated that in the next 20 years, almost $20 trillion will be moved from a senior generation to **offspring**; and that's been going on for over 200 years in geometric progression. Names like Rockefeller, Morgan, Drexel, Astor, Vanderbilt, Goldman, Lehman, Schiff, Field, Biddle, Whitney, Harriman, Mellon, Auchincloss, Schwab and Annenberg and mega-fortunes made way back when, in railroads, metals, mining, farm equipment and real estate pitch in each year to perpetuate the dynasties that founded America. Over several centuries, small families have been recreated and extended and intermarried and step-parented and fostered so that today, there are often 200 to 300 heirs funded by a single fortune. And based on successful investments even at a conservative level, what was $1 million at the turn of the century could easily be $100 million today. Money **doubles** every 14 years at five percent, so it's easy to see the relentless escalation.

Wall Street actually began in 1814 when a 32-year-old former privateer captain set up shop to speculate on commercial goods; 23 Wall Street soon became the home of Jack Morgan, and in a few years names like Kidder Peabody, Drexel, Brown Brothers, Hutton and other business wizards made the modest six-block-long street headed by a church and buttonwood tree the world capital of finance.

The typical early **habitue** of Wall Street was a Groton and Yale product, a vestryman at St. James Church, on the house committee of the Union Club, the Brook and the Gorse, and brokered for the Phippes or the Pratts or the Freylingvilles. But to spread the wealth, soon came great firms like Kuhn Loeb, Goldman Sachs and Lehman Brothers. In the free-for-all that followed for two centuries, America soared, went bust, rose, conquered, retrenched, recreated itself several times, and through it all, **prospered...** to the extent that over five million Americans today live on the proceeds of benevolent forefathers. By **passing the bucks** in arcane and innovative ways, the largesse of great periods in history, capitalistic success and the accompanying money has come to rest in the 2000s in the hands of a not so few. (Although the IRS collects about $11 billion annually in estate taxes, it's a pittance compared to what is inherited by those belonging to the "lucky sperm bank.")

As an example, when the giant Standard Oil Company of New Jersey (which controlled the various interests of John D. Rockefeller) was ordered dissolved in 1911 in an antitrust act, $1 billion of the **Rockefeller fortune** was established as a charitable trust to include the Rockefeller Institute for Medical Research, the General Education Board, the Rockefeller Foundation and a major endowment to the University of Boston; another $1.8 billion was set aside for distribution to heirs, of which there are (and have been as of now) over 350. Naturally, the more **prolific** the family, the greater potential for heirs, and the Rockefellers had no shortage of sons, daughters, grandchildren, and generally keepers of the cash.

The greatest of the ancestral families are the **du Ponts** with about 2,100 family members and some 65 more arriving each year. They comprise a dynasty worth an estimated $20 billion and present a superb example of a multi-dimensional, multifarious clan. The family as a whole was best summed up by James Warner Bellah in *Holiday Magazine* (1955):

"I have known several du Ponts. One ranks high among the world's most charming hostesses—an incisive mind denying the moated walls of great wealth and living eternally in the reality of the world. One is an insufferable travesty of Chaucer's Eglentyne, eternally prefacing a complete absence of any sound opinion with 'As a Dewopawn' (du Pont). One is a victim of sadistic family possessiveness to a point of shuddering almost visibly at the sound of the name. And one, with an excellent war record behind him, works hard at the family trade as his forebears did before him. Some are known intimately and as well in Wilmington as any run-of-the-mill neighbors in any small town. Some are towering swells, only heard from in distant places. Some people in Wilmington whisper the name in awed reverence. One prominent Wilmingtonian who bore it as a middle name never even used the initials. . . Some Delaware du Ponts live with imposing formality. Some answer their own doorbells. Some dwell in a hundred rooms. Some in three and a kitchenette. At least one has committed suicide. One held the Congressional Medal of Honor. One enclosed his 300 acres of home park with a 10-foot wall topped with jagged inset glass to 'keep all the skunks in Delaware out'—as he put it—'most of them named du Pont.' Two were United States senators. One has been married four times (you must be married five times to be an officer of that club). . . One built the Equitable Building in New York. One tried to sue half the female population of Wilmington for libel. One is a ranking tennis champion. One married an Irish barmaid between boats at Queenstown—and never came home."

In Palm Beach, imagine the ancestral funding that will follow in the evolution of the **Dixon, Kluge, Lauder, Farris, Bagley, Koch** and **Simon** families. Some $25 billion in funds is involved, and over the years, with a modicum of investment skill, that amount can double, leaving massive fortunes to generations who bear these august names. It's all a function of being geneologically fit,

The biggest single fortune being passed on in America goes to **Wallis Annenberg**, a family counselor in LA; she is the daughter of publisher Walter Annenberg and will inherit $1.6 billion. Via Annenberg's sisters—**Jan Hooker** and **Enid Haupt**—charities have been very benevolently served.

Fortunes in the $100-million range have very few places to go other than (a) the family line of succession, or (b) charities. Families in this order of finance have everything "money can buy," and unless the fortune is squandered in bad investments or some form of perversity, a charity is a likely recipient of ancestral largesse. Some of the major causes in the country—American Cancer Society, American Heart Association, Juvenile Diabetes Foundation—each have many millions pledged to their work. Donations usually come from families afflicted by various diseases, who determine to further research funding in an effort to wipe out the malady. And some noblemen actually form Institutes to combat a particular disease; shipping and real estate master **Daniel Ludwig** is leaving about half of his $1.2 billion estate to a Zurich-based cancer research organization under his name.

In another twist, the late **Paul Mellon** gave the bulk of his $450 million estate to charity, feeling that his two children, who already inherited $100 million each from their financier grandfather Andrew Mellon, have enough cash to buy whatever treasure and pleasure they want. The $100 million given to each of the Mellon children 50 years ago is now worth about $875 million.

Checking over the *Forbes 400* list shows about one-third of the wealthiest Americans came into their money through inheritance. Names like DeBartolo, Adderly, Freeman, Martin, Wilford, Marshall, Park, Spencer and Gallo appear toward the top of the list—and all are family or married names associated with massive fortunes. The power of the pass-along is staggering.

The **moment of truth** when the Reaper appears also focuses on money and the hereafter: one eccentric willed up to $1 million to a cemetery that would bury her next to her husband in her prized Ferrari, decked out in an evening gown with a bottle of Dom Perignon in hand; several decades ago, **Eleanor Ritchey**, heiress to the Quaker State Refining Corporation, left her $5 million fortune to 150 stray dogs she adopted; Russian immigrant Stanley S. Newberg left the bulk of his $8 million estate to the federal government as a special tribute to the country which allowed him to prosper (whereas the $609 million owed to the IRS by the estate of Samuel I. Newhouse was finally settled at $47 million—and all parties were happy); a **bon vivant** willed $500,000 for a major blowout for 100 of his best friends—a jet charter to Monaco, finest accommodations, gambling and a testimonial dinner, using a slide presentation of the life and times of the deceased.

Probably the frankest and **least controversial** way to check out is via the formula of French satirist **Rabelais**: *"I have nothing, I owe a great deal, the rest I give to the poor."*

—CONSANGUINITY—

*J*ust how important is **consanguinity** in climbing the social pyramid? Some say that the right upbringing is imperative to fulfillment of the family destiny. Others argue that sheer, raw ambition will triumph over an inherited, moneyed lifescript. But few protest the suggestion that *pedigree* and effective behavioral traits are the result of **genetic inheritance** and **environmental conditioning**, both of which are usually provided by parents. It's not uncommon to see a 50-year-old socialite affecting the tone, words and demeanor that her parents used in her childhood, transferring those flesh-and-blood characteristics with frightening precision. We are all a product of our early years; the path we take in life and how far we go before we arrive somewhere is fairly well preordained.

It's not by accident that seven generations of **Bachs** were great musicians; that most of the **Kennedys** followed their heritage into public service; that **Liza Minnelli** sings with the same soul as her mother **Judy Garland** did; that the **Fondas** are a dynastic entity in theater (as are the Bridges, Carradines and Douglases). Families like the **Rockefellers, McCormicks, Fields, Whitneys, Astors, Smiths, Dixons** and **Lehmans** have sustained their consanguinity through excellence in their respective fields of endeavor. It's a part of LINEAR DESTINY.

To judge just where we will go, it's important to first examine the invisible threads that tie us, like a puppet, to our past. For family destiny argues that the **choice of a life path** and the level of motivation absorbed during childhood from parents (and the home environment) is quite precise in determining exactly what, how, where and how well a person copes with life.

A number of **factors** influence our destiny and each is determined almost at the moment of birth.

First is **GEOGRAPHY**: Someone born in East St. Louis probably won't make the A list as easily as a Manhattanite; being raised in Grosse Pointe gives one an advantage over adolescence in the heart of Detroit; enjoying a **big eastern-city upbringing** provides certain advantages that aren't found elsewhere in the country. A person from Newport will automatically be embraced more quickly by Palm Beachers than someone from Memphis.

Another factor is **FAMILY UNIT POSITION:** It's axiomatic that more is expected from the **oldest child** in a family than other siblings; thus that child expects more from him/herself. If the person is an only child, much time will be spent with adults, thereby offering different mature perceptions. As a rule, the eldest child is the most ambitious and hostile; the youngest is more playful, passive and dependent.

NAME is another telling factor: The surname Vanderbilt certainly carries some rank with it; **WASP designations** (Lodge, Mellon, Phipps, Harriman) seem to create easy access in most places, and names like Ford or Marshall Field or August Busch bring both privilege and a special set of expectations which shape behavior to a large degree.

The career path of a Buddhist, Christian or Jew may ultimately cross later in life, but rarely before that, since each **RELIGION** has its own merits in being generally accepted by life-at-large. Each embraces a philosophy that guides one during early adolescence and **sets guidelines** for later questions of ethics, social acceptance, entree to the power elite and general leverage in life.

When it comes to **EDUCATION**, it's been standard over the years to think of **Ivy League** or **Seven Sister** schools as peerless, and although the curriculum of such institutions isn't superior, being part of a selective group does open doors as one progresses along the path. The mere mention of Harvard or Princeton in an interview or in idle chatter at a cocktail party raises eyebrows and interest levels. Having such a credential makes entry easier, and expectation higher—a mixed blessing.

Picasso often praised his parents for their dedication in making him superior: *"When I was a child my mother said to me, 'If you become a soldier you'll become a General. If you become a priest you'll be the Pope.' Instead I became a painter and wound up as Picasso."* So much for **FAMILIAL EXPECTATIONS.**

Rich children develop an attitude of **entitlement**—they don't aspire to be upwardly mobile since they are already up in their minds. They aren't unduly impressed by important people, and mix in with enough security to hold their own with any crowd. They, therefore, go into life with more assurance and a **success-anticipation** that sees them through early confrontations, and gains them initial acceptance.

In general, it's fairly clear that in the family the **SUCCESS OF THE PARENTS** is the prime mover in developing the ambitions and career-plots of the offspring. We all try to beat the economic, social and lifestyle levels established by our parents and are often obsessed with such achievements.

416

Winston Churchill had a poor relationship with his exalted father—Cabinet Minister Randolph Churchill—and was driven to eclipse him, which he did by becoming Prime Minister. But both were driven by the bizarre success of ancestor John Churchill, the son of a country squire, who slept with the king's mistress and conned her into buying him a commission in the king's guards, then changed sides when William of Orange overthrew King James in the glorious Revolution of 1688—his new alliance made him a duke with the biggest palace of anyone in Europe. A gentleman he may not have been, an opportunist he was, and the family career path was thus set.

Although democracy is our accepted way of life in Palm Beach and in the USA, a *pedigree* plays an important part in giving each of us the satisfaction we seek from society. *Pedigree* is a function of the factors mentioned and can't be easily assumed, presumed, contrived or bought. We are what we are; the **Gubelmann, Kenan, Matthews, Reynolds, Fanjul** names and heritage have a fixed quality about them which, in a way, determines just how those name-holders perform—what they take from life, and more importantly, **what they give to life.** Each of us realizes at some point, that our *pedigree* gives us access to very selective situations, and with access there is often acceptance which leads to commitment, and always to **responsibility.**

The most **consanguinity** can do in Palm Beach or elsewhere is get you to a level where you are accountable in what you do, because what you do profoundly affects the lives of others.

A prestigious birthright demands excellence; sometimes it's easier to be just another John or Henry or Coward.

—SINGLES & SECRETS—

*A*nyone who goes through a half-dozen or so decades, by osmosis if nothing else, picks up a lot about humankind. Just rubbing bones together, smelling each other's aromas, glancing through hazy sunlight at one you love (or hate), all without a word, tells so much about life, and the game, and what a real existence is all about. No primer is needed; the answers are there in what you see, and it's all **free**!

You've seen this kind of Palm Beach guy—he has carefully positioned himself in life to **avoid the excesses** of either happiness or pain; he's cultivated a safe and judicious shallowness and has taste but no appetite. He laughs but seldom smiles, has expectations but no hopes, is remarkably bold but lacks courage, and is frank but not sincere. He **celebrates artifice**—and is very successful at being the "extra" man, Mr. Available, charming and fitting, but never contributes anything of substance.

417

And you've witnessed the male who doesn't want **all of anybody** anymore. He wants the parts that nobody is using, and based on his premise that most married women are only half-used, he moves toward extra-marital activities. His philosophy—parts of somebody are more interesting than all of somebody.

Often you've been to parties where everything is **wishful**—the Dalmatian can wolf down $200 of caviar and nobody even notices; they're all too busy wishing they were young enough and beautiful enough and uninhibited enough to peel off their $3000 gowns or tuxes and skinny-dip.

There, definitely, are women whose **cells** are just better than others—more ripe with lifestuff or something; it's why they, those knock-out creatures, are twice as alive as the rest of us; they also seem to have a truth-radar, a lie-detecting mechanism that allows them to skip over the lie and get to the motives behind it. If there is anything wrong with women like this, only an **x-ray** could find it—and to a person, their feet look like they have trod on a lot of beaches and worn out numerous tennis shoes. These wondrous ladies may not add a lot to the libraries of life, but they certainly fill visual space on a singularly sensational basis.

And there are women, too, who are prey to the **Socratic** method. The virtue of that method is that it forces women to talk; once they talk a little, their natural volatility comes into play, and the conversation ranges from despair to meaninglessness to empty days and loveless nights, and then it segues to things like "Friends" and Madonna and the Gross National Product. By being a good Socratic listener, a gentleman can learn a lot about life over one martini.

How about the **presumptive male** who asks three questions of his female counterpart—*"Do you want to eat and go to bed; or go to bed and then eat; or eat in bed?"*

There are **well-intentioned men** who believe:

* Ladies are only a temporary answer, but if you repeat a temporary answer often enough, it acquires a degree of permanency...

* Women love to forgive you; you don't even have to apologize — just give them the opportunity to forgive you and they will, then, take you to bed...

* Women are like lawyers and torturers, more interested in process than in results...

* The surprising thing about young foolish women is how many survive to become old foolish women...

* Ladies are cutest, most animated, most vulnerable when they're expectant—keep them ever so slightly in the dark about your motives, manners and munificence.

And, of course, there are **women who believe** —

* A man who dies rich has lived a poor life; he needs a spending-partner...

* Most men get into new relationships to get out of the ones they are not brave enough to say are over...

* Although well-motivated, a lot of men are like turtles who are turned over on their backs—everybody is picking on them and they can't defend themselves well (in a way they get to like their role as martyrs), and it takes enormous effort to turn over and right themselves...

* No one can ever understand eternity until she understands the monotony of a boring male.

Some men, or women, realize the power of a **true alliance**—in which nothing can ever be the same again; the parties have tested the ultimate and they should never do that, there should always be one corner around which one doesn't go, because once there, what is left?

Women surely know men who have bought a **do-it-yourself** Rex Harrison kit but never quite mastered the instructions; and men know about women who have undergone the **same surgery** and how they love to compare scars.

When in **love**, He sees Her as soft, with flawless skin and dark eyes that speak volumes; she is a sea of silk, satin and velvet, hypnotically, magnetically beautiful; and he, hopelessly in lust, is like a locomotive that has puffed and struggled up one side of a mountain and then careened full speed down the other, totally out of control.

One thing common to both male/female is—*ex adversis felicitas crescit:* **from adversity grows happiness!**

Finally, both principals in the Great Game of Life agree that in the end, it is **time** that outlives us all and leaves us as history. Time moves relentlessly forward, the one enemy that is unchallengeable. Maybe that is why we're so easily lured into and **captured by the past;** if we could put time in a bottle (as Jim Croce suggested in song before time made off with him), hold it still and keep it from running off, we'd be in control of our destinies.

Everywhere you go, people gaze backward, because the past alone is **immutable.**

—WHICH A-LIST?—

*L*ike most games in life, the competition is fierce with applicants far outnumbering opportunities; but with the right goals and a definitive career path, you can be **a winner** and on the right **A-List** in town; or you can be on the **other** A-List.

419

Unlike (but not totally) **Hollywood**, where a casting couch is the medium for bright lights, Palm Beach puts aspirants through a series of little social tests and gambits to flush out star-quality if it's there, and to remind the wannabes that (a) life is indeed unfair, (b) there is prejudice— usually called cultural preference, (c) money buys privacy, (d) the golden rule is made by those with the gold, and (e) the vocation of marry-up can be as challenging as being a global seismologist. In showbiz, the credo— all young women have the inalienable right to dedicate their lives to the pursuit of stardom, regardless of talent—is quite acceptable; in Palm Beach, the "regardless of" gets edited out and "based on" is inserted. Merely a formality, but Palm Beach deals in **formalities**.

When a potential listee is introduced to a **One Unit Man** ($100 million) social graces suggest she says: *"Of course, I've read about you."* or *"Yes, I have met Margaret Thatcher."* or *"Oh, I love to dance."* Never-no way—should these lines escape her lovely lips: *"What's your sign?"* or *"Sorry, I don't remember your name."* or *"Didn't we meet in a previous life?"* Better than any words—let **eyes** do the talking.

Naturally, a listee-to-be has to be refined, well-mannered, speak crisply, and choose her wines with distinction; in her **entourage** should be an image-maker, personal trainer, publicist, palimony attorney and a very discerning, money-loving mentor (male or female; someone who has fought a culture war before). These good associates should advise her that **octogenarians** usually have far more $$$ socked away than to-day's counterparts because of tax loopholes in the good old days; that guys with **canes** are quite appropriate for passes (at least, they get a smile from the maitre d'); and that men who aren't necessarily in sync with **GQ fashions** are still okay (the elbow-worn blue blazer is a sign of civility).

A **wannabe/listee** need not be without convictions: if she likes Placido Domingo, she should be sure not to mention him as president of the Dominican Republic; she should know that Henry Flagler isn't the **Fonz,** that social larvae are somewhere between moths and butterflies, that social intercourse via words like **alta kokker, chauzzers** and **meshuggener** must be used selectively, and finally, that there are many, many dances but no dance cards. Romance, the dance, chance are all unwritten verities.

At a **party**, the **listee** must never get caught trying on another guest's fur coat in the bedroom; or get into an argument with Audrey Gruss; or stuff too much pastry into her small, delicate and innocent mouth; or pick up one of the hired, hairy bartenders; or expound on her fake family tree and mispronounce the name of her great-grandfather; or after two martinis revert to her old self by singing telegrams. **Flirtation** is quite in order but not with the hostess' husband or our Town's men of the cloth; and our listee **should** take it personally when the most civilized man in the room ignores her credentials but is impressed by her significant cleavage.

At the bar in his mansion, utterances **never even to be thought of** are: *"You must be crazy—you're old enough to be my grandfather!"* *"Does this mean I can move in?"* *"I'm flattered, but I really don't know if I can direct all those servants."* *"When was your latest blood test?"* *"I never get drunk, just a little tipsy."* *"Do you think your stepchildren will like me?"*

Our aspirant must also know the Palm Beach **parlance**: legend = has been; emotional problems or nervous breakdown = too many Manhattans too regularly; there are still tickets left for = a fiasco; people are talking about so-and-so = no one's even interested except the publicist; and expected at the party-of-the-year are = all the usual suspects will be boringly there.

In the case of **limos**, which should be at least an occasional accoutrement of the listee, proper **protocol** is a must: the door should always be attended by someone else; champagne should never be opened with the cork pointing at an elderly but rich and wonderful escort; no gasps are allowed even when passing the Whitehall Museum; waving to friends in the 1970 VW is not conducive to a successful relationship; schmoozing too much with the limo driver throws off strong negatives to other companions; posing for photos by cheesecaking on the Caddy's fender is **passe**; and scheduling an arrival at a ball at the same time as Mayor Lesly Smith requires a motorcycle escort and isn't sage planning.

People **come and go** like leaves in the wind, and few aspirants make it to the candle-adorned dining table for long; those who do have mastered the esoteric of convincingly falling in love or convincingly being the object of love. Or really being in love and loved. **Mating grounds** abound and the human quest for romance is insatiable. Most Palm Beachers have settled into their quite composed lives and only the strongest **primal urges** are likely to change their routines, so a bountiful young maiden with a good method and a glib tongue does have a shot at the **A-list**. But not even the most optimistic odds-makers would make it an **even bet!**

Listees who don't get their "A" usually become **groupies** attending each and every function, trying desperately to join the upper crust crowd; in between parties and fellowship they work on committees or as volunteers or as assistants to important executives, usually a high visibility job where making connections is possible. In some cases, they are not discouraged by working at these "temporary" jobs years—Hope does spring eternal.

As ancient tribes, long ago, sat around campfires and pondered their plight, so the **Survivors** gather at Palm Beach Tavern, telling stories of their conquests (the extent of their mattress money) and compliances, exchanging the latest gossip. In some arcane way, they are usually right on the money; their rumor mill is uniquely precise. They can tell you who the next "Queen of Society" will be, when the next important-people divorce is due, what unhappy husband is about to be caught *en flagrante,* what ex-VP will soon become the CEO. Their prescience comes from jungle drums that are constantly pounding away, fully aware that they, the Survivors, operate in a social jungle, where the killing fields are awesome. Yet, they persist in believing they can scale the Regal walls and become one of the Chosen. High society **is** their Jericho, and Joshua will blow his golden trumpet, and the mighty gates will fall before them.

Being optimistic for the future, these Survivors gather together for comfort, motivating each other with their dreams, always on the brink of breaking through. In the meantime, as time moves forward, they live with each other, often marry and divorce each other, never noticing how time is betraying them—new facial lines, graying temples, the need for more makeup, all the signals of being shopworn.

Ultimately the illusion is shattered by rejection, a toughening of spirit and a final realization that the odds and the price are too high to compete in the heady business of social success. And, usually, at that time, the **Listee/Survivor** begins to lead a somewhat normal, happy life, no longer full of the ogre of disllusionment and delighted to be on the **other A-List (autonomous, anonymous and adjusted!).**

—GOSSIP—

*G*ossip was called the bane and disgrace of society by George Eliot and "intellectual chewing gum" by some anonymous Bostonian Regal. Admittedly, it can be harmful, unjust, awesome in implication, false and malicious, but it also can be astute, incisive, instructive and truthful.

*"**Gossip** brings ethics home by introducing abstract morality to the mundane,"* wrote psychologists John Sabini and Maury Silver in their volume *The Moralities of Everyday Life. "Gossip is a means of social control in that it allows individuals to express, articulate, and commit themselves to a moral position in the act of talking about somebody else. Thus, it is a way that we come to know what our own evaluations really are."*

422

As in any society-driven community, Palm Beach is not without **gossip**—it is a daily routine at golf games, club outings and nocturnal pursuits. While gossip may not always be truth, it is at least openly suspect; and while it may not be fair, everyone has access to it, there are no limitations on its availability. It is simply part of our lives—part of the daily 5,000 words each person uses. Much like eye contact, a nod of the head, a wink or pat on the shoulder, gossip is a verbal means of communicating **something special**.

The word gossip derives from the Old English **godsib**, meaning one who has a spiritual affinity with another being, for example, a God-mother-or-Father. Thus, a certain familial closeness is set up which allows for intimate details of lives to be discussed and analyzed. While men worked to create the economics of life, women were left to chatter on about indiscretions/successes /failures of those within the family/ friend circle.

Gossip was formalized in the mid-1800s by a southern gent named **Ward McAllister**; he traveled extensively across the country and picked up on the nuances of societies presented in cities like San Francisco, Boston, New York and Charleston. By being an expert at what various people liked in various cities, what their dining habits were, what pretensions they had and similar information, McAllister created a list of the "Nobs" (Old Families) and the "Swells" (newcomers). For whatever reason, his list was gospel to those in the social milieu, and McAllister became a self-appointed patriarch of the social crowd. His list later reflected the "Four Hundred" who were typically invited to Mrs. Astor's annual bash (rumor has it that the limit of 400 people was imposed by the size of the ballroom) but, in fact, the list had just over 300 names on it.

McAllister had his moment of fame but was never really taken seriously by the "Nobs." He wrote a fatuous book—*Society as I Have Found It*—which led to his discovery and downfall. Just prior to the World's Columbian Exposition in 1893 in Boston, when the Mayor announced that he would give everybody who attended a "genuine" Boston welcome, McAllister retorted, *"It is not quantity, but quality that society people want. . . and hospitality which includes the whole human race is not desirable."* A war of words resulted with him as the victim; his Boston contretemps sealed his doom, and he was soon discharged from his associations and dubbed a "New York flunky."

Another social arbiter was needed—it came in the person of **Louis Keller** who started the *Social Register*. Over a 50-year period the *Register* became the dominant document appraising the social crowd. By 1922 the *Register* had editions in 21 cities and was a force among all levels of socially-oriented people. Composed largely of newspaper clippings about marriages, divorces, deaths, debutante lists, college graduations, etc., the *Register* had a secretive nature and was basically non-approachable by someone seeking a listing. But those in the know, knew that by merely asking for an application and having five solid *Register* listees send letters of recommendation, the chances of being included in the next edition were very good.

One of the odd factors of the *Register* was why certain names were dropped and others added. Outside of refusing to fill out forms and thereby opening family history to examination, or speaking out against the *Register*, properly submitted names usually appeared with regularity. **John Hay Whitney** and **Alfred Gwynne Vanderbilt** thought the *Register* was a "joke of the lowest denominator" and were thus excluded. After **Stephen "Laddie" Sanford** was dropped for marrying actress **Mary Duncan**, the late John Sanford was so exercised that he demanded the *Register* drop his entire family from the listing. *"This treatment,"* he protested *"is no better than Communism."*

The *Register* got its greatest criticism when it threw out **Charles Alden Black** of San Francisco for marrying **Shirley Temple**—which was like insulting the American flag.

When Keller died, the mantle of arbiter was passed on to the master of "Gossip Truth"—**Cholly Knickerbocher** (Maury Henry Biddle Paul of Philadelphia). He wrote multiple gossip columns under different names (Polly Stuyvesant, Billy Benedick, Dolly Madison) and was syndicated in over 50 newspapers countrywide. In 1921 he divided society into the "Old Guard" and "Cafe Society" and thus endeared himself to many of the richest people in America (the Old Guard who wanted proper identification of their credentials) and to many of the almost richest (Cafe Society types who wanted a transfer of social level). Throughout a turbulent run of two decades, Paul grew more cynical and more isolated from the true aristocrats, thereby being forced to focus on new people. As he said *"The newcomers of today are the Old Guard of tomorrow."*

The last of the arbiters was the late **Frank Crowninshield**, debonair, distinguished, cosmopolitan from the start. Over the years, he elevated gossip to a more authentic level and made ***Vanity Fair*** Magazine the classic of its time. To society he added accomplished people in the arts, theater, Hollywood and sports, and made light of the fearsome infighting climbers engaged in, seeking more to associate society with people who were loyal Americans, leaders in their fields, of excellent character, culture and taste, and having sufficient **humility**.

To its credit, gossip helps make an orderly **transition** for august families. What to one generation is Cafe Society, for example, is to the next generation real Society. And nobody devoured the subject more amusingly than the true gossip columnists of the postwar era. They created a term called *Publiciety* and went at the social clans with a vengeance. **Walter Winchell**, the most loved/hated chronicler of the time said: *"Most of the old families today have either press agents or praise-agents."* **Leonard Lyons**, commenting on the names in Cholly Knickerbocher's column, noted *"They can't be society, I know them all."* In Los Angeles, **Mrs. Cobina Wright** tried a column called "Society as I Find It" — but couldn't find IT and recast her writing as "News from Cobina Wright." **Hedda Hopper** labeled socialites as *"people who would rather go to hell than not see their names in print."* And finally, and more to the point, legendary social scribe **Joseph Xavier Dever** declared that the only society in America was the Society of Achievement. *"Family background,"* he said, *"is no longer the sole criterion of an individual's distinction."*

Anthropologists say that gossip is a "given," a universal component of human nature; condemning or ignoring it is futile, and unwise for anybody dealing with other humans as the means to an end. Unlike computer-oriented societies, Palm Beach deals with charities, funding and power, each predicated on the performance of a person, a group, a committee, **people**. Thus, the imperative of using gossip to its best advantage.

In **Palm Beach**, "Dear Abby" or the *Enquirer* or some nebulous grapevine is not significant, but verifiable gossip—"insider information," distilled gossip which equals "informed speculation," the infamous "leak" which is really a directed flow of gossip—is **vital**.

Gossip can help move **life forward** in many ways. As an **Equalizer**, the **G-word** softens the myth of the mega-rich; all the intimidating talk about how wealthy he is, or how extensive her properties are, or what company is next on the agenda for acquisition, can be put into better perspective when there's small talk about the peculiarities of the person in question. After the verbal genuflection publicly given to Megaman, small talk can be used to cut big talk down to size and as an antidote to pomposity and authority. Gossip is the Great Leveler when used to talk about the sad relationship the Queen of Society has with her children, or the terrible golf game the King pushes on his peers, or the dismal lack of happiness in the Royal Family.

As author Erica Jong suggests—*"Gossip is the opiate of the oppressed."* When someone needs to feel equal or superior, a quick route to an ego-high is to bring someone else down through verbal flak.

As a **Morale Booster**, gossip keeps the committee members who work the dull side of an event upbeat and functional; nothing can be more deadly than hour-after-hour addressing of envelopes, and nothing offers a better opportunity for some affirmative rumor-spread. In this case, gossip can be used to politic, socialize and reinforce someone's performance. Gossip implies a negative; but can be very **positive**. By the Chairman simply stating that the assembled group has addressed more envelopes in less time than in any previous effort, the word is out. Winners all!

While gossip is normally chosen by those who want to **slander** others without exposing themselves to cross-examination, facts invariably surface, usually discrediting the slanderer in the process. Thus, as a **Lie Detector**, gossip identifies those whose information **can't** be trusted and, conversely, those who **can**. Gossip is, in this instance, an ongoing credibility test everybody takes, with or without knowing it.

It's said that **hell is a place where everybody is condemned to mind his own business**—there is no hotline in the inferno, no flak, no town crier. It's surprising how **quickly** gossip gets passed from party-to-party; memos and formal communication may take weeks to reach an audience; gossip usually leapfrogs from **source-to-subject** in minutes. A Chairman might, for example, want to shake up the raffle committee by quietly passing the word to staff members that raffle sales are slipping, or the raffle prize is not exciting enough, or whatever. Not surprisingly, that word will flow with the speed of light, and in all probability, remedial action will be taken.

Gossip is a great medium of **P.R.**; the Chairman can casually suggest she's heard (from an undisclosed source) that her leadership is too rough on co-workers (when in fact, she is very patient with the less-fortunate). Her friends will instantly rally-round her with allegiance and praise, all of which simply gives her more momentum in being a bit overbearing (if that's what it takes). "Undisclosed sources" have incredible credibility when used effectively; by being good at what you do and dropping a few lines about the acceptance of your performance, generally more **favorable** response is generated.

Legends like **Voltaire** and **Dryden**, **Boswell** and **Wordsworth** reported the facts of their era with panache; they were colorful, sometimes bitchy, tough but fair, as they detailed the pecadillos of the *haut monde*, and became, as a result, accepted, often revered. To them gossip provided the means to embellish their social and literary standing.

Very importantly, gossip serves as a **Guidebook** to the prevailing rules, latitudes or morals of a given circumstance; what is considered harsh, obscene or out-of-touch is quickly put into the pipeline of words after a few meetings person-to-person. Gossip is mostly nuance in these situations, but clearly delineates what the **real** values, ethics and realities are. Rumor may have it that the chair's husband loves his cups and is a source of great embarrassment to his wife; thus, she is always harried, and indecisive. The gossip may be right on the money, and if so, committee people can adjust accordingly or confront the issue. Nobody likes to fool around with Mother Nature, or a Chairman, but for the well-being of the party, action may be required.

Although hype has its place in the world, extended hype or **untruth**, however circulated, usually is emasculated by truth. In a way, gossip expedites the process—it exposes the fraudulent, reveals the inept, sets players and pretenders up for failure. It may begin casually, but with each messenger, different layers of revelation (and danger) accumulate. The finale of a particular rumor may be accommodation, disaster or triumph, but each of the **carriers**-of-the-world is exposed for what he truly is, too.

—THE CELEBRITY CULTURE—

*T*he damndest part of celebrity is its inverse ratio—you can be trash in the grand scheme of the universe, like **Mickey Rourke**, and get a table at Elaine's, La Goulue or Tavern on the Green before an authentic gem like **Warren Buffett. Tom** and **Nicole** can stroll into "21" and be seated minutes later at a prime table while the president of New York University spends elbow time at the bar awaiting his reservation. **Sarah Ferguson**, ex-Duchess of York and a master of high visibility, rates more salutation than **Gov. George Pataki** of New York when she prances into Le Cirque.

It's all a matter of the sewer system often called **gossipocracy.** If you're on the chosen list of the news gossips, for better of for worse, it's likely your power will escalate in direct proportion to the number of mentions or column inches you get. The late **Diana, Princess of Wales**, was so revered by the press for her charm, good work, martyrdom and misalliances that she will live for a decade in the illumination of gossip inches; others like **Madonna** and **Sharon Stone**, often considered novelty-celebrity, will have run their 100 yards and become facts and faces in history while Diana will continue to be sublimated. (However, never misjudge the fickleness of humankind—the cycle of stardom goes from rejected to tolerated to approved to accepted to admired to emulated to praised to idealized to memorialized to FORGOTTEN. Don't ever *forget* that!)

Celebrity culture today equals power, and power in certain environments is tantamount to having it your way, regardless. Crude, irrational behavior, ugly appearances, an intelligence void have nothing to do with power, as defined by the media. If you have enough cache to appeal to the masses (by whatever device—a marriage or divorce, a good movie, a great season at bat, top swindle as a politician, an erotic novel or a gay play on Broadway) you're a celebrity by acclamation of the press. There was a time when celebrity meant recognition, admiration for something really well done; a brilliant performance or feat. No more!

There are probably only about 500 **meritocrats** in any given major city—the leaders, the real producers of value for their city, their firm, their organization. The mayor, top real estate developer, professional sports team owner, top media person, maybe an architect or lawyer or educator will be in that grouping. They are authentic heroes by any standard; yet most of them will get lost in the welter of hype that surrounds those who push for position at the altar of gossip. As for the **aristocrats**, the original monied socialites who don't work for a living, they aren't concerned. The media has never been good to them, it has only embellished their vulnerabilities.

Given that celebrity is power, then it is also currency, and gossip is the medium of exchange. Gossip can create careers, opportunities, relevance—it can even take a willing body from obscurity to relative fame. It all depends on what appeal there is, the public's appreciation of the person and circumstance, what people want to hear and read. Reaching a point of celebrity, regardless of qualification, is the equivalent of reaching social nirvana.

The inaccuracy of **value-bestowal** by the media is part of the problem. People like Louis Gerstner (CEO, IBM), John Malone (CEO, Telecommunications, Inc.), Bob Wright (CEO, NBC) and media mogul Michael Bloomberg are humongous businessmen who have created empires employing tens of thousands of workers. They are truly leaders in any context. Yet, their substance is always underplayed when compared to showfolk like Steven Spielberg, David Geffen, George Lucas or Michael Eisner. America prospers greatly from the former group, but is entertained by the latter—so maybe that's what America is all about. A country seeking its solutions, or at least its escape, via the screen or tube, comics or electronic games. (Fortunately, the intensity of the mass computerization of our youth is transferring much energy from superficial to intellectual pursuits; but media exposure is still a much desired goal, whatever the achievement.) We should make distinctions between social strata as related to media—there is **cafeteria** society, the lowest form; then **cafe** society, the middle ground of human intercourse and the major force of upward mobility in the 90s, and there is **real** society, the kind that is based on heritage, trust funds and generations of doing good (or at least no evil). Most celebrity we speak of is at the **cafeteria** and **cafe** level—that's where the action is, and where most of the world's yentas operate. It is the major playing field for those in the schmoozing game. Look at the superficial stardom of Kato Kaelin; a short-lived moment in the sun, not deserved, not capable of being preserved. But, for a while, the darling of the media.

Guys like **Sinatra** and **Crosby** were world-class celebrities—they took their hits for a half a century and still stood tall as they faced the final curtain. They can't be compared to anybody—they own their own league. If celebrity, power, prestige were to be measured over a period of time, maybe 25-years being the minimum, there would be few leaders. Most of what we see today is stuff that the tabloids promote—Divine Browne, Monica Lewinsky, who may be around somewhere, but their 15-minutes have dissipated quickly.

The best measure of true celebrity should be just how **utilitarian** a person is—what one really brings to the world's table, something of long-term value which does, in fact, make life better. Hardly any of the Numero Unos of today have that cache—they hit a headline, roast in the sun for a while, and because they really don't have any utility, are soon ancient history. Gossip may have given them currency but it wasn't deserved, and thus it never really translated to lasting power.

Yet, delve into the top drawers of New York City or the Hamptons and try to find your place in an atmosphere heavy with "stars," media celebs and winners. The power of the press prevails. It's very easy to feel ignored, disenfranchised and dead in the water. The fame eaters are enjoying dinner, with flashbulbs popping and eager groupies hovering about. It's almost surreal!

I wonder how **Einstein** and **Gandi** and **Albert Schweitzer** would perceive this circumstance? This circus world? Being as charitable as they were, they'd probably just say "it's hard to understand." And yes, it is hard to put into perspective. A world as scientifically and technically advanced as it is, still being pandered to by low brow characters who seem to have more clout than the true geniuses of the era.

It's an **inverse** world! If you take it seriously, you're in trouble.

Example: The skinny tables at *(the late)* Mortimer's, a real NYC social showcase, are those in front by the window where you see/are seen. If you're more than a size 8, you won't fit at those tables, so naturally the sleek, svelte women of our times are glamorized there. Heftier women sit in back. Can you imagine that women actually go into training and weight reduction programs to ultimately be accepted by the skinny tables, thereby to be part of the beautiful people?

Add **perverse** to **inverse!**

—TIPPERS—

*I*n the old days when a great transoceanic liner docked and passengers began to debark, the personal-service staff would stand along the path of exit, right hand out, palm up, and remind departing voyagers who they were and how well they had served: "Valet, sir." "Cabin steward, sir." "Barman, sir." The tipper had a final moment of contact with the tippee to resolve just how well he or she was treated. Despite the fact that this final beseechment was part of traveler protocol, it was an uncomfortable point in time for everybody; it imposed a final confrontation between the giver and receiver of gratuities, and a last opportunity for largesse or negation.

It's much better to be a **tipper** than a **tippee**, for the former has all the power. Whether it be a discreet slip of a $20 bill to a captain in a high-energy restaurant, the Christmas envelope for the building super or a payment (10 C-notes stuffed in a giftcard) to a deserving mole for info-of-import, the remuneration is controlled by the tipper. He either gains/loses face and future power by the extent of his graciousness.

Palm Beach tipping varies by the **vintage** of the tipper; the more chronology, the less the tip. Generally, members of the Old Guard are more reluctant to part with cash than their younger, flashier counterparts. The standard 15 percent is usually observed as a form of civility and few words are exchanged about the excellence of service; but harsh words have been known to fly when an irritated Brahmin gets a little lip from a service person. Usually such matters grow quite out of focus and result in the club's board of governors making decisions about the viability of the servant. In these august environments, sure death is a flip line from a waitress, like "Hey thanks, big spender." (Note: most private clubs avoid any chance of confrontation by imposing an automatic 15-20 percent gratuity on the bill.)

At one grand Palm Beach restaurant, the **captain** confides: "In this town, you're either a waiter or a millionaire. A rich guy thinks nothing of $100 deuces (a $100 tab for two) at lunch and a $40 tip. Many of the PPs *(players and pretenders)* who are single and want to impress a girl, go bonkers with tips—one guy recently gave me a C-note for a bill that was less than $80. The guys that really bother me, though, are the foreigners who feign ignorance about tipping and make a big deal about leaving very little money. Since this town is fairly small, even in season, there's a circuit of waiters who talk among themselves about patrons—waiters don't forget stiffs."

At one of our finest hotels, the **food/beverage** manager notes that famous people leave 18-20 percent and rarely are in direct contact with waiters since they usually travel with an entourage. Businessmen are the best, leaving a 25 percent tip which is split between the three-man team that serves each table—the captain, food waiter and drink waiter. Germans give a tip of twice the tax, as do the old well-offs in public eateries. Women generally don't tip as well and seem a little flustered at the moment of departure. French, English and Australians are the cheapest in

that they don't expect to return and the $10 tip can better be used buying a Palm Beach souvenir.

Restaurant steadies look at tipping as an **investment**—the better the rapport between client and captain, the more respect one has when introducing possible new business associates. As in any game of leverage, the higher (assumed or real) the level of friendship, the more impact on impressionables. Those with a little less *savoir faire* look at tipping as a form of **blackmail**—they pay as little as possible to avoid disaster (a table in Siberia, sassy waitress, shoddy service, nasty exchanges and cold food).

At the "21" Club in NYC, all **guesswork** is taken out of the tipping process. Each bill is accompanied by a slip that says—"Table service is not included on your check... and management will distribute your gratuity: waiter, 15%; captain, 5%; sommelier, 7% of wine bill. Thank you."

One of the great stories about **tipping** took place at The Breakers in the early 50s: a very proper, black-tied gent was waiting at the dining room entrance when a young Navy officer and his beaming bride walked in and asked for a table. The gent, bemused by his mistaken identity, looked the officer up and down and said "It will cost you a $100." The officer blanched. The gent continued the ruse—"A $100 is for the dance floor, $50 gets you a table near the kitchen." The flustered officer bit his lip and shoved a worn $100 bill into the gent's hand. Just then, the captain showed up—the gent introduced the officer as a great war hero and admonished the captain to give him the best table. As the couple was led off, the gent slipped the hundred back to the officer with a wink and a salute!

Strange habits prevail in **foreign** countries. In France, for example, a man seeking relief in a public toilet is likely to find a large, ample-bosomed woman glowering at him as he enters. In front of her is a saucer sprinkled with coins. Should the man fail to add to her tips, he is likely to hear some muttered curses. One is expected to pay for one's **pipi** in France.

The typical Palm Beach tip is like a **bribe**, done very discreetly. It consists of **five** stages. **First** is the **encounter**, when the captain sizes up a patron and a little power-playing results in a yeh or neh. **Second** is the **concealed note**—inside the palm, a twice-folded bill. The patron maintains direct eye contact and suggests his gratefulness for a nice table. The captain perceives the message and responds. **Next** is the **walk**; the captain drops his left hand down to his side while the patron drops his right hand; they begin walking to the table. Stage **four**—the bill is pressed by the forefinger against the captain's palm and held there until he closes his hand in one smooth **movement**. The **reward** is the **fifth** stage—smiles all around, a professional execution between tipper/tippee with no one the wiser. Cheers!

Tipping basically demands a realistic **calculation** of just how good service is; yet few people are discerning enough, or courageous enough, to deal with the issue effectively. Those in the know, however, recommend **overtipping** and suggest that life will be filled with smiling, attentively helpful people via the largesse!

—THE AFFAIR—

*S*uddenly... you're taking the dog out for walks more often on weekends; you're saving your quarters so you can use pay phones; you have several new sets of keys made, you buy the local papers and look at the want ads under apartments for rent, jobs available, used cars; you check into the gym more often and start using facial creams after shaving; you get your hair styled ala models in GQ and clean out your closet to get rid of the old, and add a few new slacks and jackets and a touch of Hilfiger; you seem to be tired more often and always a little out of breath; you are more concerned with your stock portfolio, and whereas previously you took the normal overhead of living for granted, you now scrutinize bills to see if they're necessary, and accurate; you have both fear and glee in your eye and life at home seems very tentative. The long hours you're putting in at the office get longer and one senses you're at a crossroads.

And they're right! You are about to embark on a very dangerous mission, a form of Russian roulette—you're about to have an **affair!**

The young lady in the gym with hair of Harlowesque platinum is all pecs and lats, attitude and grade-A buns, very upbeat and very uplifted. Casual chats turned into flirtation, then to a veggie salad after a workout, onto several nights of cocktails and conversation with subject matter all about cheating and passion and morality and fidelity and families, and finally to a collective commitment that an affair might be **healthy!**

Lana Turner and John Garfield in "The Postman Always Rings Twice," (1946)

Palm Beachers have a historical fix on the mating game vis-a-vis the life and times of an Island legend—**Henry M. Flagler**. As a young man, Flagler married and had two daughters and a son; his wife soon died of ill health and Flagler remarried his dead wife's nurse—**Ida**. It was a marriage founded in hell, and Flagler, ever the dashing entrepreneur, as a major stockholder in Standard Oil and the developer of much of southern Florida, soon met **Mary Lily Kenan**, a charming, well-bred Carolinean, 39 years his junior. They were smitten with each other and openly declared their love and intent to marry.

But Ida thought otherwise; she became delusional and Flagler had her committed to a mental institution, hoping that his marriage to her would be dissolved. Not so; New York state permitted divorce only on the grounds of proven adultery. In the meantime, Flagler was gifting Mary Lilly with impressive jewels and vacations and about $1 million in **Standard Oil stock**. Then he changed his residence to Florida (by then he was one of the state's most influential citizens) and cajoled a friendly legislator in Tallahassee to introduce a bill making insanity grounds for divorce. Years later it was discovered that some $125,000 had been paid

433

to the state legislature under the guise of work done on Flagler's railroad.

Mary Lily and Flagler had only 12 years of marriage together, and by most accounts, it was divine. Upon death he willed her his fortune, estimated at $10 million. A few years later, Lily married **Robert Worth Bingham**, a Louisville lawyer. Less than a year later Lily died and left her husband many millions which enriched Bingham newspaper, *The Louisville Courier Journal*. As for **Ida**, she lived on in a mental institution and died at age 82; the stock given her by Flagler in their early years together was worth over $15 million!

The Flagler/Kenan alliance was atypical and should not be viewed as a normal case history. There was money, power, motive, illegality involved. For those given to **infidelity** and an affair of a more contemporary mode, certain laws of the jungle should be observed. Although pleasure abounds in a delightful dalliance, there is always a piper to pay, and in the case of adultery, he can be awesomely satanic. Even during the illicit courtship, there are numerous requisite ploys to assure temporal ecstacy and a long life.

First, infidelity is a **lot of work**. The constant going and coming, the preoccupation, the sneaky phone calls, mood swings, unharnessed expenses, appearances, and the lying demand the ultimate from a cheating partner. It isn't easy to glide through life with nonchalance and equalibrium—every day is loaded with potential disaster.

Next, being unfaithful tests your **friendships**. From gossip to the ripple effect, your conquest will expand, and in the process, you'll have admirers and detractors. You will not be vanilla to anyone—either liked or reviled. And each perception of you will carry social weight—you'll be invited to some parties, not to others. The straights in your peer group will admonish you often and basically disenfranchise you; others, who may be enjoying a similar comradeship, will seek your kinship. After all, you're all an endangered species.

Then, consider the **wrath** of your marriage partner when she discovers your betrayal. A usually pliable and humble wife often becomes a firestorm of fierce emotion when she defends herself against the **"Other Woman"** (usually referred to as the slut, the tramp, the whore, the home wrecker or the nymph). The Other Woman justifies her position by blaming the Wife for not being desirable, not sexy enough to keep her husband on the Serta. Whatever the designations, as long as you live, your ex will be flying in your face, making your next life impossible, using children to crucify you, strangling you for money, generally peppering you with guilt, cowardice, disloyalty and, most of all, **ignorance.**

(And, it's possible, when all is said and done, and you get a divorce but defer marrying your consort, that you'll see things more clearly. And you'll wonder why you ever entertained the thought of an affair, what a miserable person your potential mate was and how much it cost you, and why it was a **horrendous idea.** Things focus more clearly when not under pressure—you'll probably want your old wife back because you realize how relatively great she was; but if she's got balls, she'll not only reject you, she'll demolition derby you right out of town.)

Finally, consider **statistics.** A typical enflamed affair lasts from 18 months to three years; it may be sheer ecstacy for some of those months, but more often than not the dalliance flames out, and wounded bodies flank you on all sides. The personal price of an unsuccessful affair equals a 10% drop in the Dow Jones. Money, integrity, honor, friendships, futures, geneology all get creamed in the process. Even a successful affair, resulting in a divorce and remarriage, always carries scars from the past.

In the new **millennium**, marriage will not change, nor will it be a relic of an obsolete culture. It will always be in upheaval because of changing mores, freedoms and fetishes, but it is one of the few sacred institutions of mankind. Marriage is alive and unpredictable, like quicksilver, always on a roll, only to be steadied by a good grasp.

Suggestion: enjoy some illicit love by seeing *The Bridges of Madison County*. Clint and Streep have a smoldering romance, good sex, and then for her, the wrenching journey back to a husband. Both realize that being faithful to self is the greatest of faiths—for then **you** become someone **you** can trust!

—THE THOROUGHLY MODERN MISTRESS—

*I*n 69 B.C., **Cleopatra** consorted with Julius Caesar and Mark Anthony; Catherine the Great and Grigori Potemkin hit it off in the 18th Century; Leon Dupuis and Rodolphe Boulanger had their hands full with Flaubert's Madame Bovary in the 19th Century, and as the 20th century dawned, stylish ladies like Simone de Beauvoir (with Jean-Paul Sartre), Ingrid Bergman (with Roberto Rossellini), Coco Chanel (with Paul Poiret), Catherine Deneuve (with Roger Vadim and Marcello Mastroianni), and Andrea Reynolds (with Claus von Bulow) played out their hand in life as consorts, concubines, companions, or simply—mistresses. **Lust never sleeps!**

In those days, life was fairly simple. Mistresses were into their medium for money, pleasure, marriage, alliances between countries, blackmail, perversion, redemption, the creation of offspring, self-gratification, but mostly, then, as now, for **power.** All the fringe benefits, the dollars and the dreams, were a function of maximizing one's position on the pyramid, and thereby getting out of the strug. Most of the girls didn't want to toil for spoils, they just wanted to be dominant in the sociochemical mix. To them, love, hate, envy, sex, bank balances, genealogies and whose diamond tiara is genuine and whose isn't, were life's vital matters.

Throughout history, mistresses have kept pace with the changing scenario of life, and have often led to the circumstance where **headlines** are made. Picasso kept media people guessing in his alliance with Francoise Gilot 80 years ago; Profumo and Christine Keeler, Papandreou and Dimitra Liani, and Alfred Bloomingdale with Vicki Morgan —were all good copy for the photojournalists. Each made history with a flash of animalism and enough panache to have mass appeal.

We know, that in the 90s, murder pays, justice weeps, viruses rule, your wife's lover is not a man, actors run for office, Mother Nature has balls and the tabloid boys have taken over. It's a world where everybody says—look at my tallest finger, and Starman & Stargirl get the best tables. Mistresses are right up there in neon.

Genteel types look at mistressing as grim-gross-disgusting-repulsive. Cafe Society shouts—nobody gives a damn who you sleep with. It's who you're seen dining with that counts. Somewhere in between—at theater, in Van Cleef, at boxing matches, on the Concorde, and usually at tryst-oriented places like Mark's Club in London, Chez Andre in Paris, Inn of the Seventh Ray in LA or Barbetta in Manhattan, a world-class mistress doles out her **largesse.** Although her duties haven't changed much in thousands of years, the thoroughly modern mistress wants more than jewelry and furs. She wants **access.**

Access to the power structure in New York, LA, Washington, London or Dallas is the new instrument for networking one's way into the top echelon. Mistresses usually study diligently, becoming knowledgable on esoteric subjects—antiques, jewelry, gastronomy, art— that elevate her credentials with the culture crowd. Noteworthy mistress **Eva Peron** became a world-power briefly, by being far more charismatic than her husband, and being an expert on the plight of the impoverished. When she made her appearance in Paris, at a world conference on poverty, in skintight gold lame, who could deny her access? A mission so noble. In fact, her mission was to further build an international power base that would help her succeed her husband as President of Argentina.

But, for the record, were a measurement made of how the top achievers in the country got there, the role of **"mentor"** would be significant. Mentorship can be applied in many ways, one of which is a gent who keeps a mistress, or the affluent lady who brings a dashing young stud up to speed. Alliances are everything. Also, a Croesus-rich mate can do wonders for an aspiring young Barbie: and unassailable clubby credentials coupled with glamor and chic are a sure ticket into the top social stratum.

Margaret Mead was fond of saying that the vow 'till death us do part' was invented at a time when life expectancy was about 36. A similar parameter exists for the mistress. She knows she'll grow older and less desirable, and that her career may last only five to ten years. People change, loves fade and are reignited, fortunes come and go. A realist understand these laws of the jungle and makes the most of the moment. The most comforting notion for a mistress is that Big Daddy will always take care of her while he's alive. But with more care and devotion, a mistress is often tempted to break the cardinal rule and fall in love with her mentor, thereby jeopardizing everything. She usually gets dumped (lust invariably can't match equity built up over several decades), and has to use her court masque in a job in interior design, real estate or in art circles. Little girl, all alone, until, hopefully, the next dalliance.

Power or money, say the cynics is life's report card. A mistress often gets A's. With a world-class bum and a conquest mentality, she can treat men like field mice and build her personal inventory, so that when time runs out she can perpetuate her lifestyle. No big deal. Just a matter of being Dickensian in matters of the heart, and Machiavellian in matters of the mind. And having just the right **index of malice.**

Marion Davies pranced across the stage in Follies in 1917; in the first row sat a large fellow named William Randolph Hearst. In due course, he sent her gifts of silver, candy, and pendants. After a special performance, he asked to meet her to shake her hand. She found a diamond watch in her glossy paw (later valued at $250,000). It was the perfect beginning to a perfect alliance, one that lasted 33 years through headlines and legal hassles and sickness, but ended as expected. When Hearst went to the Great Sky, the prancer was dropped unceremoniously, her sweet inspiration no longer recognized.

Unlike Davies, most **Palm Beach** mistresses are quite invisible. The Town is too small for an illicit romance to be public, and whatever physical interaction is required to keep the relationship in high orbit is usually done in a modest apartment or home maintained by the Master. Mistresses mostly play at the burlesque of youth; plying cosmetics with trowels and panting feverishly after the phantoms of fun, purpose and fulfillment. Alas, again, the spectre of failure looms largely—in her overwhelming zeal to be vital to the Master, a mistress often mistakes the edge of a rut for the horizon. She presumes too much, ignores storm warnings, loses direction, lets her mind fix on *forever* as the basis of the

437

relationship, deactivates her truth radar, and thereby becomes a mass of unsorted emotions. Often, through some accidental contretemps, the alliance is discovered, and Barbie becomes a classic case of Dominick Dunne's **"inconvenient woman."** She gets the social firing squad.

But the good mistress, and others of her metier, had her moment in the sun; she was a successful **connoisseur** of the human psyche and the frailty of human flesh, which enabled her to rub thighs with the power elite. In a world of despoiled innocence, that may be as good as it gets!

—MARRY ME—

*M*arriage was originally conceived as the answer to lust. When a man saw a woman he desired (usually from another tribe), he took her by force, often with the aid of a conspirator (the best man). **Capture** marriages dominated the prehistoric world, legal in England until the 13th century. Then marriages by **purchase** took over—the bride was part of a package of political alliances, bullion, real estate, social advancement, a military force and power.

The Anglo-Saxon word *wedd* suggested a promise to marry, but also exacted a pledge from the groom to contribute horses, property, silver, weapons or whatever to the bride's father. Thus a wedding was actually the purchase of a woman for breeding, and the perpetuation, thereby, of genealogy, a dynasty or even a country.

Albeit unromantic, a marriage of that type made sense—it was about money and children, and protection of the future. The notorious tyrant **Henry VIII**, who beheaded two wives and disposed of two others, sought to marry for love, but was fully aware that his first wife, Catherine of Aragon, the daughter of Spain's King Ferdinand, brought with her the prospect of an awesome land alliance that favored England. To protect his new riches, the King endured a tempestuous 22-year union with Catherine; in the finale, she got away with her head, and the land in question became a source of contention for decades.

Much of the history of marriage in America is centered around **"similar backgrounds."** Wealthy parents hoping their children will enjoy good marriages *to their kind*; bringing them up to school at Brearley, attend debutante balls, live on Park Avenue and be members of the Meadow Club. To be socially aristocratic and to join hands (and interests) with equals, and if not that, to marry up or down gracefully. Any descendant of a Fortune 500 family always the premier marital prize!

As we face the millennium, marriage is no longer an economic contract but an emotional cord that mates two people bent on achieving the top rung in whatever their medium, be it medicine, publishing, Wall Street, politics, showbiz or real estate. Books with titles like: *The Good Marriage; Love between Equals - How Peer Marriage Really Works*; and

438

Together Forever—extol the validity of power marriages, suggesting that the power of love is an immense force for a couple to use in making their mark in society, and even history.

Power marriages mate two careers; and in the process deal with love and sex and affection and passion to be sure, but equally important are subjects like managing the butler, housekeeper and nanny, who is responsible for the house on Gin Lane and the condo in Aspen, how best can kids from previous marriages be handled, whose limo will be used Saturday night, and what society function is best suited for pyramid climbing.

The power couple, as we know the term, has been in our lexicon only about 10 years. In the old days, grande dames handled society, and lovely corporate wives tirelessly advanced their hubby's career. But corporate wives had no professions as such, and generally didn't have their own money, a source of constant worry. Now women rule certain segments of business, have a hefty hand in all social events, and importantly, have their own high-powered **status**. It's natural for them to seek an equally powerful man.

Author **John Updike** writes that there are "four forces in life: love, habit, time, and boredom. Love and habit at short range are immensely powerful, but time, lacking a minus charge, accumulates, inexorably, and with its brother boredom levels all." In a **traditional marriage**, these four factors may invite an ongoing harangue between partners, adultery, fury, compromise, drugs, perverse behavior, any number of risky ventures. But the power couple has **motive**—onward/upward movement, always! Often, this kind of alliance disallows dalliance. There is no time for frivolity. Life is keyed around achievement.

And **achievement** is a great propellant. **David and Helen Gurley Brown** have been together, forever it seems; she invented the modern day Cosmo, while he still produces movies—she let him lunch with beautiful young women and in return he got to write Cosmo's sexy cover lines. **Tom Brokaw** anchors for NBC while wife **Meredith** is on the board of Gannett. **Bill Buckley** still pumps out best-sellers and makes all the money, while wife **Pat** gives all the parties—they are considered NY society's grand elite. **Felix and Liz Rohatyn, Dr. Mathilde Krim** and husband **Arthur**, and **Jim** (former AmEx CEO) **and Linda** (P.R. expert) **Robinson** still make headlines whenever they venture out. **Diane Sawyer** and **Mike Nichols** pack double-whammy, both being masters of their craft and glamorous. Maximum partnership couples—**Carolina and Reinaldo Herrera**, *Talk Magazine* editor **Tina Brown** and husband **Harry Evans**, long time force in publishing, make few moves without consent from their mates—they are synergistic in the full management of life.

Say the pundits—**power wives** are a unique multifunctional equation;

they have an impressive intellectual capacity, great vision, social presence and can be a mistress to their man while helping him strangle competition, sometimes all of this in bed. As for a **power husband**—he believes in disciplined freedom, high wit, ambition by momentum (one thing leading to another), and the rights of editorship by his mate. He accepts his human fallibility and seeks objective counsel from the love of his life.

In **Palm Beach**, marriages are a unique blend of the grand old days and the thrust of the 21st Century. Couples like **Virginia and Bill Buckley, Alma and Tony Tambone, Mary and Bob Montgomery, Jerre and Curt Gowdy, Jeanne and Frank Habicht, Angelica and Paul Ilyinsky, Betty and Alfred Fisher, Renee and Bill Lickle, Lisa and John Anderson, Jackie and Dick Cowell, Ruth and Ray Perelman, Catherine and Fred Adler, Chris and Bernard Marden, Pat and Ed Cook, Joan and Murray Goodman, Kit and Bill Pannill, Noreen and John Drexel, Jane and Guilford Dudley**, and **Tina and Bill Flaherty** fit the specs perfectly—longevity, professional success, social and community leadership, and still given to romance.

They have power—of love and like, which gives rise to leverage, and ultimately to a lofty, richly deserved status, as... **legends!**

—THE PLAYBOY—

*H*e prefers to hobnob with deposed royalty and movie or cosmetic tycoons; keeps pieds a terre on Fifth Avenue and Monte Carlo; devours vitamins; has no source of income but enjoys extensive friendships with the wealthy and is opportunistic about credit arrangements; has a vaguely continental accent; requires Roederer as his favorite tipple; visits a Swiss clinic once a year for R&R; is unmarried, dates nubile blonde models; would never consider psychoanalysis; can ride the hunt, handle a Ferrari at 100 mph and double like a demon in backgammon; likes to give blue-boxed Tiffany gifts or a single yellow rose; is courtly, funny, chic, gifted in looks and manner, a great dancer and raconteur. And macho to the bone.

And he is among the missing in today's society!

Only seniors would remember **Porfirio Rubirosa,** who died in 1965 at age 56. He was the playboy of the century—oozing charm, charisma, impeccable manners and an unparalleled way with women. In a matter of a decade Rubi married four of the world's most desirable women. First was **Flor de Oro**, daughter of Dominican Republc dictator Rafael Trujillo; that alliance got him the job as *charge d'affaires* to France (and as a major shareholder in Tru's humongous sugar holdings). Next he courted and won **Danielle Darrieux**, the most beautiful French actress of the time. After several neurotic and high-flying years, Rubi was divorced and legally took American heiress **Doris Duke** to bed; he got his walking papers from that marriage with trimmings, a hefty cash settlement. Then on to **Barbara Hutton**, another prominent heiress, where the marriage was brief but the price tag high. These marriages came on line in the 40s, and it's estimated that Rubi pulled down settlements of close to $5 million (today's equivalent: $50 million) for all his troubles. His final marriage was to actress **Odile Rodin**, who became his widow, and celebrated in style (from his estate) for many years.

Yet, true to his **playboy style**, each of his wives spoke fondly of Rubi— as a talented man, reckless but not wild, very accountable, and, importantly, as the most ardent lover since Don Juan. One amplifying story—when he was Trujillo's ambassador to Cuba during the Batista regime, pro-Castro forces tried to assassinate him by throwing a grenade through his bedroom window. Rubi was engaged in his favorite pastime; he and his lady survived the blast and went right back to their ardent undertaking, with pleasure!

Playboys were typically **gentlemen.** They said "please" and "thank you" and weren't stuffy or patronizing. They took contrarian stands but not excessively, and they generally treated everyone the same, making no distinctions among class. As Professor Henry Higgins said as a rationalization for his one-sided dealings with Eliza Doolittle in *My Fair Lady:* "It's not as though I treat you differently from anyone else. I treat you the same."

The era of the serious world-class playboy acted itself out mostly in the 50s and 60s. The economy was good, there was limited social conscience, New York and Malibu and various European capitals were perfect *rendesvous.* First-generation heiresses and the beautiful people looked for love in all the wrong places. They ignored intelligence and honesty and, instead, quested feverishly after luxury and false values. New York's **Latin Quarter, Stork Club** and **El Morocco** were the *loci* for most hardcore playboys, many of whom slipped off to San Marino, a small principality nestled in the center of Italy, to buy a title, thereby to juice up their credentials as marriage candidates. John Perona ran El Morocco with an iron fist but had great camaraderie with playboys—he loved harmless deception. At the Stork Club, ex-bootlegger Sherman Billingsly didn't like the titled crowd much. He catered to politicos, movie stars and debs; few of the premier playboys dared to face indifference from their host and simply skipped over to Billy Rose's Latin Quarter where girls of every dimension and depravity flowered. It was non-stop partying with plenty of sex, no drugs and not too much booze, but a promiscuous nuance in every exchange or transaction.

Leading men like **Prince Aly Khan, Dan Topping, John "Shipwreck" Kelly, Warren Avis, Taki Theodoracopulos, John Hay "Jock" Whitney, Warren Avis, Larry Fisher, Winthrop Rockefeller, Huntington Hartford, Howard Hughes, Bill Millner, Bob Sweeney**, Palm Beacher **Dick Cowell, Tom Corbally** and the **Princes David, Serge and Alexis Mdivani** (with p.r. flak from **Teddy Howard** and social scribbling by **Doris Lilly**) plied their trade with great *panache*, and became international celebs in the cafe society crowd. And not surprisingly, macho guys like **Hemingway** and **Gary Cooper** were impressed; they felt that **Rubi**, for example, was an artist (of the flesh) who was exceptionally good at what he did; he was tops in his profession as Hemingway was in writing and Cooper in acting. It was what we now know as "male-bonding."

So what happened to these glorious days? **Time just ran out** as it does with most social phenomena. Playboys died or were scandalized by paparazzi, heiresses got lawyered out of huge giveaways, taxes pressured all but the richest, seduction got less sophisticated, and the era of the working, **independent woman** dawned. The sweet passion and mystery of conquest gave way to the harsh realities of male/female equality, and as the 60s gave way to new decades, roles were reversed; women became the dominant aggressors in cafe society.

Maybe the **millennium** will see the return of playboys. This time a little more serious about their art, and more approving of woman as equals. If cycles play a part in the social culture of our world, the years ahead auger well for playboys, since women have been the main attraction since the mid-80s!

—SNOBBERY—

*W*hen you're **toasting** a dangerously competitive peer, you might say: "Here's to Charles, ever the master of his fate, mitigator of our furies, and mentor of those whose brains and beauty meet his notoriously high standards." Since a toast romanticizes the mundane, backlights common events to make us feel superior (as Fitzgerald wrote of Gatsby—"There was something gorgeous about him... it was his extraordinary gift for hope"), it is a perfect weapon for snobbery—it uses superlatives to set the stage for failure. It's a gracious way to raise a competitor on high for a few moments, to disarm him so that the kill is that much easier. A toast is deadly flattery, *tres amusant* to all.

Among other beliefs of the snob:

■ A man who believes that you **respect** him is easily manipulated. (Duplicity at its best. Somerset Maugham said that it is dangerous to let the public behind the scenes because they become disillusioned. "Then they become angry with you, for it was the illusion they loved." Proper respect can lead to manipulation, or simply to agreement—a far safer course.)

■ To know the right means (people) of getting something **done** is virtually to have done it. (Robert Benchley once asked the uniformed man outside the "21" Club to call him a cab. "I am an admiral," replied the man, stiffly. "In that case," said Benchley, "call me a battleship." The exchange was typical Benchley but suggests that movement is best done through intermediaries—the concierge, building super, p.r. agent, et al.)

■ Hard work is essential—other people's **hard work**—there is a big difference between working hard and simply doing hard work. (One of the most understated rich men of all time was Andrew Mellon, who amassed a fortune at the turn of the century through investments in Gulf Oil and Alcoa. He abhorred publicity and gave credit for his success to his employees. He managed to keep his name out of major newspapers until he was 66 years old and the second richest man in America after John D. Rockefeller. At this late stage in life he was proposed for Secretary of Treasury in the Harding administration but was virtually unknown in Washington. Seven of his top company officials had more name recognition than Mellon, who suggested: "They do all the work and should get all the credit.")

■ Success comes to you only when you are **on the move.** If you are to be successful, you must never stop. You stop, it goes. (When America was founded, it was dedicated to the utilitarian idea of money. The first generation of patriots resented the privileges bestowed on the colonial aristocracy by the British crown, and within a few years of the Revolution they did away with most of the hereditary fortunes vested in land. The Constitution associated liberty with property and set up government as a "broker" to deal with the wilderness and natural resources. Ever since, America has been a land of ceaseless making and unmaking, new names, new deals, new ground, new successes. Being on the move has always been the keynote.)

■ Never **stagnate.** A sign of stagnancy is doing the same thing again for the same amount of money. (This is the Prostitute's Fallacy—in the end one is doing the same thing for less money. Remember inflation!)

■ It is not necessary to know a great many **subjects;** it is more important to know your way around them. By knowing about things, you have a facility to allude to them, which is impressive—without the risk of seriously expounding on them which is oppressive. (Social scribe Stephen Birmingham, often considered the dean of society authors, was a file clerk for the Aetna Life Insurance Company. In his files he discovered correspondence about the group policy of the William H. Vanderbilt family—intimate details about the Vanderbilt private lives, the maids, gardeners, grooms, all part of the policy. From that bountiful expose of inside info, he became a writer and a major source for details on the lifestyles of American aristocrats.)

■ Once your name escapes the confines of your own school or community, it grows out of all **proportion** to your actual achievements. (Andy Warhol parlayed eccentricity into world-class celebrity, becoming an icon and leader of a movement based on his peculiarities being played out as cutting-edge behavior. In the typical post-demise euphoria when his estate brought in about $50 million at auction, Warhol became an American legend and an artistic genius.)

■ It is a mistake to play **games** at which you always lose or at which you appear ridiculous. (Do not purport sophistication on subtleties: be sure to call London's Beauchamp Place, "Beecham"; if you ride with the exclusive Belvoir Hunt, correctly call it the "beaver" hunt; you may brag about staying at Cliveden, the Astor family house/now country hotel, but be sure to call it "Clifden." The snob never mispronounces but often begrudges—it's a common calling.)

■ The snob is like a million dollar bill: if men turn you away because they haven't got change, they reveal their **poverty,** not yours. (In early America, the landed gentry gave way to New England shipping magnates, who in turn were superseded by fur traders, cotton planters, gold and silver miners, cattle barons and railroad tycoons; then Wall Street autocrats and the organizers of trusts, automobile makers, oil and agricultural moguls, dealers in religion and bootleg gin; and on to movies, microtechnology and electronic communications. In each stage of growth there was risk, overwhelming competition and a fair share of poker playing. The real winners always trust instinct and the power of bluff to win the deal, whatever it be.)

■ The Law of **Social Entailment**: if you are accepted by one man, you are also accepted by all those who accept him. (In England, the regimental tie bespeaks snobbery. In what other modern country would a thin piece of striped material worn around the neck betoken lineage and whether one is "clubable" or not?)

■ There is nothing to stop you **going** where there is nothing to stop you going. (Former Prime Minister Margaret Thatcher came from a white-

444

collar Lincolnshire background—hardly regal. But she persisted, and early in her career as the daughter of a store owner, took elocution lessons to remove her lower-class accent. Once she reached the pinnacle, comments from her political peers were consistent—"I admire her, but that accent drives me mad. Nobody is born speaking that way!")

■ The Law of **Party Parity**: anyone you meet at a party will automatically assume your right to be there and your equal status. (English actor David Niven was once at a party of peerage, and mixed well with the nobleman. At one point he observed two women coming down the stairs and commented to a man he had just met: "That's the ugliest woman I've ever seen." The man stiffened: "That's my wife." "I meant the other one," said Niven. "That's my daughter" was the unwelcome response. Niven looked the man calmly in the eye and said: "I didn't say it!" and quickly vanished. Later he encountered the same man, the event's jovial host, who winked at him and said—"I never heard it!")

■ The Law of **Osmotic Transference**: if an unknown man interviews a famous one, by the end of the interview the fame of the two men may level out based on the effectiveness of the interview. The person who fearlessly questions the right of others to be successful soon becomes so himself. (How about Oprah and Barbara Walters and Charlie Rose—all legends, for simply addressing the unknowns of celebrities and courageously asking often distasteful and embarrassing questions. A life of voyeurism for the masses.)

■ To be in time, it is necessary to be on the move. To be on the move, it is necessary to think **dialectically**. To think dialectically, it is necessary to know without illusion where you are at any given stage in life and to know your next objective. (Although a born monologist and a sometime bore, Coco Chanel was always up to speed on career pathing. She had no illusions about the fashion industry and understood that each new trans-Atlantic airplane could change the whole fashion scene, mostly by making it more accessible. She felt her peers were mostly decorators, not designers; "they take the same silhouette and add a new button or bow or hemline, and think they've revolutionized style. I'm a dressmaker. I know what women want, how they can best show their snobbery. That's why I'll always last!")

No one can force you to live life to the full, but life is there to be lived to the full.

—THE PHANTOM BALL—

T *hey are assembled at The Breakers; it's the new millennium. A century of Palm Beach lore fills the fabled halls. The high and mighty, the founders and builders, the socialites and spar-*

kling personalities, the legendary ones—they're all here for The Phantom Ball, a commemoration of 100 years of living and loving in Palm Beach, that mystical island in the Atlantic Ocean known as "The world's richest society."

And so our evening begins.

Holding court at the center of the power elite is dapper **Henry Flagler**, regaling his entourage with stories of Rockefeller, Standard Oil, the Florida East Coast Railway, the beginnings of Palm Beach and life-at-large. His wife, **Mary Lilly** (Kenan) dazzles the crowd in a stunning French gown of clinging Charmeuse satin with seed pearls. Among the Flagler guests are the **"Cap" Dimicks, the William K. Vanderbilts Jr., Andrew Carnegie, J.P. Morgan**, publisher **William Randolph Hearst** and court jester **Joe Jefferson** (who is also a builder of some repute). Most notable and rotund of the group is **President Teddy Roosevelt**, down for some fun in the sun before moving on to more international conquests. He is animated in his conversation with **Admiral George Dewey**, immaculately clad in his starched Naval officer's uniform.

Henry Flagler

A striking figure in white tie and tails is mega-architect **Addison Mizner**, strumming his fingers to the music as he cajoles members of the clans—Whitney, Phipps, Goelet, Wanamaker, Cosden, Vanderbilt, Biddle, Warburton and Stotesbury (Edward is senior partner in the firm J.P. Morgan—his wife **Eva**, the undisputed grande dame of the Island; their Philadelphia manse boasts 147 rooms). Road builder **Joseph Hugh Reese**, having just completed a highway between West Palm Beach and Stuart, is receiving plaudits like a true gentleman. Guest **Hilda Wynne** of London—winner of numerous medals and decorations during World War I—is fiddling with her lace collar while listening to **Mrs. Paris Singer**, whose husband (sewing machine money) is the popular president of the Everglades Club. Mrs. Wynne is a charming Englishwoman who has quickly taken hold in Palm Beach. They are atwitter over the Stotesbury daughter —**Mrs. Louise Cromwell Brooks** who will soon be married to **Brigadier General Douglas MacArthur**, Superintendent of the U.S. Military Academy at West Point.

446

Numerous dukes, counts, countesses and trifling nobels, many of whom have fled their native countries, are casting about for auspicious connections. Their worthless titles are derided by most of the Old Guard; yet they are charming, add panache and are rapidly making social inroads. **Major Barclay Warburton**, the high-chinned- and -chested Mayor of Palm Beach, is in spirited conversation with a marquis about the latest car—the *Winton Six*, manufactured in Cleveland. **Mrs. Edward F. Hutton**, in Renaissance dress, joins in the conversation with the eccentric **Mrs. (Zelda) Scott Fitzgerald**, who has journeyed from her New York home at the St. Moritz Hotel.

As our gala evening progresses, we encounter **Horace Dodge, Connie Lewis** and **Orson Munn** joking about their play at the 21st Annual Society baseball game. **John Sargent Pillsbury** and his wife (who live in *"La Chosa"* on Banyan Road) and former actress (biggest role—Poppy in *"The Shanghai Gesture"*) **Mary Duncan Sanford**, in a flowing pink gown (she recently married well-to-do sportsman **Stephen "Laddie" Sanford**), are amused by their brag-and-boast, as is scholarly **Warren Gamaliel Harding**, 29th President of the United States (who often vacations in a home near The Breakers). **Grand Duke Dimitri** and his wife, **Princess Anna Ilyinsky**, have recently arrived in Palm Beach with their young son—**Paul** (who will one day be Mayor of PB), and are welcomed into the fashionable group.

The prolific **Munn family** is in evidence. Gurnee (great grandson of tycoon **John Wanamaker**), Frances, Mary, Nonnie, Pauline, Ector, Carrie Louise are gaily dressed and chatting with finishing school charm. Under soft lights and coconut tree shadows, serious businessmen **Charles Amory Jr., Reginald and Dennie Boardman, Jimmy Mills, George Baker, Maurice Fatio** and **Robert Huntington** are discussing the economic fate of America. **Joseph E. Widener** (founder of Hialeah racetrack), polo man **Winston Guest** and his beautiful best-dressed listed wife **C.Z.**; Broadway biggie **Florenz Ziegfeld** (who caught the largest sailfish of the season), **Thelma Chrysler Foy** (daughter of auto magnet Walter Chrysler), **Col. Edward Bradley** (owner of the famous Bradley's Casino) bide time between cocktails and dancing.

Seen across the room in fluttering ruffles and royal puffs and bows are: **Mrs. Louis Marron**, whose fortune was made in oil and investments—she became synonymous with the Salvation Army of the Palm Beaches; **Janet Annenburg Neff Hooker**, sister of **Walter Annenburg**, once Ambassador to England—she now lives in the former home of **Peter Widener** of the horsey set; **Mrs. Woolworth Donohue**, widow of the heir to the Woolworth dime store fortune; **Mrs. John (Brownie) McLean**, leading socialite and girl-about-the-cosmos (her mother-in-law **Evelyn Walsh McLean** owned the *Hope Diamond*); **Jack Massey**,

447

holder of big hunks of Kentucky Fried Chicken stock with palsman **Bruce Norris**, Chicago playboy. **Mrs. John (Jane) Volk** listens in, the usual radiant smile on her face (her husband is one of the major architects on the Island). In playful dialogue are **Frank McMahon**, big bucks from Canada in natural gas and oil, now married to **Betty Betz** (writer for *Hearst* newspapers); **Bill Todman** of TV game show fame with hi-glam wife **Fran; Dan Moran**, former NYC cop, now husband of **Gregg Dodge**, widow of car guy **Horace Dodge Jr.**; **General Ephraim Jeffe**, (once top gun at ConEd in NYC) and his wife **Hulda**, the noted artist; Cincinnati millionaire **Horace Schmidlapp** and stunning wife, **Patricia; Verner and Permelia Reed**, Hobe Sounders; **John R. Drexel III**, socially prominent Philadelphian; **Mead Johnson**, millions from pharmaceuticals; **Sam and Dorothy Rautbord**, great art collectors from Chicago; and well-laundered Gentleman **Jim Kimberly** of Kleenex fame/fortune (a handsome devil, often called the *"Silver Fox"*).

Visiting for a week are **Ethel Merman, Irving Berlin** and **Eddie Duchin**—all currently involved in the Broadway musical, *"Call Me Madam."* The **Charles Wrightsmans** stroll the room, chumming with friends near and dear; the **Duke and Duchess of Windsor** are with the **Robert Youngs**, drawing much attention. **Eva Gabor** and **Frank J. Hale** head up the show biz crowd, and have interested **Sen. William Knowland** and **Earl E.T. Smith**, true gents to the core, in backing a play. The **Connie Macks, John S. Phipps** and the **Hon. Mrs. Frederick Guest, Mrs. Horace Elgin Dodge** (whose mansion—*"Playa Rienta,"* most fabulous of the Mizner mansions, is being auctioned), **Rose and Joe Kennedy** (proud parents of nine children), **Joe and Ruth Tankoos** (Colony Hotel owners), **Dina Merrill** (lovely daughter of **Mrs. Marjorie Merriweather Post** and wife of actor **Cliff Robertson**), and **Joe and Estee Lauder** are fox trotting in tandem with **Amb. and Mrs. Guilford Dudley, Mrs. Raymond Guest, the H. Loy Andersons** (he's a banking legend and she's a perfect role model for womanhood), **Mrs. Arthur Karoff, Otto Kahn, Tom and Peggy Bancroft, Prince Alfonso de Bourbon,**

Marjorie Merriweather Post

Barbara Hutton (the **Countess Haugwitz Reventlow**), **Mrs. Charles Lachman**, founder of St. Mary's Hospital; **Mrs. R. Stuyvesant Pierrepont**, members of the Bolton and Blossom families; **A. Atwater Kent Sr.**, (pioneer in electronics and radio), and **Sonny and Mary Lou Whitney** (who make a singular couple—she so effervescent, he so knowing) are all smiles.

Celebrities like **Douglas Fairbanks Jr., Joan Crawford, Clark Gable, Bob Hope, Valentino** and **Bill Blass** fill space at important tables. The formidable **Sir Winston Churchill** has his own table with a few international chums (he just arrived on **Aristotle Onassis'** yacht, *The Christina*). Some of the younger set—quotable children of notable parentage, observe politely, being groomed for times ahead. They give credence to the passing of the torch, and the adage—it's a wonderful thing to reach the age of 70, only it comes too late in life. As one columnist said—"Their sprinkling of bounce and pounce, French perfume, little cherry cheeks, legs that start at their chins, and honey, lilac and hot chocolate scents add a nice cachet to any paahhtee!"

The hours frivol by with fuss, flattery and deference as elegant **Rose and Mortimer Sachs, Marion Sims Wyeth, Llwyd Ecclestone, Sr.** (noted sailor and builder), fashionable **Mary McFadden** and **Patrick Lannan** (mega AT&T financier and art collector), former *Vogue* model **"Baby Jane" Holzer**, and **Jorie and Geoffrey Kent** lend their individual cachet to the event. Scores of ladies offer a glimpse at how Chanel, Balenciaga, Galanos, Mainbocher, Dior and Givenchy make their fortunes.

Although not seeking the limelight, the quiet beauty of certain ladies shines forth. Among them: always immaculate **Mrs. A. Parker Bryant**; civic leader **Helen Cluett**; **Mrs. James Abercrombie de Peyster** (her investor husband **James** is a direct descendant of the 17th century New York Mayor Abraham de Peyster); **Mrs. John R. Drexel III; Lorraine Gallagher Freimann** (Magnavox oodles); **Mrs. Alfred Kay** (revered member of the ancien regime and honorary president of the Garden Club); **Mrs. Raymond Kunkel**; Cuban-born aristocrat **Carola Mandel**, world-class skeet shooter; **Mrs. Jean Flagler Matthews** (granddaughter of Henry Morrison Flagler and restorer of *Whitehall*—the great Flagler mansion); **Mrs. Charles Merrill** (major patroness of the arts); **Mrs. Harold Payne Whitney**; the incomparable **"Sue" Whitmore** who singlehandedly staged the Red Cross Ball for many years. Several enchanting multi-marriage swans are also winging about: **Countess Dolly Hylan Hemingway Fleischmann O'Brien Dorelis** (once lady chum of Clark Gable) and **Josephine "Fifi" Widener Leidy Holden Wichfeld**. They enrich the Ball with their colorful histories.

Many members of the power clique are present; they, too, are understated but success permeates their erect-spined, manly presentation: sportsman **Dan Topping**; **Nate Appleman**, independent oil and gas producer, great servant and benefactor to the Town; **Philip Fortin** (least visible PB philanthropist); Town Council President **Robert Grace**; international yachtsman **Walter Gubelmann** (leader of The Society of the Four Arts); **Paul Maddock**, owner of Duck's Nest, the oldest house in PB; **Page Hufty**, prominent financier; underwater developer **John Perry, Jr.**; patriarch of PB's largest landowning family **Ogden Phipps**; **Charles Wrightsman** (Texas oilman and art collector); all-around good guy **Wiley Reynolds Jr.**; and man of multi talents, inventor **Victor Farris** (married to lovely English entertainer—**Celia Lipton**).

Gliding about with elan are patricians **Ginny and Ned Burke, the Alfred Fishers, Barbara and Doyle Rogers, Ambassador Francis Kellog**, chic and celebrated **Pauline Boardman, Linda and Jay Rossback**, twinkly-eyed **Betsy** and mannerly **George Matthews, Janna and Stan Rumbough**, realtor **Bill Pitt, Felix Mirando**, papa-gateau **Al Taubman**, gracious **Betty and Herb Swope, Anne and Tom Keresey**, the **Winston Guests**, the redoubtable **Alyne Massey**, gregarious **Barton Gubelmann, Lilly Pulitzer Rousseau** (her Lilly fashions dot the globe) and multidimensional **Alex Dreyfoos**. To a person, they hum and thrum with puissance.

The star-spangled manners and jolly faces of other high goal society players fill the dance floor: **Fred Melhado**, various sweet guys and dolls from the **Fanjul** clan; **Lisa and John Anderson, Jean** (frame her and she'd be a Renoir) and **T. Suffern Tailer, Chessy Patcevitch**, orchid master **Bill Pannill** with wife **Kit, Eles and Warry Gillet**, model **Betsy and Michael Kaiser**, peripatetic **Willie Hutton III** (grand-nephew of financier E.F. Hutton), **Ned and Terry Monell, Renee and Bill Lickle**, jewelry designer **Dee and Tommy Cushing, Ridgely W. Harrison, Jr.**, and the **Richard Cowells.**

Dozens of fresh new faces are evident as the ball winds down. Faces with names to remember, like **Trump, Kohl, Adler, Curtis, Gosman, Araskog, Schuler, Boalt, Burns, Cook, Keenan, Dillard, Leidy, Benjamin, Surtees, Mashek, Fomon, McFarland, Merck, Currey, Harris, Gruss, Scripps-Harvey, Gaines, Brinker, Brogan, Heeren, Goldsmith, Kent, Mahoney, Schrafft, Shields** and **Von Pantz** make their entries and exits with aplomb.

As our Phantom Ball ends, the stars have faded from the sky and night brightens into dawn. Time speeds on, Planet Earth spins on its axis and our guests are dizzy with the wonder of it all. They circle one another in lofty orbit, our Palm Beach icons, wondering how time got *away and how quickly the years pass. They reach out, caress, wipe away the tears and whisper farewells. The glamorous, nostalgic evening has affirmed what we always knew... that we care about our bright and noble friends and our Island haven....and it's another year, full of intrigue and promise...and what a **great party life is**!*

"At The Ball," from a painting by Auguste Francois Gorguet
Reproduced by courtesy of Fine Art Photographic Library

Photo: Lucien Capehart

STEPHANIA AND DONALD CONRAD
orderly and outstanding

Photo: Lisa Smith

ALMA AND ANTHONY TAMBONE
taste, gentility and grace

PATRICIA AND J. PATTERSON COOPER
peerless and picturesque producers

DEE AND TOMMY CUSHING
big believers in faith, hope and charity

BILL AND BARBIE CLAGGETT
distinguished and debonair duo

AMBASSADOR AND MRS. HENRY KIMELMAN
matchless and mannerly movers

SAM AND MARY BOYKIN
gifted, giving and glowing

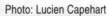

NORINA COURSEY AND MICHAEL KORS
frolicsome, fashionable and unfettered

SUGAR RAUTBORD AND PARKER LADD
plenty of cachet and exuberance

ZACK SHIPLEY AND MARY FRANCES TURNER
animated and affirmative

ALLEN MANNING AND HEATHER WYSER-PRATTE
notable and nimble doers

HERME AND DAVID MIRO
dauntless and devoted

JOHN AND ETONELLA CHRISTLIEB
spirited and splendid social spirits

AMBASSADOR AND MRS. ENRIQUILLO DEL ROSARIO
illustrious and incisive achievers

SUSAN PARTINGTON
inviting and inspiring

**BEVERLY WILKES, RON NEAL AND
MRS. JAMES CLARKE**
nimble, noble and non pareil

PETER AND ANN SUMMERS
upbeat and up-to-date

KATHY AND ALAN BLEZNAK
daring, dashing and decorous

CHAPTER XII

FINAL WORDS & WISHES

Photo: Mort Kaye Studios

ELESABETH GILLET (AND USMC ESCORT)
sovereign and scintillating

—Bon Mots—

*T*here's a cast of characters in Palm Beach—the men usually identified as the **Old Dukes, Boulevardiers, Cavaliers** or **Grandee**s; the ladies referred to as the **Grandes Dames, Queens** or **Dowagers**. Whatever the designation, they have their own language and some rather pointed and uninhibited comments on mankind:

- Don't feel bad about **growing old**; it's a privilege denied to many.
- **Good judgment** comes from experience; experience comes from bad judgment.
- The days are long, but the **years are short**.
- Here's wishing you all the happiness you can stand and just a touch of sorrow to show you the **difference**.
- There are three ways to learn: by watching, by doing, by **shock**.
- Those who **marry for money** wind up earning it.
- Beware of a **social larva**—not quite a moth, certainly not a butterfly.
- Avoid those who never even draw breath but just keep **talking**.
- Ah, the **relationships** we get into just to get out of the ones we were not brave enough to say are over.
- Do not accept **social hamsters** on their wheels; they go nowhere.
- Take no brandy from **strangers**.
- People who don't believe in God are stuck with believing in **Mankind**.
- Life's answer is that there is no answer; the bottom line is that there is no **bottom line**.
- The symbol of the irony of our lives is the **phoenix**, which must die to live.
- **Failure** is never fatal.
- Beware of **escorts** with sweet souls and limpid brown eyes whose neuroceptors are in high gear.
- There's always someone better, prettier, richer, smarter, younger, more **well-heeled**.
- Avoid people who follow you around mutely like a **giant pet**; their minds have been banalized.
- A man has only so many **yeses** in him in a lifetime; even fewer **nos**.
- Better to die of **life** than to die of irrelevance.
- A **scandal** requires no documentation; it is a fire that feeds on innuendo alone.
- Even the past is **mutable**; we change it all the time.

- Life is not only unfair; it is **untidy**.
- Very few people ever really are **alive**, and those who are, never die, even though they are gone.
- Admire, yet avoid, those who have a profound compassion for the infinite variety of **human failure**.
- For winners, insurmountable odds are **surmountable**.
- **Human beings** love to roll over on their backs just like puppies.
- Age and youth look on life from opposite ends of the **telescope**; to the one, life is exceedingly short, to the other, it is exceedingly long.

—PALM BEACH CREDO—

*D*reamers, optimists, pretenders, negativists, promoters, believers, whatever, invariably come to certain conclusions about life, founded on their own experiences; we hope this book will be an ongoing source of knowledge about Palm Beach, and **yourself**, for some time.

About Life
- Life is more than just being **alive**.
- Life is not based on the **way things are**, but on the way people think things are.
- Life is like a **maze** in which you try to avoid the exit.
- Life is **colorful**—there's red tape, red alerts and rednecks, gray matter, blue laws, blue notes, blue chips and blue bloods, backmail and blackballing, green thumbs, greenbacks and greenhorns, whitewash and white papers, pink elephants, yellow streaks, golden rules, and best of all, silver linings and rainbows.
- Life is a room full of **doors**, which close with time.
- Life in **reverse**: You get your gold watch after 40 years of hard work at the State Department; you come out of college after four years of hard play; you spin through high school and play through grammar school; you become a kid with toys and no responsibility, then a child and a little baby; you go back into the womb and spend your last nine months floating; and you finish off as a gleam in somebody's eye!
- No one appreciates life more than those who are growing **old**.
- Life's **reciprocity**—my turn today, yours tomorrow.
- Life is **tough**—it takes up a lot of your time, all your days and nights, all your weekends, and what do you get in the end? **Death**.

About You
- To seize **opportunity** may be to die; to ignore it is never to be born.

463

- To **befriend** yourself, do good for someone else.
- You don't need a weatherman to know which way the wind **blows.**
- Take away your **life-illusion**, and you limit happiness.
- There is a major **difference** between doing things that make you feel good, and doing things that make you feel good about yourself.
- The greatest **aphrodisiac** is being in charge of yourself.
- When you are in full possession of yourself, when you **know who you are, and are who you are**, the world is a trinket in your hand.

About Others
- Beware of **H&P** people; they huff and puff their way through life, always going nowhere.
- Avoid those who like the song—*Down is Up Enough!*
- **Songwriters** have the most vivid obituaries; memories never die.
- A person of **excellence** is as difficult as she is rare.
- The man who **blushes** easily can hardly be a brute.
- A **fool** at 40 remains a fool the next 40.
- When a **general** makes a mistake, all the troops suffer.
- Every **madman** thinks everybody else is mad.
- A man should make at least one bet each day; otherwise he could be walking around **lucky** and never know it.
- Beware of the man who brags he has the world's best **inferiority complex**.
- Those who truly **enjoy life** don't talk about it; they're busy doing it.
- A **learned** man always has wealth within himself.
- He who builds no **castles in the air**, builds no castles anywhere.

About The Game
- The **sun** shines for everyone.
- In a **junkyard**, you see the ultimate destruction of everything we once desired.
- **Foundations** keep shifting.
- **Order** may breed habit, but chaos breeds life.
- **Hunger** makes everything taste good.
- Never praise the day until the **twilight** comes.
- Fortune **favors** the **bold**.
- **Speak** kindly of the dead; they have no rebuttal.
- He lives twice who **lives well.**
- The best **mirror** is an old and true friend.
- There is no **leisure** if it's not used well.

• **Laughter** is a good beginning for a friendship; and the best ending for it.

• "To love" is the **greatest verb** in the world; "To help" is a close second.

FINALLY, EVEN BEING GOD ISN'T A BED OF ROSES!

❤ ❤ PALM BEACH LOVE AFFAIR ❤ ❤

*T*here once was a young man who loved the water. Often, he would walk along the beach north of **The Breakers** and feel the spray on his face. He loved to dive into an incoming wave and feel its force; but, mostly, he loved to swim far out into **the Atlantic** where he could be alone.

One day he happened upon a small shoal he had never seen before. As he explored it, he sensed the presence of another being. He turned quickly and glimpsed a **mermaid** disappearing into the ocean. He dove deeply, but couldn't find her. The next day the same thing happened, but this time the shy creature lingered for just a moment before slipping away. Each day he was able to get a little closer to her, until one day their hands touched. Though it lasted only a moment, **the touch** was full of life and excitement.

In time, they **fell in love** with each other. He would swim out each day to be with her, and they would share her world under the water. She knew where the most intricate formations were and took him to caves and ledges. She was at home with the creatures of the ocean, and they played with the dolphin, wahoo and billfish, but he found that even with air tanks, he could not go too deep or stay under too long.

In the evening they would lie together in the shallow water of the beach where they were beautifully fulfilled with each other; and as their love grew, they knew they wanted to be together always. But they realized that each was out of place in the other's world. . .

He decided to bring her onto land to show her Palm Beach, and prepared a small van with special provisions for keeping her body moist. He introduced her to flowers, trees, the joys of **Worth Avenue**, lush greens at **Wellington**, butterflies, everything. She loved the sense of sharing a life together, but after several days of being away from the ocean, she grew fatigued, and their time together had to end.

In the long run, they had to settle for a **distressing reality**. Their worlds overlapped only in shallow water at the edge of the beach. There, their joy was full; they embraced blissfully and nothing else mattered. But this time was brief, and it was not a place where they could live, this narrow margin of mutuality. So they would meet as often as possible, touch, love, rejoice in their common world, and then part.

Finally, they understood that this is the way life is; we are all somehow mermaids or men. For no one fully enters another's world, no one lingers long in the presence of another's mystery.

They came to accept this and cherished all the more each moment in which their worlds touched! ❤

Epilogue

Palm Beach

Town of Majesty
Jewel of America
Resort of Legend

Island of Miracles

*　　　*　　　*

One night as the mermaid and her man lay on the shore, waves rippling the sand, the wind sighing serenely in a world at peace. . . the sky brightened with high stars and a quiet hush moved in. The man felt his mermaid soften as her body trembled, and transformed. . . into a wondrous woman—ripe, complete, long-legged and lithesome. . .and lovely beyond words.

They rose, glorious in their happiness, and walked from the beach, together and forever, in love.

***And, of course, Palm Beach being the miracle it is. . .
They lived happily ever after!***

—INDEX—

(Note: Palm Beach is a familiar, friendly Town; most names in this Index are listed informally.)

—CONTRIBUTORS—

A *Standing Ovation* **for:** Diane Millner and Melissa Posey, who gave this book... heart and soul, mind and spirit.

Special Applause **for:** Dr. Fred Barr, Dr. Greg Boyajian, Joanne Cutner, Margie Kacoha, Lewis Kapner, Gene Lawrence, Bob Leidy, Bob Montgomery, Reid Moore, Jr., Karen Morrish, Maureen O'Sullivan, Jim Ponce, John Ryan, Kay Rybovich, David Scaff, and for Lucien Capehart, Bob Davidoff and Mort Kaye, who make Palm Beach a joyous visual delight.

For editorial inspiration, *Plaudits* **to:** Kathy Adams, Bobby Albre, Beth Amil, Cammie Anderson, Cara Anna, Agnes Ash, Muffie Potter Aston, Susan Beach, Joan Bever, James Brady, Michael Brown, Joella Cain, Jack Campo, Dale Carlson, Frank Cerabino, Elizabeth Clarke, Jeff Cloninger, Alexandra Clough, M.M. Cloutier, Jill Cooper, Norina Coursey, Dick Cowell, Pat Crowley, Cheryl Crowley, Bob Cuillo, Ted Curtis, Suzanna Cutts, Andrew J. Davis, Shannon Donnelly, Joan Durante, Michele Eassa, Sarah Flynn, Marc Freeman, Dale Fuchs, Tom Gates, Greer Gatuso, Barbara Gault, Michele Gelormine, Robert Gordon, Loretta Grantham, Susan Green, Burt Handelsman, Skippy Harwood, Joy Hearn, John Henderson, Larry Hobbs, Mary Francis Holleran, Robert Janjigian, Helmut Koller, Parker Ladd, Paula Law, Bob Leidy, May Bell Lin, Allison Malcolm, John Mariani, Barbara Marshall, Linda Marx, Enrique Maza, Maggie McCloskey, Kathy Miller, Jim Mitchell, Roy Moyer, John Murawski, Peg Murray, Shirley Murphy, Stephanie Murphy, Jesse Newman, Meredith Newton, Daphne Nikolopoulos, Jan Norris, Maria Ornelas, Jeff Ostrowski, Paul Owers, Carey O'Donnell, Clare O'Keeffe, Tim O'Meilia, Charles Passy, Amy Penn, Herbert Perez-Vidal, Joseph Polito, Dan Ponton, Peggy Rao, Linda Rawls, Paul Reid, Howard Risick, Sherman Robbins, David Rogers, Sherry Sales, Patti Sans, Arnold Scaasi, Gary Schwan, Angela Sergeant, Deirdre Shapiro, Judy Shepherd, Bob Simmons, Robert Sims, Jan Sjostrom, Jackie Slatkow, Barbara Smart, Stephanie Smith, Thom Smith, Sue Stacey, Brenda Star, Bunnie Stevens, Michael Strauss, Chris Sutherland, Catherine Tolton, Deborah Tornaben, Alan Tremain, Ava Van de Water, Ron Viejo, Janet Villella, Rob Walker, Rev. Ralph Warren, Jr., Mary Watkins, Skira Watson, Leslie Aldridge Westoff, Joan Willmott, Robert Wyner, Kyle Zimmer.